Gender and Sport: A Reader

This reader contains a range of highly influential articles that confront and illuminate issues of gender and sport whilst reflecting on the contribution of international feminist scholarship to the study of sport. It addresses the key issues, theoretical debates and empirical research that have informed the study of gender and sport and continue to do so. Key areas covered include:

- theories of gender and sport;
- historical developments;
- the media and representation;
- 'race' and ethnicity;
- men and masculinities;
- sexualities;
- bodies, physicality and power;
- policies and politics.

The articles are divided into thematic sections, each of which is supported by an editorial introduction, suggestions for further reading, and seminar questions related to each reading. The book provides an invaluable learning and teaching resource for all those concerned with sport or gender studies.

Sheila Scraton is Professor of Leisure and Feminist Studies and **Anne Flintoff** is Principal Lecturer in Leisure and Sport Studies, both at Leeds Metropolitan University.

Gender and Sport: A Reader

Edited by
Sheila Scraton and Anne Flintoff

London and New York

First published 2002
by Routledge
11 New Fetter Lane, London EC4P 4EE

Simultaneously published in the USA and Canada
by Routledge
29 West 35th Street, New York, NY 10001

Routledge is an imprint of the Taylor & Francis Group

Typeset in 10/12 pt Times by
Newgen Imaging Systems (P) Ltd., Chennai, India
Printed and bound in Great Britain by MPG Books Ltd, Bodmin

British Library Cataloguing in Publication Data
A catalogue record for this book is available
from the British Library

Library of Congress Cataloging in Publication Data
Gender and Sport : a reader / edited by Sheila Scraton and Anne Flintoff.
    p. cm.
    Includes bibliographical references and index.
    1. Sports–Social aspects.   2. Sex discrimination in sports.   3. Sex role.
4. Feminism.   I. Scraton, Sheila, 1950–   II. Flintoff, Anne, 1958–

GV706.5 .G48 2002
769'.082–dc21   2001052003

ISBN 0-415-25952-5 (hbk)
ISBN 0-415-25953-3 (pbk)

Contents

Contributors

Celia Brackenridge, Cheltenham and Gloucester College of Higher Education, UK.

Margaret Carlisle Duncan, University of Winsconsin-Milwaukee, USA.

Ben Carrington, University of Brighton, UK.

Gill Clarke, University of Southampton, UK.

Robert W. Connell, University of Sydney, Australia.

Timothy Jon Curry, Ohio State University, USA.

Shari L. Dworkin, University of California, USA.

Kari Fasting, Norwegian University of Sport and Physical Education, Norway.

Anne Flintoff, Leeds Metropolitan University, UK.

Pat Griffin, University of Massachusetts, USA.

Ann Hall, Formerly of University of Alberta, Canada.

Jennifer Hargreaves, Brunel University, UK.

Cynthia A. Hasbrook, University of Winsconsin-Milwaukee, USA.

Mary Maynard, University of York, UK.

Michael A. Messner, University of California, USA.

Camilla Obel, Canterbury University, New Zealand.

Gertrud Pfister, Freie Universitat Berlin, Germany.

Riita Pirinen, University of Tampere, Finland.

Sheila Scraton, Leeds Metropolitan University, UK.

Margaret Talbot, Leeds Metropolitan University, UK.

Nancy Theberge, University of Waterloo, Canada.

Benilde Vázquez, Instituto Nacional de Education Fisica, Spain.

David Whitson, University of Alberta, Canada.

Sharon Wray, University of York, UK.

Preface

We have developed this *Reader in Gender and Sport* out of our experience in teaching and researching in the area over the past two decades. We are aware that there are an increasing number of students on sport-related courses in the UK (which may be replicated in some other European countries and in North America and Australasia). This increase in student numbers reflects the changing nature of higher education and the increasing theoretical and vocational interest in sport studies. The availability of literature on gender and sport has failed to keep pace with the demand generated by the recent expansion of specialist courses and modules and the associated numbers of students in the area. It is often extremely difficult for both academic staff and students to access library resources that are disperse, often on different campuses and limited by the number of articles and books in stock. This dedicated *Reader in Gender and Sport* gives staff and students access to both seminal and contemporary writings in the field.

Within sport studies the contribution from feminist work centralizing gender and the experiences of women has increasingly been recognized. The chapters included in this *Reader* provide a coherent collection that demonstrates both the breadth and depth of work in the area. We have selected material that addresses the key issues, theoretical debates and empirical research that have informed the study of gender and sport over the past few decades. Importantly the collection provides access to many of the key authors who have developed this area of work and reflects the contribution of international feminist and pro-feminist scholarship to the study of sport and physical activity. The chapters include previously published work and new articles commissioned for the *Reader*. The over-arching purpose is to provide an invaluable resource for all academics and students in sport-related subjects and/or concerned with gender/women's studies.

We have divided the book into eight parts each focusing on a specific area of interest. To some extent this is a false fragmentation as all the issues discussed are intertwined and related to each other. For example, the part on '*Race*' and *Ethnicity* includes a chapter by Carrington that would also fit neatly into the part on *Men and Masculinities* and Wray's chapter, also in '*Race*' and *Ethnicity* could be situated in *Bodies, Physicality and Power*. However, the structure we use is developed in recognition that most courses/modules are divided into blocks of teaching and learning and each part provides inter-related chapters that can be used to stimulate discussion and provide resource material. The parts include theoretical questions in gender and sport (*Theorising gender and sport*); traditional areas of interest (*Historical developments: the engendering of sport; The media and representation; policy and politics*); the intersections of gender with other relations of power ('*Race' and ethnicity; Sexualities; Men and masculinities*); and more recent debates relating to the body, identities and physicality (*Bodies, physicality and power*).

We begin each of the parts with a brief introduction to the chapters and identify the learning outcomes that we would expect to be achieved through the study of this material. These are suggestions that we hope will guide students towards a more structured 'reading' of the chapters and will support their understanding of key concepts and issues. In addition we provide some further readings to extend their study. These are selected to complement those in the *Reader* and can be used to support seminar discussions or assessment work. Further support is provided by suggested seminar questions following each of the parts. A number of chapters have been edited to make them more 'student-friendly', concise and appropriate to the topic.

The *Reader in Gender and Sport* clearly reflects our own history and journey through feminist theory and practice in sport. The selection of the material, through necessity, means that many important and interesting articles have been omitted. For this we apologize but hope that the collection provides the platform for both staff and students to engage in issues relating to *Gender and Sport*. It can be used to structure a whole module or course or can be used selectively around specific topics. We have found the process invaluable and hope that the *Reader* encourages and supports more staff and students to engage critically with this important area of study.

Further key texts

Birrell, S. and Cole, C. (1994) *Women, Sport and Culture*, Champaign: Human Kinetics.
Brackenridge, C. (2001) *Spoilsports: Understanding and Preventing Sexual Exploitation in Sport*, London: Routledge.
Cahn, S. K. (1994) *Coming on Strong: Gender and Sexuality in Twentieth Century Women's Sport*, Cambridge: Harvard University Press.
Griffin, P. (1998) *Strong Women, Deep Closets: Lesbians and Homophobia in Sport*, Champaign: Human Kinetics.
Guttman, C. K. and Pfister, G. (Ed) (2000) *International Encyclopedia of Women and Sport*, New York: Macmillan.
Hall, M. A. (1996) *Feminism and Sporting Bodies*, Champaign: Human Kinetics.
Hargreaves, J. (1994) *Sporting Females: Critical Issues in the History and Sociology of Women's Sport*, London: Routledge.
Hargreaves, J. (2000) *Heroines of Sport: The Politics of Difference and Identity*, London: Routledge.
Messner, M. and Sabo, D. (1990) *Sport, Men and the Gender Order*, Champaign: Human Kinetics.

McKay, J., Messner, M. A. and Sabo, D. (2000) *Masculinities, Gender Relations and Sport: Research on Men and Masculinities*, Thousand Oaks: Sage.

Sheila Scraton and Anne Flintoff
Centre for Leisure and Sport Research
Leeds Metropolitan University
Leeds, England

Acknowledgements

We would like to thank the Centre for Leisure and Sport Research (CLSR) in the School of Leisure and Sport Studies at Leeds Metropolitan University for their support in the production of this Reader. In particular, we would like to thank Fiona Stoddart for her invaluable work in compiling the Reader and Rachel Clarke for her help with permissions. We are indebted to discussions with colleagues and to our students over the years for providing the stimulus and motivation to develop the Reader.

We are grateful to the following publishers for granting permission to reproduce the articles included in this Reader:

Allen & Unwin Publishers, Australia (Australia, New Zealand and Southeast Asia)

Connell, R. W. (2000) *The Men and the Boys*, pp. 3–5, 10–14, and 29–32.

Altamira Press, Maryland, USA

Dworking, S. and Messner, M. (1999) 'Just do . . . what? Sport, bodies, gender' in Ferree, M., Lorber, J. and Hess, B. (eds) *Revisioning Gender*.

Blackwell Publishers, Oxford (UK and Commonwealth)

Connell, R. W. (2000) *The Men and the Boys*, Cambridge: Polity Press. pp. 3–5, 10–14, and 29–32.

Frank Cass & Co. Ltd, London

Pfister, G., Scraton, S. and Fasting, K. (1999) 'Women and football – a contradiction? The beginnings of women's football in four European countries'. In Mangan, J. (ed) *Sport in Europe: Politics, Class, Gender. The European Sports History Review, Vol. I*, London: Frank Cass.

Human Kinetics, Champaign IL

Curry, T. J. (1991) 'Fraternal bonding in the locker room: a profeminist analysis of talk about competition and women', *Sociology of Sport Journal*, 8: 119–135.

Duncan, M. C. and Hasbrook, C. A. (1988) 'Denial of power in televised women's sports', *Sociology of Sport Journal* 5: 1–21.

Griffin, P. (1992) 'Changing the game: homophobia, sexism and lesbians in sport', *Quest* 44(2): 251–265.

Hall, M. A. (1988) 'The discourse of gender and sport: from femininity to feminism', *Sociology of Sport Journal*, 5(4): 330–340.

Hargreaves, J. (1993) 'The Victorian cult of the family and the early years of female sport', in E. G. Dunning, J. A. Maguire and R. E. Pearton, *The Sports Process*, Champaign: Human Kinetics, 71–83.

Whitson, D. (1994) 'The embodiment of gender: discipline, domination and empowerment', in S. Birrell and C. L. Cole (eds) *Women, Sport and Culture*, Champaign: Human Kinetics.

Leisure Studies Association, Eastbourne

Clarke, G. (1995) 'Outlaws in sport and education? Exploring the sporting and education experiences of lesbian Physical Education teachers' in Lawrence, L. Murdock, E., Parker, S. (eds) *Leisure Sport and Education*, Eastbourne: LSA Publications.

Sage Publications, London

Carrington, B. (1998) 'Sport, masculinity and black cultural resistance', *Journal of Sport and Social Issues*, January, 1: 275–298.

Obel, C. (1996) 'Collapsing gender in competitive bodybuilding: researching contradictions and ambiguity in sport', *International Review for the Sociology of Sport*, 31(2): 185–220.

Pirinen, R. (1997) 'Catching up with the men? Finnish newspaper coverage of women's entry into traditionally male sports', *International Review for the Sociology of Sport* 32(3): 239–249.

Taylor & Francis, London

Brackenridge, C. (2001) 'Men loving men hating women – the crisis of masculinity and violence to women in sport', *Spoilsports: Understanding and Preventing Sexual Exploitation in Sport*, London: Taylor & Francis.

Maynard, M. (1995) ' "Race", gender and the concept of "difference" ' in 'Feminist thought', Maynard, M. and Afshar, H. *Dynamics of 'Race' and Gender: Some Feminist Interventions*, London: Taylor & Francis.

Part I
Theorizing gender

Introduction

We begin the *Reader* with chapters that explore some of the theoretical debates within gender and sport. All the chapters in the book are informed to some extent by feminist thought. Andermahr, Lovell and Wolkowitz (1997: 76) suggest that:

> Historically, there have been many feminisms, variously grounded. Minimally, the term implies the identification of women as systematically oppressed; the belief that GENDER relations are neither inscribed in natural DIFFERENCES between the sexes, nor immutable, and a political commitment to their transformation.

A central characteristic of feminist work is *praxis* – the relationship between theory and practice. Theory is only useful if it *informs* political action and practice and if it is also *developed out of* these. As a result, different theoretical strands of feminism have emerged which focus on diverse experiences and issues.

We have selected two chapters, one that introduces some of the early theoretical debates within feminist work in sport (Hall) and one that engages with more recent questions (Dworkin and Messner). In our chapter, (Scraton and Flintoff) we provide a comprehensive overview of the different strands of feminism, tracing their development and application to sport. Throughout this part, key concepts such as sex role, ideology, patriarchy, sexuality, hegemony, difference and discourse are introduced and explored.

Ann Hall's chapter overviews some of the early theoretical developments in understanding gender and sport. These were important foundations from which more contemporary theories have emerged. She describes social, psychological research with its focus on the perceived conflict between femininity and sport, and the development of sex role theory. Both are criticized for their functionalism and their neglect of social and political factors and gendered power relations. She argues that it is time for the sociology of sport to recognize the importance of engaging in non-sexist, woman-centred and feminist scholarship. Ann Hall's work critiques the 'malestream' of sport sociology and has made a significant contribution to feminist praxis in sport.

The second chapter by Shari Dworkin and Michael Messner addresses current questions about gender in sport in relation to empowerment, difference and the complex intersection of race, class and gender. They argue that contemporary feminist theory must go beyond a simple gender 'lens' to incorporate a more sophisticated analysis that engages with debates central to post-structuralism. However, they argue against a radical deconstruction of gender, or 'men' and 'women', and conclude that it is essential to retain and build upon a concept of social structure, reasserting the significance and centrality of both gender and social class.

In the final chapter we explore the impact of feminism on the sociology of sport, and trace the developing strands of feminist thought from modernist to post-structuralist analysis. While recognizing the problems of compartmentalizing these strands, none the less it is useful to understand the historical development of feminist theory, and identify the domain assumptions which characterize liberal, socialist, radical, Black and post-structuralist approaches. Different approaches centralize particular concepts and concerns, but all have had an important role in both criticizing androcentric sport and suggesting feminist alternatives for challenging oppression.

After reading all three chapters in this section, students should:

- be able to recognize the different theoretical approaches to understanding gender and sport;
- be able to appreciate the application of theory to policy and practice;
- be introduced to the key concepts and key influential authors;
- understand the shift between modernist and postmodernist feminisms.

Reference

Andermahr, S., Lovell, T. and Wolkowitz, C. (1997) *A Concise Glossary of Feminist Theory*, London: Arnold.

Further readings

The special edition of *Women's Studies International Forum*, (1987) 10, 4 contains a number of articles which explore early theoretical positions on women/gender and sport including:

Bryson, L. (1987) 'Sport and the maintenance of male hegemony' (p. 349–360).
Lenskyj, H. (1987) 'Female sexuality and women's sport' (p. 381–386).
Rail, G. (ed) (1998) *Sport and Postmodern Times*, New York: State University of New York Press.

Although the following are not specifically concerned with sport, they provide a comprehensive introduction to the varieties of feminist thinking:

Tong, R. (1999) *Feminist Thought: A Comprehensive Introduction*, London: Unwin Hyman.
Safia Mirza, H. (ed) (1997) *Black British Feminism*, London: Routledge.

WWW sources

Women's Sport Foundation: *http://www.wsf.org.uk*
Canadian Association for the Advancement of Women and Sport and Physical Activity (CAAWS): *http://caaws.ca/main.htp*
Women Sport International: *http://www.de.psu.ed/wsi/index.htm*
Women's Sports Foundation (United States): *www.lifetimetv.com/wosport.index.html*

1   The discourse of gender and sport: From femininity to feminism*

M. Ann Hall

When we speak of the discourse of gender and sport, we are in a sense speaking about speaking. In an everyday sense, discourse is about daily conversation and the ordinary things people talk about. Our social reality is in many ways our discourse. But discourse, in the sense I wish to use it here, can also mean the way in which a particular topic or subject area is approached, the assumptions surrounding its investigation, the ways in which new knowledge is generated, and how this knowledge fits with the zeitgeist of a specific discipline or field. There is, or should be, a direct connection between ordinary social discourse and more formal, theoretical discourse about which academics continually need reminding.

I want to discuss how the formal and theoretical discourse about the relationship between gender and sport came to be, what characterizes it now, and how it could (dare I say should?) be changed. In doing so I want to argue the following: (a) that there are unrecognized gender assumptions and ideologies implicit in sport research; (b) that these gender assumptions and ideologies are rarely analyzed or related to social structure; and (c) that the only viable analyses of gender and sport are those that provide both a critical and historical analysis of the ideological foundations of our past and ongoing research. Finally, I will make some programmatic statements as to future directions in reshaping the discourse of gender and sport.

But first, let me say a brief word about my use of the term *sport*, and more important, how it should be conceptualized and theorized. The first point is that there are, both within a culture and among cultures, many diverse forms of sport. In my own society, for example, it makes sense to speak of professional sport, state-supported amateur sport, school and university sport, Olympic sports, domestic sports, youth sport, and so forth. Sport is conducted in a variety of social settings by individuals with different backgrounds, motives, and social characteristics. The second point is that play, games, and sports are real *social practices* that are reproduced and changed over time by human beings. They are not idealist abstractions with no connection to the making and remaking of ourselves as human

* Taken from, *Sociology of Sport Journal* 5 (1988): 330–340. An early version of this paper was presented at the Congress on Movement and Sport in Women's Life, University of Jyväskylä, Finland, August 17–21, 1987.

agents, nor are they simple products of material conditions. Like all other forms of culture, sport is a creation of human agency and it can be transformed.

Gender is a major social and theoretical category just as significant and perhaps more so than the more familiar sociological categories of class and race. It is a conceptual tool to understanding the social world as well as a theoretical construct that requires careful, sustained analysis. As David Morgan (1986: 31) points out, 'Feminist theory may, in part, be seen as an insistence that gender belongs up there with the more familiar categories of sociological discourse; that, indeed, it exists at the highest levels of generality.' Paradoxically, as Morgan also points out, the higher the realm of sociological discourse, the higher the level of generality, the more likely that gender differentiation yields to more abstract categories such as role, social actor, organization, system, and class.[1]

Also problematic is the tendency, certainly in North America, to translate 'gender' to mean 'woman.' Courses, symposia, and texts with the label 'gender and sport' are considered for women only and the issues discussed are relevant only to women, never to men. From a research perspective, gender differences mean that women are different from men, but rarely is the reverse question asked: How are men different from women? (Birrell, 1984). Women's experiences are seen as variations (or deviations) on men's; we know women only in relation to men. These studies become subsumed under gender research when implicit is the assumption that gender means women (and not men) or gender inequalities are subsumed under some broader category such as children, social class, athlete, and so forth.

What is the history of this discourse about gender and sport? What assumptions and ideologies are implicit here? My starting point, both within ordinary and formal discourse, is the pervasive obsession with the femininity (and masculinity) of female athletes and sportswomen but *never* with the masculinity (and femininity) of male athletes and sportsmen.

Culture, femininity, and athleticism

Since the 1960s a major focus of gender issues within North American sport sociology and social psychology has been to 'prove' that sport competition does not masculinize female participants either psychologically or behaviourally. Between 1965 and 1987 I have located over 70 published articles, conference papers, and theses directed at this 'problem.' The literature has followed, to a certain extent, the major trends in the larger sex role/sex identity research of social psychology. The earlier research was concerned primarily with the perceptions, stereotypes, and acceptance of the female athlete. Much of this work coincided with increasing numbers of female physical educators entering American and Canadian graduate programmes whose personal concerns about the myths surrounding athleticism and femininity were reflected in the thesis topics they chose. Unfortunately, much of this work was essentialist, atheoretical, and as I argued in a substantive critique of this research (Hall, 1981), harmful because it continued to perpetuate the very stereotypes we wished to eradicate.

Within the social sciences, and particularly psychology, there is a long history of assuming that so-called cross-sex behaviors and preferences (e.g., athleticism among females) were indicators of emotional disturbance or sexual deviation (Spence, Deaux, & Helmreich, 1985). To be a woman and an athlete was to be in conflict and therefore psychologically unhealthy. With the reemergence of feminism in the 1960s and the tremendous explosion of feminist scholarship over the past decade, these assumptions have not only been challenged but investigated with increasing rigor, sophistication, and tenacity. The key construct to emerge is *psychological androgyny*, whose premise is that masculinity and femininity are independent, rather than bipolar, dimensions so that individuals high on both (now called androgynes) are mentally healthier and socially more effective (Cook, 1985). Sport researchers have leapt upon the concept and their studies typically find that female athletes are more androgynous, more masculine, less sex-typed, or less feminine than female nonathletes *but* no less psychologically healthy and often with a more positive self-concept (Hall, 1981; Marsh & Jackson, 1986).

In my original critique (Hall, 1981), I attacked this research with equal rigor. My argument, briefly, was as follows: since androgyny simply combines the old dualities of masculinity and femininity, which are themselves patriarchal constructs, the concept and the working models that define it will do little to bring about real change in a society that is fundamentally oppressive to women. This of course is a political argument and one I still hold. There is also a more specific theoretical and methodological critique (see Hall, 1981). Further, the important sociological question is not that a conflict between gender and culture exists, but why it exists only in the realm of the feminine. As Rosenblum (1986) so cogently argues, a key feature in the American conception of gender is the care/autonomy distinction: femininity is equated with and displayed by care for others rather than self, whereas masculinity is characterized by autonomy, self-reliance, and achievement, requiring an asocial, even antisocial, stance to the world. Prevailing American values, however, stress achievement, individuality, and self-promotion. Femininity must forego these values to be true to a feminine morality with its emphasis on self-sacrifice and responsivity to others' needs. Therefore the conflict between gender and culture exists only in the realm of femininity because masculinity *is* culture.

This explains the almost obsessive approach, by American sport researchers in particular, to explore the conflict relationship between femininity (never masculinity) and sport, and to 'prove' that female athletic involvement has positive psychological benefits without producing a loss of femininity.[2] I would also suggest, as have others (e.g., Griffin, 1987), that in reality femininity is a thinly disguised code word for heterosexuality. The real issue behind so much attention to an athlete's femininity is the fear that she may be a lesbian. Here are the summary statements from two of the more recent studies:

> The results of this investigation show that female athletes apparently do not experience much role conflict, can be more M without being less F, and tend to have higher levels of self-concept – particularly in areas most logically

related to sporting experience. The findings strongly refute the popular myth that female athletes are not, and cannot be, feminine.

(Jackson & Marsh, 1986, p. 208)

One possible explanation concerns the relationship between engaging in gender-deviant activities and the culturally established value of the activities. Let us assume, for the purpose of argument, that masculine activities are indeed perceived as more valuable than feminine activities in our culture. For the cross-sex-typed woman, cross-gender identification may make gender-deviant behavior (participation in masculine activities) more likely.

(Matteo, 1986, p. 430)

The obvious reification (e.g., 'cross-sex-typed' and 'gender-deviant activities') present in these studies continually reaffirms the belief that very normal, self-fulfilling activities (e.g., participation in sports for girls, or dance for boys) are in fact deviant in a psychological sense. What the researchers, many of whom would describe themselves as feminists, fail to recognize is that this unavoidable reification hinders political attempts to critique (and change) the pervasive gender ideologies of our culture. Most researchers, whose cognate field is psychology or social psychology, cannot and will not understand this because of the very nature of their disciplines (Walker, 1981). In a recent summary of social psychological research on sex roles in contemporary American society (Spence *et al.*, 1985: 172), the authors admit to the following:

Assuredly the recent elevation of phenomena related to sex-roles and gender to major research topics among social and behavioral scientists have been motivated more by concern with societal action than by dispassionate scientific curiosity . . . . Attempts to describe and explain these temporal trends and their profound impact on societal institutions require an appeal to political, technological, economic, and sociological factors and to macrotheories of social change. Although not indifferent to the role of such factors, social psychologists have ordinarily left their investigation to members of other disciplines, preferring to focus (as is their wont) on the individual within the immediate group rather than on the group and larger sets of social forces.

This is all very well, and I certainly do not oppose a division of labor in our research, but in the specific case of gender and sport research it has been social psychology (to say nothing of biology and physiology) with its emphasis on the individual and individual differences, to the exclusion of social and political factors, that has largely determined the discourse about gender and sport. In part this is a reflection of the ways in which gender is taught and reproduced in our university physical education courses and curricula. The dominant framework in our programs is one that utilizes knowledge from the biological and behavioral sciences to analyze human physical performance and therefore presents gender as an issue of sex differences (Dewar, 1987). This approach focuses on individuals, and what is usually missing is an analysis of the powerful ways in which the gender system and gender ideologies inform our research. There is, in other words, no feminist analysis and critique. This is not to say that there has been no sociological discourse, feminist or otherwise, on gender and sport, but it is, as I will show now, replete with its own problems.

The inadequacy of role theory and functionalism

Much of the North American literature on gender and sport is subsumed within the general sex-roles literature that has grown from a trickle to a torrent over the last 15 years. The term *sex role* (or gender role) is now so common that many new researchers coming into the field do not realize there is a very substantive critique both of the notion of sex role and role in general. Here we see how the discourse on gender and sport has been determined more by ignorance and sloppy scholarship than by an analysis of gender ideologies and assumptions implicit in the research.

In my original 1981 critique, I outlined the major concerns about the notion 'sex roles': (a) It is sociologically illogical in that we do not speak of race roles or age roles or class roles because we do not attempt to explain differential behavior patterns on the basis of race, age, or social class alone, but we do explain them in terms of a power differential that certainly coincides with race, class, and age distinctions. (b) The notion of role focuses attention more on individuals than on social structure and depoliticizes the central questions of power and control in explaining gender inequality. (c) Terms like 'sex role stereotyping,' 'sex role socialization,' 'sex role orientation' are used as if they exist concretely rather than being analytical constructs; in other words, they become reified. (d) Role terminology is not fully applicable to gender because sex or gender, like age, race, and social class, infuse the more specific social roles one plays (e.g., teacher, athlete, coach, university professor).

Carolyn Sherif, a well-known and respected social psychologist, likened the term 'sex roles' to a 'boxcar carrying an assortment of sociological and psycho-logical data along with an explosive mixture of myth and untested assumptions' (Sherif, 1982: 392). More important, she argued that stereotypical attributions of instrumental versus expressive, which are the basis of sex roles and seen as univer-sal, are part of the very ideology that inhibit women's entry into more egalitarian role relationships with men. Her advice, never taken, was to drop the concept altogether.

Several sociologists (e.g., Coulson, 1972; Giddens, 1979), although more con-cerned with the general concept 'role' than the more specific 'sex role,' have also argued that the concept be abandoned, certainly by sociologists. Giddens points out that within functionalist theories of social systems, role (to quote Talcott Parsons) is 'the primary point of direct articulation between the personality of the individual and the structure of the social system.' For Giddens, and others who eschew func-tionalism, 'social systems are not constituted of roles but of (reproduced) practices; and it is practices, not roles which (via the duality of structure) have to be regarded as the 'points of articulation' between actors and structures' (p. 117). This is an important point because the concept of sex roles is a functionalist conception of gender deeply shaped by the concepts – instrumental versus expressive – developed by Parsons and used by others (Stacey & Thorne, 1985). The implications of this are that gender is thought to be more central to the family than to other institutions (sport is a good example here) and that gender arrangements function primarily to ensure social maintenance and reproduction. What is interesting is that functionalist assumptions seem more deeply ingrained in sociological conceptions of gender than in other forms of social inequality.

As for the sociological discourse of gender and sport, the implications I think are obvious: functionalist conceptions of gender applied to sport fail to recognize that femininity (and masculinity) are socially constructed, historically specific, and mediated by social class, race, ethnicity, and other social categories of inequality.

Social theory, sport, and feminist theory

Elsewhere (Hall, 1986) I have argued that the concept of gender is only beginning to emerge as a major social category to be treated seriously, and with some care, in our theoretically based social analyses of sport. I outlined what I consider to be the major paradigms (shared perspectives on how research should be conducted) that currently inform primarily North American sport sociology: (a) the dominant idealist/positivist paradigm whereby sport is seen as part of a larger societal system and is studied to assess how it contributes to individual personal growth and the maintenance of social order; (b) the materialist/socialist (political economy) paradigm, more Canadian in content, which focuses on the relationship of sport to the emergent features of industrial capitalism; (c) a social definition paradigm whereby the focus, in the context of sport, is on how individuals define their social situation (e.g., small groups, teams, athletic subcultures) and the meaning they attach to their actions; (d) a lesser known cultural studies paradigm, whose origins are in Britain, that examines the ways in which culture and ideology are relatively autonomous in relation to economic and political pressures and, more important, the mediating role of human agency in the making of culture (sport being an important aspect of culture); and finally (e) an emerging feminist paradigm which, quite frankly, is seeking to find its focus at present but which is concerned primarily with the 'gendered' practice of sport.

Obviously there are very different epistemological assumptions inherent in these paradigms and, as in sociology in general, the ensuing debates focus on which paradigm should take precedence. Those advocating a critical sport sociology (e.g., Marxists, socialists, feminists, cultural theorists) are at odds with the idealist/positivist paradigm because of its inability to recognize its own ideology, and with the social definition paradigm because of its seemingly apolitical stance to the social world. Feminists have been accused of substituting a logic-of-patriarchy for an equally reductionistic logic-of-capital explanation of domination, and on it goes. There has to be some paradigm resolution here, although admittedly the idcological differences between the idealist/positivist paradigm and the others is so great that we must settle for a more unified, theoretically informed, critical sociology of sport. The best possibility for resolution, it seems to me, is between the cultural studies and feminist perspectives.

What this solution recognizes is that there is a growing and sophisticated body of literature we can now define as feminist social theory. My definition of feminist in this context is taken from Acker, Barry, and Esseveld (1983: 423): 'a point of view that (1) sees women as exploited, devalued and often oppressed; (2) is committed to changing the condition of women; (3) adopts a critical perspective toward dominant intellectual traditions that have ignored and/or justified women's oppression.' Feminist social theory, as Sondra Farganis (1986a, 1986b) points out, has much in common with classical (i.e., critical) social theory, certainly as expounded by Marx, Durkheim, Simmel, Weber, and Mannheim, and more recently by the writings emanating from the Frankfurt School and the critical theory of Jurgen Habermas. What is central to classical social theory *and* feminist social theory is the critique of positivism and scientism, and more important, that theory is essential to informing practice (praxis). Whatever the theory, it must be an emancipatory one.

Nonsexist, women-centered, and feminist scholarship: transforming the discourse

I said earlier that the feminist paradigm or perspective within the sociology of sport is an emerging one whose focus at present is unclear. Some confusion and uncertainty is to be expected because modern feminist scholarship is not much more than 20 years old. It has literally exploded over the last decade, so that keeping up with the volume of papers, books, conferences, symposia, even in one field, is now impossible. For those of us whose academic careers have coincided with this political and intellectual movement, it is a terribly exciting, stimulating, if not somewhat frightening, time. We have moved far beyond the 'add women and stir' phase of our scholarship to a perspective that is highly critical and challenges the dominant intellectual traditions of our time. There has also been a substantial challenge to the sexist bias of all social science, both in content and methodology. Any researcher, male or female, who still engages in sexist or androcentric research now has no excuse (e.g., see Eichler, 1988; Eichler & Lapointe, 1985). Feminist scholarship is here to stay. Perhaps at present it only rattles the cages of the traditional disciplines, but over time it will transform the entire academy (e.g., Davis, 1985; Dubois, Kelly, Kennedy, Korsmeyer, & Robinson, 1985; Farnham, 1987; Keller, 1985; Schuster & Van Dyne, 1985; Spender, 1981). In the process, feminist scholarship and research will begin to transform individual and specific discourses, which is precisely what is happening in this tiny little field called the sociology of sport, and more specifically still the discourse of gender and sport.[3]

What, precisely, makes scholarship feminist? How do we distinguish it from nonsexist scholarship, or from woman-centered scholarship? To do feminist scholarship is to apply a fundamentally political concept – feminism – to the world of academic research. Earlier I defined feminism as a point of view that sees women as exploited, devalued, and often oppressed, and that is committed to changing their condition. To do feminist scholarship in the world of sport is to recognize that female athletes and sportswomen are devalued, often exploited, and very often oppressed. Those of us who consider ourselves feminist are committed to bringing about fundamental change in the world of sport to counter not just exploitation and oppression based on gender but also on race, class, age, ethnicity, and so on. However, there has to be some division of labor. Some choose to work in academe, focusing on research and scholarship, whereas others choose the more frontline work such as the Canadian Association for the Advancement of Women and Sport in Canada, the Women's Sports Foundation in Britain and the USA, the Women's Committee of the Norwegian Sports Federation in Norway, and others. Hopefully, those in academe and those in the frontline are working hand in hand. We can ensure that this happens by communicating with each other and respecting the value of each other's work.

Feminist scholarship must be distinguished from that which is nonsexist and that which is woman-centered. Research and scholarship in the social sciences is sexist if it is informed and shaped by a male viewpoint resulting in a distorted picture of social reality (Eichler, 1987). Research is truly nonsexist if its sexist elements have been removed from its language, concepts, questions posed, methods used, interpretations or policy recommendations made, as well as in overall perspective (see Eichler, 1988). Everyone, male or female, engaged in social science research must be forced to do nonsexist research; journals must no longer publish sexist research, and conferences must no longer be a forum for it. This obviously is no easy task.

Woman-centered research and scholarship are also sexist but in a reverse way. Studies focus totally on women, and women are seen only in relation to a social universe constructed around females (Eichler 1987). This is a gynocentric model of social reality as opposed to an androcentric one, and it has been an extremely useful and productive way to recognize and counter androcentric, sexist scholarship. It has also added immeasurably to our knowledge about women and their lives. The development of women's studies in North American universities is largely an outgrowth of this perspective.

Feminist research and scholarship are both nonsexist and woman-centered, but also much more. What that 'more' consists of is difficult to define because not only is it evolving but it constantly changes. As Dubois *et al.* (1985: 196) point out, 'it may be futile to define feminist scholarship by patroling its borders or specifying its center. Rather what gives the field coherence is the relation of the parts to the whole and its link to the more general feminist movement that brought it into being.' Certainly there are competing feminist frameworks, not unusual for a new scholarly venture, but what is at issue is the potential of feminist scholarship, as a critical mode of inquiry, to transform the traditional disciplines so they are rid of their androcentric biases.

I suggested earlier that it is time the sociology of sport recognize the theoretical importance of feminism. This means that individual scholars, both male and female, must inform themselves about feminist scholarship. Gender should no longer be considered the prime interest of a few female sport sociologists; it must interest everyone. I also suggested that sport sociologists, if they wish to be truly critical, should consider a cultural studies approach to their scholarship. Those who comprehend what this means warn that 'he or she must master a rich body of interdisciplinary literature and come to grips with several very thorny epistemological, methodological, and theoretical problems' (Loy, 1987: 131). I agree, but that is precisely what is so exciting about feminist scholarship: It is interdisciplinary, it is constantly changing, it is beginning to work through its own epistemology and methodology, and feminist social theory leads one right back to what sociologists are supposed to be doing – making sense of differing social realities.

Feminist scholarship, and the social movement from which it grows, are a direct frontal attack on the masculinity-as-culture discourse of gender and sport. Of necessity, women have had to create their own culture and communities. This has been true of women's sport. The central debate in feminism at present, however, is the extent to which gender differences, as manifested in cultural femininity and masculinity, ought to be eliminated or encouraged. The discourse about women and sport, on a practical level, is now about integration versus separation, engagement versus autonomy, and co-optation versus ostracism (see Williams, 1985). There is also a slowly growing interest in how the patriarchal and gendered practice of modern sport has shaped men's lives as well (see Carrigan, 1985; Kidd, 1987; Messner, 1985; Sabo, 1985). Slowly but surely, the discourse of gender and sport is finally moving away from an exclusive and restrictive focus on women and femininity to the nature of gendered social behavior and the impact of gendered social structures on *both* sexes.

Notes

1 Gender is also a key variable in the sense that researchers commonly use 'sex' or 'gender' as an independent variable most especially in the now voluminous work on social behavioral sex or gender differences. This is equivalent to recording one's socioeconomic status or ethnic background, and it is not without its problems. It is also not the sense in which I wish to deal with gender here. However, for an excellent summary as well as some useful suggestions, see Morgan (1986).
2 Although there has been since the 1960s an increasing number of studies that use both male and female subjects, I found only one (Caron, Carter, & Brightman, 1985) that focused exclusively on males. It found that competitive team athletes were significantly more masculine, more tolerant of premarital sexual behavior for both sexes, and showed less egalitarian views toward women than did their nonathlete and individual athlete peers. There were no differences in femininity.
3 For an example of some current work, see Hall (1987), which is a special issue of *Women's Studies International Forum* on 'The Gendering of Sport, Leisure and Physical Education.'

References

Acker, J., Barry, K., & Esseveld, J. (1983). Objectivity and truth: Problems in doing feminist research. *Women's Studies International Forum*, **6**, 423–435.

Birrell, S. (1984). Studying gender in sport: A feminist perspective. In N. Theberge & P. Donnelly (Eds.), *Sport and the sociological imagination* (pp. 125–135). Fort Worth: Texas Christian University Press.

Caron, S. L., Carter, D. B., & Brightman, L. A. (1985). Sex-role orientation and attitudes towards women: Differences among college athletes and nonathletes. *Perceptual and Motor Skills*, **61**, 803–806.

Carrigan, T., Connell, B., & Lees, J. (1985). Towards a new sociology of masculinity. *Theory and Society*, **14**, 551–604.

Cook, E. P. (1985). *Psychological androgyny*. New York: Pergamon.

Coulson, M. A. (1972). Role: A redundant concept in sociology? Some educational considerations. In J. A. Jackson (Ed.), *Role* (pp. 107–128). London: Cambridge University Press.

Davis, B. H. (Ed.) (1985). Feminist education [Special issue]. *Journal of Thought*, **20**(3).

Dewar, A. M. (1987). The social construction of gender in physical education. *Women's Studies International Forum*, **10**, 453–465.

Dubois, E. C., Kelly, G. P., Kennedy, E. L., Korsmeyer, C. W., & Robinson, L. W. (1985). *Feminist scholarship: Kindling in the groves of academe*. Urbana: University of Illinois Press.

Eichler, M. (1987). The relationship between sexist, non-sexist, woman-centred and feminist research in the social sciences. In G. H. Nemiroff (Ed.), *Women and men: Interdisciplinary readings on gender* (pp. 21–53), Toronto: Fitzhenry & Whiteside.

Eichler, M. (1988). *Nonsexist research methods: A practical guide*. London: Allen & Unwin.

Eichler, M., & Lapointe, J. (1985). *On the treatment of the sexes in research*, Ottawa: Social Sciences and Humanities Research Council of Canada.

Farganis, S. (1986*a*). *The social construction of the feminine character*. Totowa, NJ: Rowman & Littlefield.

Farganis, S. (1986*b*). Social theory and feminist theory: the need for dialogue. *Sociological Inquiry*, **56**, 50–68.

Farnham, C. (1987). *The impact of feminist research on the Academy*, Bloomington: Indiana University Press.

Giddens, A. (1979). *Critical problems in social theory*. London: Macmillan.

Griffin, P. S. (1987, August). *Homophobia, lesbians, and women's sports: An exploratory analysis*. Paper presented at the 95th Annual Convention of the American Psychological Association, New York City.

Hall, M. A. (1981). *Sport, sex roles and sex identity* (The CRIAW Papers/Les documents de l'ICRAF, No. 1), Ottawa: The Canadian Research Institute for the Advancement of Women.

Hall, M. A. (1986, November). *How should we theorize gender in the context of sport?* Paper presented at the Sport, Sex and Gender Conference, Lillehammer, Norway.

Hall, M. A. (Ed.) (1987). The gendering of sport, leisure and physical education [Special issue], *Women's Studies International Forum*, **10**(4).

Jackson, S. A., & Marsh, H. W. (1986). Athletic or antisocial? The female sport experience. *Journal of Sport Psychology*, **8**, 198–211.

Keller, E. F. (1985). *Reflections on gender and science*, New Haven: Yale University Press.

Kidd, B. (1987). Sports and masculinity. In M. Kaufman (Ed.), *Beyond patriarchy: Essays by men on pleasure, power and change* (pp. 250–265). Toronto: Oxford University Press.

Loy, J. W. (1987). Aphorisms and the advancement of learning: A Baconian rejoinder to Mr. MacAloon. *Sociology of Sport Journal*, **4**, 120–132.

Marsh, H. W., & Jackson, S. W. (1986). Multidimensional self-concepts, masculinity, and femininity as a function of women's involvement in athletics. *Sex Roles*, **15**, 391–415.

Matteo, S. (1986). The effect of sex and gender-schematic processing on sport participation. *Sex Roles*, **15**, 417–432.

Messner, M. (1985). The changing meaning of male identity in the lifecourse of the athlete. *Arena Review*, **9**, 31–60.

Morgan, D. H. J. (1986). Gender. In R. G. Burgess (Ed.), *Key variables in social investigation* (pp. 31–53). London: Routledge & Kegan Paul.

Rosenblum, K. E. (1986). The conflict between and within genders: An appraisal of contemporary American femininity and masculinity. *Social Inquiry*, **56**, 93–104.

Sabo, D. (1985). Sport, patriarchy, and male identity: New questions about men and sport. *Arena Review*, **9**, 1–30.

Schuster, M. R., & Van Dyne, S. R. (Eds.) (1985). *Women's place in the academy: Transforming the liberal arts curriculum.* Totowa, NJ: Rowman & Allenheld.

Sherif, C. W. (1982). Needed concepts in the study of gender identity. *Psychology of Women Quarterly*, **6**, 375–398.

Spence, J. T., Deaux, K. & Helmreich, R. L. (1985). Sex roles in contemporary American society. In G. Lindzey & E. Aronson (Eds.), *Handbook of social psychology (3rd ed.): Vol 2. Special fields and applications* (pp. 149–178). Reading, MA: Addison-Wesley.

Spender, D. (Ed.) (1981). *Men's studies modified: The impact of feminism on the academic disciplines.* Oxford: Pergamon Press.

Stacey, J., & Thorne, B. (1985). The missing feminist revolution in sociology. *Social Problems*, **32**, 301–316.

Walker, B. M. (1981). Psychology and feminism – If you can't beat them, join them, in D. Spender (Ed.), *Men's studies modified: The impact of feminism on the academic disciplines* (pp. 111–124). Oxford: Pergamon Press.

Williams, C. L., Lawrence, G., & Rowe, D. (1985). Women and sport: A lost ideal. *Women's Studies International Forum*, **8**, 639–645.

2 Just do . . . what? Sport, bodies, gender*

Shari L. Dworkin and Michael A. Messner

Sport has proven to be one of the key institutional sites for the study of the social construction of gender. Organized sport, as we now know it, was created in the late nineteenth and early twentieth centuries by and for White middle class men to bolster a sagging ideology of "natural superiority" over women and over race-and class-subordinated groups of men (Crosset 1990; Kimmel 1990; McKay 1991; Messner 1988; Whitson 1990). Thus, although sport was seemingly based in natural physical endowments, it was socially constructed out of the gender, race, and class-based stratification systems of Europe and the United States. [. . .]

It took a gender analysis of sports ideologies and commercialization to unravel the ways sport is organized to sell masculinity to men. Today, that same gender analysis is being applied to the deconstruction of the selling of a shifting imagery of physical femininity in women athletes. Note, however, the persistence of the gender segregation so evident in organized sport from the beginning – in nearly all cases, men's and women's sports are carefully segregated, and men's sports are still assumed to be mostly for male spectators. Women's sports, however, to be successful, have to be attractive to men as well as women viewers. As a result, notions of conventional masculinity and femininity persist. Sport, as a cultural and commercial production, constructs and markets gender; besides making money, making gender may be sport's chief function.

It may appear ironic that an institution that has continued to contribute to the reconstitution of hegemonic masculinity throughout the twentieth century has become a key site for the development of a critical feminist scholarship on gender (e.g., Birrell 1988; Birrell and Cole 1994; Bryson 1987; Hall 1988, 1996; Hargreaves 1994; Messner and Sabo 1990; Theberge 1981). In fact, it is the very centrality of the body in sport practice and ideology that provides an opportunity to examine critically and illuminate the social construction of gender (Connell 1987; Lorber 1994). [. . .]

[. . .] Sport has become a fascinating subfield in which to revisit perennial feminist questions of structure and agency, as well as to explore more recent debates

---

* Taken and abridged from, M. Ferree, J. Lorber and B. Hess (eds) (1999) *Revisioning Gender*, Thousand Oaks, California: Sage.

over embodiment, identity, and power. We begin this chapter with an examination of recent research on men and sport to reflect on the limitations of employing an analytic gender lens that ignores or marginalizes the centrality of race and class. Then we discuss the extent to which bodily agency by athletic women represents resistance to oppression by exploring three contexts: the Title IX struggle for sex equity in high school and college sports, the recent championing of women's athletic participation by corporate liberals such as Nike, and the contradictory meanings surrounding muscular female bodies.

Athletic men: paying the price

When we disentangle the historical and contemporary relationship between sport and men's power, we must recognize the distinction between sport as a cultural practice that constructs dominant belief systems and the individual experience of sport as an athletic career. Clearly, for at least the past 100 years, the dominant cultural meanings surrounding athletic masculinity have served mostly to stabilize hegemonic masculinity in the face of challenges by women, working-class men, men of color, and immigrants (Crosset 1990; Kimmel 1990). However, the experience of male athletes is often fraught with contradiction and paradox. Although many male athletes may dream of being the next Michael Jordan, very few ever actually make a living playing sports (Messner 1992). Even for extremely successful male athletes, the rigor of attaining and maintaining athletic stardom often comes at the cost of emotional and interpersonal development (Connell 1990). And although athletic masculinity symbolizes an image of physical health and sexual virility, athletes commonly develop alienated relationships with their bodies, learning to relate to them like machines, tools, or even weapons to be "used up" to get a job done. As a result, many athletes and former athletes suffer from permanent injuries, poor health, and low life expectancy (Sabo 1994; White, Young, and McTeer 1995). In particular, it is disproportionately young men from poor socioeconomic and racial/ethnic backgrounds who pay these costs.

To put it simply, young men from race- or class-subordinated back-grounds disproportionately seek status, respect, empowerment, and upward mobility through athletic careers. Most of them do not make it to the mythical "top", but this majority is mostly invisible to the general public. Instead, those very few who do make it into the limelight – especially those in sports like football or boxing, that reward the most extreme possibilities of large, powerful, and violent male bodies – serve as public symbols of exemplary masculinity, with whom all men can identify *as men*, as separate and superior to women (Messner 1988, 1992). While serving to differentiate "men" from "women" symbolically, top male athletes – especially African American men in violent sports – are simultaneously available to be used by men as cultural symbols of differences among them. African American male athletes – for instance, boxer Mike Tyson – have become icons of an atavistic masculinity, in comparison to whom White middle-class men can construct themselves as kinder, gentler "new men" (Messner 1993a). This imagery of Black men includes a package of sexual potency and muscular power wrapped in danger. Just as African American males have been used in the past to symbolize fears of a "primitive" sexuality unleashed (Hoch 1979; Davis 1981), Americans are increasingly obsessed with documenting the sexual misbehaviors of Black male athletes (Messner 1993b).

Men's sport, then, constructs masculinities in complex and contradictory ways. At a time in history when physical strength is of less and less practical significance in workplaces, especially in the professional and managerial jobs of most White, college-educated men, African American, poor, and working-class men have increasingly "taken over" the sports to which they have access. But having played sports is of little or no practical use to most of these young men once their athletic careers have ended. Athletic skills rarely transfer over into nonsports careers. The significance of successful African American male athletes in the current gender order is *not* that they challenge dominant social meanings or power relations. To the contrary, they serve to stabilize ideas of natural difference and hierarchy between women and men and among men of different social classes and races.

We can draw two conclusions from this brief discussion of men's sports. First, although we can see African American men's struggles to achieve success and respect through sport as a collective response to class and racial constraints, this agency operates largely to *reproduce* – rather than to resist or challenge – current race, class, and gender relations of power. [...] Second, we can see by looking at men's sports that *simply* employing a "gender lens" to analyze sport critically is limiting, even dangerous. The current literature supports the claim that men's sport does continue to empower "men," but for the most part, it is not the men who are doing the playing who are being empowered. Clearly, when we speak of "sport and empowerment" for men, we need to ask, Which men? These two points – that "agency" is not necessarily synonymous with "resistance," and that we need to be very cautious about employing a simplistic gender lens to speak categorically about "men and sport" – will inform our examination of women's current movement into sports.

Sex equity for "women in sport"

Since the passage of Title IX of the Education Act Amendments, adopted by Congress in 1972, girls' and women's sports in the United States have changed in dramatic, but paradoxical, ways. On the one hand, there is no denying the rapid movement toward equity in the number of female participants and programs for women and girls (Cahn 1994; Carpenter 1993). [...] These numerical increases in opportunities to participate in such a masculine-structured institution as school sports prove the effectiveness of organizing politically and legally around the concept "woman." Indeed, the relative success of this post-Title IX liberal strategy of gender equity in sport was premised on the deployment of separate "male" and "female" sports.

On the one hand, at least within the confines of liberalism, a "strategic essentialism" that successfully deploys the category "woman" can result in moves toward greater distributive justice. [...]

[...] Yet, Title IX has not yet yielded anything close to equity for girls and women within sports – more boys and men still play sports; they still have far more opportunities, from the peewee level through professional sports; and girls and women often have to struggle for access to uniforms, travel money, practice facilities, and scholarships that boys and men routinely take for granted (Lopiano 1993; Women's Sports Foundation 1997). But the dramatic movement of girls and women into sport – and the continued legal basis for challenges to inequities that are provided by Title IX precedents – makes sport an impressive example of a previously almost entirely masculine terrain that is now gender contested. The very existence of skilled and strong women athletes demanding recognition and equal access to resources is a destabilizing tendency in the current gender order.

On the other hand, there are obvious limits in the liberal quest for gender equity in sport. [...] First, as the popularity, opportunities, and funding for women's sports have risen, the leadership positions have markedly shifted away from women to men. Radical critics of sport have argued that this shift toward men's control of girl and women athletes is but one indicator of the limits and dangers of a gender-blind model of equity that uncritically adopts the men's "military model" of sport (Nelson 1991). To be sure, this shift to men coaches was heroically resisted throughout the 1970s by many women coaches and athletic administrators behind the banner of the Association for Intercollegiate Athletics for Women (AIAW). [...] Locally, most women's athletic departments were folded into male athletic departments, and the hiring of coaches for women's sports was placed in the hands of male athletic directors.

As women's sports has become controlled by men, it increasingly reflects the most valued characteristics of men's sports: "hierarchy, competitiveness and aggression" (Hall 1996: 91). In the most "feminine" sports, men coaches are simultaneously demanding the aggressiveness of adult men athletes and the sub-missiveness of little girls – a most complex gender message! A poignant example of these dangers can be seen in women's gymnastics and ice-skating, where very young girls, typically coached mostly by men coaches who are often abusive, learn to practice with painful injuries and often develop severe eating disorders in order to keep their bodies "small, thin and prepubescent" (Ryan 1995: 103). [...]

As girls and women push for equity in sport, they are moving – often uncrit-ically – into a hierarchical system that has as its main goal to produce winners, champions, and profits. Although increased participation for girls and women apparently has its benefits at the lower levels, as the incentives mount for girl and women athletes to professionalize, they increasingly face many of the same lim-itations and dangers (in addition to some others, such as sexual harassment and rape) as those experienced by highly competitive men.

"If you let me play ..."

In recent years, corporate America has begun to awaken to the vast and lucra-tive potential markets that might be developed within and subsidiary to women's sports.

[. . .] In recent years, athletic footwear advertisements by Reebok and Nike have exemplified the ways that corporations have made themselves champions of women's athletic participation. In the early 1990s, Reebok was first to seize the lion's share of the female athletic shoe market. But by the mid-1990s, Nike had made great gains with a highly successful advertising campaign that positioned the corporation as the champion of girls' and women's rights inside and outside of sports. One influential TV spot included images of athletically active girls and women, with the voice-over saying things like, "If you let me play, I'll be less likely to drop out of school," and "If you let me play, I'll be better able to say no to unwanted sexual activity." These ads made use of the research findings from such organizations as the Women's Sports Foundation, documenting the positive, healthy, and empowering aspects of athletic participation for girls. Couching this information in the language of individual empowerment, Nike sold it to girls and women in the form of athletic shoes.

To be sure, the power of these commercials lies partly in the fact that they almost never mentioned shoes or even the Nike name. The message is that individual girls will be happier, healthier, and more in charge of their lives if we "let them play." The Nike "swoosh" logo is subtly displayed in the corner of the ads so that the viewer knows who is the source of these liberating ideas. It is through this kind of campaign that Nike has positioned itself as what Cole and Hribar (1995) call a "celebrity feminist," a corporate liberal entity that has successfully appropriated and co-opted the language of individual empowerment underlying the dominant discourse of opportunity for girls and women in sports. Aspiring athletes are then encouraged by slick advertising campaigns to identify their own individual empowerment – in essence, *their relationship to feminism* – with that of the corporate entity that acts as a celebrity feminist. If "feminist identity" can be displayed most readily through the wearing of the Nike logo on shoes and other athletic apparel, then displaying the Nike "swoosh" on one's body becomes a statement to the world that one is an independent, empowered individual – a successful young woman of the nineties.

There are fundamental limitations to this kind of "empowerment." If radical feminists are correct in claiming that patriarchy reproduces itself largely through men's ability to dominate and exploit women's bodies, we might suggest a corollary: Corporations have found peace and profit with liberal feminism by co-opting a genuine quest by women for bodily agency and empowerment and channeling it toward a goal of physical achievement severely limited by its consumerist context. The kind of collective women's agency that emphasizes the building of institutions such as rape crisis centers, domestic violence shelters, and community women's athletic leagues is a *resistant agency* through which women have empowered themselves to fight against and change the institutions that oppress them. In contrast, individual women's agency expressed as identification with corporate consumerism is a *reproductive agency* that firmly situates women's actions and bodies within the structural gender order that oppresses them.

In addition, Nike's commitment to women's liberation is contradicted by its own corporate practices. In 1996, when it posted its largest profits, and its CEO Phillip

Knight's stock was estimated to be worth $5 billion, the mostly women Indonesian workers who manufactured the shoes were paid about $2.25 a day. Workers who attempted to organize for higher pay and better working conditions were fired (Take Action for Girls 1996). Meanwhile, U.S. women's eager consumption of corporate celebrity feminism makes it almost impossible for them to see, much less to act upon, the exploitation of women workers halfway around the globe. [. . .]

Liberal feminism in sport has come full circle: a universalized concept of "women" was strategically deployed to push – with some impressive but limited success – for equal opportunities for women in sport. As these successes mounted, a key ideological support for hegemonic masculinity – the naturalized equation of male bodies with athletic ability and physical strength – was destabilized. But corporations have recently seized upon the individualist impulse of female empowerment that underlies liberal feminism, and have sold it back to women as an ideology and bodily practice that largely precludes any actual mobilizing around the collective concept of "women." Individual women are now implored by Nike to "Just do it" – just like the men "do it." Undoubtedly, many women strongly approve of, and feel good about, the Nike ads. But Nike's individualized and depoliticized "feminism" ignores how individuals who "do it" with Nike are implicated in an international system of racial, gender, and class exploitation of women workers in less developed nations.

Just as we argued in our discussion of the limits of sports for raising the status of working-class and African American men, here, too, gender analysis alone is not enough. It is not just muscular, or athletic, or "fit" bodies that must be considered in women's liberation – it is also laboring bodies as well. In fact, as we will argue next, a danger in contemporary reductionist understandings of empowerment as being synonymous with the development of one's body is that concentrating on toning muscles can easily transfer energies – especially those of women privileged by class and race – away from collective organizing to change institutions that disadvantage all women, but especially those who are poor, working-class, and racially disadvantaged.

Women and muscles

In addition to the ever-increasing numbers of women who compete in high school and college sport, more and more women today engage in fitness activities, lift weights, and enjoy the power of carrying musculature. [. . .] New bodily ideals can be said to have broadened from thin and slim to tight and toned, with an "allowance" for "substantial weight and bulk" (Bordo 1993: 191). By some standards, today's more muscular woman can be viewed as embodying agency, power, and independence in a way that exemplifies resistance to patriarchal ideals. However, just as within sport, women's bodily agency in fitness activities can be contradictory. Is this bodily agency resistant and/or empowering, or is the fit, muscled ideal simply the latest bodily requirement for women, a form of "self-surveillance and obedience" in service to patriarchal capitalism (Bartky 1988)?

Some feminists argue that when women exercise their agency to develop bodily mobility and muscular power, these activities are self-affirming for women and antithetical to patriarchal definitions of women as passive, docile, and weak (MacKinnon 1987; Nelson 1991; Young 1990). By fighting for access to participation in sport and fitness, women have created an empowering arena where the meaning of gender is being contested and renegotiated, and where active rejections of dominant notions of femininity may be forged (e.g., Bolin 1992; Gilroy 1989; Guthrie and Castelnuovo 1992; Kane and Lenskyj 1998; Lenskyj 1987; McDermott 1996; Theberge 1987). Other feminists, however, offer compelling counterarguments. First, there is the question as to whether bodily "empowerment" is merely a modern version of the "docile body," the intensely limiting and oppressive bodily management and scrutiny with which women learn to be complicit (Bordo 1993). For some women (especially those who are White, middle-class, and married heterosexuals) this complicit agency might result in more work on top of their already stifling "second shift" (Hochschild 1989) – a "third shift" that consists of long doses of effort invested in conforming to the latest touted bodily "requirement." It is these women, whose daily lives in families and careers might leave them feeling less than empowered, who would then respond to advertisements that encourage them to participate in sport and fitness in order to feel a sense of empowerment through their bodies. Couched in the logic of individualism and the Protestant work ethic, it seems that a woman needs only enact her free will and "just do it" in order to "have it all." But "doing it" the corporate individualist way involves a radical turning inward of agency toward the goal of transformation of one's own body, in contrast to a turning outward to mobilize for collective political purposes, with the goal of transforming social institutions. Clearly, despite its uplifting tone and seemingly patriotic commitment to American women, corporate slogans such as Nike's beg several questions, such as: Just do *what* And *for whom?*

Just as the cult of true womanhood excluded numerous women from its "ideal" in the early nineteenth century, a similar conceptual vacuum arises here. After all, the dominant fitness industry message very likely "has no relevance to the majority of working-class women, or to Black women, or those from other ethnic minorities" (Hargreaves 1994: 161). [. . .]

Just as images of physically powerful and financially successful African American men ultimately did not challenge, but instead continued to construct a stratified race, class, and gender order, current images of athletic women appear to represent a broadening of the definitional boundaries of what Connell (1987) calls "emphasized femininity" to include more muscular development. But the resistant possibilities in images of athletic women are largely contained by the continued strong assertion of (and commercial rewards for) retaining a link between heterosexual attractiveness and body image. For instance, many lauded Olympic track star Florence Griffith-Joyner's muscularity as a challenge to the dominant image of femininity and to images of men as physically superior. However, Griffith-Joyner's muscularity existed alongside "rapier-like" nails, flowing hair, and spectacular outfits, which ultimately situated her body and its markings firmly within a commercialized modernization of heterosexual femininity (Messner forthcoming).

Now more than ever, the commodification of women's bodies may mean that when women "just do it," they are "just doing" 1990s "heterosexy" femininity. In the media, these bodies are not unambiguously resistant images of powerful women, but rather an ambivalent framing or subtle trivialization or sexualization of women's bodies that undermines their muscles and their athletic accomplishments (Duncan and Hasbrook 1988; Messner, Duncan, and Wachs 1996; Kane 1995; Kane and Lenskyj 1998). Female bodybuilders in particular illustrate these gender ambiguities. Research demonstrates that women can and do press and contest the limits of emphasized femininity. However, their agency is contained by the structure, rules, and ideologies of women's bodybuilding. [. . .]

Researchers who study women's participation in fitness activities find the same tendency to adhere to emphasized femininity as is shown by women athletes and bodybuilders. They tend to avoid lifting weights "too much" for fear of being "too big." Instead, they engage in long doses of cardiovascular work, which is thought to emphasize tone and leanness (Dworkin forthcoming; Markula 1996). Just as women in male-dominated occupations often hit a glass ceiling that halts their professional advancement, there appears to be a glass ceiling on women's musculature that constrains the development of women's muscular strength. Defined according to the latest commodified eroticization of heterosexual femininity, most women (with differences by race, class, sexuality, age) remain acutely aware of how much muscle is "allowed," how much is "still" attractive.

Conclusion

Through an examination of gender, bodies, and sport, we have made three main points in this chapter that may illuminate more general attempts to understand and change the current gender order. First, although sport has been an arena for contesting the status quo by men of color and by White women and women of color, the positive results have been individual rather than collective. A few star athletes have become celebrities, but their popularity has not raised the overall status of disadvantaged men and women (although it may have upgraded the physical potentiality of middle-class White women). Second, whatever sport has accomplished in terms of equity, women's and men's sports are still segregated, and men's sports are still dominant in commercial value and in the media. Third, rather than breaking down conventional concepts of masculinity and femininity, organized sport has overblown the cultural hegemony of heterosexualized, aggressive, violent, heavily muscled male athletes and heterosexualized, flirtatious, moderately muscled female athletes who are accomplished and competitive but expected to be submissive to the control of men coaches and managers.

The link in all these outcomes is that organized sport is a commercial activity first and foremost. Organized sport is financially underwritten by corporations that sell shoes and clothing to a public looking for vicarious thrills and personal "fitness." The corporations capitalize on the celebrity of star athletes, who use individual achievements to make more money, rather than to help upgrade the communities from which they have come. Their endorsements sell individual achievement and conventional beauty and sexuality as well as Nikes and Reeboks. A further negative consequence to the upbeat message of "Just do it" is that many of the appurtenances of sport and fitness are produced by the labor of poorly paid, malnourished, and probably physically unfit women workers.

Does this mean that women's agency in sports and other physical activities is a dead end that should be abandoned by feminist activists? Absolutely not. We think that sport is like any other institution: We cannot abandon it, nor can we escape from it. Instead, we must struggle within it. [...] We think feminists need to fight on two fronts in the battle for equity in sports. On the one hand, we must continue to push for equal opportunities for girls and women in sports. On the other hand, although the research points to benefits for girls and women who play sports at the lower levels, many of the girls and women who are professionalized into corporate sports can expect – just as most of their men counterparts in corporate sports can – to pay emotional and physical costs.

But in challenging women's uncritical adoption of the dominant values of corporate sport, we must be cautious not to fall into the same trap as have past activists for girls' and women's sports. In the 1920s and 1930s, in the wake of two decades of burgeoning athleticism by girls and women, medical leaders and physical educators responded with what now appear to be hysterical fears that vigorous physical activity for girls and women carried enormous physical and psychological dangers (Cahn 1994). The result of these fears was the institutionalization of an "adapted model" (i.e., "tamed down" sports for women) that served to ghettoize women's sports, leaving the hegemonic masculinity of men's sport virtually unchallenged for the next 40 years. Given this history, today's advocates of women's sports walk a perilous tightrope. They must assert the positive value of vigorous physical activity and muscular strength for girls and women while simultaneously criticizing the unhealthy aspects of men's sports. A key to the accomplishment of this task must involve the development of a critical analysis of the dominant assumptions, beliefs, and practices of *men's* sports (Thompson 1988; Messner and Sabo 1994). In addition, we need to continue to explore feminist alternatives, for women and for men, to the "military model," with its emphasis on heroism, "playing through pain," and winning at all costs (Birrell and Richter 1987; Nelson 1991; Theberge 1985).

The activist fight for women and girls as a group will not be helped by simplistic scholarship that acts as a cheering section for numerical increases in women's athletic participation, or for the increasing visibility of women's athletics in televised ads. Nor will a simple "gender lens" that views sport uncritically in terms of undifferentiated and falsely universalized categories of "men" and "women" take us very far in framing questions and analyzing data. Different groups of men and of women disproportionately benefit from and pay the costs of the current social organization of sports. We need an analytic framework that appreciates the importance of class, racial, and sexual differences among both men and women while retaining the feminist impulse that places the need to empower the disadvantaged in the foreground.

Data from empirical observation of sport demonstrate the absence of absolute categorical differences between "men" and "women" – instead, there is a "continuum of performance" that, when acknowledged, can radically deconstruct dichotomous sex categories (Kane 1995). Obscuring this continuum are the social processes through which sport constructs and naturalizes differences and inequality between "men" and "women." Does this observation lead us down the path of radical deconstruction? We think the discussion in this chapter demonstrates just the opposite. The current post-structuralist preoccupation with deconstructing binary categories like "men and women" (e.g., Butler 1990; Sedgewick 1990) has produced new discourses and practices that disrupt and fracture these binaries (Lorber 1996). Yet simply deconstructing our *discourse* about binary categories does not necessarily challenge the material basis of master categories to which subordinate categories of people stand in binary opposition: the capitalist class, men, heterosexuals, Whites. In fact, quite the contrary may be true (Stein and Plummer 1994). As many feminists have pointed out, although it is certainly true that every woman is somewhat uniquely situated, a radical deconstruction of the concept "woman" could lead to an individualism that denies similarity of experience, thus leading to depoliticized subjects. We would argue that it is currently corporations such as Nike that are in the forefront of the widespread development of this sort of depoliticized individualist "empowerment" among women. Radical deconstruction, therefore, is very much in the interests of the most powerful institutions in our world, as it leaves us feeling (at best) individually "empowered," so long as we are able to continue to consume the right products, while making it unlikely we will identify common interests with others in challenging institutions.

Rather than a shift toward radical deconstruction, the research on gender, bodies, and sport suggests that it is essential to retain and build upon the concept of social structure, with its attendant emphasis on the importance of people's shared positions within social institutions (Duncan 1993; Messner 1992). Such a materialist analysis reveals how differential access to resources and opportunities and the varieties of structured constraints shape the contexts in which people think, interact, and construct political practices and discourse. A critical analysis of gender within a materialist, structural analysis of institutions entails a reassertion of the crucial importance (though not necessarily the primacy) of social class. Interestingly, as recent intellectual trends have taken many scholars away from the study of institutions toward a preoccupation with individuals, bodies, and difference, the literature has highlighted race, gender, and sexual identities in new and important ways, but social class has too often dropped out of the analysis. As we have demonstrated, discussions of the possibilities and limits of women's agency in gender equity struggles in sport, the co-optation of feminism by Nike's "celebrity feminism," and the current encouragement of physical fitness for middle-class women all need to be examined within the context of distributive justice. We also need a clear analysis of the position of women and men as workers in organized sport; as marketable celebrities; as workers in sweatshops making sport shoes, clothing, and equipment; and as consumers of these products and symbols. This analysis must be informed by feminist theories of the intersections of race, class, and gender (e.g., Baca Zinn and Dill 1996). Politically, this work can inform an alliance politics that is grounded simultaneously in a structural analysis of power and a recognition of differences and inequalities between and among women and men.

References

Baca Zinn, Maxine and Bonnie Thornton Dill. 1996. "Theorizing difference from Multiracial Feminism." Feminism Studies 22: 321–31.

Bartky, Sandra L. 1988. "Foucault, Femininity, and the Modernization of Patriarchal Power." In *Feminism and Foucault: Reflections on Resistance*, edited by I. Diamond and L. Quinby. Boston: Northeastern University Press.

Birrell, Susan. 1988. "Discourses on the Gender/Sport Relationship: From Women in Sport to Gender Relations." *Exercise and Sport Sciences Review* 16: 59–200.

Birrell, Susan and Cheryl L. Cole. 1990. "Double Fault: Rence Richards and the Construction and Naturalization of Difference." *Sociology of Sport Journal* 7: 1–21.

——, eds. 1994. *Women, Sport, and Culture*. Champaign, IL: Human Kinetics.

Birrell, Susan and Diana M. Richter 1987. "Is a Diamond Forever? Feminist Transformations of Sport." *Women's Studies International Forum* 10: 395–409.

Bolin, A. 1992 "Vandalized Vanity: Feminine Physique Betrayed and Portrayed." Pp. 79–90 in *Tattoo, Torture, Mutilation, and Adornment: The Denaturalization of the Body in Culture and Text*, edited by Frances E. Mascia-Lees and Patricia Sharpe. Albany: State University of New York Press.

Bordo, Susan. 1993. *Unbearable Weight: Feminism, Western Culture, and the Body*. Berkeley: University of California Press.

Bryson, Lois. 1987. "Sport and the Maintenance of Masculine Hegemony." *Women's Studies International Forum* 10: 349–60.

Butler, Judith. 1990. *Gender Trouble: Feminism and the Subversion of Identity*. New York: Routledge.

Cahn, Susan K. 1994. *Coming on Strong: Gender and Sexuality in Twentieth Century Women's Sport*. New York: Free Press.

Carpenter, Linda Jean. 1993. "Letters Home: My Life with Title IX." Pp.79–94 in *Women in Sport: Issues and Controversies*, edited by Greta L. Cohen. Newbury Park, CA: Sage.

Cole, Cheryl L. and Amy Hribar. 1995. "Celebrity Feminism: Nike Style Post-Fordism Transcendence, and Consumer Power." *Sociology of Sport Journal* 12: 347–69.

Connell, R. W. 1987. *Gender and Power*. Stanford, CA: Stanford University Press.

——, 1990. "An Iron Man: The Body and Some Contradictions of Hegemonic Masculinity." Pp. 83–95 in *Sport, Men and the Gender Order: Critical Feminist Perspectives*, edited by Michael A. Messner and Donald F. Sabo. Champaign, IL: Human Kinetics.

Crosset, Todd W. (1990). "Masculinity, Sexuality and the Development of Early Modern Sport." Pp. 45–54 in *Sport, Men and the Gender Order: Critical Feminist Perspectives*, edited by Michael A. Messner and Donald F. Sabo. Champaign, IL: Human Kinetics.

Davis, Angela Y. 1981. *Women, Race, and Class*. New York: Random House.

Duncan, Margaret Carlisle. 1993. "Beyond Analyses of Sport Media Texts: An Argument for Formal Analyses of Institutional Structures." *Sociology of Sport Journal* 10: 353–72.

Duncan, Margaret Carlisle and Cynthia A. Hasbrook. 1988. "Denial of Power in Televised Women's Sports." *Sociology of Sport Journal* 5: 1–21.

Dworkin, Shari L. Forthcoming. "A Woman's Place Is in the … Cardiovascular Room? Gender Relations, the Body, and the Gym." In *Athletic Intruders*, edited by Anne Bolin and Jane Granskog. Albany: State University of New York Press.

Gilroy, S. 1989. "The Embody-ment of Power: Gender and Physical Activity." *Leisure Studies* 8: 163–71.

Guthrie, Sharon R. and Shirley Castelnuovo. 1992. "Elite Women Bodybuilders: Model of Resistance or Compliance?" *Play and Culture* 5: 378–400.

Hall, M. Ann. 1988. "The Discourse of Gender and Sport: From Femininity to Feminism." *Sociology of Sport Journal* 5: 330–40.

——, 1996. *Feminism and Sporting Bodies: Essays on Theory and Practice*. Champaign, IL: Human Kinetics.

Hargreaves, Jennifer. 1994. *Sporting Females: Critical Issues in the History and Sociology of Women's Sport*. New York: Routledge.

Hoch, Paul. 1979. *White Hero Black Beast: Racism, Sexism and the Mask of Masculinity*. London: Pluto.

Hochschild, Arlie R. 1989. *The Second Shift*. New York: Avon.

Kane, Mary Jo. 1995. "Resistance/Transformation of the Oppositional Binary: Exposing Sport as a Continuum." *Journal of Sport and Social Issues* 19: 191–218.

Kane, Mary Jo and Helen Lenskyj. 1998. "Media Treatment of Female Athletes: Issues of Gender and Sexualities." In *MediaSport: Cultural Sensibilities and Sport in the Media Age*, edited by Lawrence A. Wenner. London: Routledge.

Kimmel, Michael S. 1990. "Baseball and the Reconstitution of American Masculinity, 1880–1920." Pp. 55–66 in *Sport, Men and the Gender Order: Critical Feminist Perspectives*, edited by Michael A. Messner and Donald F. Sabo. Champaign, IL: Human Kinetics.

Lenskyj, Helen. 1987. "Female Sexuality and Women's Sport." *Women's Studies International Forum* 4: 381–86.

Lopiano, Donna A. 1993. "Political Analysis: Gender Equity Strategies for the Future." Pp. 104–16 in *Women in Sport: Issues and Controversies*, edited by Greta L. Cohen. Newbury Park, CA: Sage.

Lorber, Judith. 1994. *Paradoxes of Gender*. New Haven, CT: Yale University Press.

——, 1996. "Beyond the Binaries: Depolarizing the Categories of Sex, Sexuality, and Gender." *Sociological Inquiry* 66: 143–59.

MacKinnon, Catharine A. 1987. *Feminism Unmodified: Discourses on Life and Law*. Cambridge, MA: Harvard University Press.

Michael A. Messner and Donald F. Sabo. Champaign, IL: Human Kinetics.

Markula, Pirkko. 1996. "Firm but Shapely, Fit but Sexy, Strong but Thin: The Postmodern Aerobicizing Female Bodies." *Sociology of Sport Journal* 12: 424–53.

McDermott, Lisa. 1996. "Towards a Feminist Understanding of Physicality within the Context of Women's Physically Active and Sporting Lives." *Sociology of Sport Journal* 13: 12–30.

McKay, Jim. 1991. *No Pain, No Gain? Sport and Australian Culture*. Englewood Cliffs, NJ: Prentice Hall.

Messner, Michael A. 1988. "Sports and Male Domination: The Female Athlete as Contested Ideological Terrain." *Sociology of Sport Journal* 5: 197–211.

Messner, Michael A. 1992. *Power at Play: Sports and the Problem of Masculinity*. Boston: Beacon.

——, 1993a. "Changing Men and Feminist Politics in the United States." *Theory and Society* 22: 723–37.

——, 1993b. "White Men Misbehaving: Feminism, Afrocentrism, and the Promise of a Critical Standpoint." *Journal of Sport and Social Issues* 16: 136–44.

Messner, Michael A. Forthcoming. "Theorizing Gendered Bodies: Beyond the Subject/Object Dichotomy." In *Exercising Power: The Making and Remaking of the Body*, edited by Cheryl L. Cole, John Loy, and Michael A. Messner. Albany: State University of New York Press.

Messner, Michael A., Margaret Carlisle Duncan, and Faye Linda Wachs. 1996. "The Gender of Audience-Building: Televised Coverage of Men's and Women's NCAA Basketball." *Sociological Inquiry* 66: 422–39.

Messner, Michael A. and Donald F. Sabo. 1990. "Towards a Critical Feminist Reappraisal of Sport, Men and the Gender Order." In *Sport, Men and the Gender Order: Critical Feminist Perspectives*, edited by Michael A. Messner and Donald F. Sabo. Champaign, IL: Human Kinetics.

——, 1994. *Sex, Violence and Power in Sports: Rethinking Masculinity*. Freedom, CA: Crossing Press.

Nelson, Mariah Burton. 1991. *Are We Winning Yet? How Women Are Changing Sports and Sports Are Changing Women*. New York: Random House.

Ryan, Joan. 1995. *Little Girls in Pretty Boxes: The Making and Breaking of Elite Gymnasts and Figure Skaters*. New York: Warner.

Sabo, Donald F. 1994. "Pigskin, Patriarchy, and Pain." Pp. 82–88 in *Sex, Violence and Power in Sports: Rethinking Masculinity*, by Michael A. Messner and Donald F. Sabo. Freedom, CA: Crossing Press.

Sedgewick, Eve K. (1990). *Epistemology of the Closet*. Berkeley: University of California Press.

Stein, Arlene and Ken Plummer. 1994. "'I Can't Even Think Straight': Queer Theory and the Missing Sexual Revolution in Sociology." *Sociological Theory* 12: 178–87.

Take Action for Girls. 1996. "The Two Faces of Nike." *Take Action for Girls Newsletter* 1 (November): 2.

Theberge, Nancy. 1981. "A Critique of Critiques: Radical and Feminist Writings on Sport." *Social Forces* 60: 341–53.

——, 1985. "Toward a Feminist Alternative to Sport as a Male Preserve." *Quest* 37: 193–202.

——, 1987. "Sport and Women's Empowerment." *Women's Studies International Forum* 10: 387–93.

Thompson, Shona M. 1988. "Challenging the Hegemony: New Zealand Women's Opposition to Rugby and the Reproduction of Capitalist Patriarchy." *International Review of the Sociology of Sport* 23: 205–12.

White, Philip G., Kevin Young, and William G. McTeer. 1995. "Sport, Masculinity, and the Injured Body." Pp. 158–82 in *Men's Health and Illness: Gender, Power, and the Body*, edited by Donald F. Sabo and Frederick Gordon. Thousand Oaks, CA: Sage.

Whitson, David. 1990. "Sport in the Social Construction of Masculinity." Pp. 19–30 in *Sport, Men and the Gender Order: Critical Feminist Perspectives*, edited by Michael A. Messner and Donald F. Sabo. Champaign, IL: Human Kinetics.

Women's Sports Foundation. 1997. *The Women's Sports Foundation Gender Equity Report Card: A Survey of Athletic Opportunity in American Higher Education*. East Meadow, NY: Women's Sports Foundation.

Young, Iris M. 1990. *Throwing Like a Girl and Other Essays in Feminist Philosophy and Social Theory*. Bloomington: Indiana University Press.

3 Sport feminism: The contribution of feminist thought to our understandings of gender and sport

Sheila Scraton and Anne Flintoff

Introduction

In this chapter we seek to provide a thorough overview of the distinctive strands of second wave feminist thought and how they have been applied within sports feminism. There are in existence comprehensive critiques of the 'malestream' of sport sociology and the contribution of feminism in challenging the male dominance of this academic area of study (Hall 1988, 1996; Hargreaves 1994). We are interested in taking a 'journey' through contemporary feminist thought, interrogating how it has contributed to our understanding of sport and the impact (if any) that it has had on policy and practice. This journey through feminism and sport demonstrates that gender relations are not static but change over time. Equally all theories are fluid and dynamic, do not emerge from a vacuum but build on, develop and challenge knowledge and understanding that has gone before. How we understand and explain gender and sport is influenced by social, political and economic change and by developments both within and outside sport. Sport itself is dynamic and can be altered by shifting gender relations and can itself, be part of the processes that challenge and shift hegemonic notions of gender.

Fundamentally, feminism has been about seeking to change and equalize the social relations within which women are oppressed and disadvantaged. However, the reason that there have developed different feminist positions is because there have been (and continue to be) differences in definition of the 'oppressor' and where the source of oppression lies. Indeed the use of the terms 'oppression' and 'oppressor' is itself a source of contention as some feminists would use more moderate language in relation to women's inequality or subordination (Whelan 1995). Thus, as feminism has developed both theoretically and politically so it has become more complex with the development of many feminisms or distinctive strands of feminist thought each focusing on specific areas and issues.

In this article we outline the main features of the major strands in contemporary feminist thought. It is important to note at this point, that to separate out and 'label' different feminisms is to a certain extent a false distinction. There are many overlaps between different positions, writers shift their own understandings and 'new' feminisms emerge out of existing theoretical positions. However, in order to provide an adequate journey through feminist thought it is important to recognize that there have been different approaches within feminism each of which has posited different 'causes' or 'solutions' to gender inequalities. Rather than perceiving the different strands as having clear boundaries and being totally distinct from each other, it is more useful to think of 'waves' of theory. Each wave grows out of and contains aspects of the wave that started further out from the shoreline. Thus liberal feminism developed as a wave of theory reflecting and influencing women's experiences at a certain point in our history in the 1960s and 1970s. Out of this wave developed radical and socialist feminism each of which incorporated some of the arguments from liberal feminism but provided explanations centred on very different understandings and concerns. More recently in the 1990s we have post-structuralist theory once again building from and challenging what has gone before. However, at no point is one theory totally replaced by another. We still have liberal feminist thought as well as feminists who take a radical or socialist theoretical and political stance. The 'new' post-structuralist wave(s) of theory reflects perceived major political, economic and social shifts at the end of the twentieth century and addresses some very different questions and concerns to those central to the earlier second wave feminist theories. Yet to understand 'new' theory it is important that the foundations or early waves of theory are recognized. We can then be in a position to decide ourselves whether some of the 'old' questions of early feminism are now outdated and surpassed by new more relevant concerns or whether some questions and issues continue to be pertinent for our sporting lives in the twenty-first century.

Throughout our journey through feminist thought we focus on some of the key issues and explanations that have received attention by sport feminists. This further highlights how different feminist approaches can provide different and sometimes competing 'readings' of the same sporting issue. For example, in trying to understand and explain why women have not participated in football (soccer) to the same extent as men we could offer an explanation based on their lack of access and opportunity and their socialization into feminine sports (a liberal approach). Alternatively we could look more specifically at the male control of the governing bodies of football across the world and understand this in relation to patriarchal power (a radical approach). During our engagement with the diverse strands of feminism, we highlight the theoretical shift over the past three decades in sport feminism from an early emphasis on women's shared oppression and inequality to a concern with difference. Through focusing on difference there is increasingly an exploration of the diversity of women's experiences with new questions and issues raised. These include, for example, questions relating to gendered sporting bodies, diverse and fluid identities and the potential of sport to transgress the traditional boundaries of femininity and masculinity. We hope that by taking you on this journey through the development of feminist thought in sport you will come to appreciate the complexities and excitement offered by feminist theories and their contribution to our understandings of gender and sport.

Strands of feminist thought

Feminist theories can be characterized as founded on liberal democratic beliefs (liberal feminism), structural power relations (radical, socialist) and post-structuralist notions of difference and power as plural and productive (black feminism, post-structural feminism). To reiterate what we stated in the introduction, these are broad categories that do not do justice to the overlaps and the complexities within and across the different strands. However, in order to apply feminist theories to sport it is important to understand how and why different feminisms have developed and how they give primacy to different factors. There is not the space to engage in a full debate about all the strands of feminist thought, which can be accessed elsewhere (Tong 2000; Whelehan 1995). The following highlights some of the key points underpinning the development of different feminisms and their application to understanding gender and sport.

Liberal democracy

Liberal feminism developed from Western liberal philosophical positions that go back to the seventeenth century. Early feminism was based on the demand for women to have equal rights to those that men held 'naturally'. The legacy of liberal feminism is in the early writings of Mary Wolstencraft, John Stuart Mills and Harriet Taylor (Rossi, 1970) who challenged essentialist notions of femininity and the dichotomy that posited rationality as masculine/male and emotionality as feminine/female. They argued strongly that women are denied their rights through their lack of suffrage (legal rights), their lack of property rights and particularly in their restricted access to education.

Modern liberal feminism bears the legacy of this tradition in liberal thinking and consequently focuses its attention on equality of access and opportunity. It is because girls and women have not had the same access and opportunities as boys and men that they have been disadvantaged and therefore denied their rights. This lack of opportunity is seen in different socialization practices (in the family and schooling) and through gender stereotyping and discrimination. Consequently changes in the law via legal reform and in educational practices are seen to be essential for the liberation of women.

The underlying assumption of a liberal feminist approach to sport is that sport is fundamentally sound and represents a positive experience to which girls and women need access. It is argued that differences in female sports participation are the results of socialization practices carried out by institutions such as the family, the media and school (Greendorfer 1993; Oglesby 1978). For example, girls are socialized into 'feminine' activities such as netball, gymnastics, or hockey and into a 'feminine' physicality, and boys are socialized into 'masculine' sports such as football, rugby or cricket and into a 'masculine' physicality (Scraton 1992). Furthermore, discriminatory practices prevent women from having equal access to sport opportunities. These include unequal access to facilities and resources; for example, in most private golf clubs 'lady' players have limitations on when they can play, usually being restricted to one day at a weekend or tee times later in the day (Crosset 1995; Rogers 1988); and despite two decades of debates about equal opportunities in education there is evidence to suggest that opportunities for sport participation for girls is still less than that for boys (Office for Standards in Education 1995). Women remain under-represented in the decision-making positions in sport and in higher coaching and leadership posts (Knoppers 1994; White and Brackenridge 1985). Legal restrictions also act to reduce women's opportunities for sports involvement. The UK Sex Discrimination Act 1975 excludes sport from its remit and as a result sports clubs are not required to provide equal access and opportunities for girls and women (Talbot 1993).

Liberal feminism has placed these issues on the agenda of sports organizations, governing bodies, schools and other institutions involved in delivering, providing and developing sport. Pressures from activists working on women and sport initiatives (e.g., Women's Sports Foundation (WSF); Women's Sport International (WSI); the Windhoek Agreement) and the application of theory to practice have resulted in the opening up of opportunities for some women, and issues of equity and equality becoming part of the mainstream sports agenda (United Kingdom Sports Council 1998). There are few sporting contexts where equal opportunities are not paid lip service, although the reality of experience for some women involved can be very different!

These early feminist critiques are valuable for their rejection of biological explanations for women's subordination in sport, and for establishing that gender is socially constructed. They are important, also, for documenting the real distributive inequalities between men's and women's sport and for highlighting the significance of women role models, both as participants and decision makers in sport. Many of the questions raised by early liberal feminists remain pertinent to contemporary sport practice. Private sport clubs remain outside the equal opportunities legislation, so discrimination can and does continue, although both individuals and groups of women continue to put up resistance on a daily basis. Physical education in schools still offers different activities that are gender defined, and teaching can produce dominant gender ideologies (e.g., Scraton and Flintoff 2001). Women are still not in decision-making positions in sport, although some small inroads have been made onto committee structures (Talbot 2001).

However, the focus on socialization and sex-role differentiation by liberal feminism is now seen as problematic because it tends to see women as an homogeneous group. Early policy initiatives, for example, identified 'women' as a target group, with little regard paid to the differences between women (White 1995). This approach also unquestioningly accepts men's sport practices and organization, and defines women and their world, not sport itself, as the problem. This approach can be described therefore, as an implementary approach in that the focus is very much on reform, rather than on a fundamental challenge to the broader structural power relations of sport. Although liberal feminism has been very influential in challenging existing policy and practice, critics of this approach argue that it remains locked in a concern about differences between men and women with the fundamental aim being for women to gain access to the same opportunities as men.

This fails to question the underpinning structures of society and the institution of sport to which women are fighting to gain access. What is seen to be missing is an analysis of gender *relations* rather than simply sex difference. What we understand about 'masculinity' at any one time is always defined *in relation* to 'femininity'. However, these ideas are not just relational, but are also *hierarchical*, where one set of attributes and associated activities (men's) are viewed as more important than the others (women's). Gender relations can therefore be defined as relations of power 'whereby men as a group have more power over women than women have over them; they are socially constructed, not biologically given; and they are not fixed but rather subject to historical change and can be transformed' (Hall 1990: 226). For some feminists the questions are much more about the power relations between women and men and the structures and institutions of society that maintain and reproduce these inequalities. Thus gaining access to an unequal society is insufficient and there needs to be a more fundamental challenge to structural power relations.

Structural power relations

Radical feminism developed out of radical politics in the 1960s and 1970s. There has always been a strong link between radical activism and the theories that developed to explain women's oppression. Fundamentally their explanation is concerned with underlying structural power relations that are the result of the systematic maintenance of male power through patriarchy, whereby men as a group dominate women as a group. Patriarchy as a concept has received critical attention over the past few decades with many attempts to provide clear definitions that recognize its complexity (Millet 1971; Walby 1990). Radical feminists explore the nature of oppression through the personal experiences of women (the 'personal is political') and centralize sexuality as a major site of men's domination over women through the social institutionalization of heterosexuality (Rich 1980). This has led to an analysis of compulsory heterosexuality and lesbian feminism. Rich (1980) argues that heterosexuality is defined as the norm both for individuals and within institutional settings, thus it becomes the only *legitimate* form of sexuality. Compulsory heterosexuality acts as a form of social and sexual control by normalizing and naturalizing (hetero)sexuality. Through this, radical feminists argue, male power is manifested and maintained. Male violence against women is understood as part of this social control of women and is fundamental to women's oppression (Dworkin 1981). As men and male power is seen to be the primary cause of women's oppression and inequality, a response has been to celebrate women's values (Rich 1980), raise women's consciousness and to develop a separatist philosophy. The degree to which separatism is developed differs from women-only events and spaces to the adoption of a total separatist lifestyle.

Whereas liberal feminists argue that women have unequal access to decision making positions, radical feminists are more interested in the power over women by men that is maintained within and through sport. Central to men's domination over women is how men's sexuality functions to control women in their work, sport, leisure and schooling. This control operates in both the private and public spheres and benefits all men regardless of their desires and objectives. Radical feminists working in sport have been interested in the role of sport in the social construction of male sexual dominance and female sexual submission. For example, Llenskyj (1986; 1994) argues that discussions about 'femininity' in sport should be better focused on sexuality, such is the strong association between gender and sexuality. Femininity should be viewed as a code name for heterosexuality. Through sport, females are encouraged to develop an acceptable 'femininity' central to which is heterosexual attractiveness and availability. Women's involvement in sport is controlled and restricted through their clothing and their need to present a 'heterosexy' image (Griffin 1992; Llenskyj 1994). For example, the clothing for international women's beach volleyball competitions states that the bikini bottoms must not have a side deeper than 6 cm. This is less to do with appropriateness of dress for the sport and more about the objectification of women's bodies. Women's objectification in sport is evidenced further in the media portrayal of sportswomen through an emphasis on their appearance, sexuality and their motherhood/domestic role in the family (Creedon 1994; Hargreaves 1993; Pirinen 1997; Wright and Clarke 1999). This takes place in our print and broadcast media and is supported by the 'use' of women as display in male sports such as motor racing and boxing (Hargreaves 1993).

Radical feminists have contributed to our understandings of lesbianism and homophobia in sport. Research in this area shows how lesbians in sport and physical education are constructed as deviant, silenced, delegitimized and stigmatized as abnormal. Importantly, they demonstrate, also, the negotiations and resistances developed by lesbians to maintain a presence in homophobic sport contexts (Cahn 1994; Clarke 1998; Griffin 1998; Lenskyj 1991). They do this by the development of various strategies including avoidance, the construction of complex boundaries around themselves, deflection and 'playing' the heterosexual (Clarke 1995). This work has been extended by male pro-feminist writers to an analysis of gay men's position and experiences in sport (Messner 1992; Pronger 1990; 1998).

Radical feminists' work on male violence to women has been applied to sport by demonstrating the continuum of violence from sexually derogative comments to sexual abuse and rape (Brackenridge 2001; Brackenridge and Kirby 1997). Within sport, this is a relatively new area of concern dealing with important and sensitive issues; male violence is experienced in sport, both 'on and off the field'. Examples include domestic violence and male professional sportsmen; the sexual abuse and rape of athletes by male coaches; and sexual assaults by male student-athletes on University campuses in the USA (Crosset *et al.* 1995; Kirby and Greaves 1996; Fasting *et al.* 2000).

A radical feminist approach to understanding sport emphasizes the importance of consciousness raising about violence and sexual abuse and supports the development of anti-discriminatory policies challenging homophobia and discrimination against lesbians and gays. Radical feminism has made an important impact on gender relations particularly through influencing institutional understanding of male violence (domestic violence units in the police, rape as male power) and the significance of women-only space in providing further opportunities for women in a range of areas. This separate provision ranges from local initiatives (e.g., women-only sessions in leisure and sport centres) to large scale, international sporting events (e.g., women's sports organizations, the Women's International and British Games 1924, and the Gay Games). Furthermore, a radical feminist approach to sport suggests the need to reconstruct or recreate sport into forms that celebrate women's values rather than those more traditionally associated with masculine aggression and competition (Birrell and Richter 1987; Mitten 1992).

However, radical feminism is criticized for its tendency to essentialism and biological reductionism. There is a real danger in celebrating the importance of women's values that femininity is reified and becomes fixed and reduced to a biological explanation. In addition the concentration on patriarchy and the shared oppression of women by men is seen to fail fully to explore the divisions between women based on class, 'race' and ethnicity.

Whereas patriarchy is seen to be the primary structure of oppression in radical feminism, *Marxist feminism* identifies gender inequalities as deriving from capitalism, class and economic exploitation. The sexual division of labour is fundamental to this approach and focuses on how capital benefits from women's unpaid domestic labour and their maintenance of the future labour force (childcare) and the day-to-day care of male labourers. Because of this narrow focus on capitalism, *socialist feminism* looks more specifically at the relationships between class and gender and the systems of capitalism and patriarchy. To a large extent socialist feminism has replaced the economic determinist approach of Marxist feminism and remains the feminist approach that seeks to explore the complex dynamics of class and gender relations. Women's oppression cannot simply be explained by class relations and the sexual division of labour (Marxist feminism) or by men's power over women (radical feminism). Socialist feminism attempts to provide a more comprehensive explanation that incorporates both of these areas.

A major problem for socialist feminists is how the relationship between class and gender can be theorized without giving primacy to one over the other. This has become more complex as socialist feminists have responded to the work of black feminists (which is discussed in the next section) who have argued powerfully against the ethnocentricity of white feminism. Socialist feminism has responded by looking more closely at the inter-relationships of gender, race and class located within capitalism, patriarchy and neo-colonialism. A strength of socialist feminism is that it addresses differences between women and continues to try to provide a comprehensive theoretical position that draws from and develops the issues relating to class, race and gender inequalities. However, both radical feminists and black feminists argue that in the final analysis socialist feminism gives primacy to class and economics and underplays other structural relations.

Within sport, socialist feminism highlights the part played by women in servicing both men's and children's sports. For example, women often provide the refreshments at male sporting events; they wash sports clothing for their partner's or men's teams; and they transport their children to sports events and support them in their activities often to the detriment of their own leisure and sporting activities. This sexual division of labour extends into employment in the sports organizations and sports clubs, where women are often found in servicing and supporting roles (e.g., women as secretaries, women as cleaners). Women's dual role in the paid labour force and domestic labour impacts on their time and energies available for sport and recreation (Green *et al.* 1987). As more women move into the paid labour market this becomes increasingly significant, particularly as contemporary evidence shows that there is not a corresponding shift of more men into domestic labour (Silva 2000; Speakman and Marchington 1999). Socialist feminism has been critical of the disparities between men's and women's opportunities for sponsorship, prize money, and sporting careers (Hall 1996).

Apart from exploring the complex inter-relationships between capitalism and patriarchal power relations, socialist feminism has shifted the emphasis from solely concentrating on women's experiences to looking more critically at gender. In order to do this there has developed a focus on the exploration of male power through hegemonic masculinity (Connell 1987, 1995). This has now developed into a large area of study (*men and masculinities*) and has created the space for men to engage with feminist theorizing. This remains a contentious area (as to whether men can be feminists or engage with feminist theories) but the research and writings of pro-feminist men have contributed to our knowledge of men's power and how men have to change if gender relations are to be equalized. The early work by Sabo and Runfola (1980) recognized the significance of feminist work to an understanding of men and sport but it is primarily through the work of Sabo (1985), Messner (1992), and Messner and Sabo (1990) that there has developed critical theoretically informed studies of men, masculinity and sport. This work looks at the historical construction of masculinity and muscularity through sport, male hegemony and hegemonic masculinity and the relationship between masculinity, male power and sport. Importantly it explores how men as a group enjoy privileges in sport through the construction of unequal gender relations; how men also pay the cost for their adherence to narrow definitions of masculinity; and the importance of differences and inequalities between men (Messner 1992; 1997).

Post-structuralist feminisms

Although we begin this discussion by looking at *Black feminism*, it is difficult to know whether to place their work under the heading post-structuralist or structural power relations. Black feminists have challenged the dominant white feminist theorizing and activism since the early days of second wave feminism, arguing that they have been largely excluded and made invisible (Hill Collins 1991; hooks 1981; 1984; 1989). Race and ethnicity have been marginalized and black women's experiences have been ignored or placed at the periphery of theorizing. For example, black women's experiences in the labour market are not only disadvantaged and structured by their economic position and sexism but are also determined by racist structures that are a product of imperialism and colonialism. Black feminists highlight the fact that the sites of their oppression may be different to those of white women. For example, many white women have seen the family as a major site of their oppression by both men and the sexual division of labour. Yet for some black women the family is an important site for their resistance and solidarity, where they have control and can yield power (Hill Collins 1991). By focusing only on gendered power relations, white feminist theories have neglected to problematize racial power as central to the production of white feminist knowledge. White women within the feminist movement have not only failed to address the marginalization of black women, but have failed to seriously interrogate their own whiteness. Whiteness is the taken-for-granted central position that relegates blackness to 'otherness' (Mirza 1997). The invisibility and marginalization of black women in feminism:

> ... speaks of the separate narrative constructions of race, gender and class; it is a racial discourse, where the subject is male; in a gendered discourse, where the subject is white; and a class discourse where race has no place
>
> (Mirza 1997: p. 4)

We have chosen to begin the section on post-structural feminisms with an introduction to black feminism because not only have black feminists argued for the identification of racist structures as important determining features of their lives, but they have also prioritized differences between women, black identities and subjectivities.

Much of the current discourse about women and sport remains ethnocentric and is viewed through a 'gendered lens' (Dworkin and Messner 2001). There is little work that could be defined as offering a black feminist perspective on sport. As Birrell (1990: 193) concludes 'we need to increase the awareness of issues in the lives of women of colour as they themselves articulate these issues'. Although written over a decade ago, there is little evidence that these omissions have been addressed. Birrell (1990) argues that most of the work that has been done on black women and sport has been categoric (emphasizing differences between categories) or distributive (providing statistics on inequality of opportunity, access and distribution of resources) (see also Smith 1992). Often the early work on gender, race and sport has tended to present a simplistic, additive, theoretical model of black women and sport where black women's experiences are simply 'added on' to an understanding of gender oppression (Scraton 2001).

Raval (1989) provides one of the first critiques in the UK from the position of a South Asian woman in challenging the appropriateness of white, male academics researching the sporting experiences of black and South Asian women (e.g., Carrington *et al.* 1987). She argues that their conclusions pathologize South Asian culture, and universalize the notion of South Asian women, failing to recognize differences between these women in relation to ethnicity, religion and class. More recently, the work on the racialization and gendering of sport has been developed by Benn (1996) on teacher education; Zaman (1997) on the perceptions of Muslim young women of Islam well-being and physical activity, and Wray (2001) in relation to physical activity and mid-life Muslim, Pakistani women. This work is located within a theoretical framework of difference that challenges the universalistic approaches of the liberal and structural feminist analyses. In North America and Australia there is an increasing body of work on minority ethnic women and their experiences of sport (Paraschak 1997) and in the UK, Hargreaves (2000) provides the first major publication that focuses on different groups of women and their experiences and struggles in sport including South African, Muslim and Aboriginal women.

Most of the research on race, ethnicity and sport has been androcentric and has focused on black sportsmen (Carrington and Wood 1983; Cashmore 1982; Fleming 1994; Jarvie 1991). This work has centralized race and ethnicity but has under-theorized the relationships between gender, race and ethnicity. More recent analyses are beginning to explore these relationships through a deconstruction of hegemonic masculinity. The image of athletic masculinity is not only about being a man, a dominant powerful image seen in opposition to a subordinate femininity, it is also a racialized image that distinguishes between black athleticism and white athleticism (Dworkin and Messner 2001; Messner 1993). Sport can be an important site of masculine self expression for black males that can provide some means of resistance but can also serve to reinforce and lock them into their marginalized positions within a racist society (Majors 1990; Messner 1997). Carrington's (2001) work on race, racism and cricket in the UK is an example of the development of a critical engagement with the complexities of black masculinity and sport. His work suggests that an understanding of sport as a site of black cultural resistance to racism does not recognize that this is black *male* resistance, often dependent on gendered power relations. Messner (1997: 77) in his discussion of racialized masculinity politics reiterates Carrington's analysis in suggesting that:

> . . . in foregrounding the oppression of men by men, these studies risk portraying aggressive, even misogynist, gender displays primarily as liberating forms of resistance against class and racial oppression. What is obscured or even drops out of sight is the feminist observation that these kinds of masculinity are forms of domination over women.

The policy and practical responses to black feminism have included some greater awareness of the needs of different women. This has included specific community based strategies, for example, to encourage South Asian women into physical activity and active lifestyles (Scraton and Stoddart 2000) and more macro surveys of the sporting experiences and aspirations of people from minority ethnic communities (Rowe and Champion 2000). Although some sports organizations may have anti-racist policies, these have had little impact on the experiences of black sportsmen and women (Long, Hylton, Welsh and Dart 2000). Indeed, the sporting world has some way to go before the concerns of black feminists become central to sporting practice.

Post-structuralist feminists provide conceptual challenges to the macro analyses of the structural feminist approaches discussed earlier. They argue that it is no longer relevant to seek *the truth* or a single explanation to a particular issue.

They reject the view that it is a lack of equal access or opportunity (liberal), patriarchy (radical), capitalism (Marxist) or a combination of patriarchy and capitalism (socialist) that explains women's oppression. Rather they focus on difference and diversity and argue that the very term 'women' has little significance in the fragmented and changing world that we live in today. Post-structuralist accounts draw on the work of Foucault (1980; 1983) who challenges the structuralist definitions of power (top down, repressive) and considers power as plural and productive in a multiplicity of sites such as the body, discourse, knowledge, subjectivity and sexuality (Wearing 1998). Foucault highlights the significance of discourses, such as medical, scientific and sexual, through which meanings and people are made, and importantly, through which power relations are maintained and changed. His conception of power provides opportunities for women's resistance and struggle, with more of an emphasis on the everyday experiences and agency of individual women. Post-structural feminism argues for the deconstruction of the term 'woman' and the diversity of femininities. As Wearing (1998: 148) argues in relation to the de-valuing and the delegation of nurturing, caring tasks to women:

> If... the concept of 'woman' is open to diversity, to change and to re-definition, there is the possibility of rewriting the script for women so that these tasks are re-valued and other avenues for a sense of self-worth are opened up.

Post-structuralist feminism challenges the dichotomy of femininity/masculinity and argues for multiple femininities, which can be experienced both between women, and by individual women as diverse subjectivities and identities (Butler 1990). However, it has been criticized for its potential for slipping into a relativism that emphasizes difference and thus loses the notion of women's shared experiences in relation to gender. The issues central to the concerns of post-structuralist analyses are also considered to be somewhat distanced from the everyday realities of many people's lives (Dworkin and Messner 2001).

Post-structural feminist analyses of sport are as yet relatively undeveloped. However there are some exciting areas that are emerging (Rail 1998). The focus on the body in post-structuralism more generally is particularly appropriate for analyses of gender and sport. Foucault's work has been used to explore the notion of the 'docile body' and disciplining the body. Bordo (1993) shows how women engage in self-surveillance of their bodies, disciplining themselves through diet and exercise. Markula (1995) looks at aerobics as a site for disciplining the female body, but concludes that although they work hard to achieve the ideal body, women also gain pleasure, self-confidence and self-esteem through their aerobics workout.

Sport has been analysed in relation to its role in the maintenance of binary oppositions such as man/woman; heterosexual/homosexual; white/other; healthy/sick, and also for its potential to transgress gender, and deconstruct these binaries (Caudwell 1999; Obel 1995; Pronger 1990; 1998). For example, both Sykes (1998) and Clarke (1995; 1998) show how the boundaries between heterosexuality and lesbianism are maintained within and through sport, whilst recognizing, also, the power of individual women to resist and transgress these boundaries. Caudwell's work on women who play football deconstructs the dichotomies of sex/gender and masculinity/femininity through an interrogation of the concepts of 'butch' and 'female masculinity' (Halberstrom 1998). Work on bodybuilders and boxing similarly show how women's engagement in sport traditionally defined as male challenges the boundaries of femininity and masculinity through the development of strong, muscular sporting bodies (Halbert 1997; Obel 1995).

Wright (1996) focuses on the significance of language and discourse for post-structuralist analyses of sport. Through an analysis of language between students, and teachers and students, Wright shows how their verbal interactions construct, and are constructed within, gendered discourses about bodies in physical education. Students' talk constructs male and female bodies and their physical abilities in relation to one another as 'complementary'; male bodies are described as strong, independent and skilled and female bodies as the opposite – fragile, nurturant and less physically able. Therefore language is crucial in the maintenance of these boundaries and has the potential to deconstruct binary relationships.

Although engaging with difficult concepts and theoretical developments, post-structuralist accounts of sport raise some important and significant areas of study. Importantly they shift the focus from the structural constraints on women and sport to possibilities of empowerment and resistance through sport. They emphasize the social construction of gender and sexuality and thus show how 'false' binaries can be challenged and transgressed.

Conclusion

This journey through feminism and its application to gender and sport has through necessity been relatively short and selective. However, we hope that it has provided some initial understanding of how feminist theories have developed and the range of interesting questions and issues that they have posed for the world of sport. As different strands of feminist thought have developed so different questions and explanations have emerged. We want to leave you with some questions that we consider are pertinent for any theoretical consideration of gender and sport.

- Have women gained equal access to sport? We know that there has been a considerable opening up of opportunities and access for many women in sport. They now compete in more events in the Olympics; women play sports traditionally associated with men such as football (soccer), rugby, ice hockey and so on. Do inequalities of access remain and if so why?
- How has men's sport changed? Whereas access and opportunity for women to participate has become a 'mainstream' issue, there appears to be little evidence of equity in relation to control and decision making in sport (coaches, managers, sponsorship etc.). Has the association between hegemonic masculinity and sport become redefined?
- Who services sport today? Have we moved to a position where women and men both take responsibility for servicing their children's sport, sports

associations and clubs and so on? Do both women and men now have *choice* in relation to their sporting activities?

- How do we understand difference in relation to gender and sport? How significant are *individual* differences or is difference relevant to our understanding of *groups* of women and men (for example, lesbian and gays, disabled sports people, minority ethnic groups, working class athletes). In other words can there still be a notion of 'shared' inequalities?
- How significant is *gender* in a rapidly developing and changing social, economic, cultural and political world? Are materialist analyses still relevant or is it more significant to look at questions around bodies, subjectivities and individual empowerment rather than the 'old' questions regarding structural analyses of power?

This final question is important. We would argue that there are some new and exciting questions raised in post-structuralist accounts of sport but that this does not mean that all the 'old' questions have been answered or that they are no longer significant. We return to the notion of waves of theory. Each wave is important and has contributed to our understandings. However, each strand of feminist thought continues to develop as sport, also, changes and adapts to new times. Until there exists true equality for *all* people in the sporting world, feminist theoretical debates will continue to have an important part to play in our understandings and in the development of sporting policies and practices.

References

Benn, T. (1996) 'Muslim women and physical education in initial teacher training' *Sport, Education and Society* 1(1): 5–21.

Birrell, S. (1990) 'Women of color; Critical autobiography and sport', in M. Messner, and D. Sabo (eds) *Sport, Men and the Gender Order*, Champaign, IL: Human Kinetics.

Birrell, S. and Richter, D.M. (1987) 'Is a diamond forever? Feminist transformations of sport', *Women's Studies International Forum* 10(4): 395–409.

Bordo, S. (1993) *Unbearable Weight: Feminism, Western Culture and the Body*, Berkeley: University of California Press.

Brackenridge (2001) 'Men loving men hating women – the crisis of masculinity and violence to women in sport', in S. Scraton and A. Flintoff (eds) *A Reader in Gender and Sport*, London: Routledge.

Brackenridge, C. and Kirby, S. (1997) 'Playing safe? Assessing the risk of sexual abuse to young elite athletes', *International Review for the Sociology of Sport* 32(4): 407–18.

Butler, J. (1990) *Gender Trouble: Feminism and the Subversion of Identity*, London: Routledge.

Cahn, S. (1994) *Coming on Strong: Gender and Sexuality in Twentieth Century Women's Sport*, New York: Free Press.

Carrington, B., Chivers, T. and Williams, T. (1987) 'Gender, leisure and sport: a case-study of young people of South Asian descent', *Leisure Studies* 6(3): 255–80.

Carrington, B. (2001) 'Sport, masculinity and black cultural resistance', in S. Scraton and A. Flintoff (eds) *A Reader in Gender and Sport*, London: Routledge.

Carrington, B. and Wood, E. (1983) 'Body talk: Images of sport in a multi-racial school', *Multiracial Education* 11(2): 29–38.

Cashmore, E. (1982) 'Black Youth, Sport and Education', *New Community* 2, Winter.

Caudwell, J. (1999) 'Women's football in the United Kingdom: theorizing gender and unpacking the butch lesbian image', *Journal of Sport and Social Issues* 23(4): 390–402.

Clarke, G. (1995) 'Outlaws in sport and education? Exploring the sporting and education experiences of lesbian physical Education teachers' in L. Lawrence, E. Murdoch, S. Parker (eds) *Leisure, Sport and Education*, Eastbourne: LSA Publications.

Clarke, G. (1998) 'Queering the pitch and coming out to play: lesbians in physical education and sport', *Sport, Education and Society* 3(2): 145–60.

Connell, R. (1987) *Gender and Power*, Stanford, CA: Stanford University Press.

Connell, R. (1995) *Masculinities*, Sydney: Allen and Unwin.

Creedon, P. (ed) (1994) *Women, Media and Sport: Challenging Gender Values*, London: Sage.

Crosset, T. W. (1995) *Outsiders in the Clubhouse: The World of Women's Professional Golf*, New York: State University of New York Press.

Crosset, T., Benedict, J. R. and McDonald, M. A. (1995) 'Male student-athletes reported for sexual assault: A survey of campus police departments and judicial affairs offices', *Journal of Sport and Social Issues* 19(2): 126–40.

Dworkin, A. (1981) *Pornography: men possessing women*, London: Women's Press.

Dworkin, S. and Messner, M. (2001) 'Just do . . . what? Sport, bodies, gender' in S. Scraton and A. Flintoff (eds) *A Reader in Gender and Sport*, London: Routledge.

Fasting, K., Brackenridge, C. H. and Sundgot Borgen, J. (2000) *Sexual Harassment In and Outside Sport*, Oslo: Norwegian Olympic Committee.

Fleming, S. (1994) 'Sport and South Asian youth: the perils of 'false universalism' and stereotyping', *Leisure Studies* 13: 159–73.

Foucault, M. (1980) *Power/Knowledge: Selected Interviews and Other Writings 1972–77*, Colin Gordon (ed.), Brighton: Harvester Press.

Foucault, M. (1983) 'The subject and power', in H. Dreyfus and P. Rabinow (eds), *Michel Foucault: Beyond Structuralism and Hermeneutics*, Chicago: Chicago University Press, pp. 208–20.

Green, E., Hebron, S. and Woodward, D. (1987) *Women's Leisure, What Leisure?* London: Macmillan.

Greendorfer, S. (1993) 'Gender role stereotypes and early childhood socialisation', in G. L. Cohen (ed.) *Women in Sport: Issues and Controversies*, Newbury Park, CA: Sage, pp. 3–14.

Griffin, P. (1992) 'Changing the Game: Homophobia, sexism and lesbians in sport', *Quest* 44(2): 251–65.

Griffin, P. (1998) *Strong Women, Deep Closets: Lesbians and Homophobia in Sport*, Champaign, IL: Human Kinetics.

Halberstrom, J. (1998) *Female Masculinity*, London: Duke University Press.

Halbert, C. (1997) 'Tough enough and woman enough', *Journal of Sport and Social Issues*, 21: 7–36.

Hall, M. A. (1988) 'The discourse on gender and sport: from femininity to feminism', *Sociology of Sport Journal* 5(4): 330–40.

Hall, M. A. (1990) 'How should we theorise gender in the context of sport', in M. Messner and D. Sabo (eds) *Sport, Men and the Gender Order: Critical Feminist Perspectives*, Champaign: Human Kinetics.

Hall, M. A. (1996) *Feminism and Sporting Bodies*, Illinois, Human Kinetics.

Hargreaves, J. (1993) 'Bodies matter! images of sport and female sexualisation', Brackenridge, C. (ed.) *Body Matters: Leisure Images and Lifestyles*, Eastbourne: LSA.

Hargreaves, J. (1994) *Sporting females: Critical Issues in the History and Sociology of Women's Sport*, London: Routledge.

Hargreaves, J. (2000) *Heroines of Sport: Politics of Difference and Identity*, London: Routledge.

Hill-Collins, P. (1991) *Black Feminist Thought: Knowledge, Consciousness and the Politics of Empowerment*, London: Routledge.

hooks, b. (1991) *Ain't I a Woman: Black Women and Feminism*, Boston, Massachusetts: South End Press.

hooks, b. (1984) *Feminist Theory: From Margin to Center*, Boston, Massachusetts: South End Press.

hooks, b. (1989) *Talking Back: Thinking Feminism, Thinking Black*, Boston, Massachusetts: South End Press.

Jarvie, G. (1991) *Sport, Racism and Ethnicity*, London: Falmer.

Kirby, S. and Greaves, L. (1996) 'Foul play: Sexual abuse and harassment in sport', paper presented to the Pre-Olympic Scientific Congress, Dallas, USA, July 11–14.

Knoppers, A. (1994) 'Gender and the Coaching Profession', in S. Birrell and C.L. Cole (eds) *Women, Sport and Culture*, Champaign: Human Kinetics.

Llenskyj, H. (1986) *Out of Bounds. Women, Sport and Sexuality*, Toronto: Women's Press.

Llenskyj, H. (1991) 'Combating homophobia in sport and physical education', *Sociology of Sport Journal* 8: 61–9.

Llenskyj, H. (1994) 'Sexuality and femininity in sport contexts: issues and alternatives', *Journal of Sport and Social Issues* 18, 4: 356–76.

Long, J., Hylton, K., Welch, M., Dart, J. (2000) *Part of the Game: An Examination of Racism in Grass Roots Football*, London: Kick It Out.

Majors, R. (1990) 'Cool pose: black masculinity and sports', in M. Messner and D. Sabo (eds) *Sport, Men and the Gender Order*, Champaign, IL: Human Kinetics.

Markula, P. (1995) 'Firm but shapely, fit but sexy, strong but thin: the postmodern aerobicising female bodies', *Sociology of Sport Journal* 12: 424–53.

Wolstonecroft, M. (1975) *A Vindication of the Rights of Woman*, C.H. Poston. (ed.), New York: Norton. (Original work published 1792).

Messner, M. (1992) *Power at Play: Sports and the Problem of Masculinity*, Boston: Beacon Press.

Messner, M. (1997) *The Politics of Masculinities: Men in Movements*, Thousand Oaks: Sage.

Messner, M. (1993) 'White men misbehaving: feminism, Afrocentrism and the promise of a critical standpoint', *Journal of Sport and Social Issues* 16: 136–44.

Messner, M. and Sabo, D. (1990) *Sport, Men and the Gender Order: Critical Feminist Perspectives*, Illinois: Human Kinetics.

Rossi, A. S. (1970) (ed.), John Stuart Mill and Harriet Taylor Mill, *Essays on Sex Equality*, Chicago: University of Chicago Press.

Millet, K. (1971) *Sexual Politics*, New York: Equinox Books.

Mirza, H. (1997) *Black British Feminism: A Reader*, London: Routledge.

Mitten, D. (1992) 'Empowering girls and women in the outdoors', *Journal of Physical Education, Recreation and Dance* 63, 2: 56–60.

Obel, C. (1995) 'Collapsing gender in competitive bodybuilding: Researching contradictions and ambiguity in sport', *Review for the Sociology of Sport* 31(2): 185–202.

Office for Standards in Education (OFSTED (1995) *Physical Education and Sport in Schools: A Survey of Good Practice*, London: DFEE.

Oglesby, C.A. (1978) (ed.) *Women and Sport: From Myth to Reality*, Philadephia: Lea and Febiger.

Paraschak, V. (1997) 'Variations in race relations: sporting events for native peoples in Canada', *Sociology of Sport Journal* 14(1): 1–22.

Pirinen, R. (1997) 'Catching up with the men? Finnish newspaper coverage of women's entry into traditionally male sports', *International Review for the Sociology of Sport* 32/3: 239–49.

Pronger, B. (1990) *The Arena of Masculinity: Sports, Homosexuality and the Meaning of Sex*, London: GMP Publishers Ltd.

Pronger, B. (1998) 'Outta my endzone: sport and the territorial anus', *Journal of Sport and Social Issues* 23(4): 373–89.

Rail, G. (1998) (ed.) *Sport and Postmodern Times*, Albany: State University of New York Press.

Raval, S. (1989) 'Gender, leisure and sport: a case study of young people of South Asian descent – a response', *Leisure Studies* 8: 237–40.

Rich, A. (1980) 'Compulsory heterosexuality and lesbian existence', *Signs* 5: 631–60.

Rogers, B. (1988) *Men Only: An Investigation into Men's Organisations*, London: Pandora.

Rowe, N. and Champion, R. (2000) *Sports Participation and Ethnicity in England: National Survey 1999/2000*, London, Sport England.

Sabo, D. (1985) 'Sport, patriarchy, and the male identity: new questions about men and sport', *Arena Review* 9: 1–30.

Sabo, D. and Runfola, R. (eds) (1980) *Jock: Sports and Male Identity*, Englewood Cliffs, NJ: Prentice-Hall.

Scraton, S. (1992) *Shaping Up to Womanhood: Gender and Girl's Physical Education*, Buckingham, England: Open University Press.

Scraton, S. (2001) 'Reconceptualising race, gender and sport: the contribution of Black feminism' in Carrington, B. and Macdonald, I. (eds), *Racism and British Sport*, London: Routledge.

Scraton, S. and Flintoff, A. (2001) 'Sport feminism: the contribution of feminist thought to our understandings of gender and sport', in S. Scraton and A. Flintoff (eds), *A Reader in Gender and Sport*, London: Routledge.

Scraton, S. and Stoddart, F. (2000) *An Evaluation of the Zindagi Project*, Leeds: Leeds Metropolitan University.

Silva, E. (2000) 'The material and the moral in everyday Life', paper presented at 'Nation, Culture, People' conference, Open University, Milton Keynes. May.

Smith, Y. (1992) 'Women of color in society and sport', *Quest* 44: 228–50.

Speakman, S. and Marchington, M. (1999) 'Ambivalent patriarchs: shift workers,' breadwinners and housework', *Work, Employment and Society* 13(1): 83–105.

Sykes, H. (1998) 'Turning the closets inside/out: towards a queer-feminist theory in women's physical education', *Sociology of Sport Journal* 15: 154–73.

Talbot, M. (1993) 'A gendered physical education: equality and sexism', in J. Evans (ed.), *Equality, Education and Physical Education*, London: Falmer.

Talbot, M. (2001) 'Playing with patriarchy; the gendered dynamics of sports organisations', in S. Scraton and A. Flintoff (eds), *A Reader in Gender and Sport*, London: Routledge.

Tong, R. (2000) *Feminist Thought: A More Comprehensive Introduction*, Boulder, Colorado: Westview, 2nd edition.

United Kingdom Sports Council (1998) *Women and Sport from Brighton to Windhoek: Facing the Challenge*, London: United Kingdom Sports Council.

Walby, S. (1990) *Theorizing Patriarchy*, London: Routledge.

Wearing, B. (1998) *Leisure and Feminist Theory*, London: Sage.

Whelehan, I. (1995) *Modern Feminist Thought*, Edinburgh: Edinburgh University Press.

White, A. (1995) 'Towards gender equity in sport: an update on sports Council Policy development', in A. Tomlinson (ed.), *Gender, Sport and Leisure: Continuities and Challenges*, Brighton: Chelsea School Research Centre, University of Brighton.

White, A. and Brackenridge, C. (1985) 'Who rules sport? Gender divisions in the power structure of British sports organisations from 1960', *International Review for the Sociology of Sport* 20(1/ 2): 95–105.

Wray, S. (2001) 'Connecting ethnicity, gender and physicality: Muslim Pakistani women, physical activity and health', in S. Scraton and A. Flintoff (eds), *A Reader in Gender and Sport*, London: Routledge.

Wright, J. (1996) 'The construction of complementarity in physical education', *Gender and Education* 8(1): 61–79.

Wright, J., and Clarke, G. (1999) 'Sport, the media and the construction of compulsory heterosexuality: a case study of women's rugby union', *International Review for the Sociology of Sport* 34(3): 227–43.

Zaman, H. (1997) 'Islam, well-being and physical activity: perceptions of Muslim young women', in G. Clarke and B. Humberstone (eds), *Researching Women and Sport*, London: Macmillan.

Seminar questions

Chapter 1

1 How has sex role theory been applied to understanding gender and sport? What are Hall's main criticisms of this approach?
2 How would you distinguish between non-sexist and feminist scholarship?

Chapter 2

1 What are Dworkin and Messner's arguments for the limitations of adopting simply a gender 'lens', and what do they advocate instead?
2 Critically assess Nike's contribution to the empowerment of women in sport.

Chapter 3

1 What are the strengths and weaknesses of the different strands of feminist thought?
2 Assess the adequacy of post-structuralist feminism for addressing questions in contemporary sport practice.

Part II
Historical developments: The engendering of sport

Introduction

Feminists have argued that women have been 'hidden from history'. Most of the historical accounts of sport have focused on men's experiences, and women's experiences have been ignored or marginalized. Hargreaves (1994: 42) notes that:

> Although the first women's suffrage movement in England was set up in 1866, no real step forward in political emancipation for women was achieved during the nineteenth century, and feminism did not reach its peak until the early twentieth century. It was at this time that women's sports expanded rapidly and when there were increasing opportunities for working class as well as for middle class women. However, the balance of power between men and women in sports was always desperately uneven. Victorian and Edwardian sports were major male preserves that generated and reproduced patriarchal assumptions.

Historical accounts are important because they help us understand from where contemporary debates and practice have emerged. Women's struggles and resistances in sport today need to be situated in an historical understanding of patriarchal power relations. This helps us to appreciate the gains women have made in the sporting arena, but also highlights the continuing inequalities that women face. It is important to understand the historical construction of femininity and hegemonic masculinity and also how these gendered images and ideas become commonplace and accepted.

The two chapters in this section were selected to explore different kinds of historical insights into women's sports. The first chapter by Jennifer Hargreaves focuses on an important era (middle of the nineteenth century to the early years of the twentieth century) in the development of women's sport. The second chapter looks specifically at one sport (women's football) but explores its development in different countries. They both show how men have been involved in both supporting and limiting women's opportunities for sport.

Jennifer Hargreaves discusses the way in which the ideology of Victorian familism impacted on women's lives in and out of sport in the 1800s. Central to this ideology was that women were the guardians of morality. This involved them being responsible for a passive heterosexuality, and through their role as mothers, the care and continuation of the family. Although women did become more active in sport and physical activity during this period, they did so within the boundaries of dominant expectations of femininity.

The authors of the second chapter, Gertrud Pfister, Kari Fasting, Sheila Scraton and Benilde Vazquez look specifically at the development of football (soccer) for women in four European countries, England, Germany, Norway and Spain. They show how gender relations in football are reflected in, and reflect, the particular historical and cultural differences between countries. Nevertheless, there are universal features of gender that are evident across sport in the different countries. The chapter analyses the close relationship between masculinity and football and the consequences of this for women.

After reading both the chapters in this section, students should:

- understand the construction and strength of ideologies of femininity, masculinity and sexuality and their significance for the development of modern sport;
- learn about the hidden history and development of women's sport;
- appreciate the significance of cultural context for women's opportunities in sport;
- recognise men's power and its influence on women's struggles to participate in sport.

References

Hargreaves, J. (1994) *Sporting Females: Critical Issues in the History and Sociology of Women's Sports*, London: Routledge.

Further readings

Cahn, S. K. (1994) *Coming on Strong: Gender and Sexuality in Twentieth Century Women's Sport*, Cambridge: Harvard University Press.

Crossett, T. (1990) 'Masculinity, sexuality and the development of early modern sport', in M. Messner and D. Sabo (eds) *Sport, Men and the Gender Order: Critical Feminist Perspectives*, Champaign: Human Kinetics.

Fletcher, S. (1984) *Women First: The Female Tradition in English Physical Education 1880–1980*, London: Athlone.

Llenskyj, H. (1986) *Out of Bounds: Women, Sport and Sexuality*, Toronto: The Women's Press.

4 The Victorian cult of the family and the early years of female sport*

Jennifer Hargreaves

In this chapter it is argued that during the formative years of female sport – that is, from the middle of the nineteenth century to the early twentieth century – the legitimate use of the female body was redefined to symbolize a more active (yet when compared with men nevertheless still subordinate) role. This development is extremely complex and difficult to analyse because it touches on many different domains, for example, the biological, psychological, medical, moral, and military domains. Importantly, it also incorporates elements of Social Darwinism.[1] However, because of the limited space available here, I have chosen to focus on the Victorian cult of the family because it was a unifying feature of nineteenth-century bourgeois ideology and acted as a dominant constraining force on the early development of women's sport. Furthermore, Victorian familism highlights the specific nature of some of the contradictions facing the nineteenth-century sportswoman that have had repercussions for the development of women's sport until the present day.

It has been argued that the association of women with the domestic sphere and their role in the nuclear family was a modern invention dating approximately from the eighteenth century.[2] However, it became a popular idea that defined what a woman was and that directly related to her being female. The solidification, most notably of the bourgeois family, developed concomitantly with the consolidation of industrial capitalism, and by the turn of the century it was a key institution in the 'social mythology that helped to keep women relatively powerless'.[3] The underlying assumption about the family as the 'natural unit' existing in separation from the total social formation was an intrinsic part of a system of patriarchy with which many women colluded, bound up as it was with ideas about family arrangements, gender identities, sexual mores, and women's biological, psychological, and moral characteristics.

The idealised model of the respectable family centred on the man as the 'head of the household', operating mainly in the economic sphere, the provider of the material requirements of his family and its dominant authority figure. The relationship between the man and the woman was viewed as a reciprocal one in that the

* Taken from, E. Dunning *et al.* (eds) (1993) '*The Sports Process,*' Champaign: Human Kinetics.

woman's dependent role as wife, housekeeper, and childbearer, which confined her to 'the inferior world of the family ... left the bourgeois man "free" to accumulate capital' in order to maintain her adequately.[4] Additionally, the woman was viewed as the family member whose moral influence should be impeccable. It was from the 'saintly mother' in the home that children first learned about the sexual division of labour and associated attitudes of obedience, hard work, honesty, and loyalty. Thus the family was effectively cemented and its continuity ensured.

This model of the Victorian family may have been a reality for the affluent middle classes, but it was an impossibility for the majority of working-class families, who depended not only on the wife's wage labour to finance the home, but also, in many cases, on the labour of children as well.[5] Nevertheless, in the public image, the woman's work role was always secondary to her role within the family, which constituted the Victorian ideal of the sexual division of labour.

The assumption that this was the 'natural order of things' was underpinned by an implicit belief that the differences between men and women were biologically determined and hence immutable. Women, it was argued, were eminently suited, because of their innate physical and emotional characteristics, to staying at home and being good wives and mothers, and, by the same argument, were poorly equipped for the productive sphere. This was an integral element of the rhetoric of Social Darwinism. It incorporated the medical case for women's physical inferiority, which was employed to justify 'maternity as the "highest function" of womanhood – essential to the healthy progress of the nation'.[6]

The extent to which this vision of family life was a reality is less important than the way in which it was elevated as a concept that permeated social consciousness. Its development to a form of institutionalized sexism dominated social relations, thus giving them a material base in the work and family domains and also in the educational and leisure contexts. I suggest that the early years of women's sport gave ideological legitimation to the confinement of women to their separate, private sphere of the home, and to the existing pattern of biological and social reproduction in the home. 'Behaving like a lady' meant adopting the bourgeois values associated with being female, and it appears to have been a prerequisite for the nineteenth-century sportswoman. I have characterised early forms of female sport and physical activity to show how they incorporated the ideology of the family and I shall deal first with conspicuous recreation. Such activities as croquet, early tennis, and spectating at the races were all parts of a process of consumption linked to the technological developments that revolutionized industrial methods of production. The increasing specialisation of labour created a multitude of new jobs for working-class women. At the same time, however, it narrowed the lives of middle-class women and robbed them of their economic usefulness.[7] The idleness of the bourgeois lady became symbolic of her husband's or her father's material success; her finery reflected his affluence, and the way she organized her leisure defined his social standing.

The life-styles of the middle classes, in particular, reflected the increased opportunity for acquisitiveness associated with the garden suburbs that flourished from the middle of the century onward as swelling numbers moved into detached, semi-detached, and terraced houses in the newly developed areas.[8] The insular, self-contained nature of these modern homes made the family a spatially segregated recreation unit, with the woman as its focal object who publicized the spending power of her husband or her father. Middle-class homes became more 'palatial' and gardens became part of the improved amenities of domestic life for the middle classes. By the mid-Victorian period, the bourgeois family had reached a plateau of prosperity sufficient for domestic duties to be taken care of by a growing army of servants. Even when growth and prosperity seemed to suffer a more general contraction from the mid-1870s, the Victorian bourgeoisie were able to resist any serious curtailment of expenditure and consumption and this was reflected in all forms of women's leisure. A whole 'consumer-amusement market' for the family developed,[9] and the resultant conspicuous display of affluence was symbolic of the increasing economic dependence of middle-class women on men. It was, also, a reflection of the middle classes increasingly divorcing themselves from their inheritance of thrift and frugality and indulging more openly in social pleasure.[10]

Lavish, extravagant clothes and accoutrements were worn to afford evidence of a life of leisure, but they restrained women from performing any but the smallest and meanest of movements. The bourgeois lady remained, even on the tennis court, the wifely ornament of beauty, a physically incapacitated player, inhibited and subdued by convention and, as Veblen put it, 'bound by the code of behaviour as tight as the stays she was compelled to wear'.[11] At competitive events such as horse racing, regattas, or cricket matches, women reinforced the superiority of men by adopting a spectator role as members of an admiring female audience watching the physical antics of men. And women were also absorbed into the leisure sphere by the provision for them of 'gentle, respectable games', eminently suited to the 'weaker sex', and exemplified by croquet and its indoor derivatives like 'Parlour Croquet', 'Carpet Croquet', or 'Table Croquet'.[12]

Prints and photographs provide some of the scant evidence available that this model of the conspicuous sporting lady prevailed throughout the nineteenth century, and even beyond 1900. For example, in his *Edwardians at Play*, Brian Dobbs includes 50 engravings, prints, and photographs, many of which feature women spectators: sitting in the stands in flamboyant, wasp-waisted dresses, or walking in a leisurely and self-conscious fashion through the grounds. The one illustration of a woman participant shows her to be a most decorative lady partnering the sporting Prince of Wales at lawn tennis. She is undoubtedly wearing corsets, has a most fashionable pair of shoes, a pretty hat perched on her head, and even with a racquet in her hand looks for all the world unable to move an inch or two in any direction.[13]

'Tight croquet', as it was originally called, featured all the most pronounced manifestations of bourgeois 'conspicuous recreation'.

> Nobody could have called it a good game played, as it was, with only one hand in order that the womenfolk might be able to guard their complexions from the sun ... a game of frills and fancies, of petticoats, giggles and maidenly blushes.[14]

Croquet was a highly sociable and fashionable pastime and became something of a craze so that 'hardly a house with a lawn was without its croquet set.[15] Tennis also became a mania for the affluent; it 'swept like a wind of change through the quiet countryside and brought the sexes together on the courts in a wave of exciting activity'.[16] For example, tennis parties 'were the highlight of Cambridge society in the 80s and 90s', although by this time the game had become a good deal more active for women and tennis attire was less restricted – the ladies sometimes tying their long dresses back with an apron.

Generally speaking, women's participatory role in conspicuous recreation embodied the characteristics of passivity rather than activity, subordination rather than ascendancy. The female croquet and tennis player represented an embellishment of men; such games had no natural, organic connection to physical action of the sort that epitomizes the essence of sport as we know it today. Women were obliged to show restraint, be refined and respectable, and confirm at all times the 'ladylike' modes of behaviour prescribed for them. In the home context, the 'playing of games' became an important, fashionable accomplishment for middle-class women, in the same category as those much admired genteel activities like playing the piano, singing, drawing and painting, reciting poetry, and doing needlework. It was a new, comparatively enjoyable way for the middle-class wife to display her talents as a 'cultured' lady of whom her husband could be truly proud, and since the daughter's chief objective was to find herself a husband,[17] it gave her scope to disport herself in appealing fashion to the opposite sex, in a seemingly innocent and acceptable form. Furthermore, playing games in the family context was viewed as positively desirable, as well as respectable, because it reflected the close-knit nature of family relationships and promoted the image of family life. The range of family sports increased to include various forms of hockey, badminton, cricket, bowls, and skittles.

The schooling of middle-class girls provided an ideal preparation for all the features of 'conspicuous living' in the ambit of the family. The 'accomplishments' were given primacy in the majority of private girls' schools until 1850, and remained a feature of the curriculum, in a decreasing number of schools, for around 50 more years. Insofar as it is possible to describe the crocodile walks and calisthenics and social dance as forms of physical education, done as they were in a self-conscious manner and in the restricting and fashionable clothes of the time,[18] then it is possible to observe that they invoked an attitude – a way of thinking and feeling – about what it was to be feminine, which became internalized and hence 'real'. This image of femininity can be recognised as the same one that applied to 'conspicuous recreation' in the sphere of the home and the family and so they mutually reinforced one another.

Another feature of bourgeois conspicuous living for middle-class women was the development of therapeutic forms of exercise. Middle-class women fulfilled their own stereotype of the 'delicate female' who took to her bed with consistent regularity and thus provided confirmation of the dominant medical account that this should be so. Women 'were' manifestly physically and biologically inferior because they actually 'did' swoon, 'were' unable to eat, suffered continual maladies, and consistently expressed passivity and submissiveness in various forms. The acceptance by women of their own incapacitation gave both a humane and moral weighting to the established scientific so-called 'facts'. One way to avoid constitutional degeneration – a benefit to women as well as to the nation as a whole – was by way of medically prescribed exercise, and middle-class women with affluent husbands made ideal patients who, in addition, supported the economic status of doctors. Gentle exercises, remedial gymnastics, and massage were the prescribed treatments for a whole range of female complaints and became integrated into a new 'medical-business-complex'. There was a boom in the number of clinics, health spas, and seaside holidays and a proliferation in the number and type of personnel employed. A new range of semispecialists such as dieticians, masseuses, and remedial gymnasts emerged,[19] and students trained at the new specialist colleges of physical education were incorporated into this movement to service the bodies of middle-class ladies. The prescribed treatments promoted the identification of these women patients as a group who had similar delicate natures and built-in frailties. Rude health in this context was considered quite vulgar – gentle exercise on the other hand was intended to enable women to return to the ambit of their families in order to service their husbands and children and to be able to procreate successfully. Throughout the 1880s, the stereotype of the middle-class lady with her associated limitations remained intact, in one form or another, in the family setting, and she supplied the predominantly institutionalized female image of the late nineteenth century that provided a backward-looking scenario for the 'new woman' to enter.

Gradually, a qualitatively different image connected with the notion of 'positive health' evolved, but it coexisted with a body of medical opinion opposing exercise for women because it was claimed to be damaging to health – a position that was in evidence for a long time. For example, in 1837, riding was condemned because it was believed to produce an 'unnatural consolidation of the bones of the lower part of the body, ensuring a frightful impediment to future functions . . .'[20] and not so differently, in 1910–1911, it was claimed that emphasis on games and athletics was likely to do irreparable damage to the adolescent girl and that hockey, specifically, could disable women from breastfeeding.[21]

These positions for and against exercise for women were not really in opposition in that they were both related to women's procreative functions and were underpinned by a belief in Social Darwinism and its concern for the future of the human race and the national good by transposing the 'laws' of nature to social phenomena. Only exercise of a suitable kind, in moderation, without overindulgence or risk of strain, was considered to enhance the health of women and their potential to conceive healthy children. In other words, there was a unity of the medical and moral opinions concerning female sport and exercise. This trend can also be viewed as part of the discourse of sexual constraints embodied in Victorian familism. As Foucault says:

There was scarcely a malady or physical disturbance to which the 19th century did not impute at least some degree of sexual aetiology and which were susceptible to pathological processes and requiring therapeutic interventions.[22]

The prudishness associated with sport was also a way of censoring sex. In all forms of exercise for women, a 'proper' demeanour, decency, and modesty were required: The avoidance of overexertion, bodily display, and sensual pleasure was essential. The growing dominance of this position as the century progressed explains how the eroticism of the false contours of the flamboyant dresses worn for 'conspicuous recreation' were replaced by the blouses and skirts of the hockey era, which, though more natural and flowing, covered all possible parts of the body from sight. As activities took on a more vigorous form, the sporting attire for ladies became distinctly shapeless and 'sexless'. The blue serge box-pleated gymslip, with tights sewn into knickers, and black and brown woollen stockings and laced shoes were the attire worn increasingly by numbers of lady gymnasts and games players right into the 1920s.[23] A *Daily News* report of 1890 describes how 'Their costume consists of a dark blue tunic and knickerbockers with a red sash with falling ends tied at the side. A knot of blue ribbon ties the bodice in front, and the stockings are dark blue with red ribbons'.[24] The splashes of colour added a 'feminine' touch to the proceedings but in no way affected the strict uniformity and depersonalising nature of their clothing.

The implication that sport could detract attention from sexuality was made quite explicit in the 1912 *Handbook for Girl Guides*:

> All secret habits are evil and dangerous, lead to hysteria and lunatic asylums, and serious illness is the result. Evil practices dare not face an honest person; they lead you on to blindness, paralysis and loss of memory.[25]

The precise nature of the practices was not specified but we may guess what they were because cold baths and healthy exercise were the preferred antidote to sexual desire.

An important feature of late Victorian mores was the de-emphasis of the sensuous nature of women and the predominance given to their actions, missions, qualities of character, and home life.[26] Their conscience or soul, duty or reason, were expressions of the highest part of their nature, whereas the body or appetite, or animalism – in reality the sexual instinct or desire – represented the lowest part of female nature.[27]

Moral purity continued to be embraced by better-off middle-class families whose reputations rested upon the chastity of their daughters. Opposition to sports that were viewed as a threat to this convention was commonplace. Cycling for women was described as an indolent and indecent practice that could even transport girls to prostitution; it was said to be an activity far beyond a girl's strength and one that made women incapable of bearing children. Cycling, it was said, 'tends to destroy the sweet simplicity of her girlish nature; besides, how dreadful it would be if, by some accident, she were to fall into the arms of a strange man'.[28]

In the context of swimming, the closeness of near-naked bodies smacked of depravity. Separate swimming was rigidly adhered to until the 1920s, and even then, in some areas, mixed participation was only possible in the guise of family bathing. There were separate entrances for men and women, and strict rules of procedure disallowed men from getting out of the water on the 'women's side' of the pool, and vice versa.[29] Even as a feature of the seaside family holiday, bathing was organised with great propriety to avoid embarrassment and to ensure absolute modesty and morality.[30]

It is clear from the account so far that changes in women's sport were not abrupt or dramatic but rather a process of adjustment and accommodation, new forms of activity being formulated concomitantly with established conservative attitudes. Patriarchal ideology was the most consistent and sustaining set of values that women learnt to accommodate to, although there was no reason to suspect that the new sportswomen did not believe its basic premises anyway. In order to achieve social approval for their involvement in sport, women had to demonstrate that femininity and more active participation in physical activity were not incompatible. If the activity could be shown to have a utilitarian function, if there was no associated immodesty or impropriety, and if women remained cautious regarding other levels of exertion, then they could extend their physical horizons without threatening their existing social relationships with men – in fact, they could actually show that they positively supported their men in their ventures into sport. In all the different forms of sport, this process of accommodation can be seen and those from the most wealthy sections of society were no exception.

The following examples from pre-1900 publications concerned exclusively with women in sport had distinctly aristocratic overtones, but interestingly rested upon similar justifications to those of the sports of other social groups. I have characterised these as *elite sports* and they exemplify the moral imperatives of women's sport. An unusually diverse assortment of activities – riding, hunting, team and tandem riding, tiger shooting, deer stalking and driving, covert shooting, kangaroo hunting, cycling, and punting – were all deemed highly suitable and desirable pastimes for rich women with a potential to enrich their lives in respect, most particularly, to their essential femininity, to the state of their moral welfare, and to their general health. For example:

> Women . . . who were afraid neither of a little fatigue nor of a little exertion are the better, the truer, and the healthier and can yet remain essentially feminine in their thoughts and manners.[31]

This account by Lady Grenville rests upon the implicit assumption that there are innate psychological differences between the sexes and that women 'characteristically' possess an improving nature, an ethical disposition that can 'refine the coarser ways of men . . . contribute to the disuse of bad language', and lead the way to 'habits of courtesy and kindness' in the world of sport. We read that riding tends greatly to moral and physical well-being and improves the temper, the spirits, and the appetite.[32] It is stated that hunting in the shires provides a healthy way of making a man active and training his character, while the woman's most significant contribution as she rides by his side through the countryside is 'tact, kindness . . . courtesy and politeness . . . part of our ideal lady's nature . . . which go a long way towards what is called "Keeping the country together" '.[33] It was recognized that the woman's innate potential to employ her moral influence to improve the condition of the nation was as possible in the realm of sport as in her family role. The influence of the patrician elements, especially, set the cultural tone of women's sport and complemented the restrictions imposed by Social Darwinist beliefs.

The equating of moral rectitude with physical well-being was a fundamental feature of sport in the physical education colleges for women and in the more advanced schools for middle-class girls. Like the mother to her children, the college principals and the physical education mistresses were the moral exemplars for their students and pupils. The first principal of Bedford College (founded in 1903) was described by an old student as 'a sort of moral yardstick', and one who firmly believed that 'the discipline of the school emanates from the gymnasium'.[34] This idea was an element of the ethos of the physical education profession that made an indelible mark on its future development in the twentieth century. Madam Bergman-Österberg, the first principal of Dartford College, was herself an uncompromising disciplinarian who demanded from her students the highest standards of behaviour. She was an autocrat who controlled her students' activities in every practical detail, forbidding them to visit each other's rooms, enforcing an early lights out, imposing cold baths, and refusing weekend leave except in special circumstances.[35] In this way, Madame Bergman-Österberg intended to raise the level of health, intellect, and morality of her students. Her support of female emancipation was effectively a nationalist sentiment, confirming the contemporary Social Darwinist position about the vital importance of motherhood in evolution, and encompassing a belief that the educational arrangements should be geared to the role of women as mothers.[36] Familism was, therefore, incorporated into the rhetoric, ideology, and practical arrangements of college life at Dartford, and later in the other specialist colleges. It was argued that the complete course of training was, in itself, an education for a future life as a wife and mother. 'The outdoor exercise and the training here [at Dartford]', Madame Bergman-Österberg said, would fit a girl 'to become the organiser of the perfect home, or the trainer of a vigorous and beautiful new generation'.[37]

Previous medical accounts of the female constitution had directed attention to the physiological vulnerability of the woman's procreative capacity. In a way, they were now turned around by the notion that Swedish gymnastics, with its systematised attention to every part of the human anatomy, could promote healthy procreative functions. The woman's body and her ability to bear healthy children were idealised by Madame Bergman-Österberg:

> [Gymnastics] is the best training for motherhood. Remember it is not 'hips firm' or 'arms upward stretch', it is not 'drill', but it is moulding and reshaping and reforming the most beautiful and plastic material in the world, the human body itself.[38]

The physical education of women gained considerable ground by widening the definition of how they could legitimately use their bodies, but although the freedom gained had some reality in relation to what went on before, it was a very limited version of being free and natural. Women's freedom to move rested upon the assumption about the different, innate characteristics and needs of men and women, 'Gymnastics'. Madame Bergman-Österberg claimed, 'develop body, mind and morals simultaneously' and are a 'vital factor in making manly men and womanly women'.[39]

Encapsulating the physical notion of motherhood was the belief that national efficiency inevitably depended upon a strong tradition of home life. The college, in loco parentis, reproduced the structure and ideologies of the 'perfect' Victorian home with the college principal as both father and mother figure rolled into one – the 'head of the house', the ultimate authority and the inculcator of high moral standards. 'If you want to see something of the home life of my girls, you have come at the right moment' was Madame Bergman-Österberg's greeting to a visitor.[40] 'A small college admits also of home life', she said, 'always essential to woman's happiness, and never more so than during the period of youth'.[41] The students represented the children in their relationship to the principal, and the teaching staff were also, symbolically, part of the same family – their authority over the students was analogous to the authority of an older over a younger sibling. At Dartford, the staff as well as the students were all referred to as 'Madame's girls'.

These familistic authority relations were also reproduced in the student body; the 'college mother' had a responsibility for her 'college daughter' to see that she was integrated into the family community. In a very practical and taken-for-granted way, the general living arrangements of the college household consolidated the ideas about what middle-class family life should be like – meal times especially were formal occasions, with everyone in evening dress, and the principal sitting at the 'head of the table'. A student from Anstey College said, 'At meal times, in keeping with Rhoda Anstey's idea that we were one family, the whole company sat at one vast Victorian dining table'.[42] An old student at Bedford College observed, 'The first refresher course was like a family gathering'.[43] The idealization of the family was both a central feature of patriarchal ideology and of the version of feminism in the physical education colleges; it was an integral part of everyone's living and thinking. The theory and practice of familism in the colleges reproduced the structure and morality of the patriarchal Victorian bourgeois home and reinforced conventional sexual divisions in society.

Many of the students trained in the colleges became involved in voluntary philanthrophic activities as well as teaching, which seems to reflect a shift from their stereotypical and static wifely roles to a less insular social position that involved an increasing participation in public life. However, their widening sphere of action posed no threat to the traditional family structure – their benevolence was confirmation of a deeply moralistic attitude extending from the home into the community. The absence of any pecuniary profit established the impeccable nature of the enterprise. Feminists themselves often adopted a contradictory position: on the one hand subscribing to a lessening of inequalities between men and women, on the other implicitly accepting the notion of innate differences that predisposed women to certain occupations – 'best suited to work in the fields of Education and Pauperism'.[44] The National Association of Girls' Clubs was instituted in the 1880s, and its associate members included clubs organized by the Church of England, the Girls' Friendly Society, and Mothers' Unions. These clubs offered hockey, swimming, and gymnastics for their 'improving' qualities.[45] Youth work of this sort provided an opportunity for enlightened women to escape from the confines of domesticity without contradicting prior duty to home and family. Middle-class women were the main carriers of ideology within their family context, and their work teaching sport in clubs and elementary schools was an extension of this role where they became carriers of bourgeois ideology into the lives of the working class.

Early rationalised forms of sport were shared between sports clubs, girls schools, universities, and the colleges of physical education and began to unfold during the last third of the nineteenth century. They represented organized forms of sport and included competitive team games with codified rules and bureaucratic procedures. In all forms of rationalised sport, women had to accommodate to public hostility – the freer the activity in terms of bodily and spatial mobility, the more powerful was the opposition, always based on moral and biological criteria. In 1884, when women were first allowed at Wimbledon, it was declared that 'tournament play was all too tiring for the weaker sex',[46] but athletics was viewed more seriously as synonymous with indecency – a corrupting influence for a 'properly brought up girl'. In addition, it was considered to be a form of exercise unsuited to women's physiques that would produce an unnatural race of Amazons, thus destroying the prospect of motherhood and hence affecting the deterioration of the human race.[47]

The proliferation of twentieth-century women's sports such as golf, tennis, badminton, skating, hockey, netball, lacrosse, rounders, cricket, gymnastics, swimming, and athletics only became possible because they occurred in separate spheres from the sports of men. By being insular, sportswomen did not constitute a challenge in their relationship to men. If men and women never opposed one another in open competition, the newly learned female 'aggressiveness' and 'competitiveness' could be defined as qualitatively different from men's. Although sportswomen opened a new 'social space' in which they exerted power, it was thought that the power they wielded was not always progressive. The division of social space between men and women was characteristic of the nineteenth century – part of the dominant worldview of that century. Separate male and female sport did nothing to minimize the polarization between masculine and feminine that was manifest in the separate spheres of private (or family) life and public life.

Sport was still overwhelmingly a symbol of masculinity – the core manly virtues of courage, aggression, and the competitive 'instinct' were intimately associated with it. The cult of athleticism was in essence a cult of manliness, and so, if women joined in on equal footing, they could hardly be simultaneously projected as sexual objects by men, whose position was clear.

> Beauty of face and form is one of the chief essentials (for women) but unlimited indulgence in violent outdoor sports, cricket, bicycling, beagling,

otter-hunting, paper-chasing, and – most odious of all games for women – hockey, cannot but have an unwomanly effect on a young girl's mind, no less on her appearance. . . . Let young girls ride, skate, dance and play lawn tennis and other games in moderation, but let them leave field sports to those for whom they were intended – men.[48]

Nevertheless, women's participation in the traditionally all-male competitive sports was symbolic of their competition with men, and they faced harsh ridicule about their de-sexing characteristics. It was imperative, therefore, for women games players to be in every way 'ladylike' in their behaviour both on and off the pitch. It is difficult to conceive of hockey being played by Victorian women in contemporary ladylike fashion since it is a potentially vigorous, aggressive, and dirty game – but that was what was achieved. The ball was frequently lost under the long skirts of the players, who wore hats, and usually gloves as well, and who tackled each other at all times 'gently and fairly'. In 1897 there was a complaint in a game at Frances Holland School that hockey players 'keep the ball too much under their petticoats'.[49] I suggest that even after the turn of the century, as women's games-playing skills increased with the increased freedom of movement afforded by tunics and divided skirts, they nonetheless created and reproduced traditional gender divisions. The ambivalence of, and irony in, the way women accommodated to their role in sport is unwittingly, but perfectly, encapsulated in the compliment paid to a headmistress about the behaviour of her cricket team: 'Your girls play like gentlemen, and behave like ladies'.[50]

Notes

1 For a full discussion of the formative years of female sport see J.A. Hargreaves, 'Playing Like Gentlemen While Behaving Like Ladies: The Social Significance of Physical Activity for Females in Late Nineteenth and Early Twentieth Century Britain' (unpublished M.A. dissertation, University of London Institute of Education, 1979).

2 E. Janeway, in H. Eisenstein, *Contemporary Feminist Thought* (London, 1984), p. 9.

3 Eisenstein, ibid.

4 S. Rowbotham, *Hidden from History* (London, 1973), p. 3.

5 R. Baxandall, E. Ewen, and L. Gordon, 'The Working Class Has Two Sexes', *Monthly Review*, 28 (July–August 1976).

6 C. Dyhouse, 'Social Darwinist Ideas and the Development of Women's Education in England, 1880–1920', *History of Education*, 5 (1976), 41–42.

7 V. Klein, *The Feminine Character: History of an Ideology* (London: 2nd ed., 1971), p. 14.

8 G. Best, *Mid-Victorian Britain* (London, 1971), p. 18.

9 P. Bailey, *Leisure and Class in Victorian England* (London, 1978), p. 18.

10 S. Margetson, *Leisure and Pleasure in the Nineteenth Century* (New York, 1969). The principles of duty, self-sacrifice, and discipline were no longer so emphasised with a resultant tendency for the opulent leisure patterns of the upper classes to be imitated.

11 T. Veblen, *The Theory of the Leisure Class* (London, 1934), p. 181.

12 B. Jewell, *Sports and Games: Heritage of the Past* (Tunbridge Wells, 1977), pp. 96–98. A whole range of commercialized indoor versions of games was produced including

billiards, snooker, German billiards, bagatelle, versions of shove halfpenny, quoits, skittles and table skittles, and Aunt Sally.

13 B. Dobbs, *Edwardians at Play* (London, 1973), p. 8.

14 N. Wymer, *Sport in England* (London, 1949), p. 226.

15 Jewell, op. cit., p. 96.

16 Margetson, op. cit., p. 211.

17 Ibid., p. 100.

18 M.C. Borer, *Willingly to School: A History of Women's Education* (Guildford, 1976), pp. 240–243.

19 L. Duffin, 'Conspicuous Consumptive', in S. Delamont and L. Duffin (Eds.), *The Nineteenth Century Woman: Her Cultural World* (London, 1978), pp. 31–32, 41.

20 D. Walker, *Exercises for Women* (London, 2nd Ed., 1937), quoted by R.A. Smith, *American Women's Sports in the Victorian Era* (Pennsylvania State University, 1972), p. 8.

21 L. Murray, 'Womens Progress in Relation to Eugenics', *Eugenics Review II* (1910–1911), quoted in C. Dyhouse, 'Social Darwinist Ideas about the Development of Women's Education in England, 1880–1920, *History of Education*, 5 (1976).

22 M. Foucault, *The History of Sexuality* (Harmondsworth, reprinted 1981), p. 65.

23 L. Desmond, 'Gymnastics in the Roaring Twenties', *B.A.G.A. Journal* (Autumn 1973), 6.

24 Cited by A. Winter, *They Made Today: A History of the Hundred Years of the Polytechnic Sports Clubs and Societies* (London, 1979).

25 K. Middlemass, *High Society in the 1900s* (London, 1977), p. 146. From the Handbook for Girl Guides (London, 1912).

26 H.E. Roberts, 'Marriage, Redundancy or Sin', in M. Vicinus (Ed.), *Suffer and Be Still: Women in the Victorian Age* (Indiana, 1973).

27 P. Cominus, 'Innocent Femina Sensualis in Unconscious Conflict', ibid., p. 156.

28 C. Willett Cunnington, *Feminine Attitudes in the Nineteenth Century* (London, 1935), quoted in M.A. Hall. 'The Role of the Safety Bicycle in the Emancipation of Women', Proceedings of the Second World Symposium of the History of Sport and Physical Education (London, 1971), p. 245.

29 A. Rawlinson, personal interview (2 July 1979). When training for the 100-yard and 200-yard backstroke events he had to take his mother with him in order to gain entry during family bathing sessions.

30 B. Levitt Whitelaw & E. Adair Impey, *Letters of Remembrance* (1965), p. 8. Dartford College Archives.

31 Lady Grenville (Ed.), *Ladies in the Field: Sketches of Sport* (Ward and Downey, 1984), p. iv.

32 Ibid., p. 3.

33 Ibid., pp. 31, 76–77.

34 M. Squire, 'Margret Stansfield 1860–1951. Teaching a Way of Life', in E.W. Clarke, *Nine Pioneers of Physical Education* (London, 1964).

35 Kingsfield Book of Remembrance, Dartford College Archives.

36 Madame Osterberg, 'Madame Bergman–Österberg's Physical Training College', *Educational Review, XIII* (1896), 7.

37 Ibid.

38 L.D. Swinerdon, Madame Bergman-Österberg's Physical Training College Report 1895, Dartford Archives.

39 Ibid.

40 S. Mitford, 'A Physical Culture College in Kent'. *The Girl's Realm* (April 1899) 555.

41 Madame Osterberg, 'The Principal's Report, Madame Bergman-Österberg's Physical Training College Report 1898', Dartford College Archives.

42 C. Crunden, *A History of Anstey College of Physical Education 1897–1972* (Anstey College of Physical Education, 1974).

43 Quoted by I.M. Webb, 'Women's Place in Physical Education in Great Britain, 1800–1966, with special reference to teacher training' (unpublished thesis, University of Leicester, 1967).

44 J. Wedgewood, 'Female Suffrage, Considered Chiefly with Regard to Its Indirect Results', in J. Butler (Ed.), *Women's Work and Woman's Culture* (London, 1869).

45 H. Meller, *Leisure and the Changing City 1870–1914* (London, 1976), p. 177.

46 Wymer, op. cit., p. 250.

47 Winter, op. cit., p. 12.

48 Dobbs, op. cit. Quote from *Badminton* magazine (1900).

49 Borer, op. cit., p. 292.

50 J.F. Dove, 'Cultivation of the Body', in D. Beale *et al.*, *Work and Play in Girls' Schools* (London, 1891), p. 407.

5 Women and football – a contradiction? The beginnings of women's football in four European countries*

Gertrud Pfister, Kari Fasting, Sheila Scraton and Benilde Vázquez

Our interest in the history of women's football developed from our involvement in the project 'The experiences and meanings of physical activities in women's lives: an intercultural comparison in four European countries.' As part of this research project we carried out 240 in-depth, qualitative interviews with women tennis players, gymnasts and footballers in England, Germany, Norway and Spain (highly competitive and recreational). In our analysis of the data from the footballers it became obvious that in order to understand their experiences as sportswomen, it was important to locate women's football in its specific historical and cultural context. This essay first examines how football spread as a male domain to various countries in Europe in the period up to 1945 and to the end of the Second World War. This is followed by a reconstruction of the first attempts by women to participate in physical activities in general, as well as football in particular. Here, we focus specifically on the following questions: under which conditions and circumstances did women succeed in penetrating this male terrain? Which reasons and arguments were put forward either to support or hinder the participation of women in this 'unfeminine' sport? Are there noticeable differences in the development of women's football in the different countries? And, finally, what explanations can be given for differences as well as similarities in this development?

We take as our starting point that body and movement are both 'biologically grounded'[1] and are, to a large extent, shaped by culture. This means that on the one hand the sexual hierarchy 'embodies' itself in men and women and that, on the other, body and movement cultures play a role in constructing the gender order. As a result of body and movement being 'engendered' in this fashion, sports have developed either a masculine or feminine image and thus appeal to men and women in different ways.[2] Further, the myths of masculinity and femininity which are associated with different body or sport practices are dependent on the prevailing social and gender orders. This can be demonstrated with many examples taken from the history of physical activities in Europe. From the very beginning, the participation of men and women in certain forms of physical exercise or certain

* Taken and abridged from J. Mangan (ed.) *Sport in Europe: Politics, Class, Gender. The European Sports History Review, Vol. I*, London: Frank Cass.

types of sport was tied to numerous rules and norms pertaining to gender. It was above all women who – in compliance with existing gender roles – were barred from sporting activities. One of the sports which in many countries was regarded as a male preserve was the game of football.

The cross-cultural comparison will, it is hoped, throw light on the factors which gave rise both to opportunities and to problems not only in women's football but also in women's sports more generally. One of the major aims of the article, furthermore, is to identify common features and differences of culture and thus to uncover structural links between women's sport and the special circumstances of women's lives. [. . .]

Women and football from its beginnings to the Second World War

Germany

The German 'games movement', which from the beginning of the 1880s had propagated physical exercise, especially with games practised in the open air derived from *Turnen*, also sought to attract girls and women because of the belief that 'strong offspring can only be born of strong mothers'. Among the activities that were recommended for girls were ball games in which the ball was only allowed to be moved by kicking it with the feet, for example, 'football in the round'. Like all *Turnen* games, this type of football game completely lacked both a competitive impulse and any orientation towards performance. Although P. Heineken claimed in 1898 that 'for many years football has been played by girls, too, and they enjoy playing it',[3] he gives neither details nor the slightest evidence for his assertion.

While proponents of sport, as well as of the games movement, wished to restrict 'proper' football to boys and men, there were advocates of women's football to be found among the first women doctors, who were in favour of physical fitness for women. These included A. Fischer-Dückelmann and H.B. Adams-Lehmann, both of whom encouraged the women readers of their popular guidebooks to practise sports as they pleased, and keep active, building up strength and stamina through exercise.[4] Fischer-Dückelmann even went as far as recommending football for women, provided that they wore the right clothing. As far as we know, this unconventional proposal was never put into practice; throughout the 1920s there was absolutely no question about the fact that the football field was no place for women. 'All types of sport which exceed women's natural strength, such as wrestling, boxing and football, are unsuitable sports for women and are, moreover, unaesthetical and unnatural in appearance' in Vierath's lapidary comment in his book *Moderner Sport*, published in 1930.[5] Reasons why women should be prohibited from playing football were seldom given. In 1927 an article appeared in *Sport and Sonne* under the heading 'Should the female sex play football?' The author had been prompted to put this question (understood merely rhetorically here) because of the 'great women's football associations which exist' in England.

According to the author, German women disapprove of football, first, because the 'rough way' in which the game is played is contrary to women's sensibilities and, second, because the game is not suited to the 'build of the female body'.[6] A rare reference to women football players – and one, moreover, which did not contain a fundamental rejection of the game played by women – can be found in the 1930 edition of the journal *Leibesübungen*. A report on the founding of a women's football club in Frankfurt included the following comment: 'The lady footballers ... intend to play a cheerful, combative kind of football. Whether it will be worse than hockey, we will have to wait and see. .... It will be interesting to see what will come of this venture.'[7] Today we know that nothing came of this venture. At first, the 35 young women who had founded a women's football club in 1930 trained regularly on Sundays. Reports of this 'scandal' in the press led soon to a 'storm of indignation', and many of the players yielded to pressure from both their families and the general public and left the club, which was subsequently disbanded in 1931.[8] On the whole, reports of women's football in Germany are rare, most of them being critical opinions voiced about football-playing women in England or France.[9] One women's magazine, the *Damenillustrierte*, commented in 1927, 'Women may be playing football in England and America, but it is to be hoped that this bad example is not followed in German sport'.[10] This hope came true and it took until 1970 before the German Football Federation officially allowed German women to play football.

England

The development of women's football in England, the motherland of this game, was much more comprehensive. As early as in 1894, a 'British Ladies' Football Club' was founded and in the following year football matches were played between various women's teams.[11] A match took place in 1895, for example, between a team from the north and a team from the south of England. A detailed report of the match appeared in the *Manchester Guardian*, although the reporter restricted himself almost exclusively to a discussion of the women's outfits.[12] The general public gradually became aware of this new sensation and a women's football match played in Newcastle in 1895 was attended by 8,000 spectators. In Scotland, too, a number of women began to take interest in this new game in the 1890s, and Lady Florence Dixie, a well-known writer and suffragette (who also supported women sitting astride a horse instead of riding side-saddle) managed a 'travelling ladies' football team'.

Football matches did take place, apparently, between women's and men's teams, although in 1902 the English Football Association forbade the clubs which belonged to the association from playing against women's teams. Whereas the first women football players were looked upon as a curiosity and the games they played were treated as some kind of fairground spectacle, women's football developed during the First World War into a popular sporting event. The women, who had to take the men's places in the factories, sought distraction and recreation in the game of football, and were even supported in this by their employers, who were interested in maintaining and improving the health and fitness of their workers – and possibly in promoting their firm's name, too. Furthermore, the boom in women's football was due to the national enthusiasm for the war effort since the matches were played to raise money for charity. On Christmas Day, 1917, for example, a game took place between Dick, Kerr's Ladies and another team from Preston with 10,000 spectators looking on. The money taken at the gate, all of £ 600, was donated to a fund for wounded soldiers. The character of the events – occasionally against men's teams or games played in fancy costumes – indicated that more importance was attached to the charitable purpose rather than to sporting performance. In this context playing football was not seen as a sign of moral decadence but as evidence of the patriotism of the women playing football. And when games were played to raise money for charity, the women had a great advantage over the men since they were, after all, an attraction for the masses hungry for sensation. The number of spectators grew to such an extent that the Football Association allowed its clubs to put their grounds at the disposal of the women: 'By early 1920 it was no idle kick about on a ploughed field with a few curious onlookers on the touchlines; it was Stamford Bridge, White Hart Lane and Goodison Park, all bastions of the male preserve with packed terraces enjoying an entertaining match for a good cause.[13]

During the First World War women's teams were set up in a number of companies, among them the five Lyons Ladies teams whose players worked in Lyons cafes in and around London. Women's football matches were organised, also, by sports clubs and in 1921 there were about 150 women's teams in England, the main centres of women's football being the Midlands and the North.

The most successful women's team was Dick, Kerr's Ladies FC. This team was founded in 1917 by workers at Dick, Kerr's, a munitions and engineering factory, and its first game, played in the same year, was organised by a woman named Grace Sibbert. She was replaced as the team's manager by Alfred Frankland and under his management Dick, Kerr's Ladies went from success to success. In 1920, for example, they played almost every Sunday – a total of 30 games over the whole year, of which they won 25 and, of the rest, three were draws. In their most famous match they beat St. Helens 4–0 at Goodison Park before a crowd of 53,000 spectators.[14]

Women's football even became international, with English teams first of all playing teams of Scottish and Irish women. In Spring 1920, for example, Dick, Kerr's Ladies defeated a Scottish team with a score of 20–0.[15] In the same year a match between Dick, Kerr's Ladies and a French team caused much excitement in the English press. The French team (accompanied by Alice Milliat, who later became president of the International Federation of Women's Sports) was given a tremendous reception on its arrival in Preston and was followed through the streets of the town by an enthusiastic crowd. In the week that followed, they played four games in four different English towns. In October of the same year, the players from Preston travelled to France on an exchange tour, which turned out to be another highlight of women's football. In 1921 a match was played between a French team and the Plymouth Ladies and in 1922 Dick, Kerr's Ladies even travelled to the United States and Canada, where they earned great respect from the spectators for their performance against men's teams.

The standard of women's football had risen considerably since its early years and players now trained regularly and systematically not only in order to improve their condition but also to refine their ball skills and practise tactical moves.

However, the rise of women's football did not meet with approval from every quarter, and in the phase of 'normalisation' after the war, there were calls also, for a return to normality in the gender order. In the press and elsewhere in public life, heated debates flared up on the question of women's football: 'It was the most ludicrous exhibition of the noble sport I have ever witnessed,' commented a reader of the *Western Morning News* in 1921.[16] On the one hand, women football players were criticised for their lack of skill; on the other hand, if they did demonstrate ball-playing qualities, they were attacked because of their lack of femininity. Moreover, the arguments which were put forward against women's football were not only of an aesthetic or moral nature, but also to a great extent medically motivated.

The women players were anxious to rebut such accusations and made every effort to try and convince the public that playing football was neither dangerous nor harmful: 'If football was dangerous, some ill-effects would have been seen by now,' observed the team captain of Huddersfield Atalanta FC in 1921. She said that she felt much better than she had the previous year and even the housework was no longer a problem since she was 'refreshed' after playing football.[17] One problem was certainly the fact that after the war the argument of raising money for charity as a legitimisation of women's football matches began to lose its validity. In addition, since the standard of football the women played was relatively high, it could no longer be declared to be a harmless pastime; on the contrary, it was hard 'unfeminine' sport. Further, the matches between women's teams seemed to divert public attention from boys' and men's football. In the reactionary political climate of the post-war years, in which women 'by a national campaign in the press and in Parliament should be persuaded, even forced back into the home',[18] women's football seemed to upset the long awaited reshaping of the gender order. The real threat appeared to come from the joint activities of the women: 'The success of single women in public life threatened the status quo. Independent women were accused of sex hatred and pilloried for preferring their own sex to men. Amid a wholesale effort to revive marriage and delicate womanhood, single women and their communities were covertly and overtly attacked.'[19]

The 'official' explanation for taking measures against women's football matches was based on the alleged lack of clarity about how revenues from the games were used. In 1921 the Football Association decided that women's teams would have to seek the permission of the FA before matches could take place at the grounds of clubs belonging to the FA. At the end of 1921, a resolution was passed by the FA's advisory committee in which it was observed: 'The game of football is quite unsuitable for women and should not be encouraged.[20] Football clubs were now urged to stop the practice of putting their grounds at the disposal of women's teams.

The women, of course, objected strongly to this; the captain of the Plymouth Ladies accused the FA of living 'a hundred years behind the times', adding that behind the measure lay 'purely sexual prejudice'. Looking back, Gail Newsham came to a similar evaluation of the events: 'The chauvinists, the medical "experts" and the anti-women's football lobby had won – their threatened male bastion was now safe.[21]

The FA's decisions were the first steps in the decline of women's football in England, especially since it meant the end of, at least some, appearance of official recognition. The end of support from established football clubs made it necessary for the women to organise their own matches and, in 1921, 25 women's clubs came together to form the English Ladies' Football Association (ELFA). By the time the Association held its second meeting, the number of affiliated clubs had already risen to 60. Nevertheless, the ELFA was faced with enormous difficulties, since it lacked not only support, but also, an organisational basis. A great part of the credit for the success of women's teams was due to their managers and trainers, who had had long years of experience and formed the necessary contacts.[22] After the FA's decision it was difficult 'to find grounds that were not used by FA affiliated clubs, referees who were not associated with affiliated football, and even the professional players who had helped train the women and refereed matches had to be careful of associating with the ladies' teams'.[23]

Little is known to date about the activities of women footballers in the period which followed: 'Undoubtedly, the women's game continued in a more or less "underground" fashion, staging matches at local festivities and for fund-raising and charity events.[24] Dick, Kerr's Ladies, at any rate, continued to play football until 1965; through the years the team played a total of more than 800 games, winning the great majority of them.

Spain

During the Second Republic, Spanish women began to take a more active part in sports. Photographs, moreover, provide conclusive evidence that some women even dared to take part in football games. However, little is known up to present about the development of women's football in Spain. Pointing to the tendencies towards modernisation and the new freedoms gained by women during that period, Garcia Bonafé noted: 'El futbol femenino cuenta con representacion en diversos clubs y el esqui incluye categoria oficial para mujeres.[25] Nevertheless, Spanish women's football was short-lived. In the Franco régime women were made aware, once again, of their roles as mothers, which could or should not be, combined with sporting activities.

Norway

Similarly in Norway we found few traces of women's soccer before the Second World War. In a German magazine, *Damen-Sport Damen-Turnen*, of 1919, a very short note was published about a soccer match between a women's and a men's team in Kristiania. 'It seems this game was not to be taken too seriously. Newspaper reports talk about 'standing ovations' and 'enthusiastic applause'.[26] No further information about this game is available.

Another sign of women playing football is a game which took place in Brumundal in mid-summer 1931.[27] When there was a soccer match between a team of women and a team of older men. It was common at that time, the author writes, to arrange amusing soccer matches between different groups. An announcement in *Hamar Arbeiderblad* (a newspaper) states: 'Humorous soccer match. Women's team against old men'. The result of this match is not known, but according to the author it inspired some sportswomen in the district to start a women's team. The women in Hamar took the initiative to develop their own team as an alternative to their 'sweethearts' team. They arranged and played matches between themselves and were supported by the men in the club (Hamar idrettslags soccer group). The women's 'baptism of fire' was a match against Bolton Wanderers that consisted mainly of English tourists. This historic match took place in connection with a tournament called 'the olympic games' held in Hamar on 19 July 1931. The result is unknown, but according to the newspaper *Hamar Arbeiderblad* it was a victory for the Norwegian women's team. Following this success, they started to look for other female opposition and managed, finally, to find some women from Kapp sports club who had played some soccer on playgrounds, with the support of their fiancés. This sports club put together a women's team and played against Hamar in August 1931. Hamar won 3–0. This is probably the first recorded soccer match between two Norwegian women's teams.[28]

Football and masculinity

In each of the countries studied, these initiatives did not seem to lead to an upswing of women's football. Indeed, many female players quickly gave up playing. Although there is no evidence for why these women gave up football, we can assume that they were constrained by dominant ideals of acceptable female behaviour. In all the countries, femininity and soccer was looked upon as a contradiction which could only be tolerated in a 'humorous' situation. Women entering male domains were regarded as ridiculous. In Norway, the strong resistance to women's sporting competitions seems to have rendered female football unthinkable.

In this concluding section we focus on two key questions. First, why did women who wished to play football not succeed in building up a women's soccer movement? Second, why did attitudes towards women's football differ in the countries studied?

It can be assumed that in all four countries opposition to women's football was closely connected to the characterisation of the game as a competitive sport.[29] In contrast to the games of the German *Turnen*, or to games such as hockey, football was considered to be competitive, strenuous, aggressive and potentially dangerous. On these grounds, football was disapproved of even for boys and men by German *Turnen* and physical education teachers. In 1928, for example, Fischer attested in his popular book on 'body culture' to the 'markedly combative character' of football[30] and advised women to play team handball, an 'altogether more subdued and civil game'.[31] In none of the countries under study did football, based as it was on performance and competition, appear to be reconcilable with the prevailing ideals of femininity. It did not matter, of course, for such images to be effective, that the qualities attributed to football were based on imagination and association and did not necessarily have much to do with the reality of this game.

The body, physical activity and forms of presenting oneself (including sport) play a major role in the reproduction of the gender order. Ideologies and myths, concerning the body and the limits of physical achievement with regard to both sexes, are key factors in reinforcing and reproducing structures. From the beginning, people were afraid that women's sport would have adverse and undesirable effects on both gender identity and gender hierarchy. Sport, or certain sports at least, have continuously provided a means, right up to the present day, of constructing and demonstrating masculinity.[32] As mentioned above, the development of football in England was closely connected with the construction of 'martial masculinity'. The ideology of militarism was an inherent part of the ideology along with the practice of team games. Mangan has demonstrated that 'it was team games like rugby and cricket that were supposed to give Englishmen an inherent superiority when it came to the supreme sacrifice in battle'.[33]

Dunning (1994) was able to reveal, using the example of rugby, that sport is especially vital as a resource in shaping male identity in times in which the balance of power between the sexes is undergoing change. Football teams (and this can be seen in the rituals that they enact) may be regarded as male preserves and male allegiances.[34] Male allegiances are formed precisely through the exclusion of women and the rejection of femininity and all the qualities attached to it such as softness and tenderness. Efforts to keep women away from football fields can, therefore, be interpreted as attempts to preserve and protect the domains and the privileges which men have secured for themselves.

Further, it must be taken into consideration that in the countries studied, football is – more or less – a national sport – the sport with which the (male) population or, at least groups of the population, identify. National sport and myths of masculinity are intricately interwoven: 'Each country's national sport contributes towards producing and securing the male identity specific to that particular country. This explains not only why in all societies the national sport is a male preserve . . . but also why it is linked to sexual demands, needs and anxieties.[35]

On the whole, in all the countries the aim was to preserve the gender order both inside and outside sport. That the differences between the sexes should disappear, that women should become more masculine, that 'certain limits' should be exceeded – this was more or less strictly rejected.[36]

Women's football – similarities and differences

The development of women's sport, and of women's football in all countries involved, shows clearly that universal ideologies of femininity and masculinity cut across culture and nation.[37] Sport was associated with hegemonic masculinity and, therefore, women faced barriers to their entering and participating in physical activities. Competition was a contested terrain for women in all four countries researched. However, women's competitive sport increased after the First World War in Germany and, to a lesser degree, in England. There was considerable resistance to competitive sport for women in Norway, and, during the monarchy, in Spain. The general judgement of football as a male combative sport and attitudes towards women football players were in many respects very similar in all the countries studied. Everywhere football was viewed as a challenge to hegemonic beliefs around appropriate femininity relating to women's role as mothers, their physicality and sexuality. The power and influence of the myths of femininity were, however, different in the countries involved. The ideology of motherhood was especially strong and powerful in Spain.

Why, then, was women's football tolerated in England, at least for some time, but spurned in Germany and Norway? Why were women prevented from playing football under the monarchy in Spain, but started to participate in football in the Second Republic? Were women's sports in England more developed and 'progressive' than in Germany or Norway? This latter hypothesis is not supported by the relatively broad-minded attitude to women's sports generally in Germany, which is reflected in the way women's athletics was encouraged.

Explanations for the differences in the development of women's football need to be situated in their specific social, political and economic contexts. If we use the percentage of women in the labour force as an indicator for women's 'emancipation', there are large differences between the countries involved. However, we have to take into consideration that working outside the home does not necessarily equate with 'liberation' or 'empowerment'. In Germany in 1933, 36% of the economically active population were women. In Great Britain the percentage was 30% (1931), in Norway 27% (1930) and in Spain 14% (1920) and 12% (1940).[38] At least for Spain it is clear that women's role was to be housewives and mothers.[39] This conclusion can be drawn, also, in relation to the introduction of political and civil rights for women. Moreover, the development of women's political rights seemed to be linked to their ability to access sport. In Norway, women gained civil rights in 1888 and the right to vote in 1913, in Germany in 1896 and 1919 respectively, in Great Britain 1888 and 1928 and in Spain 1875 and 1931.[40] However, political influence was denied to women (and men) in Spain during the dictatorship of Franco. The presented data may help to explain the exclusion of women from football in Spain during monarchy. That Spanish women started to play soccer at the same time as their role changed during the Second Republic is clear evidence that women's sport was closely connected with the political situation.

It is probable that the short success of women's football in England, as well as in Spain during the Second Republic, was made possible by the particular historical constellations and specific contexts. For women's football in England, the First World War undoubtedly played a considerable role. If women had to take the place of men in numerous fields of life, then why not in sport, too? Lopez (1997) explains the popularity of women's football in England in the following terms: 'Women were able to take the opportunity to play because millions of men went off to fight the invading Germans at the war front in France, many never to return. Therefore, not only did women have to fill the void in the factories left by the absent men and take on their traditional work role, but they also took on traditional male pastimes such as football.'[41] In England, where football already had a long tradition, the First World War and the necessity of raising funds for charity provided women with a suitable opportunity of taking up a sport which had hitherto been a male preserve. As many of the players came from the working class, it was easy to look upon the games as entertainment for the masses, instead of earnest sport; the respectability of middle-class girls was in no way compromised. Last but not least, football was not the only sport in England which was regarded as a 'male preserve'. Rugby constituted an alternative path to the demonstration and the preservation of manhood.

That it did not occur to German women to play football during this period may have been connected to the widespread misgivings which people had about this competitive game. After all, football had not found universal acceptance in Germany at that time. Moreover, German women were provided with an alternative to sports, which emphasised performance and competition, in the form of *Turnen*. In handball, they had a substitute for the combative team game of football.

In Norway, by contrast, women were largely confined to gymnastics, which was considered to be the feminine form of physical exercise. In Norway, as has been described above, until the Second World War even athletics was held to be incompatible with femininity and, as in England, the few women's football games that were played were perceived as 'humorous' or a spectacle.

In neither Germany, Norway nor Spain was there a women's sports association that could have organised and supervised women's football. In England, the tradition of gender segregation in physical education and sport and the existence of the English Ladies' Football Association may have contributed to the continuity of a women's football movement, however marginal. From the early 1930s, due to factors including an economic recession, social upheavals and political developments, traditional ideals of womanhood and the family gained new significance in all the countries under study. In a period in which criticism of emancipation and new culture was rife, there was no room for women's football.

Soon after the Second World War initiatives were taken by women in Germany and England to become officially licensed to play football. However, it was not until the 1970s that a new women's football movement began to develop worldwide – a movement which in the meantime has succeeded even in having women's football recognised as an Olympic discipline.

Notes

1 Ute Frevert, '*Mann und Werb und Werb und Mann.' Geschlechterdifferenzen in der Moderne* (Munich, 1995).
2 The term sport is used in many European countries in a broad sense: it is often synonymous with physical activities.

3 Ph. Heineken, *Das Fußballspicl*, p. 228.
4 A. Fischer–Dückelmann, *Die Frau als Hausärztm* (Dresden, 2 edn 1905), H.B. Adams Lehmann, *Das Frauenbuch* (Stuttgart, sine anno).
5 W. Vierath, *Moderner Sport* (Berlin, 1930). p. 61.
6 *Sport and Sonne* (1927), p. 24. Unfavourable comments on football in other countries are to be found, for example, in an article in *Sport and Gesundhert* (1938), 9, 18.
7 Quoted in G. Pfister, *Frau und Sport. Fruhe Texte* (Frankfurt, Fischer, 1980), p. 179.
8 B. Schreiber-Rietig, 'Die Suffragetten spichen Fuß Ball'. *Olympisches Feuer* (1993), 2, 36–41. See also *Das Illustrierte Blatt*, dated 27 March 1930.
9 *Sport and Gesundhert* (1932), 1, 16; *Sport on Bild*, dated 22 Nov. 1895, 334. See also *Sport on Bild*, dated 5. 2. 1987, p. 87; *Berhner Illustrierte Zeitung* (1933), 11, 401.
10 *Die Damenillustrierte* (1927), Special Issue 'Frauensport', 7.
11 The following text is based on information in D.J. Williamson, *Belles of the Ball* (Devon, 1991) (hereafter *Belles*); Williams and Woodhouse, 'Can play, will play'? Women and Football in Britain', pp. 85–111 (hereafter 'Can play') and S. Lopez, *Women on the Ball I Guide to Women's Football* (London, 1997) (hereafter *Women*).
12 D.J. Williamson, *Belles*, p. 4.
13 Ibid., p. 12.
14 S. Lopez, *Women*.
15 Williams and Woodhouse, 'Can play', p. 91
16 D.J. Williamson, *Belles*, p. 47.
17 Quoted in Williams and Woodhouse, 'Can play', p. 85.
18 E. Roberts, *Women's Work, 1840–1940* (London, 1988)
19 M. Vicinus, *Independent Women. Work and Community for Single Women, 1850–1920* (London, 1985), p. 285.
20 D.J. Williamson, *Belles*, p. 69.
21 Quoted in S. Lopez, *Women*.
22 D.J. Williamson, *Belles*, p. 10.
23 S. Lopez, *Women*, p. 4.
24 Williams and Woodhouse, 'Can play', p. 94.
25 M. Garcia Bonafé, 'Los Inicios del Deporte Femenino' in Vjuntament de Barcelona (ed.), *Mujer y Deporte* (Barcelona, 1989), p. 32.
26 *Damen-Sport Damen-Turnen* (1919), p. 156.
27 R -K Tukikilsen, *Norsk Kvinnefotball En historisk undersckelse om norsk kvinnefot balls utaiklung Master thesis* (Hogskolen i Levanger, 1993).
28 Kretsstyrets moteprotokoll. Bergen og Fylkene Arbeideridrettskrets, 1932–1934.
29 See especially E. Dunning, 'Sport as Male Preserve: Notes on the Social Sources of Masculine Identity and its Transformations', in S. Birell and Ch. Cole (eds.). *Women, Sport, and Culture* (Champaign: Human Kinetics, 1994), pp. 163–9.
30 H. W. Fischer, *Körperschonhert und Korperkultur* (Berlin, 1928), p. 73
31 Ibid. p. 78
32 See also M. Messner, 'Sports and Male Domination: The Female Athlete and Contested Ideological Terrain', in Birell and Cole, *Women, Sport, and Culture*, pp. 65–81.
33 Mangan, 'Games Field', 140.
34 For the *Turnen* movement as male allegiance which combined a glorification of masculinity and nationalism, see G. Pfister, 'Physical Activity in the Name of the Fatherland: Turnen and the National Movement (1810–1820)', *Sporting Heritage*, 1 (1996), 14–36.
35 M. Klein (ed.), *Sport and Geschlecht* (Reinbek, 1983), p. 18; see also G. Pfister, 'Physical Activity in the Name of the Fatherland'.
36 H.W. Fischer, *Korperschönhert und Körperkultur* (Berlin, 1928), p. 10.
37 Because of the restricted space we could not discuss the connections between gender, sport and class which showed specific patterns in the different countries.

38 B.R. Mitchell, *European Historical Statistics* (London, 1976); these numbers have to be interpreted very carefully because it is difficult to compare the available statistics which are based in each country on different material. See for a more detailed discussion about similarities and differences of womens roles in Europe the article in volume 5 of the *History of Women* edited by Thebaud (1995). In the contributions of this series edited by Georges Duby and Michel Perrot special emphasis is laid on the role of women in France and England.

39 See especially, Ackelsberg, *Free Women.*

40 M. Sineau, 'Recht and Demokratie', in G. Duby and M. Perrot (eds.), *Geschtchte der Frauen*, Vol. 5 (Frankfurt, 1995), pp. 529–59; S. Lopez, *Women*, p. 2.

Seminar questions

Chapter 4

1   What were the key elements of the ideology of familism and how did these work to limit the early involvement of women in sport?
2   How was the ideology of femininity reproduced within girls' physical education?

Chapter 5

1   How did football develop in the different countries and what factors impinged on this?
2   How did men and masculinity influence the development of women's football?

Part III

The media and representation

Introduction

Feminist analyses of the media have identified both the gendered representation of women and their marginalization within it. This marginalization is both in terms of their position within the industry (for example, the limited number and gendered location of journalists, commentators and photographers) and the amount and quality of coverage. The media is an example of a powerful patriarchal institution that is largely owned and controlled by men. The media is important in the production and reproduction of gendered ideologies and in communicating our commonsense understandings of women's and men's position within sport.

The two chapters in this part both consider the media representation of women in different sporting contexts. Both chapters provide empirical evidence, one drawing on televised coverage of an individual and a team sport, and the other, a content analysis of print media coverage of sports traditionally associated with men. Both argue that media images and representations contribute to wider gendered power relations.

Margaret Duncan and Cynthia Hasbrook's chapter is an early examination of media representations of women and sport. It is significant because it centralizes power in its analysis; it argues that the denial of power in televised women's sports is part of the imbalance of power for women in society more generally.

The empirical evidence involves an examination of basketball and surfing, both of which deliver conflicting messages about female athletes. Positive portrayals of women athletes are counter posed with subtle trivializations that deny power to women.

The more recent chapter by Riitta Pirinen focuses on Finnish newspaper coverage of women's entry into traditional male sports (boxing, ski jumping, hammer throwing, triple jump, and pole vault). She argues that the media's discursive struggles over gender are more evident in these 'new' sports for women than in the coverage of more traditional female sports. Dominant discourses of trivialization/marginalization and equal opportunities are revealed through an examination of the different textual strategies used by the newspapers. Although written nearly ten years apart, these chapters illustrate the continuing significance of the media and its role in the (re)production of gendered power relations.

After reading both the chapters in this part, students should:

- evaluate gendered images and representations of women in the media;
- consider issues of control and power in different forms of media;
- critically assess the representation of women in different sports.

Further readings

Creedon, P. (1994) (ed.) *Women, Media and Sport: Changing Gender Values*, London: Sage.

Fusco, C. and Kirby, S. (2000) 'Are your kids safe? Media representations of sexual abuse in sport', in S. Scraton and B. Watson (eds) *Sport, Leisure Identities and Gendered Spaces*, Eastbourne: Leisure Studies Association Publications.

Hargreaves, J. (1993) 'Bodies matter! Images of sport and female sexualisation', in Brackenridge, C. (ed.) *Body Matters: Leisure Images and Lifestyles*, Eastbourne: Leisure Studies Association.

McKay, J. and Huber, D. (1992) 'Anchoring media images of technology and sport', *Women's Studies International Forum* 15(2): 205–18.

Wright, J. and Clarke, G. (1999) 'Sport, the media and the construction of compulsory heterosexuality', *International Review for the Sociology of Sport* 34(3): 227–43.

6 Denial of power in televised women's sports*

Margaret Carlisle Duncan and
Cynthia A. Hasbrook

The starting point for this investigation was our observation, by no means original, of a curious phenomenon: women's participation in team sports and certain "male appropriate" individual sports is *decisively* lower than men's participation in these sports. More significant yet, though, is the disproportionate amount of television coverage devoted to team sports, particularly men's team sports, and to "male appropriate" individual sports. By comparison, females competing in team contests and certain individual sports receive a negligible amount of air time. Why are team sports and certain individual sports considered to be a male domain? Why is there such a notable lack of female participation in these areas? And why are these imbalances underscored by disproportionate media coverage, especially television coverage? Much has been written about this asymmetry, but few authors have provided sufficient explanation.

Metheny's classic work (1965) in the area of feminine sporting images suggests that social sanctions powerfully shape female participation in sport. She observes that female participation in certain forms of competition (sports that feature body contact, face-to-face opposition, moving a heavy object, or propelling oneself over long distances) appear to be categorically unacceptable in our society. Metheny traces the social prohibitions relating to such participation to "differences between the ways in which males and females may use their own bodily forces in the mutual action of procreation." She argues that "the female role [is] construed in passive terms as the act of receiving and nurturing new life rather than creating by personal intent expressed in terms of bodily force [as the male does]" (p. 52).

More recent work on this subject by Boutilier and SanGiovanni (1983) offers insights quite similar to those of Metheny:

> Girls and women continue to receive social acceptance for individual sports more readily than for team contests. Social approval for sports such as tennis, golf, and gymnastics is high. As non-contact individual sports, they offer the dual "benefits" of continued segregation of the female athlete from teammates and the continued confirmation of the participant's "femininity." (p. 43)

* Taken and abridged from, *Sociology of Sport Journal* 5 (1988): 1–21.

Yet team sports offer their participants rewards that individual sports cannot, benefits from which women might greatly profit. As the two authors point out a team player learns valuable skills – cooperation and negotiation for example – and enjoys the pleasures of camaraderie and group cohesiveness.

Boutilier and SanGiovanni hypothesize that women's participation in certain individual sports is more socially acceptable than their participation in team sports because the former (golf, gymnastics, swimming) allow women to remain true to the female stereotype: glamorous, graceful, nonsweaty, and definitely *not* roughed up by contact with other women. While both Metheny (1965) and Boutilier and SanGiovanni's (1983) formulations of socially sanctioned female images may provide a partial explanation for the dearth of women in team sports and certain individual sports, it surely is not wholly satisfactory in this time of changing definitions of femininity and masculinity.

Studies on media depictions of female athletes reveal even more striking patterns of asymmetry and exclusion, but again do not provide compelling explanations for these patterns. For example, Rintala and Birrell's study (1984) of a youth sport magazine, *Young Athlete*, clearly points up a pattern of female exclusion from team sports in media depictions:

> One of the more striking patterns in representation by sport focuses on team sports. As the data . . . illustrate, girls are markedly under-represented in team sports. Three team sports are overwhelmingly composed of females: field hockey (99%), softball (98%), and volleyball (93%). Yet photographs of these sports did not reflect the female dominance of them: only 59% of the field hockey players, 51% of the volleyball players, and 33% of the softball players in *Young Athlete* were females. . . . females are grossly under-represented in all team sports, even those they do in fact dominate.

Rintala and Birrell do not venture an explanation for this exclusionary practice, apart from alluding to the financial rationale of the magazine (the issues featuring female athletes on the cover or stories about females in team sports do not sell as well, according to the publisher). That, unfortunately, tells us very little. Why don't these issues sell as well?

Obviously there is no easy answer to this question. However, several researchers hint at an area which, if more fully investigated, might yield a plausible explanation for these patterns of asymmetry and exclusion, and particularly the media's disregard of women in team sports and certain individual sports. In her article on the politics of women's sports. Susan Birrell (1984) argues that "positions of power invariably rest in the hands of the overclass; access to opportunities, *rewards, power* and other rights and privileges are under their control" (p. 25). And Don Sabo, in his article on sport, men, and masculinity (1985), echoes Birrell's argument as he observes that men assume roles of power and prestige in sport (as coaches, players, managers, and owners) while women hold mainly subservient positions. In the sporting world, of course, men constitute the overclass; women are subject to their will. Thus, power, or lack of it, is the issue that surfaces in these discussions of women's participation in sport.

Power is introduced in an abbreviated but tantalizing way in the chapter on psychological dimensions of sport written by Susan Birrell in Boutilier and SanGiovanni's (1983) book. This chapter makes a direct connection between participation in team versus individual sports and a power motive. Birrell argues that sport contains both an achievement element and a competitive element and that the two are not identical, nor are they necessarily balanced. That is, in some sports athletes measure themselves against an inanimate standard of excellence (the clock, a perfect score of 10, their previous personal best, and so on) and do not directly compete against others. These sports are preponderantly *individual* sports. Birrell hypothesizes that athletes participating in such sports are motivated primarily by achievement concerns.

In other sports, the athletes compete directly against one another in the sense that they can control, influence, or overpower their opponents; they can immediately see the effects of their own actions on their opponents' performances. Such sports are predominantly *team* sports, and Birrell theorizes that athletes participating in this group of sports are motivated primarily by a need for power. Thus, it is primarily team sports that allow athletes to directly exercise their power, to see the immediate, direct consequences of that power, and to satisfy their need for power. Since women are frequently excluded from participation in team sports, particularly by the media, they are also denied the opportunity to directly wield power and influence in the sporting world.

Power is an issue that often surfaces in media studies about females. For example, Annette Kuhn (1982) dedicated the better part of her book, *Women's Pictures: Feminism and Cinema*, to showing how film frequently functions to repress the feminine (female sexuality and female discourse) in patriarchal societies such as our own. A number of studies focusing specifically on television portrayals of females reach similar conclusions. Douglas Kellner (1982) argued that certain kinds of television symbols having a potent effect on consciousness and behavior serve to encourage sexism, which is basically an issue of power. Kellner cited, among others, the example of the television mini-series "Loose Change." In it, women trying to be free in the 1960s got their just rewards in the 1970s. Happiness was the reward of those who conformed to the existing social order (an order in which women are submissive and are fulfilled by love and marriage). Pain and punishment were the lot of those who defied it.

Fiske and Hartley (1978) in their book, *Reading Television*, observed that in the world of television, "white females rarely, if ever, appeared in occupations that allowed them to exert power over others" (p. 26). Michael Real (1982), commenting specifically on television portrayals of the Super Bowl, pointed to the total male domination of this sporting event and then argued, "if one were to create from scratch a sport to reflect the sexual ... priorities of the American *power structure*, it is doubtful that one could improve on football" (p. 227; emphasis added). Thus in Real's argument, this male domination of a television sport is clearly linked to the prerogatives of power in American society; by extrapolation, the absence of females during televised coverage of football, and the Super Bowl in particular, suggests that these are prerogatives from which women are excluded. Thus, this media studies literature appears to confirm what the sport literature suggests – that television depictions of females may function to symbolically deny power to women, either on a conscious or subconscious level.

In light of this suggestion found in both bodies of literature – sport studies and media studies – we shall frame our research question in the following way: Does the relative exclusion of women from team sports and from certain individual sports constitute a symbolic denial of power? It appears that society and one of its most influential institutions, the mass media, discourage female participation in team sports by labeling it unfeminine and by ignoring women's team sporting events. The same phenomenon occurs when women participate in particular individual sports, those considered to be more appropriate for males than females because of the "unfeminine" demands made on strength and endurance or because of the risk involved. Perhaps, then, sport provides us with a model for the exercise of power in our society; sport tells us, through its lopsided distribution of women into "female-appropriate" individual sports, men into team sports and certain "mainly" individual sports, how this power is withheld from women and how it is accorded to men.

We shall attempt to answer this question by concentrating on a particularly influential social medium: television. We will examine televised depictions of women's sports and will focus on team sports and individual sports that have traditionally been considered men's sports. The commentary and visuals on these tapes of women's sports will be compared with televised depictions of men's sports – both team and individual events. The men's and women's sports are as evenly matched as possible, both in nature and in magnitude. Our sample will be deliberately restricted; it is not intended to be an exhaustive study but rather an exploratory investigation. [...]

Texts

The texts selected for this investigation are the televised transcripts of the 1986 NCAA women's (Lexington, KY) and men's (Dallas, TX) basketball championship games (team competitions), of the 1985 (Oceanside, CA) Stubbies Pro International Surfing Championship (both women's and men's competitions; this is an individual sport regarded as masculine). [...]

In our sample we had hoped to include more women's team competitions but, significantly, television networks *simply do not broadcast them*, apart from the rare basketball championship. [...]

Basketball

Basketball, on the one hand, is one of the premier women's intercollegiate sports. It draws larger crowds and generates more revenue than most other women's sports. Yet on the other hand, basketball is viewed by many as one of the least feminine of women's sports in that it is an aggressive, physical-contact sport that pits women against women in face-to-face opposition. Unlike men's intercollegiate basketball, women's intercollegiate basketball receives little media attention. Although the major television networks broadcast many of the men's National Collegiate Athletic Association (NCAA) games each season, women's games are rarely aired. One fairly recent exception to this practice was the broadcasting of the women's NCAA Division I basketball championship game. The live national broadcasts of the 1986 men's and women's NCAA Division I basketball championship games will serve as the basis for our first analysis.

The television broadcast of the women's game was ambivalent in the sense that although the game was booked and aired as an intercollegiate basketball championship game and indeed had every outward appearance of being just that, what one would have expected to be the essence of the broadcast – an analysis of the game and play of the teams – was largely absent. We argue that this ambivalence represents a symbolic denial of power and, more specifically, a symbolic denial of sport. This symbolic denial of sport takes on two general forms: a denial of team and a denial of game.

Denial of team

Basketball is a team sport. Though each team consists of a group of individuals, one team is viewed as competing against another, and the team is seen as the central unit of focus rather than the individual. To overlook or ignore this central focus constitutes a denial of team.

Focus on the individual rather than on the team in the women's game was well established from the beginning of the telecast. The viewing audience was introduced to the women's championship game between the University of Southern California "Lady Trojans" and the University of Texas "Lady Longhorns" by commentary about Cheryl Miller, one of the top female basketball players in the country (CBS, 1986a). The audience was not introduced to USC seeking their third national title in 4 years, but to Cheryl Miller "seeking her third NCAA title in 4 years." Nor were viewers introduced to USC's opponents, the Texas Lady Longhorns; rather, they were introduced to Cheryl Miller's opponents: "*her* opponents, the Texas Lady Longhorns." In contrast, during the opening commentary of the men's game the audience was introduced to the Duke Blue Devils and to the Louisville Cardinals without an emphasis on any particular player (CBS, 1986b).

The play-by-play commentary that followed in the women's game further established the lack of focus on the team and the central focus on individuals. Individuals, not teams, were named as bringing the ball down the court, setting up the plays, losing the ball out-of-bounds, scoring points, rebounding, and fouling. The following examples were typical: "Beverly Williams starts Texas out and ties it up at 2"; "Here's Fran Harris moving inside. The 6-foot senior has given Texas a 4-point lead"; "And here comes Kamie Ethridge"; "Here is Fran Harris"; "Cynthia Cooper brings it down"; "Cooper cuts it to 4"; and "The foul sends Cooper to the line." Very seldom was reference made to the play of either team by school name or by mascot. Emphasis on individual female players' personal backgrounds – their injuries, their families, and their personality characteristics – underscored the lack of commentary about the team in the women's game.

Conversely, the play-by-play commentary in the men's game emphasized the team rather than the individual, as the following comments demonstrated: "controlled by Louisville"; "Duke goes into a man-to-man"; Louisville 2-2-1 full-court pressure"; "They get it to. . ."; "They have shown great interior motion"; "Here come the Blue Devils"; "Cardinals turn it over"; "outscoring the Louisville backcourt"; "rebound by Duke"; "over to Louisville, last touched by Duke"; and "hard to get lob pass over Louisville".

This failure of the women's game commentary to focus on the team constitutes a denial of team, unlike the men's game commentary whose focus might well be described as a confirmation of team.

Denial of game

[. . .] During the basketball championship broadcast, the physical skills of the female basketball players were virtually ignored; what the commentary focused on instead was their movement, and this movement was depicted in primarily aesthetic terms. It was variously described as "so fun to watch," "beautiful," "very pretty," "nice," and "fine." In contrast to this aesthetically focused depiction, the physical prowess of the male players was often referred to as "athletic skill." Such skill was labeled "great," "powerful," and "pure." And the physical skill of the male players was also in part attributed to their knowledge of the game.

Commentary about the game play of individual male players often suggested knowledge and mental powers, for example, "brilliant shot," "smart foul," and "smart play." Not one remark could be found in the commentary of the women's game attributing knowledge or mental powers to female players or their play

In the women's championship, the degree of technical analysis and commentary on strategy within the game was all but absent. Instead of providing technical commentary, the announcer focused on personal sketches of the female players. [. . .] In contrast, the commentary in the men's game was a technical play-by-play analysis including such technical jargon and references to strategies as: "2–2–1 full-court press," "1–4 offense," "weak post," "no weakside help," "backdoor," "baseline," "great weakside defense," "screened out," "double screen," and "blocked out." Seldom did the commentators take time during the game to share personal information about various male players. [. . .]

Thus, while the commentary within the men's championship game recognized and therefore affirmed the game elements of physical skill, knowledge, and strategy, the commentary associated with the women's game overlooked and thus symbolically denied these elements. In this sense, the televised commentary of the women's game constituted a denial of game, while the televised commentary of the men's game constituted a confirmation of game.

Berger (1972) argues that "every image embodies a way of seeing" (p. 10), and points out the ways in which men and women have been differentially depicted in paintings and photographs throughout history. For this reason, we might have expected quite contrasting *visual* presentations of men's and women's basketball. However, this was not the case; there was little difference between the televised visual depiction of the men's game and that of the women's game. Perhaps this is because there are fewer opportunities in the live televising of a fast-moving subject, such as a sporting contest, to "construct" images than there are in the production of a painting, photograph, or prerecorded, edited television program.

What we found, then, is manifest evidence of ambivalence in the *narratives* of women's basketball on television. This ambivalence revealed itself quite decisively in contradictory network messages: that the women's competition was an important intercollegiate basketball championship, but that the women's competition was neither a real team sport nor a real game.

Surfing

Surfing is an individual sport that has traditionally been considered a man's sport. [...] Although many girls and women do surf, the stereotype of a surfer is a bronzed, muscular man (or boy). Perhaps this stereotype exists because surfing involves some risk, particularly when the waves are high and punishing and the undertow is dangerous.

We investigated the televised transcripts of the 1985 Stubbies Professional International Competition which included both a men's and a women's division (ESPN, 1985/1986). Because this competition was not aired live (was in fact rebroadcast some months later), what was shown was a kind of montage – alternating highlights of both men's and women's divisions interspersed with interviews and photo essays. The film editors clearly took advantage of their opportunities to cut and splice and so produced some very interesting and telling effects.

The broadcast began with a very short interview, as the male announcer asked the female commentator, "Who's gonna win?" The next minute was devoted to a photo essay: a collage of shots, each lasting no longer than 1–2 seconds, some stills, some in motion, all set to music. The subject of all 21 of these shots was local color; they were all beach or surf scenes. But the majority of these shots (11) did not show men and women surfing; instead they focused on women's bodies or part of their bodies. By focusing on these anatomical parts, the camera depicted women in primarily sexualized ways. Women were fragmented, reduced to faces, bikinied torsos, breasts, bottoms, thighs. In all but three of these shots women were clearly spectators and were in passive positions, reclining, sitting, observing, or making minute adjustments to their hair, visors, sunglasses, bikinis. Of all 21 shots, only one showed a recognizably female surfer actually in the water, riding a wave. There were two other shots of women who were surfers. In one, two women were carrying their boards down the beach and the camera focused on their undulating backsides. In the other, two women with their boards were standing motionless on the beach, watching the sea. The remaining shots were of crowd scenes, a T-shirt that announced the name of the competition, and of male surfers. There was only one shot that might possibly be construed as a "beefcake" shot, and in that case the camera was focusing on the announcer with his shirt off. The rest of the shots that featured men (six) showed them in action, riding the waves, except for one close-up of a man waiting in the water to catch a wave.

The next part of the broadcast featured a male commentator and showed a recap of the men's performances earlier in the week, leading up to the semifinals, an interview with the beach marshall who explained the judging, and interviews with several leading competitors in the men's division. Then the camera showed crowd scenes and a few close-ups of particularly attractive women in bikinis, focused on the men's semifinals, and cut to footage of the leading men's performances as the announcer described their various feats and strengths. Next the focus switched to the women's competition. A female commentator narrated this section and began interviewing a woman (presumably an expert analyst) on the subject of the top four female competitors. Footage was shown from the women's semifinals, and two leading surfers were interviewed. More footage from the semifinals was shown, and then a prerecorded interview interrupted the sequence of surfing scenes. This interview featured the first female surfer, the grown-up Gidget, who talked about how she was the only girl who surfed when the sport first became popular. The rest of the broadcast continued along these lines: alternating footage of the men's and women's competition, brief interviews with the competitors, and camera shots of the beach scene. It was during the segments of the men's competition that the camera displayed bikinied women in various poses on the beach. Approximately equal time and emphasis were given to the men's and women's competitions.

The commentary accompanying the footage of the male surfers' performances and that which accompanied the female surfers' performances seemed quite comparable. The announcers described the maneuvers of both men and women in a positive yet critical light. The surfers' strengths were emphasized, as were particular virtuoso moves. For example, Debbie Beachum analyzed leading competitor Tricia Gill's performance in this way:

> There goes Tricia taking the top off that wave, getting some maneuvers, getting high, getting some speed down the face of this wave. Good wave for Tricia. Coming back into the white water of the wave so she can get the momentum all the way to the beach. She's so light on her feet she's able to get all that way into the jetty. Coming back, cutting back, nice backside turn, good wave for Tricia Gill, real good, strong wave for Tricia.

The male announcer described top competitor Tommy Curren's performance in a similar fashion:

> Here's Tommy Curren up and riding, really light and quick on his feet. He covers a lot of ground, makes it to the next section, full roundhouse cutback! Watch how he throws his hands and his shoulders in the direction he's turning. Re-entry, great spray.

If one were to concentrate only on the audio portion of this surfing competition, one might get the impression that male and female athletes received similar treatment by the television network. The commentary that accompanied the surfing footage suggested that male and female competitors were equally skilled and competent in their sport. However, the video portion seriously undercut the impression of female competence. From almost the beginning, the photo essay trivialized women, both spectators and surfers. Women were objectified and demeaned as the camera focused on their breasts, bottoms, and faces. Women were presented in postures of passivity: lying on the sand, observing the ocean, posing on the rocks. Even those women who were clearly atheletes – those filmed with their surfboards – were shown in ways that largely denied the seriousness of their sporting endeavors; the camera focused on their bottoms as they carried their boards down the beach. Throughout the broadcast, especially during the men's competition, the camera kept returning to attractive bikinied women who populated the beach. The message was unmistakable: women are of a class, decorative objects, not serious competitors. Like the women's basketball commentary, these visual representations constituted a kind of denial of game or sport. They emphasized the sexual desirability of women while ignoring the women's surfing prowess, the physical skill and strategy which give to surfing its sporting qualities.

Against this treatment of women we juxtapose the depictions of men. In the photo essay, men were portrayed mostly in active, athletic postures – skillfully riding the crest of a wave, vigorously paddling out to catch a wave – where their skill, strategy, knowledge, and competitiveness (the elements of game or sport) were foregrounded. There were no shots of men to imply passivity, none that blatantly objectified their bodies.

What we found, then, was a clear-cut instance of ambivalence in the treatment of female surfers. Television's message was indeed contradictory. The audio said that women are capable, strong, talented athletes who were participating in an exciting sport; the video said that women are passive, decorative objects who beautify a nonsport. [. . .]

Conclusion

We stated at the outset of our investigation that evidence of ambivalence would constitute an affirmative answer to our research question: that sport as it is depicted by one of society's most influential mass media, television, symbolically denies power to women. The televised texts of women's basketball and surfing provided a wealth and profundity of ambivalence. Each television broadcast included fundamentally contradictory depictions of female athletes. That is, we found ambivalence in positive portrayals stressing women's strength, skill, or expertise along with negative suggestions that trivialized the women's efforts or implied that they were unsuited to sport (i.e., that they were in some respect weak, inferior, or incapable, that the sports in which they participated were not *true* sports). In addition, we discovered several clearly defined moments of resistance – which added to the overall ambivalence – wherein women symbolically affirmed their strength and power.

In the commentary of one of the few women's team sports nationally televised, the NCAA women's basketball championship, we found denial of team and denial of game, thanks to the lack of technical analysis and discussion of team strategy. Both suggested that the sport in which the female basketball players were participating was not a true sport but rather a pale imitation of real (men's) basketball. This suggestion contrasted with the outward appearance of the sport broadcast – in which the game was booked and aired as an intercollegiate basketball championship. And so this may be considered a highly ambivalent portrayal of sportswomen.

In surfing we found that although the narratives describing male and female surfers were quite comparable and emphasized the skill of the athletes – male and female – the visuals fragmented and objectified women by presenting them in a highly sexualized way, focusing on certain body parts and depicting women in mostly passive poses. Thus, while the commentary suggested that female surfers were strong and capable, this positive portrayal was undermined by the visual implication that women were decorative sex objects, unsuited to any endeavor as active and demanding as sport. This juxtaposition of positive audio with negative video created a deeply ambivalent depiction of female athletes. [...]

In brief, this evidence of ambivalence suggests that one of society's most influential mass media, television, symbolically denies power to women by its exclusionary and denigrating tactics. It excludes women by its brute neglect of women's sport, the failure to televise women's team sports for example. When women are allowed inside TV's hallowed arena, it denigrates them by conjoining images of female strength with images of female weakness, as much of the textual analysis has demonstrated.

Our next step is to argue that this denial of power to women in the sporting world is harmful and wrong-headed. We can do so on a number of grounds: health, personal, developmental, moral. We have already pointed out some of the benefits of team sports for women, benefits such as camaraderie with other women, cohesion, and teamwork, which women have been denied for too long. We could add to this a discussion of the health and fitness benefits of participation in some of the more vigorous and challenging "men's sports." In more abstract terms, we certainly could argue for a more equitable distribution of power on the ground that imbalances of power tend to create a number of injustices, which include among other things a sporting underclass that is denied the pleasures of the privileged class.

But there is another and equally compelling argument for redressing these inequities in the sporting world. It is a truisim among sport scholars that sport and society constitute a dialectic. From the most elementary sport sociology textbooks to the most sophisticated articles, our attention is called to this fact: that society shapes sport, and reciprocally, sport shapes society. As Felshin (1974) so aptly puts it, "Sport expresses the context of culture in its existence and modifies the culture by its existence" (p. 180). This latter part of the dialectic deserves our attention now. Sport is not merely a reservoir of social attitudes, norms, and values; it also has the potential for actively modifying larger social practices. Because of this potential, we can never be content with the way things are, nor can we lay the blame on society or the mass media for the exclusionary and discriminatory policies of sport. That would be missing the point. When we discover the kinds of great inequities that our study has revealed, we as sport and leisure educators have an ethical obligation to try to change the structures of sport – to strongly encourage female participation in team sports, to petition the media to present sporting women as athletes and not as objects of sexual gratification. And we should do so not merely to improve the lot of women in sport, although that in itself is an eminently worthy goal. We should do so in the knowledge that our acts in the sporting world will reverberate throughout society. A more equitable balance of power in sport can lead to a more equitable balance of power in other social spheres.

Acknowledgement

The first author gratefully acknowledges the Center for Twentieth Century Studies at the University of Wisconsin-Milwaukee for its support of this research.

References

Berger, J. (1972). Ways of seeing. London: British Broadcasting Corporation.

Birrell, S. (1984). Separatism as an issue in women's sport. *Arena Review*, **8**(2), 21–9.

Boutilier, M. A., & SanGiovanni, L. (1983). *The sporting woman*. Champaign, IL: Human Kinetics.

CBS Television Network (1986a, March 30). NCAA Women's Division I Basketball Championship. USC-Texas. Lexington, KY.

CBS Television Network (1986b, March 31). NCAA Men's Division I Basketball Championship. Duke-Louisville. Dallas, TX.

ESPN Television Network (1985). Rebroadcast of the 1985 Stubbies Pro International Surfing Tournament in Oceanside, CA, on June 30, 1986.

Felshin, J. (1974). The social view. In E. W. Gerber, J. Felshin, P. Berlin, & W. Wyrick (Eds.), *The American woman in sport* (pp. 179–279). Reading, MA: Addison-Wesley.

Fiske, J., & Hartley, J. (1978). *Reading television*. New York: Methuen.

Kellner, D. (1982). Television, ideology, and emancipatory popular culture. In H. Newcomb (Ed.), *Television: The critical view* (3rd ed, pp. 386–421). New York: Oxford University Press.

Kuhn, A. (1982). *Women's pictures: Feminism and cinema*. London: Routledge & Kegan Paul.

Metheny, E. (1965). *Connotations of movement in sport and dance*. Dubuque, IA: W.C. Brown.

Real, M. R. (1982). The Super Bowl: Mythic spectacle. In H. Newcomb (Ed.), *Television: The critical view* (3rd ed, pp. 206–39). New York: Oxford University.

Rintala, J., & Birrell, S. (1984). Fair treatment for the active female: A content analysis of *Young Athlete* magazine. *Sociology of Sport Journal*, **1**, 231–50.

Sabo, D. (1985). Sport, patriarchy, and male identity: New questions about men and sport. *Arena Review*, **9**(2), 1–30.

7 Catching up with men? Finnish newspaper coverage of women's entry into traditionally male sports*

Riitta Pirinen

This chapter analyses how the struggle over gender relations in sport is articulated in the Finnish media. I argue that media texts may be seen both as an embodiment of specific discourses that constitute gender relations in sport, and as a social practice that reproduces these discourses. I begin by briefly discussing these discourses and then show how they are articulated in coverage of five sports in which women are relative novices: boxing, ski jumping, hammer throwing, triple jump and pole vault.

Dominant discourses on gender relations in sport

In most western countries, men's participation in sport has traditionally been regarded as a 'natural' phenomenon, whereas women's involvement in this traditionally androcentric arena has often been viewed as anomalous. Women athletes have often encountered forceful opposition and have constantly had to struggle for recognition and entitlements (Hargreaves, 1994; Laine, 1989a; 1996; Lenskyj, 1986; Olofsson, 1989; Peyton and Pfister, 1989). At the beginning of this century, women's involvement in competitive sport was restricted to a handful of 'appropriate' sports, such as tennis, golf and swimming. However, over the past few decades the number of sports open to women has expanded considerably, and women now compete in most official national championships and are entering traditionally all-male sports in increasing numbers. However, the struggle to secure equality is far from over, as both popular and academic debates on women's participation in sport show.

These debates on gender relations can be fruitfully examined as discourses. A discourse refers both to a social construction of 'reality' and a form of knowledge (Fairclough, 1992; Foucault, 1986). Thus, gender relations in sport is a discursive formation that is continually constituted by all statements that determine, name, describe, explain and evaluate men's and women's positions in institutionalized, competitive, physical activities. Discourses on these gender relations are (re)produced both in and through medicine, sports sciences, physical education,

* Taken from, *International Review for the Sociology of Sport* 32(3) (1997): 239–49.

sporting organizations, the feminist movement and the mass media. Further, these discourses are not typical of the sports institution alone – they have counterparts in many other public arenas (e.g., science, politics, business).

I suggest that there are three dominant discourses on gender relations in sport: trivialization/marginalization; equality; and separatism. In trivialization/ marginalization discourses, gender relations are constituted as a hierarchy of male domination/female subordination. In most western countries justifications of inequality between men and women in sport have generally involved two complementary strategies: a positive representation of men's achievements and a negative portrayal of women's. On the one hand, it has commonly been argued that competitive sports are primarily suited to men because they have 'inherent' athletic abilities (e.g., competitiveness, strength, stamina, courage, self-confidence, dominance and aggression). On the other hand, for decades women have been marked as the 'weaker sex'. For instance, restricting the number of competitive sports and events for women at the Olympics has usually been justified in terms of the supposedly 'intrinsic' limitations of their biological make-up (Hakulinen, 1996; Hargreaves, 1994; Laine, 1989a, 1996; Lenskyj, 1986; Olofsson, 1989; Peyton and Pfister, 1989).

Moreover, continuing inequalities between men and women in sport have also been legitimized on the grounds that the latter will suffer mental and physical harm during competition, especially in those sports labelled as 'typically' masculine. Women have also been trivialized by comparing female athletes' performances and achievements to those of men. Consequently, sports-women's accomplishments have tended to be framed as 'other than' or 'less than' those of men (Hakulinen, 1996; Hargreaves, 1994; Laine, 1989a, 1996; Lenskyj, 1986; Olofsson, 1989; Peyton and Pfister, 1989).

Equality discourses have articulated equality of opportunity principles for girls and women. This has involved unmasking discriminatory practices and removing barriers that prevent girls' and women's full participation in sport. For example, liberal feminists have argued that it is cultural conceptions of femininity, rather than any 'inherent' limitations of women's bodies, that present the major obstacles to their full participation in physical activity. Women do, in fact, possess athletic abilities, but a lack of support and training facilities has provided them with insufficient opportunities to develop their skills. Women's full involvement in competitive sports has also been justified by the argument that women can gain many enriching experiences, like an increase in self-confidence (Hakulinen, 1996; Hargreaves, 1994; Laine, 1989a, 1996; Lenskyj, 1986; Olofsson, 1989; Peyton and Pfister, 1989). Equality discourses aim to ensure that girls and women have the same opportunities as boys and men, but do not question the hegemonic values of competitive sports.

In separatist discourses, competitive sport has been criticized for its harmful features such as aggression, violence, hierarchy, male power, sexism, heterosexism, homophobia, racism and commodification. Radical sport feminists in England and the United States, for instance, have created women-only competitive or

non-competitive practices and activities outside the male-dominated sports system (Birrell and Richter, 1987; Hargreaves, 1994). Finnish women's gymnastics
is just one example of many alternative models for women's physical activity that
have provided opportunities for female bonding, empowerment and a sense of
control of one's own body (Laine, 1989b; Laitinen, 1989).

The sports media and the construction of gender relations

Sports media texts play a significant role in producing, reproducing and transforming these discourses on gender relations. For instance, studies conducted in
a variety of countries have shown that both the electronic and print media generally marginalize and trivialize sportswomen's achievements (Alexander, 1994a,
1994b; Blinde *et al.*, 1991; Crossman *et al.*, 1994; Daddario, 1994; Duncan,
1990; Duncan and Hasbrook, 1988; Hargreaves, 1994; Kane and Parks, 1992;
Lee, 1992; Lumpkin and Williams, 1991; McKay and Huber, 1992; Messner
et al., 1993; Pirinen, 1995). For example, women's sports, and women's team
sports in particular, have been underrepresented in the mass media. Female athletes
have received most coverage in individual sports and in those that are traditionally 'acceptable' for women (e.g., tennis, swimming, synchronized swimming,
figure skating, gymnastics). Women have also been represented according to
cultural stereotypes that associate femininity with weakness, dependency, emotion and submissiveness. They also have been framed in terms of their status in
the private sphere (e.g., as daughters, girlfriends, wives or mothers). Furthermore, the media have also tended to objectify women in ways that resemble
soft-core pornography. Women's sport and women's achievements and records
have often been compared to men's sport and achievements. This is hardly relevant since men and women rarely compete against each other. This indirect and
direct comparison has been applied in ways that ignore women's performances
and achievements.

This chapter attempts to increase our understanding of how discourses on gender
relations in sport are (re)produced in media texts associated with newspaper coverage of five sports in which women are relative newcomers: boxing, ski jumping,
hammer throwing, triple jumping and pole vaulting. Boxing, ski jumping, hammer
throwing, triple jumping and pole vaulting have for a long time been preserved as
a bastion of men and hegemonic masculinity (the pole vault and hammer throw
will not be officially included in the women's programme of the world track and
field championships until 1999). Finnish women have been able to take part in
these sports for a long time, but it was not until the 1990s that the first official
national championships were held. The only exception is ski jumping, in which
official championships are still not held.

Articles on women's entry into these sports provide interesting data for an analysis of discourses about gender relations, because the discursive struggles are much
more direct and visible than in routine coverage of sport. The textual analysis
addressed the specific questions of how these women were represented, and what
sorts of textual strategies were applied in constructing gender relations.

Data

The data were systematically collected from the sports pages of Finland's largest circulating daily, *Helsingin Sanomat (HS)* in 1994 and 1995 (all excerpts cited have been translated into English). The sample consisted of 35 articles on hammer throwing, triple jumping and pole vaulting; five on ski jumping; and four on boxing. *HS very rarely* reported on women's participation in these sports, with coverage typically restricted to records in the hammer throw, triple jump and pole vault. Most articles consisted of less than 20 lines of text and a headline that usually described the main incident (e.g. 'George sets new world record in pole vault' [*HS*, 18 December 1995: D6]; 'Anni Paananen triple jumps a new Nordic record' [*HS*, 4 February 1995: C9]). These short articles briefly mentioned the name of the athlete, the place where the event was held, the sport in question and that a record had been set. Four other short pieces also indicated that women would be competing in new sports at the international level (e.g.'Women's pole vault and hammer throw to become official European Championships events' [*HS*, 16 October 1994: C9]).

Other articles varied in length from about one-quarter to almost half a page and usually carried photos of women athletes. The articles described the events in considerable detail and referred to the athletes' sporting careers, performances and opinions about sport. Comments were also made with regard to whether or not the sports concerned were considered appropriate for women. Some of these articles also carried results from other women's and men's events, even though the headline referred to records set by women athletes. Women's records were discussed only in one or two paragraphs. The reporter's name was only rarely given.

Results

Elements of both the trivialization/marginalization and equality discourses were identified in the articles, whereas separatist discourses were not evident.

The trivialization/marginalization discourse

The trivialization/marginalization discourse framed women's involvement in new sports as unimportant and portrayed sportswomen's abilities as limited. The sections below provide some examples of the textual strategies that tended to mark women's performances as both different from and inferior to men's.

Women as second-rate athletes

Women boxers, ski jumpers, hammer throwers, triple jumpers and pole vaulters were represented as second-rate through implicit contrasts with male standards. These comparisons made sportswomen's performances appear as qualitatively inferior to those of sportsmen. The national and international records and championships achieved by women athletes in new sports were often deprecated and received peripheral coverage. In fact, outstanding performances by sportswomen received little coverage or were even used to argue that their entry into new sports was insignificant. This was clearly seen in an article on how results in women's pole vault had developed during the 1990s:

> Emma George, the Australian who recently set a new world record in women's pole vault serves as an excellent example that this sport is still very much in its infancy. In the space of one year the former long jumper improved from an amateurish 305 to the current world record at 428. George's rapid development is clear evidence that the results of women pole vaulters are still modest indeed.
>
> (*HS*, 30 December 1995: C7)

Although George's rapid development could have been represented as an indication of her outstanding athletic talent, the text represented it as evidence of the sport's immaturity. Describing the efforts of women pole vaulters as 'modest' implies a comparison with the world record in men's pole vault (over 6 metres).

Another strategy for devaluing women's achievements was via insinuations that the female athletes did not have to work, train or compete as hard for their success as their male counterparts, or that it was easy for women to set new records and to win championships in new events. For example, an article on the Finnish track and field championships demeaned the women's triple jump by implying that it was possible to get gold and silver medals without hard work and discipline:

> The triple jump is and will remain a sideline . . . . During the past two years Gustafsson [the winner] has trained specifically for the triple jump one single time. That the women's triple jump is still a sport in its infancy is underlined by the fact that the silver medal also went to a jumper for whom this sport is a sideline.
>
> (*HS*, 24 July 1995: B2)

The Finnish women's boxing championships were also represented as inconsequential. In 1995 only two women participated in the national championships, which was won by a woman who had never before taken part in boxing competitions. One article framed the victory as having been attained too easily. For example, the headline proclaimed that, 'One "proper" match ensured the title' (*HS*, 6 March 1995: D5). In Finnish, quotation marks are used both to challenge and invert the meanings of words, so the quotation marks around the word 'proper' were actually intended to signify an 'improper' competition, thus belittling the women's efforts. Women's boxing competitions were also disparaged because of the rule differences between men's and women's competitions. Since women are prevented from striking opponents with full blows, another article described the 1994 championship as pointless: 'Women's boxing, at first experience, was a disappointment, just as aimless as a football match without goal-areas'

(*HS*, 23 December 1994: C8). According to the reporter, the match appeared as 'peaceful dancing around', 'dancing in emptiness' or 'disco-dancing' rather than boxing.

Allegations of women's limited athletic abilities were also manifest in articles on ski jumping. For instance, in 1994 and 1995, Matti Pulli, national director of the ski jumping team, was quoted as saying that the sport was too demanding for women. The article in 1995 included his comments on the unofficial women's ski jumping competition that was arranged in connection with the 1995 World Skiing Championships in Thunder Bay, Canada. Attention was focused in a highly dramatic way on women who failed in their jumps:

> Pulli was alarmed to see a Swedish girl fall on landing and lose consciousness. The trainer of the Swedish team ... was equally shocked, rushing over to his protégé. The girl escaped with only a shaking.
>
> (*HS*, 20 March 1995: D3)

In contrast to this emotional and sensational representation of the Swedish woman jumper's fall, accounts of men's mishaps tend to be depicted as annoying setbacks – a misfortune that can happen to even experienced jumpers. This article not only constructed women as lacking the requisite athletic abilities by highlighting their 'poor' performances, but also derided their superior performances. For instance, in discussing the national record jump of Tiina Lehtola, Pulli was quoted as saying that:

> I remember when Tiina Lehtola did 110 metres on the big hill at Ruka. As far as I understand it was such an unnerving experience for her that she gave up the sport there and then.
>
> (*HS*, 20 March 1995: D3)

This account links three different elements into one causal chain: the 110-metre jump, the male expert's assumptions about Lehtola's frame of mind, and her decision to give up the sport. An athlete who decides to give up a sport will consider many different factors. The simplistic explanation given here is based on the stereotyped assumptions of a male 'expert' that women lack the sufficient mental and physical abilities for the strenuous realm of ski jumping. The same article contained sarcastic commendations on good jumps of the women in Thunder Bay (e.g., 'With the speeds they were coming down, even an iron rod would have gone a long way' [*HS*, 20 March 1995: D3]).

Other articles impugned women's performances by alleging that their techniques were defective. For example, an article on the Finnish track and field championships ridiculed both women pole vaulters:

> The jumps had a comic appearance about them, with the girls' bodies and the poles almost equally stiff in the jump.

and hammer throwers:

> Punttila made a magnificent throw upon three spins, but the technique of the other throwers hardly warranted any praise. The woman who appeared to be the most lightweight contestant very nearly flew off along with the hammer ...
>
> (*HS*, 10 July 1994: C3)

One recurring strategy used by sports journalists to trivialize and marginalize sportswomen is to concentrate on their looks (Duncan, 1990; Duncan and Hasbrook, 1988; Hargreaves, 1994; Klein, 1988; Pirinen, 1995). This sort of objectification was conspicuous in some articles. Consider, for instance, the following description of the international triple jump event for women in Barcelona: 'Picture pretty Tshen breaks the magic distance of 15 metres in the triple jump ...' (*HS*, 12 March 1995: C6). An article about the national hammer throw event for 13–14-year-old girls stated that it:

> ... was good fun watching the event. The 25 young girls hardly resembled average heavyweight male throwers. The competitors were small and slender. No one let out bloodcurdling roars.
>
> (*HS*, 18 June 1995: C7)

This description emphasized the differences between men and women. The 'real' hammer thrower (the heavyweight male athlete) was characterized by masculine appearance and behaviour; by comparison the small and slender young girls appeared to lack physical strength. Both articles represented female athletes as targets of the objectifying gaze and thus belittled their athletic skills.

The equality discourse

The discourse of equality was embodied both in descriptions of the barriers and problems facing women in new sports, and in portrayals of sportswomen's abilities and outstanding achievements.

Problems facing women in new sports

Some texts stressed that women's participation in new sports had been undermined by prejudice, lack of training facilities and limited opportunities to compete. For instance, there are very few competitions for women ski jumpers, so if they want to gain more experience they have to compete in men's events. This has obviously had adverse effects on the motivation of women athletes, as indicated by the young women interviewed in one article:

> 'When you're competing with men you know beforehand that you've got no chance. If we had our own events for girls, it would encourage us to try harder', says Sjögren from Kouvola.
>
> (*HS*, 20 March 1995: D3)

Other articles illustrated how female athletes were treated unequally in competitions. One article described how the 1995 national track and field championships were arranged in a way that placed the women's triple jump, pole vault and hammer throw at the margins of the main programme. For instance, women's competition in these three events was scheduled early in the morning, and because the spectators did not begin to arrive until later in the afternoon, they attracted very few spectators. Mention was also made of the biased treatment of the country's top female hammer throwers:

> Women hammer throwers are still more or less unknown out on the track. At Lapua, the officials turned hammer throwers away from the press conference because they didn't believe women had won medals at the Championships. (*HS*, 24 July 1995: B2)

Female athletes in new sports have often been the targets of negative comments by male spectators. For example, one article described how male spectators laughed and criticized women pole vaulters and hammer throwers at the national championships in track and field (*HS*, 10 July 1994: C3). Some articles also mentioned the appeals that had been made to national and international sports organizations in order to improve women's position in new sports. For example, the international boxing association and national skiing association had received petitions:

> The international association still takes a rather indifferent attitude towards the growing role of women. Member countries are free to organize national events, but as yet there are no plans to stage major competitions.
> (*HS*, 6 March 1995: D5)

> In recent years the national skiing association has been receiving appeals to have women [ski jumpers] included in their training and competition program. However, there has been no positive response.
> (*HS*, 20 March 1995: D3)

However, the reasons for women's subordinate status received little attention in these texts. For example, the articles did not attempt to discuss the structural bases of sexual prejudice and discrimination in sporting organizations. A good starting point for this discussion might have been to highlight how the predominance of men and the underrepresentation of women at the top levels of sports organizations affect the opportunities of sportswomen.

Women as outstanding athletes

There were some examples of 'positive' representations of women in new sports. But the articles that represented women in the same way as men were relatively brief. A typical example of equal representation was an article which stated that:

> Russia's Inna Lasovskaja broke the women's indoor triple jump world record. She won the event in the national championships with the world record at 14.78. This was the second time that Lasovskaja, 24, broke the world record during the current indoor season. In mid-January she set a new record at 14.61.
>
> (*HS*, 29 January 1994: C8)

Assertions of women's restricted athletic abilities were also challenged at times. Although one article argued that ski jumping was too demanding for women, the other article on the same page opposed this view. For example, the conventional view that courage is an exclusively male characteristic was rejected by presenting examples of outstanding bravery among female athletes ('Women certainly don't lack the courage, that should be clear from such sports as downhill skiing and boxing' *HS*, 20 March 1995: D3). Confidence was also described as a quality that female ski jumpers could improve by training:

> If you start when you are young, that makes it easier to move on to the big hill.... When you move on step by step to bigger hills, your courage will increase as you go along, and you will hardly even notice it.
>
> (*HS*, 20 March 1995: D3)

The texts also contained comments which maintained that women actually possessed the physical and mental capacities to perform in their new sports. The ski jumping article not only made the point that the female body constituted no obstacle in the sport, but also suggested that it might even be better suited to ski jumping than the male body. Given their lighter bone structure, young women might be able to gather more speed than men on the approach: 'In ski jumping girls might even be better than boys. Some say that the reason why they are bypassed is precisely that they might be even alarmingly good' (*HS*, 20 March 1995: D3).

The assumption that women had limited athletic abilities was also challenged by representing females as multi-sport participants:

> In addition to athletics, she also does cross-country skiing, biathlon, and orienteering.
>
> (*HS*, 18 June 1995: C7)

> She had great stamina to build on, thanks to badminton and squash.
>
> (*HS*, 6 March 1995: D5)

> I've always been interested in boys' sports, such as motorcycle racing. I also play football and do karate, says Pyykkö.
>
> (*HS*, 20 March 1995: D3)

Finally, it was also argued that women's 'poor' performances did not lie in their limited athletic competencies, but rather in the fact that they were involved in new sports and had not yet had enough time to train and adopt the techniques. One article on a hammer throwing competition pointed out that, because women were still new to the sport, the steel ball often flew off in the wrong direction and hit the side netting (*HS*, 18 June 1995: C7). Another article on ski jumping likewise suggested that women's problems with their technique were due to insufficient training:

> ... their position in the air is too upright. But that is a matter of technique that can always be improved by practice.... Practice will help to give girls more thrust to their jump. And in any case it's the timing of the jump and the ability to fly that matter most.

> (*HS*, 20 March 1995: D3)

Conclusions

In this chapter I have attempted to describe some of the textual strategies applied in constructing gender relations in sport. It was found that the discourses were contradictory. In the trivialization/marginalization discourse, gender relations were constructed as hierarchical power relations. Women participating in new sports were portrayed as 'less than' and 'other than' their male counterparts. This was done by giving women's new sports scant coverage and by framing women's achievements as inferior to men's. Sportswomen's abilities were called into question by making sarcastic comments on successful performances and by sexually objectifying women athletes.

The equality discourse was usually articulated via women's outstanding performances which resembled corresponding representations of male athletes. Furthermore, the argument that women have limited athletic abilities was challenged and women's 'poor' performances were explained by arguments that they have had neither the time nor opportunity to practise the techniques required in the new sports. The texts also described the barriers and problems that women have faced in new sports, such as prejudiced attitudes, limited opportunities to compete and unequal treatment in competitions.

Although the trivialization/marginalization and the equality discourses have opposite functions, they also have certain features in common. That is, both discourses position male sport and male athletes as the norm against which female comparisons are made. In the trivialization/marginalization discourse, doubts were cast over women by comparing them with a male standard. In the equality discourse, the aim was to guarantee the same rights and opportunities for women athletes as men enjoy. In summary, both discourses support and reproduce the masculine values and practices of competitive sport.

This study dealt with women in new sports, so it would be interesting to analyse articles on the same sports, say, five years from now, in order to discern if there have been any changes in the articulation of the discursive struggle over gender relations. Some questions that might be worth asking then are: Have strategies of trivialization/marginalization changed? Do journalists still rely on quotes from male experts to construct discourses about women's alleged frailty? Or, Are female ski jumpers trivialized by comments on their looks or only by limited coverage?

Acknowledgement

I would like to thank two anonymous reviewers and the editor for their helpful comments on an earlier draft of this chapter.

References

Alexander, S. (1994a) 'Gender Bias in British Television Coverage of Major Athletic Championships', *Women's Studies International Forum* 17: 647–54.
Alexander, S. (1994b) 'Newspaper Coverage of Athletics as a Function of Gender', *Women's Studies International Forum* 17: 655–62.
Birrell, S. and Richter, D. (1987) 'Is a Diamond Forever?: Feminist Transformations of Sport', *Women's Studies International Forum* 10: 395–409.
Blinde, E., Greendorfer, S. and Shanker, R. (1991) 'Differential Media Coverage of Men's and Women's Intercollegiate Basketball: Reflection of Gender Ideology', *Journal of Sport and Social Issues* 15: 98–114.
Crossman, J., Hyslop, P. and Guthrie, B. (1994) 'A Content Analysis of the Sports Section of Canada's National Newspaper with Respect to Gender and Professional/Amateur Status', *International Review for the Sociology of Sport* 29: 123–34.
Daddario, G. (1994) 'Chilly Scenes of the 1992 Winter Games: The Mass Media and the Marginalisation of Female Athletes', *Sociology of Sport Journal* 11: 275–88.
Duncan, M.C. (1990) 'Sports Photographs and Sexual Difference: Images of Women and Men in the 1984 and 1988 Olympic Games', *Sociology of Sport Journal* 7: 22–43.
Duncan, M.C. and Hasbrook, C. (1988) 'Denial of Power in Televised Women's Sports', *Sociology of Sport Journal* 5. 1–21.
Fairclough, N. (1992) *Discourse and Social Change*, Cambridge: Polity Press.
Foucault, M. (1986) *The Archaeology of Knowledge*. London: Tavistock.
Hakulinen, T. (1996) 'Keskustelu kilpaurheilun sopivuudesta naisille kävi kiivaana 1920-luvun lopussa' (Is Competitive Athletics Suitable for Women? Discussion of the 1920s), in A. Nevala (ed.) *Olympialaiset ja naisliikunta satavuotiaat*. (The Olympic Movement and Women's Physical Culture, both 100 years of Age). Kitee: Suomen urheiluhistoriallinen seura.
Hargreaves, J. (1994) *Sporting Females: Critical Issues in the History and Sociology of Women's Sports*. London: Routledge.
Kane, M.J. and Parks, J. (1992) 'The Social Construction of Gender Difference and Hierarchy in Sport Journalism – Few New Twists on Very Old Themes', *Women in Sport and Physical Activity Journal* 1: 49–83.
Klein, M.L. (1988) 'Women in the Discourse of Sport Reports', *International Review for the Sociology of Sport* 23: 139–52.
Laine, L. (1989a) 'The "Nature" of Woman – the "Nature" of Man. The Effects of Gender Images on Organizing Sports in Finland in the 1920s and 1930s', in M. Raivio (ed.) *Proceedings of the Jyväskylä Congress on Movement and Sport in Women's Life* (Vol. 1: Reports of Physical Culture and Health). Jyväskylä, Finland: Likes.

Laine, L. (1989b) 'In Search of a Physical Culture for Women. Elli Björksten and Women's Gymnastics', *Scandinavian Journal of Sport Sciences* 11: 15–20.

Laine, L. (1996) 'Kuinka ylittää rajat? Naiset pohjoismaiden urheilujärjestöissä' (How to Cross Borders – Women in Sports Organisations in the Nordic Countries), in A. Nevala (ed.) *Olympialaiset ja naisliikunta satavuotiatt.* (The Olympic Movement and Women's Physical Culture, both 100 years of Age). Kitee: Suomen urheiluhistoriallinen seura.

Laitinen, A. (1989) 'Future Perspective of Women's Movement Culture', in J. Hovden and K. Pedersen (eds) *women in Sport – Sport for Women? Constructing Scenarios and Utopias from a Woman-centred Perspective.* Report from a Nordic Research Seminar, Finnmark.

Lee, J. (1992) 'Media Portrayals of Male and Female Olympic Athletes: Analyses of Newspaper Accounts of the 1984 and the 1988 Summer Games', *International Review for the Sociology of Sport* 27: 197–219.

Lenskyj, H. (1986) *Out of Bounds: Women, Sport and Sexuality.* Toronto: The Women's Press.

Lumpkin, A. and Williams, L. (1991) 'An Analysis of Sports Illustrated Feature Articles, 1954–1987', *Sociology of Sport Journal* 8: 16–32.

McKay, J. and Huber, D. (1992) 'Anchoring Media Images of Technology and Sport', *Women's Studies International Forum* 15: 205–18.

Messner, M., Duncan, M.C. and Jensen, K. (1993) 'Separating the Men from the Girls: The Gendered Language of Televised Sports', *Gender & Society* 7: 121–37.

Olofsson, E. (1989) *Har kvinnorna en sportlig chans? Den svenska idrottsrörelsen och kvinnorna under 1900-talet* (Have Women Chances in Sport? Swedish Sports Movement and Women in the 20th Century). Kungälv: Umeå Universitet.

Peyton, C. and Pfister, G. (eds) (1989) *Frauensport in Europa. Informationen – Materialien* (Women in Sport in Europe). Hamburg: Czwalina.

Pirinen, R. (1995) 'Naisurheilijat näyttävät naisilta. Tekstimuotokuvia naisurheilijoista' (Representations of Female Athletes in Women's Magazines), in A. Tuomisto and H. Uusikylä (eds) *Kuva, teksti ja kulttuurinen näkeminen* (Photographs, Texts and the Cultural Ways of Seeing). Helsinki: SKS.

Seminar questions

Chapter 6

1 How does the media representation of women in basketball and surfing contribute to a denial of power for women?
2 Duncan and Hasbrook's analysis of power in sport draws on Boutillier and San Giovanni's distinction between individual and team sports. How useful is this in understanding the nature of gender power relations in media representations of women's sport?

Chapter 7

1 What examples of trivialisation/marginalisation and equality discourses are identified in the articles analysed by Pirinen?
2 What evidence is there in the media that similar discourses are represented in other sports in different cultural contexts?

Part IV
'Race' and ethnicity

Introduction

Black feminist analyses of sport, as discussed in Part One, identify the ethnocentricity of much feminist work. In sport this is particularly evident, with little work focusing on black and Asian women's experiences of sport or theoretical accounts which centralize 'race', racism and ethnicity. Much of the work which does focus on 'race', ethnicity and sport concentrates on black sportsmen. The limited work that there is in relation to black sportswomen tends to stereotype, marginalize or pathologize their experiences. It is partly as a result of questions raised by black feminists that issues relating to difference and diversity are now at the forefront of contemporary sport feminism. It is only more recently that whiteness has begun to be critiqued and understood as a power relation constructed in and through sport.

Each of the three chapters in this part focus on different questions in relation to 'race', gender and culture. The first chapter by Mary Maynard engages with the theoretical debates about difference and diversity in feminism. The other two chapters draw on empirical research; the first exploring the experiences of mid-life Pakistani women in physical activity (Wray) and the second, black masculinities in a Caribbean Cricket Club in the United Kingdom (Carrington). All the chapters demonstrate the importance of recognizing the difference and the need to move beyond the ethnocentricity of white feminism and sport sociology.

Although not located within sport studies, the chapter by Mary Maynard provides a good introduction to the theoretical debates and issues around the intersections of 'race' and gender. She begins her chapter with a useful discussion of terminology, in particular 'race' and black. The chapter goes on to explore the different approaches to 'race' and gender, and provides a detailed discussion of the concept of difference. She critiques two alternative approaches to difference, one based on experience and the other on post modernist fragmentation. She argues that although these approaches to diversity are important, their use alone marginalizes other important issues such as racism and material relations of power.

The second chapter, by Sharon Wray, explores how ethnic and cultural identities are constructed and reproduced through physical activity. It draws on empirical data from a research project that involved participant observation, focus groups and in-depth interviews with women aged between 36 and 56 years of age. The women identified themselves as Muslim Pakistani women and they were attending exercise classes that consisted of floor exercises and running. The chapter is a fascinating exploration of the connections between ethnic and gender identities and identifies how femininity is constructed and experienced for these women through racialized power relations that regulate their ethnic identity. It highlights the interconnections between ethnicity, gender and physicality, an area that requires further research and consideration.

Ben Carrington's chapter offers an interesting alternative focus for an understanding of ethnicity, gender and sport/physical activity. He develops an account of the meanings associated with sport in relation to black masculinity and the use of sport as a form of cultural resistance to white racism. Drawing on ethnographic research of a Caribbean Cricket Club in the north of England, he identifies three themes: cricket and its role in the contestation of racial and gendered identities; the construction of black sports institutions as black spaces; and the use of a black cricket club as the symbolic marker of community identity. The chapter shows how sport can provide an arena for some black men to lay claim to a masculine identity as a means of restoring a unified sense of racial identity. However, this is a complex process and the marginalization and silencing of women is acknowledged as black resistance often becomes equated with black *male* emancipation.

After reading all these diverse chapters, students should:

- be able to recognize and understand the different approaches to difference and diversity in contemporary feminist theory, with particular reference to 'race' and ethnicity;
- be able to appreciate the connections between gender and ethnic identities and their implications for physical activity provision and the development of active lifestyles;
- understand the role of sport as an arena for cultural resistance and identity for black sportsmen.

Further readings

Benn, T. (1996) 'Muslim women and physical education in initial teacher training', *Sport, Education and Society* 1(1): 5–21.

Birrell, S. (1990) 'Women of color, critical autobiography and sport', in M. Messner and D. Sabo (eds) *Sport, Men and the Gender Order: Critical Feminist Perspectives*, Champaign: Human Kinetics.

Messner, M. A. (1993) 'White men misbehaving: feminism, afrocentricism and the promise of a critical standpoint', *Journal of Sport and Social Issues* 16: 136–144.

Scraton, S. (2001) 'Re-conceptualising 'race', gender and sport: the contribution of black feminism', in B. Carrington and I. McDonald (eds) *Racism and British Sport*, London: Routledge.

Zaman, H. (1997) 'Islam, well-being and physical activity: perceptions of Muslim women', in G. Clarke and B. Humberstone (eds) *Researching Women and Sport*, London: Macmillan.

8 'Race', gender and the concept of 'difference' in feminist thought*

Mary Maynard

This chapter is concerned with theorizing the interrelationships between 'race' and gender oppression and the extent to which this is furthered by using the concept of 'difference'. It hardly needs stating that second-wave Western feminism has come under sustained criticism for its universalistic, homogenized and 'white' assumptions about women, since so much has been written on the subject (Frye, 1983; Collins, 1990; hooks, 1982, 1984, 1989, 1991; Ramazanoglu, 1989; Spelman, 1988). Much of this critique has concentrated on diversity among women, rather than, as previously, the things that might be said to unite them. Not only do women diverge in terms of how 'race', ethnicity, class, age, sexuality and disability effect their experiences, other factors, such as historical context and geographical location, also need to be part of the framework of feminist analyses.

One of the central ways in which this concern with diversity has developed is through an emphasis on the concept of 'difference'. Although the concept has no one connotation, as will be discussed, its implications of plurality and multiplicity have been regarded by many as providing the necessary antidote to the former unquestioning use of the unified terms 'woman' or 'women'. It is now commonplace to read books and articles, often written by white feminists, exhorting us to remember that there are differences between women and that these need to be taken account of in our work. Less likely to be found, however, are indications of what difference actually means and how it can be made a constructive part of empirical research, theoretical analysis or practical political action in order to bring about change.

My concern in this chapter is to question how useful the notion of 'difference' is for feminism, particularly when dealing with issues to do with 'race' and ethnicity. It should be pointed out from the beginning that I am certainly not denying the significance of diversity among women and the need for feminists to rethink their intellectual and political practice in the light of this. The problem is, rather, the extent to which using ideas about difference enables us to explore, not just the ways in which women may be distinguished from each other, but the mechanisms and

* Taken from, H. Afshar and M. Maynard (eds) (1994) *Dynamics of 'Race' and Gender: Some Feminist Interventions*, London: Taylor and Francis.

processes through which distinct and specific forms of subordination are brought about. I argue that to focus on 'difference' alone runs the risk of masking the conditions that give some forms of 'difference' value and power over others. In the context of 'race' and ethnicity this can lead to the marginalization of issues such as racism, racial domination and white supremacy.

The chapter has five sections. The first section briefly considers some linguistic and terminological difficulties. The second provides a context for those that follow by considering some problems with existing literature and the ways in which Western feminists have grappled with the 'race' and gender dynamic. The third section focuses on the idea of 'difference' and the main ways in which it has been used in the feminist literature of Britain and the United States. In the fourth, attention is turned to some of the problems in discussing 'difference', particularly when focusing on 'race'. The final section suggests some possible ways forward.

Terminological disputes

It is impossible to embark on any discussion of 'race' without first drawing attention to the problematic nature of the term, along with others associated with it. Disputes on the topic are legion. It has long been recognized that races do not exist in any scientifically meaningful sense. Nonetheless, in many societies people have often acted, and continue to act, as if 'race' is a fixed objective category. These beliefs are reflected, as Solomos has pointed out, in both political discourse and at the level of popular ideas (Solomos, 1989). Common-sense understandings of 'race' have concentrated on such variables as skin colour, country of origin, religion, nationality and language.

Some commentators, such as Miles, have suggested that 'race' should be dispensed with as an analytic category (Miles, 1982). This is partly because the very use of the term reproduces and gives legitimacy to a distinction that has no status or validity. It thus helps to perpetuate the notion that 'race' is a meaningful term. Although this may be the case at one level, to deny the significance of 'race' like this also obscures the ways in which it has 'real' effects, both in material and representational terms (Anthias, 1990). Donald and Rattansi have suggested that instead of starting with the question as to whether 'race' exists, it is more useful to ask how the category operates. 'The issue is not how *natural* differences determine and justify group definitions and interactions, but how racial logics and racial frames of reference are articulated and deployed, and with what consequences' (Donald and Rattansi, 1992, p. 1). Such an approach is useful because it can be used to chart the nature of the concept's shifting boundaries, while also permitting analysis of its ontological effects.

Another major confusion in the literature, as well as in everyday usage, is between the terms 'race' and ethnicity. Anthias distinguishes the two, defining 'race' as relying on 'notions of a biological or cultural immutability of a group that has already been attributed as sharing a common origin' (Anthias, 1990, p. 20). She describes ethnicity as 'the identification of particular cultures as ways of life or identity which are based on a historical notion of origin or fate, whether mythical or 'real' (*ibid.*). The term ethnicity has been preferred to that of 'race' in some quarters, largely because it is viewed as supposedly having fewer essentialist connotations (Rothenberg, 1990). This overlooks the fact that it is quite possible for the concept to be used in an essentialist way, as Gilroy describes in his discussions of how black people's identification with ethnic absolutism has, indirectly, endorsed the explanations and politics of the new right (Gilroy, 1987, 1992). The idea of ethnicity is also linked to liberal notions of multi-ethnic societies and multi-culturalism, which have a tendency to obscure the force of racism with their celebration of a benign pluralism. Yet, in as much as ethnicity can provide the grounds for inferiorization, oppression, subordination and exploitation, it too may constitute the basis for racism (Anthias, 1990). As Anthias argues, 'the markers and signifiers that racism uses need not be those of biology and physiognomy but can be those of language, territorial rights or culture' (Anthias, 1990, p. 24). For this reason, 'race' and terms such as ethnicity and ethnic group are often used interchangeably. In this chapter the term 'race' is used, with some reluctance, in the same way as by Omi and Winant who see it as 'an unstable and 'decentred' complex of social meanings constantly being transformed by political struggle' (Omi and Winant, 1986, p. 68).

A further issue of language which requires clarification relates to the use of the term 'black'. Initially this was employed as a political category to signify a common experience of racism and marginalization and the gulf this creates between white people and those whom they oppress, on both an institutional and a personal basis. Hall has described, for example, how the idea of 'The Black Experience' provided the basis for a new politics of resistance and critique of the way black peoples were positioned as 'other', irrespective of their different histories, traditions and identities (Hall, 1992). Recently, however, usage of the term 'black' has been criticized for the way in which it has tended to refer only to those of sub-Saharan African descent, for its American connotations, for its denial of the existence and needs of other cultural groups, and for assigning the label to those who do not necessarily define themselves in this way (Brah, 1992). Although feminists are beginning to acknowledge these difficulties, there is still a tendency to use the term in a homogenizing way. While the development of black feminism has been significant in challenging the fallibilities and inadequacies of white women's accounts, it is important to remember that such criticisms are not the prerogative of those from particular groups alone, nor do they come solely from those living in Western countries.

Understanding 'race' and gender: approaches and positions

One of the difficulties in trying to establish a perspective from which to consider how 'race' and gender interact is the polarized way in which research and thinking on the two subjects has previously developed. While white feminist work has been much criticized for its silence on matters of 'race', the fact that analyses of 'race' often disregard gender is frequently ignored. The study of racism and of racialized social structures, as Solomos notes, can be traced back to the work of classical social theorists and nineteenth-century political thinkers (Solomos, 1989). As a field of social science enquiry, however, the analysis of 'race' and race relations is usually taken as originating with a number of American social theorists (for example, W. E. B. Du Bois, E. Franklin Frazier, Charles S. Johnson, Robert E. Park, Louis Wirth) who wrote from the 1920s to the 1950s. During this period this group of writers helped to establish what came to be defined as the study of race relations, particularly through their work on segregation, immigration and 'race' consciousness in the USA (Solomos, 1989). It was this body of writing, in particular, which influenced those working on 'race' in post-war Britain and America.

Subsequently the analysis of the social meaning of racial divisions moved through a number of stages. In Britain there was an early concern with the arrival of immigrants, when they were black and from what was called the New Commonwealth, and the problems they supposedly presented in terms of accommodation, integration and assimilation into the host country's customs and mores. This gradually gave way, in the context of the 1970s concern with inequalities, to a focus on institutional and other forms of racism. Much of the emphasis here was on capitalism and/or class analysis and the extent to which an understanding of racial divisions could be subsumed within this. As a result of such debates, attention was eventually turned to the implications, both past and present, of slavery, colonialism and imperialism. More recently work has moved from what had tended to be a preoccupation with economic and material concerns to the role of the state, cultural phenomena and discourses in maintaining and challenging the racialized status quo.

The point about these developments is that, although a vast body of literature on 'race' has been generated, little of it, with a few notable exceptions, has been gendered.[1] When women were included it was often in a highly stereotypical fashion as wives, mothers and daughters. Instead, the focus has been overwhelmingly on the lives of black men, which have also largely been discussed from a white male point of view. It has also tended to concentrate on the public zones of the economy, employment, policing and law and order. The contribution of this work to an understanding of black women's lives, as with that of much of the Western feminist literature, has been minimal.

One field of enquiry which is notable for its concern with non-white, non-Western women's lives has been Development Studies. Although very little of this was recognized before the publication in 1970 of Ester Boserup's *Women's Role in Economic Development*, a considerable body of work on the subject has now been produced. This has been not so much a polemic about the racism of white feminism as a major scholarly intervention which broadens our understanding of the nature of women's lives in various parts of the world. It demonstrates that notions such as the family, citizenship, nation and state mean different things to women in 'third world' situations, to those in a white European or North American context. One change in the argument of this literature, which can be perceived over time, is from a perspective which aimed to integrate women into existing development theories and models to one designed to replace these with a more feminist framework

(McFarland, 1988). It is interesting, however, that the academic studies of development and of 'race' rarely draw from each other and have tended to progress in parallel. (Work on colonialism and imperialism and, increasingly, on nationality and nationhood would be exceptions here.) In addition, mainstream feminist work, which has concentrated on women in the West, has paid little attention to the ideas and implications of the literature on women and development. Rather, it has tended to treat it as a separate concern, providing the comparative and contrasting examples to Western phenomena which are regarded as more central and mainstream. Thus the polarized nature of many approaches to issues of 'race' and of gender has obscured questions of the possible relationships which might exist between them.

It is the critiques of white feminism made by black feminists which have forced consideration of the implications of 'race' and racism for the study of women. Black feminists have pointed to the inherent racism of analyses and practices which assume white experiences to be the norm, use these as the basis from which to generate concepts and theories, and fail to acknowledge the internal differentiation of black women (Amos and Parmar, 1984; Anthias and Yuval-Davis, 1983; Collins, 1990; hooks, 1984). Yet early attempts to theorize the interconnection of 'race' and gender have themselves been criticized. These merely add 'race' into the already existing feminist theoretical frameworks. They imply that 'race' simply increases the degree of inequality and oppression which black women experience as women and that oppression can be quantified and compared (Collins, 1990). This ignores the fact that 'race' does not simply make the experience of women's subordination greater. It qualitatively changes the nature of that subordination. It is within this context that writers have turned to the idea of 'difference' as a concept with the potential to encompass the diversities which ensue.

The concept of 'difference'

The concept, 'difference', has a long history in relation to Western feminism. Although the word was not used, as such, by first-wave feminists, the degree to which women were the same as or different from men, as well as divided by factors such as class, formed the basis of discussions about their roles, their rights and their potentialities in nineteenth-century society (Gordon, 1991). Subsequently, second-wave feminists have, implicitly or explicitly, employed the term to point to the inequalities and disadvantages that women experience when compared to men, as well as to revalue some aspects of femininity that had previously been denigrated. Thus there have been analyses of women's language and conversational styles, discussions as to whether they have different ways of writing, as well as research into, for example, their servicing of the household, discrimination in paid employment and risks from male violence. Recently, however, 'difference' has been used with another connotation by Western feminists, referring to the differences between women themselves, rather than just between two genders. There have been two formulations of this: one which focuses on the diversity of experience, the other concerned with difference as informed by postmodernist thinking.

One way of conceptualizing difference, then, is in experiential terms. The idea that women's experiences should be fundamental to its work has been one of feminism's central tenets. A focus on experience has been seen as a way of challenging women's previous silence about their own condition and in doing so confronting the 'experts' and dominant males with the limitations of their knowledge and comprehension. Feminism must begin with experience, it has been argued, since it is only from such a vantage point that it is possible to see the extent to which women's worlds are organized in ways which differ from those of men (Smith, 1988). Focusing on black women's experiences highlights the ways in which 'race' plays an important part in their social and economic positioning.

It has been shown, for example, how 'race' significantly affects black women's experiences of and treatment in areas such as education, the health service and the labour market (Brah, 1991). The influence of 'race' on how black women are represented in popular culture and the mass media has also been demonstrated (Modleski, 1986). 'Race' also has profound consequences in terms of the kinds of environments and circumstances in which women live around the world, as witnessed by the appalling famines in Africa and ethnic cleansing in the former Yugoslavia. All these things are, of course, mediated by other factors, such as class, nationality and able-bodiedness.

Focusing on how different experiences can result from the influence of 'race', however ascribed and perceived, has also made difference visible in two other senses. The first is an acknowledgment that the impact of 'race' may mean that the chief sites of oppression are not the same for black and white women. Black feminists have shown, for example, that for some women the family can be an arena for resistance and solidarity against racism and does not necessarily hold such a central place in accounting for women's subordination as it may do for white women (Carby, 1982; hooks, 1984). The second way in which a previously hidden form of difference has become visible is in the fact that 'race' is not a coherent category and that the lives of those usually classified together under the label 'black' can themselves be very different. Thus, culture, class, religion, nationality etc., in addition to gender, can all have an impact on women's lives. In Britain, for instance, there are many differences *within* the cultures of people of South Asian, African and African–Caribbean descent, as well as between them (Brah, 1992). The idea of difference, therefore, emphasizes differentiation and diversity. It challenges the homogeneity of experience previously ascribed to women by virtue of being 'black'.

Some commentators, particularly those sympathetic to postmodernist thought, have argued against a notion of difference based on experiential diversity. Barrett, for instance, criticizes this formulation, in a general sense, for being rooted in an unproblematized and taken-for-granted notion of common sense and for its implicitly relativistic view of knowledge (Barrett, 1987). Black writers, however, have emphasized the importance of recognizing that experience does not necessarily equal 'truth'. Rather, it provides the basis from which to address both the similarities and the contradictions in women's lives and to develop theories as to how these might be understood collectively (Brah, 1992; Collins, 1990). As

Brah says, the notion of experience is important 'as a practice of making sense, both symbolically and narratively; as struggle over material conditions and over meaning' (Brah, 1992, p. 141). She makes the useful distinction between 'the *everyday of lived experience and experience as a social relation'*. Experience in the former sense relates to an individual's biography. In the latter sense it refers to collective histories and the ways in which groups are positioned in social structural terms (Brah, 1991, 1992). Brah argues that although the two levels are mutually interdependent, they cannot be reduced to each other. 'Collective experience does not represent the sum total of individual experiences any more than individual experiences can be taken to be a direct expression of the collective' (Brah, 1991, p. 172). She thus alerts us to some of the tensions and complexities of discussing difference in terms of experience.

The second way in which the concept of difference is employed is in the work of postmodernists. It goes without saying that there is little agreement over what the term means and much dispute as to whose work should or should not be included within its rubric.[2] While not dismissing the legitimacy of these debates, it is possible, for the purposes of this chapter, to describe some common themes.

The postmodernist position is, broadly speaking, characterized by the view that there is no objective social world which exists outside of our preexisting knowledge of or discourse about it. There is, thus, much scepticism about the possibility of distinguishing between 'real' aspects of the social world, on the one hand, and the concepts, modes of understanding and meanings through which they are apprehended, on the other. Postmodernism is locked into confrontation with modernist modes of thought, which are premissed upon the search for grand theories and objectivity and the assumption of a rational and unified subject. In contrast, postmodernism emphasizes fragmentation, deconstruction and the idea of multiple selves. It decentres the subject, reducing it to a mere nodal point at the intersection of a plethora of discourses (Felski, 1989). Such an approach offers both a critique of conventional epistemology, of how we gain knowledge about the social world (this includes, at its extreme, a complete disavowal that this is possible), and a view of subjectivity as both ephemeral and transitory (Baudrillard, 1990; Boyne and Rattansi, 1990; Foucault, 1989; Lyotard, 1984; Nicholson, 1990).

Postmodernism is, then, about difference in a number of senses. It can include 'difference' in the Derridean sense of the disjuncture between objects of perception and the meanings these have as symbols or representations (Derrida, 1978). Hence, phenomena such as objects or identities depend upon language, 'which simultaneously stands for and stands *in the place of* the things words represent' (Poovey, 1988, p. 51). It can refer to the multiplicity of voices, meanings and configurations which, need to be considered when trying to understand the social world and which, supposedly, negate the possibility of any particular authoritative account (Lyotard, 1984). Postmodernism can also relate to the multitude of different subject positions which constitute the individual. It challenges the perceived essentialism of modernist thinking by positing difference as being at the centre of the postmodern world and by championing deconstruction as the method through which this is to be analyzed. In all of this *discourse*, rather the supposedly modernist concern with structure, is the central conceptual preoccupation (Walby, 1992). Although postmodernist writing tends to be very abstract, ungendered and indifferent to issues such as those of 'race', some black and white feminist writers have contemplated its significance for their work (Barrett, 1992; Flax, 1987; Hall, 1992; hooks, 1991; Nicholson, 1990; Poovey, 1988; Spivak, 1988, 1990).

The two connotations of difference which have been discussed, that based on experience and that on a postmodernist fragmentation, are clearly separate and rooted in what might be regarded as oppositional philosophies. Yet, their consequences for the study of 'race' and gender, and what makes them so appealing, are surprisingly similar. To begin with they both share an emphasis on heterogeneity, together with, quite rightly, a distrust of analyses which make sweeping generalizations and develop grandiose theoretical frameworks about the nature of 'race' and gender oppression. Both challenge the unquestioning, fixed polarizations of black versus white and the heterosexist male versus female. In the diversity-of-experience approach this enables consideration of oppressive relationships between women and between men, dispelling the idea that oppression only occurs between white and black people and between men and women. It also allows for the possibility, as black women have argued, that not all men are 'enemies' and that men and women can unite in struggle (hooks, 1991).[3]

Both formulations of difference, in varying ways, subvert the unity and meaning of terms such as 'race', 'black', 'patriarchy' and 'woman'. (It is interesting that 'white' and 'man' seem to have been relatively untouched by such deconstructionist treatment.) The implication is that these kinds of categories are too internally differentiated to be useful. This, in turn, has led to a concern with subjectivity and identity. hooks, for example, whose recent work incorporates strands of both the difference of experience and the postmodernist approaches, argues for the necessity of reformulating outmoded notions of identity (hooks, 1991). These impose an essentialist, narrow and constricting idea of 'blackness', often related to colonial and imperialist paradigms. Similar arguments have been made about the deterministic and stereotyped definitions of womanhood and of femininity. Instead, an emphasis on difference allows for multiple identities and can open up new possibilities for the construction of emancipatory selves. The likely liberatory effects of this have been outlined both for black peoples (for example, Hall, 1992; hooks, 1991) and, through the deconstruction of femininity and celebration of its multiple forms, for women (Flax, 1987; Skeggs, 1991a). One constructive consequence of this is that 'blackness' and 'womanhood' come to be associated with some positive connotations and are not just seen in terms of oppression (Brah, 1991). Difference, then, not only challenges the passive labels of 'black woman' or 'white woman', it transcends such classifications, suggesting alternative subject formulations.

The dangers of difference

The previous discussion has indicated some of the reasons why Western feminists have seen the idea of difference as attractive, particularly when considering how to analyze the implications of 'race' and gender for each other. Yet there are dangers in accepting the concept uncritically in either of the two formulations described. What Poovey has referred to as 'this brave new world of the reconceptualized subject' may be implied by the term, but it does not necessarily follow from how it is used in current practice (Poovey, 1988, p. 60). Numerous writers, for instance, have pointed to, and been critical of, the political conservatism that characterizes much postmodernist thinking, arguing that it is incapable of making any statements of an evaluative or ethical nature and has masculinist underpinnings (Callinicos, 1989; Habermas, 1987; Hartsock, 1987; Norris, 1992; Skeggs, 1991b). Others have criticized the difference-as-experience approach because of its 'us' and 'them' connotation. It can imply the existence of a supposed norm that applies to some women but not to others, so that it is the women who are not white who are the different ones (Spelman, 1988). Whiteness here is not itself seen as a racialized identity and one that, additionally, may need to be deconstructed. White people are not racialized in the way that black people are and 'race' is seen to be a problem for the latter and not for the former. Such a stance leads to the proliferation of discrete studies of a wide variety of experiences, but makes no effective challenge to the categories or frameworks within which they are discussed. Acknowledging that 'race' gives rise to forms of difference, for example, is not the same as paying attention to *racism* as it exists in the social world or feminist work. As Spelman argues it 'suggests a setting of tolerance, which requires looking but not necessarily seeing, adding voices but not changing what has already been said' (Spelman, 1988, p. 162). This runs counter to the expressed aim of making diversities visible, in that the power to name and define still resides with white women at the 'centre' (hooks, 1984).

Another difficulty inherent in using the idea of difference, in both the experience and postmodernist forms, is the endless possibilities for diversity which are created. There are several dangers associated with this. One relates to a potential slide towards the much critiqued position of liberal pluralism which sees the social world simply in terms of an amalgam of differing groups or individuals (Allen, 1972). In such pluralism difference tends to be treated as existing all on one plane or on the same level. All forms of diversity are lumped together as examples of difference, implying that they are similar phenomena with similar explanations. This kind of parallelism was heavily critiqued by Hazel Carby over a decade ago (Carby, 1982). So many forms of difference are created that it becomes impossible to analyze them in terms of inequality or power, except in the Foucauldian sense of discourse. Under pluralism, differences in access to resources or life chances etc. become largely explicable in terms of personal culpability or luck. The possibility of offering more structured socio-political explanations disappears, except in a localized sense, because these, necessarily, must be rooted in generalizations which cannot be made. There is, therefore, the danger of being unable to offer any interpretations that reach beyond the circumstances of the particular.

There are other problems also related to the pluralistic assumptions of difference. For instance, it tends to emphasize what divides women, at the expense of those experiences that they might possibly share or have in common. Yet since cultural differences are not absolute, the similarities as well as the diversities need to be acknowledged. Pluralism also encourages a cultural relativism of the 'anything goes' variety in its approach to diversity. In discussing this, Berktay has argued that some feminists, in their struggle to overcome ethnocentric bias, both tolerate and rationalize practices towards women in other societies which they would not find acceptable in their own (Berktay, 1993).

One of the reasons for these difficulties is that difference, as an organizing concept, tends to detract from our ability to consider the relationships between things and the possible consequences in terms of domination and control which ensue. Writing about American society, Gordon claims that it is, therefore, 'a step backward to think about the experiences of minority and white women as merely different. They have intersected in conflict, and in occasional cooperation but always in mutual influence' (Gordon, 1991, p. 106). Thus feminist concerns about 'race' and about gender should, necessarily, be based not so much in understanding difference, as it is currently articulated, as in getting to grips with hierarchy and power (MacKinnon, 1987). The force of racism, as Rothenberg points out, is in the assigning of *value* to difference, which is then used to justify denigration and aggression, and not in difference per se (Rothenberg, 1990). Yet there is a tendency in some of the current writing to discuss and deconstruct both 'race' and gender as if they have no links to racism and patriarchal oppression. It is the argument of this chapter that a focus on difference alone is not sufficient to take account of these latter dimensions of power.

Finally, some further points need to be made about politics and the debate about difference. One difficulty that has been discussed in the literature concerning difference in terms of experience is that of political agency and the basis from which women might 'act' politically. Much has been written about the pitfalls of identity politics, in which women have retreated into ghettoized lifestyle politics defined in terms of personal experience and shared subjectivities alone (Adams, 1989; Brah, 1991, 1992; Harriss, 1989; hooks, 1991; Parmar, 1989). This has been criticized for using the language of 'authentic subject experience', an emphasis on the accumulation of oppressed identities leading to a hierarchy of oppression, and being divisive, thus making it difficult to work collectively across experiences (Parmar, 1989). Instead, Brah has recently advocated a politics of *identification*. This regards coalitions as politically possible through the recognition of the struggles of other groups and not just those of one's own, including, on a global scale, those of communities who may never actually meet face to face (Brah, 1991).

For the postmodernist accounts of difference, however, the position is even more vexed. The deconstruction of the self into multiple modes and forms of identities, existing only at the intersection of discourses, raises questions about self-conscious activity. Paradoxically, although everything is about the subject, no one in postmodern analyses actually appears to *do* anything. Subjectivities are seemingly overdetermined by the discourses in which they are constituted, and thus lacking in both intentionality and will. How far are individuals aware of the possibilities which, it is said, some of the recent discourses of the new ethnicities and femininities open up to them (Brah, 1992; Hall, 1992; Skeggs, 1991a, 1991b)? Are these discourses available to all women and black peoples in the same way?

Or is it, perhaps, only some, the more privileged, who are in a better position to take advantage of and use the new forms of representation which ensue?

These are not intended to be idle questions, for behind them lies an important point. The deconstruction of categories such as race and gender may make visible the contradictions, mystifications, silences and hidden possibilities of which they are made up. But this is not the same as destroying or transcending the categories themselves, which clearly still play significant roles in how the social world is organized on a global scale. Thinking through and imagining beyond labels such as 'race' and gender, for those in a position to do so, is one important part of challenging both their legitimacy and their efficacy. A reworking of language alone, however, does not make them go away.

Rethinking difference

The concept of difference is not sufficient or weighty enough to encompass all the dimensions that analyses of 'race' and gender need to include. This is not to suggest that it has not been of enormous *political* significance to black peoples especially, both in terms of naming their oppressions and in forming identities which can provide the bases for collective struggle (Brah, 1992; Parmar, 1989). Rather, it is an *analytical* tool that its value is limited. Although usefully drawing attention to diversity, it cannot, on its own, account for power; how this comes to be constructed as inferiority and the basis for inequality and subordination. There is, therefore, a need to shift the focus of analysis from difference alone to the social relations which convert this difference into oppression (Bacchi, 1990).

Amid the contemporary theoretical hype about postmodernism, such a position stands likely to be accused of an unfortunate hankering after a, supposedly, discredited form of modernist thought. Barrett has recently written, for example, about an 'extensive 'turn to culture' in feminism' with a corresponding shift away from a social structural model, focusing on 'capitalism, or patriarchy, or a gender-segmented labour market or whatever' (Barrett, 1992, p. 204). Instead the emphasis is, she claims, on culture, sexuality, symbolization and representation. Yet, it is one thing to argue that such a change has taken place (and it is certainly debatable as to whether it has occurred to quite the degree suggested) and something completely different to imply that this renders a concern with materiality redundant. It is, after all, possible to acknowledge the significance of culture and discourse and some of the problems to which they may give rise in speaking about the social world, without denying that events, relations and structures do have conditions of existence and real effects outside the sphere of the discursive (Hall, 1992). To recognize that how things are represented is constitutive and not merely reflexive of how they appear to be is, surely, to do no more than accept another version of a concern for the methodological difficulties of studying social phenomena with which the social sciences have always been plagued.

Feminist analyses which are concerned with 'race' and gender, not just as subjects for study, but for the power relations to which they give rise and which need actively to be challenged, thus need to take account of several things. The first is the material, as well as the cultural, dimensions of social life and the social relations which emerge from and interact with these. This does not mean a return to the old mechanistic assumptions, embedded in non-Marxist as well as Marxist thought, in which culture, beliefs and subjectivity are determined by social structure or the economic. It *does* mean that access to and quality of resources (such as food, shelter, money, education), as well as the restrictions resulting from the lack of them and from violence, harassment and abuse, need to be taken into account. The interaction between these things, how they are represented and their relationship to more specifically cultural phenomena may be complex and contradictory. They are, nonetheless, mediating factors in any social circumstances and cannot be ignored in analyzing the situations of black and white women.

A second important issue in considering race and gender is to problematize the label 'white' (Ware, 1992). It was pointed out earlier that whiteness is not seen as a racial identity. When questions of 'race' are raised this usually means focusing on black peoples, its victims, who are thereby constructed as 'the problem'. Yet the processes of racism and racial oppression might be better understood by concentrating, as well, on the exercise and mechanisms of white privilege and power. This does not necessarily mean focusing only on situations where black and white peoples interact. It is as important to look at the taken-for-granted everydayness of white privilege, as well as circumstances in which it is more directly expressed. Also significant in this context is the process of unravelling what the term 'white' actually means, for it is by no means a homogeneous category. It should not be forgotten, for instance, that it is not necessary to be black to experience racism, as the experiences of the Jews and the Irish and current events in Europe testify. Further, the meanings of the categories black and white are not constant. Those labelled one way under certain socio-cultural conditions may find the label changes under others.

A third matter of significance in the analysis of 'race' and gender is the need to end the continual splitting of racial and gender identities and positions, as if they can be dichotomized. It is necessary, instead, to focus on the ways in which each is implied in and experienced through the other, and not separately. Much of the work of hooks, for instance, has focused on how both 'race' and class influence the degree to which male domination and privilege can be asserted and how racism and sexism are interlocking systems of domination which uphold and sustain one another. It thus does not make sense to analyze 'race' and gender issues as if they constitute discrete systems of power. For this reason Gordon has suggested concentrating analytically, instead, on such questions as the racialized aspects of gender, gender as a concept with class characteristics, the racialized aspects of class, and so on (Gordon, 1991).

Such an approach is likely to involve concentrating on culturally and historically specific circumstances, reversing the flow of theory away from the grand abstract theorizing of the metanarrative type dismissed (yet still used) by postmodernists. This does not mean, however, that generalizations about the relationship between 'race' and gender can never be made, as some have claimed (Knowles and Mercer, 1992). While it is clear that *universalizations*, with their implications for the whole world, are untenable, it is possible to talk in qualified terms about general properties, and through comparison to highlight differences and similarities, where these clearly arise from substantive material.

Finally, this chapter has argued that the current tendency to treat difference as *the* major organizing category in understanding 'race' and gender is misplaced. Although diversity is clearly one important element, to focus on this alone is to marginalize other issues, not least of which are those of racism, power and other forces of oppression. It is not the case that women are constructed differently in any absolute way and clearly evident that they share experiences across cultures. Nor is it necessary to abandon categories, such as woman or 'race', in order to recognize that they are internally differentiated. These categories may not be unitary, but this does not mean that they are now meaningless. As Stanley has argued, such terms stand for 'the social construction of a particular set of people facing – albeit with large internal differences – a common material reality because [it is] one based in a common oppression/exploitation' (Stanley, 1990, p. 152). Thus material reality is taken to include representations and categorizations themselves, as well as physical material circumstances. Thus there is no need to conclude, as many now seem to, that such a position leads to essentialism (Riley, 1988). For if the argument depends, as it does, on the idea of social construction, then it is obvious, as Brah reminds us, that it is 'commonality derived from historically variable experience and as such remaining subject to historical change' which is involved (Brah, 1992, p. 174). Discussions of difference have, rightly, drawn attention to serious problems which existed in the narrowly defined nature and overgeneralizations of previous work about women by Western feminists, one from which a concern for 'race' was almost entirely lacking. Their overemphasis on fragmentation, however, offers neither political nor intellectual support in confronting the oppressions with which feminism has historically been concerned. It runs the risk, in fact, of overlooking the very existence of such oppressions.

Acknowledgements

The author is grateful to Haleh Afshar, Anne Akeroyd, Sheila Allen, Bunie Matlanyane Sexwale, Bev Skeggs and Erica Wheeler for comments on an earlier draft of this chapter.

Notes

1 Some of the notable exceptions would include Davis, 1981; Gutman, 1976; Morrissey, 1989; Phizacklea, 1983, 1990; Westwood and Bhachu, 1988.
2 It is possible, for instance, to distinguish the poststructuralist work of someone like Foucault, which emphasizes how meanings and subjectivity are constituted through discourse, from the postmodernism of Baudrillard and Lyotard which sees the social world in terms of wholesale disinformation and manipulation and the construction of language games. Felski points out that the latter are more likely to situate what they regard as a crisis of truth and representation as occurring within a particular period. Thus it may be

linked to a supposedly new stage of capitalist development, variously described as late capitalism, post-capitalism or disorganized capitalism (Felski, 1989).

3 This argument was foreshadowed by other writers, for example Rowbotham (1972).

References

Adams, M. L. (1989) 'There's No Place Like Home: On the Place of Identity in Feminist Politics', *Feminist Review*, no. 31.

Allen, S. (1972) 'Plural Society and Conflict', *New Community*, vol. 1, no. 5.

Amos, V. and Parmar, P. (1984) 'Challenging Imperial Feminism', *Feminist Review*, no. 17.

Anthias, F. (1990) 'Race and Class Revisited – Conceptualising Race and Racisms', *Sociological Review*.

Anthias, F. and Yuval-Davis, N. (1983) 'Contextualising Feminism: Gender, Ethnic and Class Divisions', *Feminist Review*, no. 15.

Bacchi, C. L. (1990) *Same Difference: Feminism and Sexual Difference*, Sydney, Allen and Unwin.

Barrett, M. (1987) 'The Concept of Difference', *Feminist Review*, no. 26.

Barrett, M. (1992) 'Words and Things: Materialism and Method in Contemporary Feminist Analysis', in Barrett, M. and Phillips, A. (Eds) *Destabilizing Theory: Contemporary Feminist Debates*, Cambridge, Polity.

Baudrillard, J. (1989) *Selected Writings*, Ed. M. Poster, Cambridge, Polity.

Baudrillard, J. (1990) *Revenge of the Crystal: A Baudrillard Reader*, London, Pluto.

Berktay, F. (1993) 'Looking from the 'Other' Side: Is Cultural Relativism a Way Out?', in de Groot, J. and Maynard, M. (Eds) *Women's Studies in the 1990s: Doing Things Differently?*, London, Macmillan.

Boserup, E. (1970) *Women's Role in Economic Development*, London, Allen and Unwin.

Boyne, R. and Rattansi, A. (Eds) (1990) *Postmodernism and Society*, London, Macmillan.

Brah, A. (1991) 'Questions of Difference and International Feminism', in Aaron, J. and Walby, S. (Eds) *Out of the Margins*, London, Falmer Press.

Brah, A. (1992) 'Difference, Diversity and Differentiation', in Donald, J. and Rattansi, A. (Eds) *'Race', Culture and Difference*, London, Sage.

Callinicos, A. (1989) *Against Postmodernism: A Marxist Critique*, Cambridge, Polity.

Carby, H. (1982) 'White Woman Listen! Black Feminism and the Boundaries of Sister-hood', in Centre for Contemporary Cultural Studies *The Empire Strikes Back*, London, Hutchinson.

Collins, P. H. (1990) *Black Feminist Thought*, London, Unwin Hyman.

Davis, A. (1981) *Women, Race and Class*, London, The Women's Press.

Derrida, J. (1978) *Writing and Difference*, London, Routledge and Kegan Paul.

Donald, J. and Rattansi, A. (Eds) (1992) *'Race', Culture and Difference*, London, Sage.

Felski, R. (1989) 'Feminist Theory and Social Change', *Theory, Culture and Society*, vol. 6.

Flax, J. (1987) 'Postmodernism and Gender Relations in Feminist Theory', *Signs*, vol. 12, no. 4.

Foucault, M. (1989) *The Archaeology of Knowledge*, London, Routledge.

Frye, M. (1983) *The Politics of Reality: Essays in Feminist Theory*, New York, The Crossing Press.

Gilroy, P. (1987) *There Ain't No Black in the Union Jack*, London, Hutchinson.

Gilroy, P. (1992) 'The End of Antiracism', in Donald, J. and Rattansi, A. (Eds) *'Race', Culture and Difference*, London, Sage.

Gordon, L. (1991) 'On "Difference" ', *Genders*, no. 10.

Gutman, H. (1976) *The Black Family in Slavery and Freedom, 1750–1925*, New York, Vintage.

Habermas, J. (1987) *The Philosophical Discourse of Modernity*, Cambridge, Polity.

Hall, S. (1992) 'New Ethnicities', in Donald, J. and Rattansi, A. (Eds) *'Race', Culture and Difference*, London, Sage.

Harriss, K. (1989) 'New Alliances: Socialist Feminism in the Eighties', *Feminist Review*, no. 31.

Hartsock, N. (1987) 'Rethinking Modernism', *Cultural Critique*, Fall.

hooks, B. (1982) *Ain't I A Woman*, London, Pluto.

hooks, B. (1984) *Feminist Theory: From Margin to Centre*, Boston, South End Press.

hooks, B. (1989) *Talking Back*, London, Sheba.

hooks, B. (1991) *Yearning*, London, Turnaround.

Knowles, C. and Mercer, S. (1992) 'Feminism and Antiracism: An Exploration of the Political Possibilities', in Donald, J. and Rattansi, A. (Eds) *'Race', Culture and Difference*, London, Sage.

Lyotard, J.-F. (1984) *The Postmodern Condition*, Manchester, Manchester University Press.

McFarland, J. (1988) 'The Construction of Women and Development Theory', *Canadian Review of Sociology and Anthropology*, vol. 25, no. 2.

MacKinnon, C. (1987) *Feminism Unmodified*, Harvard, Harvard University Press.

Miles, R. (1982) *Racism and Migrant Labour*, London, Routledge and Kegan Paul.

Miles, R. (1989) *Racism*, London, Routledge.

Modleski, T. (Ed.) (1986) *Studies in Entertainment: Critical Approaches to Mass Culture*, Bloomington and Indianapolis, Indiana University Press.

Morrissey, M. (1989) *Slave Women in the New World*, Lawrence, Kansas, University Press of Kansas.

Nicholson, L. (Ed.) (1990) *Feminism/Postmodernism*, London, Routledge.

Norris, C. (1992) *Uncritical Theory*, London: Lawrence and Wishart.

Omi, M. and Winant, H. (1986) *Racial Formation in the United States*, London and New York, Routledge and Kegan Paul.

Parmar, P. (1989) 'Other Kinds of Dreams', *Feminist Review*, no. 31.

Phizacklea, A. (Ed.) (1983) *One Way Ticket: Migration and Female Labour*, London, Routledge.

Phizacklea, A. (1990) *Unpacking the Fashion Industry*, London, Routledge.

Poovey, M. (1988) 'Feminism and Deconstruction', *Feminist Studies*, vol. 14, no. 1.

Ramazanoglu, C. (1989) *Feminism and the Contradictions of Oppression*, London, Routledge.

Riley, D. (1988) *'Am I That Name?' Feminism and the Category of 'Women' in History*, Basingstoke, Macmillan.

Rothenberg, P. (1990) 'The Construction, Deconstruction, and Reconstruction of Difference', *Hypatia*, vol. 5, no. 1.

Rowbotham, S. (1972) *Women, Resistance and Revolution*, London, Allen Lane.

Skeggs, B. (1991a) 'A Spanking Good Time', *Magazine of Cultural Studies*, no. 3.

Skeggs, B. (1991b) 'Postmodernism: What is all the Fuss About?', *British Journal of the Sociology of Education*, vol. 12, no. 2.

Smith, D. (1988) *The Everyday World as Problematic*, Milton Keynes, Open University Press.

Solomos, J. (1989) *Race and Racism in Contemporary Britain*, London, Macmillan.

Spelman, E. (1988) *Inessential Woman*, London, The Women's Press.

Spivak, G. C. (1988) *In Other Worlds*, London, Routledge.

Spivak, G. C. (1990) *The Post-Colonial Critic*, London, Routledge.

Stanley, L. (1990) 'Recovering Women in History from Feminist Deconstructionism', *Women's Studies International Forum*, vol. 13, nos 1/2.

Walby, S. (1992) 'Post-Post-Modernism? Theorizing Social Complexity', in Barrett, M. and Phillips, A. (Eds) *Destabilizing Theory*, Cambridge, Polity.

Ware, V. (1992) *Beyond the Pale: White Women, Racism and History*, London, Verso.

Westwood, S. and Bhachu, P. (Eds) (1988) *Enterprising Women: Ethnicity, Economy and Gender Relations*, London, Routledge.

9 Connecting ethnicity, gender and physicality: Muslim Pakistani women, physical activity and health

Sharon Wray

Introduction

Research has focused attention on the links between techniques aimed at disciplining the body, such as exercise and dietary regulation, and the construction of feminine identities and bodies (see e.g., Duncan 1994; Germov and Williams 1996; Johnston 1998; Maguire and Mansfield 1998; Markula 1995). These analyses have developed theoretical links between physical activity and the construction of femininity and masculinity. However these writings do not explore how ethnic and cultural identities are constructed and reproduced through physical activity. They also ignore the connections between cultural and ethnic collective identities and the production of locally situated feminine identity. As Birrell (1989) has argued it is possible to examine the discursive configurations of power contained within gender and ethnicity by focusing on physicality. This type of analysis acknowledges the interconnections between ethnic and gender identities and the importance of theorizing patriarchy as a contextually situated power relation (Maynard 1994). This chapter is concerned with theorizing and elucidating the relationship between ethnicity, femininity and physicality.

The chapter has five sections. The first provides an outline of the methodological approach of the research on which the chapter is based. The second outlines some of the theoretical issues relating to the conceptualization of identity, embodiment and exercise. The third section draws on empirical data from the research to consider the relationship between ethnic and feminine identities. The research participants' experiences of exercise and health are discussed in the fourth section. The chapter concludes by suggesting that future analyses of physicality need to pay more attention to how ethnic and cultural difference affects women's perceptions and experiences of their bodies.

Methodology

The chapter draws on a sub-set of qualitative data generated from doctorate research into the cultural construction of different identities and bodies at mid-life (1997–2000). The three methods of data collection utilized throughout the five months of my stay included participant observation, three focus groups and nine semi-structured in-depth interviews. The women were aged between 36 and 56 years of age. Focus groups were chosen as a means of learning about the women's lives more generally and to give participants the opportunity to influence the design and direction of the research (Morgan and Krueger 1993). Issues arising from the focus group sessions informed the construction of the interview themes and questions. This ensured that the resulting interview data was grounded in the cultural and ethnically situated experiences of the participants (Glaser and Strauss 1967; Smith 1987). As the women preferred to speak in Punjabi an interpreter translated during the focus groups and interviews. The wider research sample included participant observation and semi-structured interviews with African–Caribbean and white women.

The longstanding methodological debate concerning the impact of outsider–insider identities on the collection of data (Merton 1972) is limited because it is assumed that the researcher is either an insider or an outsider. In reality the location of the researcher within the field is mediated through a multiplicity of shifting perspectives, identities and biographies that are variously (re)constructed through interaction. This makes it likely that a researcher will inhabit outsider, and insider space simultaneously (Wolf 1996). Within the research setting my white, feminist and working class identities and accompanying status positions, shifted continuously.

Connecting physicality, gender and ethnicity

As a conceptual category, self-identity has received much attention in recent discussions on the changes associated with postmodernity (Bauman 1996; Butler 1990; Castells 1997; Hall 1990). It is suggested that an effect of postmodernity has been the destabilization of the notion of 'the rational self as a focus for a fixed and determined identity' (Seidler 1994: 170). Instead it is argued that identities are complex and fragmented. In postmodern society people are supposedly free to construct identities and selves through culturally available images and consumer goods. Furthermore that identity as a reflexively organized project has extended to the body (Giddens 1991). Consequently the consumption of material goods and images has become central to the satisfaction of emotional desires: bodies have become the 'ultimate resort of identity' (Hartmann-Tews et al. 1995: 42).

Current feminist theories recognize the importance of theorizing difference and deconstructing the universalised identity category of 'woman' (Abu-Lughod 1993; Bhopal 1998; hooks 1982; Nicholson 1990; Walby 1992). Avtar Brah conceptualizes difference in two ways. First she suggests that 'difference may be construed as a social relation construct within systems of power underlying structures of class, racism, gender and sexuality' (1992: 171). Second, she argues difference 'may also be conceptualized as experiential diversity', as in the everyday lives of women (1992: 171). These conceptualizations are not separate rather they are integral parts situated within a shifting matrix of experience.

Nevertheless the process of deconstructing the identity 'woman' is itself fraught with problems. Issues of representation and self-representation underscore questions relating to the formation of collective identities, which may be labelled as 'misplaced essentialisms' (Werbner 1997: 228). Therefore to speak of 'communities', 'cultures' or 'ethnicities' inevitably reproduces essentialist discourse. It is then important to recognize that identities are complexly situated within networks of continually contested sites of representation. Werbner (1997: 230) comments on this issue by stating:

> The argument about ethnic naming highlights the fact that it is not only Western representations of the Other which essentialize. In their performative rhetoric the people we study essentialize their imagined communities in order to mobilize for action. In this regard, the politics of ethnicity are a positive politics.

Therefore the politics of identification and representation are linked to politicized individual rights, such as the freedom to express cultural beliefs and values. Cultural identities are historically located within a shared culture and exist in a transformative state of becoming as such they are politically unstable (Hall 1990). However although particular norms, beliefs, and values bind these identities they are not closed and sealed off from others but are relational to them (Gilroy 1992).

Previous research in the area of gender embodiment and identity has highlighted the significance of the exercise class, particularly aerobics, as an arena for the construction of feminine identities and bodies (Bartky 1998; Markula 1995; Wolf 1991). However within this setting women do not form the homogenous group that much of this research implies. There are important differences between and within groups of women in terms of their experiences of the class, their expectations of exercise and how they feel about their bodies. Consequently the extent to which women feel compelled to discipline their bodies to a westernized feminine ideal differs. Perceptions of body image and identity exist in relation to each other, constantly disrupting expectations of body performance and appearance. These are in turn linked to gendered contextually located taboos and sanctions (Butler 1990). Culturally specific rules and taboos govern bodies in different ways. Vom Bruck (1997) notes how Yemeni Muslim women's bodies are culturally defined according to moral codes and practices. Specifically 'the body must not be communicated – it must not be seen, smelled, heard or touched' (Vom Bruck 1997: 179). This contrasts with Western codes of femininity that define women's bodies as the 'object and prey' of men (de Beauvoir 1972: 42).

It is clear that bodies signify cultural and ethnic identities that are read by others. The meanings attached to them are located within unstable competing and conflicting discourses (Weedon 1999). These visible characteristics are manipulated within a hierarchy of difference. For example, images of slim, fit bodies are constructed as the feminine norm under the gaze of western culture. Significantly aspects of discourse on feminine beauty are contained within other discourse. As Duncan (1994: 55) notes 'beauty is advanced under the cover of the rhetoric of health' in a deceit that is very persuasive so that health comes to be linked to feeling good about your self and this is, in turn, dependent upon the appraising gaze of others. The discourse of 'feeling good and looking good' mobilizes and promotes scientific/medical knowledge in the fight against flabby thighs and sagging bodies. Exercise and diet regimes are promoted as empowering for women because they transform the appearance of bodies to the specific norms of health and beauty that pervade Western culture. As Naomi Wolf puts it 'health makes good propaganda' and moreover, as a dominant discourse, it is ethnocentrically based on westernized scientific/medical interpretations of healthy lifestyle and feminine beauty (1991: 30). The effects of this are highlighted when, for example, 'Asian' women are expected to participate in Western based exercise regimes that contradict their culturally located feminine identities.

Identifying as a Muslim Pakistani woman: ethnic and feminine identities

The Pakistani women who participated in the research defined themselves as Muslim, this was the collective identity of the group (Castells 1997). This identity carried the most symbolic significance:

> Muslim is the most important. (*Jamilla*)

> I see myself as Muslim I am a Muslim. (*Zahira*)

Tasneem articulates the embodied visibility of this self-representation of identity:

> You can just . . . you can just see I am Muslim.

The women shared a commitment to the imagined moral and aesthetic community identities associated with being 'Muslim' (Anderson 1982; Castells 1997; Werbner 1997; Yuval-Davis 1997). However the myth of a culturally pure identity category of Muslim is always already illusionary, alongside notions of an 'ideal' Muslim woman. Contradictory discourses circulate around these invented identities, creating ambivalence, uncertainty and ever shifting boundaries. As Khan (1998: 469) explains:

> Orientalism and Islamism act as two contradictory poles of desire/affirmation and aversion/disorientation and help to reinforce a structured ambivalence within the notion of the ideal Muslim woman.

Khan (1998) further argues that Muslim women caught between these two contradictory positions create a 'third space', an imaginary space that posits Muslim identity and culture as a multiple, dynamic site. This suggests that though a collective identity may serve as a means of resisting western globalizing influences, women actively resist undesirable aspects of collective identity. The dialogical relationship between changing Islamic and localized Muslim identities is evident in the following interview extracts:

> I like to go to prayer reading the Koran and reading in Urdu. I have been in England for twelve years and being a Muslim is the same as being in Pakistan. Being a Muslim is very important to me (*Zahira*).

> Yeah, I very religious, very, very strong. Pray all the time pray and uh feel very clean. Myself, children pray all the time and uh heart very clean. I'm not jealous all the time I'm very happy with everyone. No difference I have no difference with Muslim, Hindu, Christian, Sikh, I love everyone (*Arshad*).

For both Zahira and Arshad, Islam is extremely important in sustaining both individual and collective Muslim identities. Through prayer and reading the Koran, Zahira and Arshad signify their belonging to an imagined global community (Anderson 1982). Moreover their identification with Muslim lifestyle and beliefs positions them within a specific geographical space of attachment. However this space is not an essentialized place of origin but rather a temporary place of identification. It is a contextually located space where 'maps of subjectivity and identity, meaning and pleasure, desire and force are articulated', and empowerment through collective agency realized (Grossberg 1996: 102). The women's collective Muslim identities were not 'fragmented' but were subject to continual change within the boundaries of shared cultural and historical narrative (Castells 1997; Hall 1990).

A relationship exists between racialized ethnic identities and the construction of feminine gender identity. Gender identity is therefore performed differently across ethnicity and culture. Certainly women are aware of cultural standards of beauty that construct particular bodies as desirable and undesirable (Shildrick 1997; Tseelon 1995; Wolf 1991). Images of slim, fit, bodies are constructed as *the* feminine norm under the gaze of western culture. However the extent to which these markers of femininity are internalized, differs across ethnicity. Some of the women participating in the research were concerned about their appearance:

> In your 30s you start thinking about your face . . . like getting wrinkles . . . eyes getting darker around here (underneath). (*Tasneem*)

> We want to look slim and young like the women in the magazines and films.
> (Focus group discussion)

> She (*Tasneem*) says that if you don't wear jewellery you won't be like a lady. Like . . . you look nice with the jewellery . . . it is part of being a woman . . . to wear jewellery. Tasneem says that it is what makes the difference between a man and a woman, he doesn't have the jewellery.
> Most women wear jewellery, bangles and rings, sometimes from Pakistan (*Tasneem*)

For Tasneem jewellery was an important symbol of womanliness and a marker of culturally located femininity (Birrell 1989). Zahira also commented on the importance of jewellery as a prop used to denote aspects of her feminine identity:

> I don't like make-up, it's not real when you take it off you still look the same. Natural is more beautiful I like jewellery it looks nice, makes you feel and look good.

Bodily adornment is closely associated with the construction and enactment of feminine identity. It may serve as a means of empowerment as a statement of womanliness and status, or as a means of control an indicator of cultural norms and values (Wilson 1978). Nevertheless, the majority of the women did not express a desire to match the shape of their bodies and facial appearance to a Western feminine ideal:

> I wouldn't have a face-lift even if I had the money (*Naseem and Shazeem in agreement*). I would consider it if I had the money (*Tasneem*). You might have your face done and look physically different, but inside you are still old (*Parveen*). I'd never have my face done (*Zahira*). We are not worried about how we look . . . this is not the problem . . . but about what is happening inside our body (*Afshan*).
>
> (Focus group discussion)

Health was an important priority amongst the women. They were concerned about avoiding debilitating illnesses, such as arthritis and heart disease. Indeed some of the women had been advised by their GPs to attend an exercise class.

Exercise and healthy lifestyle

The exercise classes attended by the women were held twice weekly in a community centre. Sports equipment was not used as the main exercise activities consisted of floor exercises and running. The women spoke of their reluctance to join leisure centre exercise classes:

> I used to go to . . . uh . . . the leisure centre. And then one time I went to Islamic class . . . and they were saying that, you know, in Islam . . . uh a woman should not show her body to anybody . . . not even to another woman. So then I uh ... . I stopped going there. And I stopped going because I had to change my clothes in front of other ladies (*Jamilla*).
>
> I have an idea that they (women in the class) feel that maybe some men, some gentlemen, may be there (leisure centre classes). And you know this is a problem for Muslim ladies. And they feel shy 'somebody looking at me'. Every ladies they need exercise but they feel shame, just shame, they're shy (*Arshad*).

We need somewhere where we can wear our clothes and not get changed. Also sometimes the cost is too high (*Parveen*).

From these examples it is clear that Muslim women are more likely to participate in exercise if the facilities and types of exercise, do not disrupt their ethnic/religious identity. The cultural code of *izzat*, signifying 'honour, self-respect' and pride, is evident in the women's responses (Wilson 1978: 5). Parveen's comment on the high cost of leisure centre classes highlights the effects of socio-economic position on participation. The shyness articulated in Arshad's remark suggests that difference may be racialized within public spaces. Consequently attending a class at a leisure centre may be an event filled with uncertainty, and the possibility of rejection (Brah 1996). In contrast to this their regular exercise class provided a 'safe' space free from the speculative gaze of the 'other'. For example, the women did not have to change their clothing so did not break cultural rules regulating the visibility of their bodies. Also the door was kept locked so they were able to avoid the panoptic gaze of men, thereby maintaining the code of *izzat* (Foucault 1977). This was noted in my research diary:

> The door to the room is locked throughout the session. It is reopened for latecomers and in each instance the door is partly opened, until the person on the other side is revealed. Nazir tells me that the door is always locked to prevent men looking in.

Responsibility for maintaining the code of *izzat* is primarily aimed at women. This responsibility is reinforced through cultural practices and taboos relating to physical activity, dress, and diet (Sahgal and Yuval-Davis 1992).

> Women in their 'proper' behaviour, their 'proper' clothing embody the line which signifies the collectivity's boundaries; who belongs and who has particular rights
>
> (Yuval-Davis 1997: 46)

In this sense, women's 'bodies speak without necessarily talking, because they become coded with and as signs' (Grosz 1993: 199). The *dupata* (headscarf), particularly the way it is worn, 'shows to the righteous and inquisitive observers always present in the Asian communities, just how modest a woman is (Wilson 1978: 38). Participating in the classes gave the women an opportunity to temporarily discard signs of normative Muslim feminine identity like the *dupata*. For example, Jamilla and Tasneem removed their traditional clothing and wore leggings and tee shirts to exercise in:

> In the class some of the women chat loudly and run. They remove their *dupata*. Tasneem always changes into leggings and tee shirt. The atmosphere in the class is charged with enthusiasm and energy, the women look and act differently when they leave – more relaxed and happy. Their

body language changes. They walk faster and carry their bodies more confidently.

(Research diary)

However this was not always the case, older (aged 50–60) women in the group were less likely to remove traditional clothing and more likely to control their body movements when exercising.

The women spoke of the health benefits associated with exercise when discussing their initial decision to participate:

> This (exercise) is very good for the body both inside and outside is very good. Blood circulation very good heart beating very good. If I go to exercise all the body joints work well. And the stomach go down too, and the bottom go too down (laughs). And uh I'm really quick again at doing the work, and very smart (*Arshad*).

> I am a diabetic and need to lose weight, so after I have exercised I get weighed, if I lose I feel good (*Parveen*).

Although health was cited as the most important reason for participating in physical activity, health and fitness discourse was often intertwined with that of feminine beauty:

> We exercise to keep fit and to be more slim and health (*Tasneem and Jamilla*).

> We come because we have aches and pains . . . high blood pressure, arthritis, feeling out of breath, but also to become slim (*Afshan and Zahira*).

The classes also provided a space for the women to socialize and construct social selves and identities separate to those of mother and wife:

> There is more than physical well being gained from these sessions. Most of the women have been attending on a regular basis for two or more years and have built up friendships. They talk to each other throughout the session despite being asked not to by the instructor.

(Research diary)

> I have made friends since I came here and we have trips. We're I think we're going to Scarborough this time (*Zahira*).

Subsequently, although health and body image issues served as an initial catalyst to attending, it was nevertheless the social aspect that transformed the sessions into a positive leisure experience. The pursuit of fitness may indeed 'be promoted by individualization' (Hartmann-Tews and Petry 1995: 39). However this does not necessarily mean that it is experienced as a solitary event.

Health, medical discourse and diet

Medical discourse encourages women to regulate and control their appetite in the interests of health (Bordo 1993; Chernin 1983; Turner 1996). Health promoters rely on medicalized versions of scientific knowledge, as both source of and justification for the production of rules and regulations governing discourse on healthy lifestyle. Indeed science is central to the production of 'not just gender, but race and other systems of domination' (Hill Collins 1999: 268). Scientific discourse can be thought of as part of a grid of disciplinary coercion's regulating women's bodies through the jurisprudence of medical knowledge (Foucault 1981). This knowledge is a technique of power. It is deployed to discipline and regulate bodies according to the latest scientific findings and claims relating to healthy lifestyle. Further medical discourse isolates and targets groups within the population differently. This has the effect of reproducing existing Western dominant power relations, and simultaneously reinforcing stigmatizing misconstructions about ethnic and cultural difference. Douglas (1995) argues a multicultural approach underpins the health promotion programmes and strategies used to target ethnic communities. Campaigns informed by this approach 'are based upon the notion that black and minority ethnic communities have different cultures and languages (Douglas 1995: 74). However this approach is problematic because it places too much emphasis on cultural difference, and too little on the material causes of ill health associated with discrimination, such as sexism and racism. Norma, the white non-Muslim instructor at the Asian Women's exercise class, regarded the women's lifestyles as a culturally located problem:

> There is a lot more cultural pressure on the Asian women so there are a lot more problems to um . . . as far as promoting a healthy lifestyle. I mean they can come here and they can do their exercises, they can come here and you can tell them what they should eat but there's the pressure. Some of them are living in the house with the mother-in-law, some of them even . . . have even got three women running the kitchen in the house. The health promotion play this year was about a young woman who'd come out of hospital with a baby she wanted to be healthy. The husband and the father-in-law smoke and she doesn't want smoke near her baby, but she can't say anything. She wants to get her weight down but no, they won't eat curry without the butter because that makes the sauce. So they haven't got the freedom to take it on board.

Living in an extended family was seen as having a negative effect on Asian women's opportunities to live a healthy lifestyle. Clearly this view fails to acknowledge the effects of gender, racism and social class on lifestyle, and the heterogeneity within categories of ethnic identities. Moreover what actually constitutes a 'healthy lifestyle' is *uncritically* based on Western scientific knowledge, regulating diet and exercise. Western health discourse is normalized as a consequence of this process. Despite this the women in the research resisted the fitness instructor's attempts to change their lifestyles. This resistance was most evident in their response to requests to change their diet:

> Norma stresses the message "less fat, more fruit and vegetables". The women respond by saying, "but how can we use less butter in curries?" Norma again asks them to cut down on oil and fat, she explains they contain the same calories. She asks them to eat half the fat they are currently eating. The women respond saying "but it doesn't taste the same!" One of the women walks towards Norma and says "if I eat less my face will change, my eyes will sink and my cheekbones stick out". Norma replies saying this will not happen as she isn't asking them to lose weight but to eat sensibly. The women resist these attempts to change their diets.
>
> (Research diary)

The healthy diet message was reinforced during the weekly ritual of stepping on the weighing scales. The women's weight was recorded and congratulations offered when weight was lost. However on gaining weight women were questioned about their eating habits and responded with a shrug of the shoulders and an embarrassed smile. A confessional atmosphere accompanied this panoptic ritual, and the women often tried to avoid it (Foucault 1981):

> The session commences with a weigh-in but some of the women are reluctant to step on to the scales. Norma has to "chase up" three of the women who have managed to avoid the scales for two weeks. Taking the hand of one of these women she pulled her towards the scales saying "come on now . . . have you been bad?"
>
> (Research diary)

Despite this the women very rarely lost weight. As Douglas notes, food may be defined as good/bad in accordance with religious norms and values that link it to different types of 'symbolic systems of purity' (1970: 48). Food is not simply a neutral matter. Rather it symbolizes the social relations of a particular culture or ethnic group. In choosing to eat certain food individuals reinforce and maintain cultural and religious boundaries of resistance (Douglas 1970). Subsequently eating the 'wrong' food may breach these identity boundaries. For these women the risk to be avoided is not simply based on health but is also linked to the pollution of moral well being and the negotiation of a sense of cultural belonging:

> I eat chapatti, pakora, samosa, yoghurt and curry, mostly. I enjoy my food and like to make it special. God gives me everything. I don't eat takeaway foods only home made. Some things I can't eat because I am Muslim. I fast on about thirty days and I'm not feeling hungry because God gives me everything. Some things I don't eat because I am Muslim . . . you know? I know fat is very bad for me but . . . um I'm not bothered (Arshad).

Her religious and cultural beliefs and values govern Arshad's choice of food. To some extent she is able to resist the regulatory effects of western scientific and medical discourse on diet because local religious and cultural social relations, define what constitutes good and bad food. Food is used to demarcate and signify the boundaries of Muslim and Western identities and the rituals associated with diet and eating 'enable[s] people to know their own society' (Douglas 1970: 153).

Conclusion: connecting ethnicity, gender and physicality

Examining the connections between ethnic and gender identities reveals 'the ways in which each is implied in and experienced through the other' (Maynard 1994: 21). The women in this study chose to attend an exercise class to benefit their health rather than to reconstruct the appearance of their bodies. They did not express a desire to regulate their bodies to the westernized feminine ideal but instead constructed feminine identities that were circumscribed by ethnic and religious identities. The act of resisting Western hegemonic norms regulating feminine identity and healthy lifestyle, maintained the identity boundaries of Pakistani Muslim womanhood. Femininity is, therefore, constructed and experienced through the racialized power relations that regulate ethnic identity in Western society. Subsequently it does not make sense to analyse these embodied identity positions separately. Rather, analysis of how women construct bodily identities through physical activity should begin by examining the culturally and historically specific circumstances that regulate this process (Maynard 1994).

Another important issue in understanding women's experience of physical activity and health concerns the different symbolic significance attached to women's bodies across ethnicity, culture, time and space. It has been argued that women's bodies symbolize the boundaries of collective ethnic, religious and cultural identities (Douglas 1970; Vom Bruck 1997; Wilson 1978; Yuval-Davis 1997). Women spoke of the cultural norms that had the potential to constrain the type of physical activities they could participate in within designated spaces. In this, spatial separation is based on gendered codes of correct behaviour for Muslim women that are embedded within discourse on religious obligation (Afshar 1998). Locally constructed taboos, norms and values regulate women's perceptions and experiences of their bodies. Failure to observe these codes was interpreted as a rejection of Islam and Muslim cultural identity. The evidence discussed in this paper suggests that the cultural code of *izzat* may restrict Pakistani Muslim women's participation in particular types of physical activity. This is evident in the women's reluctance to join leisure centre exercise classes where they felt it might be impossible to avoid showing their bodies to others. This is not to say that this is a cultural 'problem'. Rather, it is to say that the providers of exercise classes and other physical activities should be aware of the needs of all community members. A better understanding of the interconnectedness of issues relating to 'race', ethnicity, gender, and physicality is, therefore, essential if opportunities for all to participate are to improve. This requires recognition of restrictions occurring as a consequence of cultural norms, socio-economic position, and the fear of racism.

A further issue highlighted in this paper is the connection between medicalized health discourse and the (re)construction of ethnic and feminine identities. The meaning and significance attached to health and fitness discourse differs in relation to ethnic and cultural locality. In Western secular culture foods may be defined in medical discourse as dangerous to health. This type of discourse often contrasts with local religious and cultural discourse regulating diet (Douglas 1970; Kelleher and Islam 1996). The effect of these competing discourses is apparent in the women's responses to Western health promotion rhetoric. Although the women did want to improve their health and were aware of the risks attached to eating particular foods they, nevertheless, resisted the dictates of Western health discourse. Instead they were influenced by religious and cultural discourse on correct diet. Rejecting Western discourse on health disrupts the knowledge, values, and beliefs embedded within it. Hence by actively asserting their belonging to Muslim collective identity, the women simultaneously rejected hegemonic Western identities and representations of the body.

Finally, it is clear that any analysis of the interconnection between ethnicity, gender and physicality needs to be contextually located. In this paper it has been argued that feminine identity maps on to ethnic identity. Subsequently, theorizing identities as separate and unrelated conceals the historical and cultural power relations that circumscribe women's bodies and, moreover, how this effects women's participation in physical activity.

References

Abu-Lughod, L. (1993) *Writing Women's Worlds: Bedouin Stories*, Berkeley: University of California Press.

Afshar, H. (1998) *Islam and Feminisms: An Iranian case study*, Basingstoke: Macmillan.

Anderson, B. (1982) *Imagined Communities: Reflections on the Origins and Rise of Nationalism*, London: Verson.

Bartky, S. L. (1998) 'Foucault, Femininity and the Modernization of Patriarchal Power', in R. Weitz (ed.) *The Politics of Women's Bodies: Sexuality, Appearance and Behaviour*, London: Polity Press.

Bauman, Z. (1996) 'From pilgrim to tourist – or a short history of identity', in S. Hall and P. du Gay *Questions of Cultural Identity*, London: Sage.

Bhopal, K. (1998) 'South Asian women in east London: religious experiences and diversity', *Journal of Gender Studies* 7(2): 143–156.

Birrell, S. (1989) 'Racial relations theories and sport: suggestions for a more critical analysis', *Sociology of Sport Journal* 6: 212–227.

Brah, A. (1992) 'Women of South Asian origin in Britain: issues and concerns', in P. Braham, A. Rattansi and R. Skellington (eds) *Racism and Anti Racism: Inequalities, Opportunities and Policies*, London: Sage Publications.

Brah, A. (1996) *Cartographies of Diaspora: Contesting Identities*, London and New York: Routledge.

Butler, J. (1990) *Gender Trouble: Feminism and the Subversion of Identity*, London, New York: Routledge.

Castells, M. (1997) *The Information Age: Economy, Society and Culture, Vol. II: The Power of Identity*, London: Blackwell.

Chernin, K. (1983) *Womansize: The Tyranny of Slenderness*, London: The Women's Press Limited.

de Beauvoir, S. (1972) *The Second Sex*, Harmondsworth: Penguin.

Douglas, M. (1970) *Purity and Danger: An Analysis of Concepts of Pollution and Taboo*, London: Pelican.

Douglas, J. (1995) 'Developing anti-racist health promotion strategies', in R. Bunton., S. Nettleton, and R. Burrows (eds) *The Sociology of Health Promotion: Critical Analyses of Consumption, Lifestyle and Risk*, London: Routledge.

Duncan, M. (1994) 'The politics of women's body images and practices: Foucault, the panopticon, and Shape magazine', *Journal of Sport and Social Issues* 18(1): 48–65.

Foucault, M. (1977) *Discipline and Punish*, London: Penguin. (1981) *The History of Sexuality Volume One*, London: Penguin.

Germov, J. and Williams, L. (1996) 'The sexual division of dieting: Women's voices', *The Sociological Review* 44(4): 630–647.

Giddens, A. (1991) *The Consequences of Modernity*, Cambridge: Polity.

Gilroy, P. (1992) The Black Atlantic: Double Consciousness and Modernity, Cambridge Mass: Harvard University Press.

Glaser, B. and Strauss, A. (1967) *The Discovery of Grounded Theory*, Chicago: Aldine.

Grosz, E. (1994) *Volatile Bodies: Towards a Corporeal Feminism*, Indiana University Press.

Hall, S. (1990) 'Cultural identity and diaspora', in J. Rutherford (ed) *Identity: Community, Culture, Difference*, London: Lawrence and Wishart.

Grossberg, L. (1996) 'Identity and cultural studies: Is that all there is?' In, S. Hall, and P. Du Gay (eds) *Questions of Cultural Identity*, London, Thousand Oaks, New Delhi: Sage Publications.

Hall, S. (1991) 'The local and the global: globalization and ethnicity', in A. King (ed) *Culture, Globalization and the World-System*, London: Macmillan.

Hartmann-Tews, I. and Petry, K. (1995) 'Individualisation and changing modes of consuming in sport – Some gender aspects', in A. Tomlinson (ed) *Gender, Sport and Leisure Continuities and Challenges*, Chelsea School Research Centre, Topic Report 4.

Hill-Collins, P. (1999) 'Moving beyond gender: Intersectionality and scientific knowledge', in M. Marx Ferree., J. Lorber, and B. B. Hess (eds) *Revisioning Gender*, London: Sage Publications.

hooks, b. (1982) *Ain't I A Woman? Black Women and Feminism*, Boston: South End Press.

Johnston, L. (1998) 'Reading the sexed bodies and spaces of gyms', in H. Nast and S. Pile (eds) *Places Through The Body*, London: Routledge.

Kelleher, D. and Islam, S. (1996) 'How should I live?' Bangladeshi people and non-insulin-dependent diabetes', in D. Kelleher and S. Hillier (eds) *Researching Cultural Differences in Health*, London: Routledge.

Khan, S. (1998) 'Muslim women: negotiations in the third space', *in Signs: Journal of Women in Culture and Society* 23(2): 464–494.

Maguire, J. and Mansfield, L. (1998) "No-body's perfect": Women, aerobics, and the body beautiful', *Sociology of Sport Journal* 15: 109–137.

Markula, P. (1995) 'Firm but shapely, fit but sexy, strong but thin: the postmodern aerobicizing female bodies', in *Sociology of Sport Journal* 12: 424–453.

Maynard, M. (1994) "Race", gender and the concept of 'difference' in feminist thought', in H. Afshar and M. Maynard (eds.) *The Dynamics of 'Race' and Gender: Some Feminist Interventions*, London: Taylor and Francis.

Merton, R. K. (1972) 'Insiders and outsiders: a chapter in the sociology of knowledge', *American Journal of Sociology* 77: 8–47.

Morgan, D. L. and Krueger, R. A. (1993) 'When to use focus groups and why', in D. L. Morgan, (ed) *Successful Focus Groups: Advancing the State of the Art*, London: Sage Publications.

Nicholson, L. (ed) (1990) *Feminism/Postmodernism*, New York: Routledge.

Sahgal, G. and Yuval-Davis, N. (eds) (1992) *Women and Fundamentalism in Britain: Refusing Holy Orders*, London: Virago.

Seidler, V. J. (1994) *Recovering the Self: Morality and Social Theory*, London: Routledge.

Shildrick, M. (1997) *Leaky Bodies and Boundaries: Feminism, Postmodernism and (Bio) Ethics*, London: Routledge.

Smith, D. E. (1987) *The Everyday World as Problematic: A Feminist Sociology*, Boston: Northeastern University Press.

Turner, B. S. (1996) 'The discourse of diet', in M. Featherstone *et al.* (eds) *The Body: Social Process and Cultural Theory*, London: Sage.

Tseelon, E. (1995) *The Masque of Femininity*, London: Sage.

Vom Bruck, G. (1997) 'Elusive bodies: The politics of aesthetics among Yemeni elite women', in *Signs: Journal of Women in Culture and Society* 23(1): 175–214.

Walby, S. (1992) 'Post-post-modernism? Theorizing social complexity', in M. Barrett, and A. Phillips (eds) *Destabilizing Theory*, Cambridge: Polity Press.

Weedon, C. (1999) *Feminism, Theory and the Politics of Difference*, Oxford: Blackwell Publishers.

Werbner, P. (1997) 'Essentialising essentialism, essentialising silence: ambivalence and mulitiplicity in the constructions of racism and ethnicity', in P. Werbner and T. Mahmood (eds) *Debating Cultural Hybridity: Multi-Cultural Identities and the Politics of Anti-Racism*, London: Zed Books.

Wilson, A. (1978) *Finding A Voice: Asian Women in Britain*, London: Virago Press.

Wolf, D. L. (1996) 'Situating feminist dilemmas in field work', in D. L. Wolf (ed) *Feminist Dilemmas in Fieldwork*, London: Westview Press.

Wolf, N. (1991) *The Beauty Myth: How Images of Beauty are Used Against Women*, London: Vintage.

Yuval-Davis, N. (1997) 'Women citizenship and difference', in *Feminist Review: Citizenship: Pushing the Boundaries* 57: 4–27.

10 Sport, masculinity and Black cultural resistance*

Ben Carrington

> On sport's level playing field, it is possible to challenge and overturn the dominant hierarchies of nation, race, and class. The reversal may be limited and transient, but it is nonetheless real. It is, therefore, wrong to see black sporting achievement merely as an index of oppression; it is equally an index of creativity and resistance, collective and individual. (Marqusee, 1995, p. 5)

This chapter traces the meanings associated with cricket in relation to Black masculinity by examining the role of sport as a form of cultural resistance to the ideologies and practices of White racism. [. . .]

The theoretical arguments are explored in detail by an extensive empirical analysis. Drawing on participant observation and indepth semistructured interviews, an account is given of how a Black cricket club in the north of England is used by Black men as both a form of resistance to White racism and as a symbolic marker of the local Black community. Three themes are traced in this regard, namely (a) the construction of Black sports institutions as Black spaces, (b) the use of Black sports clubs as symbolic markers of community identity, and (c) the role of cricket as an arena of both symbolic and real racial and masculine contestation. The theoretical framework developed and the empirical analysis presented begin to provide a more critical understanding of the complexities of racial identity construction and resistance in sport than has so far been developed within the sociology of sport. The chapter, therefore, attempts to improve on and advance the state of knowledge concerning the meanings, importance, and social significance of sport within Black communities, which, as a number of commentators have acknowledged, (Hargreaves, 1986; Williams, 1994) is currently inadequate. [. . .]

Black masculinity and the limits to sports sociology theorizing

In analyzing the historical development and social significance of sports during the 19th and early 20th centuries, it is now commonplace within the sociology of sport to assert that sport functioned as a key male homosocial institution whereby

* Taken and abridged from, *Journal of Sport and Social Issues* 22(3)(1998): 275–298.

'manly virtues and competencies' could be both learned and displayed as a way of avoiding wider social, political, and economic processes of 'feminization.' Sport, in effect, symbolized and reinforced a patriarchal structure of domination over women. However, such accounts have consistently failed to acknowledge that this view can only be sustained if the inherently racialized nature of social relationships and the position of Blacks, and in particular Black males, within Western societies, generally, and within sport, in particular, is ignored. Historically, the entry of Black males into the social institutions of sport was conditional with formal segregation, particularly in the United States, often imposed. When Black males did compete directly and publicly with Whites, such competition was organized on the premise that the 'White man' would eventually win, thereby maintaining the racial order, and where this could not be guaranteed the prohibition of Blacks was quickly instated.

Thus, the claim that is repeatedly made concerning sport's early development as the preservation of male authority needs to be critically reexamined as it more accurately relates to the preservation of certain notions of White male identity and authority. To acknowledge this challenges many of the Eurocentric accounts that have themselves been guilty of reproducing racist discourses that have denied both the importance, and the very presence, of Black peoples throughout the modern history of the West.

One notable exception to such accounts can be found in the work of Michael Messner (1992), who has argued that men's historical and contemporary experiences in sport clearly demonstrate that it is overly simplistic to view sport as a patriarchal institution that reinforces men's domination and power over women. Rather, 'the rise of sport as a social institution in the late nineteenth and early twentieth centuries had at least as much to do with men's class and *racial relationships* [italics added] with other men as it did with men's relations with women' (Messner, 1992, p. 17). Messner continues,

> We can see that the turn-of-the-century 'crisis of masculinity' was, in actuality, a crisis of legitimation for *hegemonic* masculinity. In other words, upper- and middle-class, white, urban heterosexual men were the most threatened by modernization, by changes in the social organization of work, by the New Woman's movement into public life, by feminism, and by the working-class, ethnic minority, immigrant, and gay men. (p. 18)

Such a radical reconceptualization of the meaning of sport's historical development would help us to better understand the heightened significance of sport within colonial and contemporary societies and, specifically in relation to this article, the critical role that sport continues to play in narrating relations between Black men and White men. Clearly, the historical position of Black males does not fit those models of analysis developed within the sociology of sport that have constructed a universal and nonraced male subject who obtains and reproduces his dominance over women in a society conceptualized as lacking racial inequalities. Kobena

Mercer (1994) has drawn attention to these questions in criticizing the Eurocentrism of many of the theoretical approaches to masculinity that have stubbornly refused 'to recognize that not all men in the world are white or even that white masculinities are informed by the ethnicity of whiteness' (Mercer, 1994, p. 153). The historically constructed social position of Black males, which raises profound questions for contemporary sports sociology theorizing, is accurately described by Mercer when he writes,

> Whereas prevailing definitions of masculinity imply power, control and authority, these attributes have been historically denied to Black men since slavery. The centrally dominant role of the white male slave master in eighteenth- and nineteenth-century plantation societies debarred black males from patriarchal privileges ascribed to the masculine role. . . . In racial terms, black men and women alike were subordinated to the power of the white master in hierarchical social relations of slavery, and for black men, as *objects* of oppression, this also cancelled out their access to positions of power and prestige which in gender terms are regarded as the essence of masculinity in patriarchy. Shaped by this history, black masculinity is a highly contradictory formation of identity, as it is a *subordinated* masculinity. (pp. 142–143)

It is clear then that we need to move toward more sophisticated and nonreductionist models of analysis that do not treat the significance of race as being epiphenomenal to the development of modern sports and that take seriously the 'intersectionality' (Brah, 1996) of race, gender, nation, class, and the other multiple relational identities individuals have.

The racial signification of sport

[. . .] Given that sport is one of the few arenas where public displays of competition, domination, and control are openly played out (Birrell, 1989), it is not surprising, as bell hooks (1994) suggests, that, historically, 'competition between black and white males has been highlighted in the sports arena' (p. 31).

Messner (1992), drawing on a Gramscian analysis of the hegemonic nature of sport, highlights the way in which sport provides opportunities for subordinated groups to challenge the established order. Messner argues that subaltern groups are able to 'use sport as a means to resist (at least symbolically) the domination imposed upon them. Sport must thus be viewed as an institution through which domination is not only imposed, but also contested; an institution within which power is constantly at play' (p. 13). Therefore, within racially inscribed societies we can see how the sociocultural, psychological, and political meanings of public displays of sporting contestation come to take on specifically racial significance [. . .].

Michael Messner's (1992) arguments pertaining to the role of sport in allowing for the realization of a masculine identity for subaltern groups is relevant here. Messner suggests that 'subordinated groups of men often used sport to resist racist, colonial, and class domination, and their resistance most often took the form of a claim to "manhood" ' (p. 19). It is precisely this attempt to reconstruct Black masculinity, which colonialism had configured 'as feminised and emasculated' (Vergès, 1996, p. 61), that is central to Frantz Fanon's (1986) analysis of colonial racism, and further shows why it is impossible to separate, in any simple way, questions of masculinity from race. For Fanon, the claim to manhood is realized via a claim to *black* manhood because it is on the basis of the Black male's racialized identity, that is, because he is Black, that his masculine identity is denied: 'All I wanted was to be a man among men' (Fanon, 1986, p. 112). Confronted with this denial, or lack of recognition, Fanon responds, 'I resolved, since it was impossible for me to get away from an *inborn complex*, to assert myself as a BLACK MAN. Since the other hesitated to recognize me, there remained only one solution: to make myself known' (p. 115).

It is not surprising then that it is the traditionally highly masculinized arena of sports through which Black men often attempt to (re)assert their Black identity, that is, gender acts as the modality through which a racialized identity is realized (Gilroy 1993, p. 85). [...] Sports can therefore be seen at one level as a transgressive liminal space where Black men can attempt, quite legitimately, to (re)impose their subordinated masculine identity through the symbolic, and sometimes literal, 'beating' of the other, that is, White men. Therefore, what we might term the 'racial signification of sport' means that sports contests are more than just significant events, in and of themselves important, but rather that they act as a key signifier for wider questions about identity within racially demarcated societies in which racial narratives about the self and society are read both into and from sporting contests that are imbued with racial meanings.

Cricket, colonialism, and cultural resistance

> The whole issue [of racism] is quite central for me, coming as I do from the West Indies at the very end of colonialism. I believe very strongly in the black man asserting himself in this world and over the years I have leaned towards many movements that follow this basic cause.
>
> (Richards, 1991, p. 188)

It is within this context that we can begin to more fully understand the centrality of sports to Black resistance. [...] In the Caribbean, complex class, gendered, and racial antagonisms within the Caribbean itself, and of course between the West Indians and the British, were most often played out in the arena of cricket. C.L.R. James's (1963/1994) seminal work *Beyond A Boundary* is testament to what he saw as the inherent relationship between culture, and in particular cricket, politics, and Black resistance in the anticolonial struggles of the time. James argued that cricket was central in helping to shape a political sense of West Indian identity during the period of colonial rule by the British. In a way, cricket could be seen as being more than a metaphor for Caribbean politics; in many ways, *it was* Caribbean politics.

Cricket, in particular, due to its position both as perhaps *the* cultural embodiment of the values and mores of Englishness and its 'missionary' role within

British imperialism and colonialism, occupied a central site in many of the anti-colonial struggles both within the Caribbean and elsewhere within the Empire. Thus, the game itself assumed political importance in narrating unequal power relations between the British and the West Indians: 'beating them at their own game' taking on deeper and more profound meanings. [. . .] Cricket, especially for certain generations of West Indian men, came to occupy a central position in their social identities, whether they were living in the Caribbean or elsewhere within the Black diaspora. [. . .] It is to ground these theoretical issues, relating to the importance of cricket and notions of cultural resistance in the lived experiences of Black men, that I now turn.

The setting: the racialization of Chapeltown

This study focuses on the Caribbean Cricket Club (CCC), which is situated near an area of Leeds, a large city in the north of England, where the majority of the city's Asian and Black residents live. The 1991 census data for Leeds showed that those classified as Black-Caribbean numbered just under 7,000, of whom nearly 60% lived within the two wards known as Chapeltown (Policy Research Institute [PRI], 1996). Because of the relatively large concentration of Black people, Chapeltown has come to be known in the city as a Black area, and as such, has been subject to a racialized discourse, fueled by local and national media representations (Farrar, 1997) that have labeled the area (and by default the Black residents of Chapeltown) as a deviant, dangerous, and sexually promiscuous place.

In keeping with many of Britain's multiracial, inner-city areas, Chapeltown is a largely working-class area with few public amenities and considerable economic problems, such as higher-than-average levels of unemployment and poor housing conditions (Farrar, 1997; PRI, 1996). Partly as result of these socioeconomic conditions, the area has twice seen major disturbances, which attracted both regional and national attention in 1975 (see Farrar, 1981; Gilroy, 1987; Sivanandan, 1982) and during the summer of 1981, when many areas of Britain were gripped with violent Black and working-class political revolts (see Farrar, 1981). Despite, and probably because of, these economic conditions and the difficulties faced by the city's Asian and Black populations, the large number of political and cultural organizations in the area, of which the cricket club is a central part, have maintained, and even increased, their importance to social life.

The club: Caribbean Cricket Club

The CCC is one of the oldest Black sports clubs in Britain. It was originally formed in the late 1940s as a social and sporting club by a group of West Indian soldiers who had fought in the Second World War and had settled in the city (Wheatley, 1992; Zulfiqar, 1993). Over the years, the club became more successful, culminating in the late 1970s when it won the league three years running and won the treble on a number of occasions. In the late 1980s, the CCC moved on to play in one of the strongest leagues in Yorkshire County, the Leeds League, where it has played for the past 10 years. It currently has three senior men's teams and three junior boy's teams. Nearly all of the senior players are Black except for three Asian players and three White players.

The club's current ground, called The Oval, is a relatively new acquisition. With money from the local council, wasteland just outside of Chapeltown was transformed, over many years, into a cricket pitch and a few years later the club's current pavilion was built – the plaque inside proudly confirming the opening as 'The Realisation of a Dream.' The surrounding area is largely overgrown grassland, overlooked by a working-class council estate and tower blocks on one side, with a panoramic view of the city's skyline on the other.

The clubhouse has been the constant subject of vandalism and break-ins over the years – another break-in occurred during the research, in which the television, phone, drinks, and money from the till and pool table were stolen. The most serious setback to the club has been an arson attack that unfortunately destroyed nearly all of the club's memorabilia. This has left the clubhouse looking somewhat empty without all the team photos that usually adorn cricket clubhouses. There is often talk within the club that such attacks are racially motivated, with the prime suspects being the youths from the nearby, predominantly White, council estate, although on each occasion the police have been unable to prosecute anyone. Earl, the third team wicket-keeper, suggested,

> I think it's down to, 'Oh, it's a Black club, we don't want them to get far.' I think it's a racial thing again because I've seen words daubed up, 'Niggers Out,' and things like that. Because once you've been done over once, and it happens again, you know there is a pattern to it.

The spacious wasteland of the surrounding area tends to attract youngsters riding motorbikes and sometimes cars. Presumably due to this activity, a police car or two, and sometimes even a police helicopter, will circle the ground (as occurred on my very first visit to a game at the club). The well-documented history of police and state regulation, surveillance, and harassment of Black community spaces within Britain (Gilroy, 1987; Hesse, 1997b; Keith, 1993; Sivanandan, 1982), a key factor in the disturbances in Chapeltown in 1975 and 1981, gives this constant police activity (that symbolically infringes on the bounded space of the club) heightened significance. This inevitably leads to the feeling among many that the police are keeping an eye on the club as much as looking out for the joyriders. The location of the club and its somewhat troubled history seems to give the club and its members an embattled feel and adds to the widely held notion of the club's struggle both on and off the pitch.

Black space as cultural resistance

I wish now to explore briefly how members of the club use the CCC as a discursively constructed Black social space. In relation to the racialization of space, Farrar (1997) remarks,

> In everyday speech, many residents of an urban area of black settlement would readily comprehend a phrase such as 'black space' ... in terms of their effort to forge discourses and practical activities in a particular part of town which are, to some extent, 'free' from the discourses and practices which they associate with a coercive white power structure. Establishing nearly autonomous territory is the conscious aim of all sorts of actors in the black inner city – in churches, mosques, temples, community centers, clubs, pubs, and in certain 'open' spaces. (p. 108)

Such movements to create nearly autonomous spaces are an attempt to resist what might be described as the 'terrorizing white gaze' (hooks, 1992) within public spaces. Here, Black people, and Black bodies, become subject to a panoptic form of 'white governmentality' (Hesse, 1997b) that seeks to oversee, control, and regulate the behavior of Black people and is underpinned by the constant threat of racial harassment and violence. In this sense, we can see how the club's significance goes beyond merely being a cricket club and assumes a heightened social role as a Black institution within a wider White environment, providing many of the Black men with a sense of ontological security. This can operate on a number of related levels, from being a space removed, albeit not entirely, from the overt practices of White racism, as a social and cultural resource for Black people, and as an arena that allows for Black expressive behavior. These elements can be traced in the various ways in which the importance of the CCC was discussed by its members. The club was often labeled by the players and members in the interviews and discussions as a *Black space*, by which was often meant a place where Black people could be themselves (for example, in being able to tell certain jokes and speak in Caribbean patois), free from the strictures imposed by the White gaze. Thus, the club's importance transcended its sporting function.

The current chair and manager of the CCC, Ron, came to Leeds in the late 1950s and joined the CCC in the 1970s, when in his early 20s. For Ron, it was important to acknowledge the historical social role of the club within the area. When asked whether he saw the club as being more than just a sporting club, he replied,

> Oh yeah, because when it started in '47 it wasn't just a sports club, it was a focal point for those people who were black and in a vast minority, because in 1947 I don't think there were the amount of black people in Leeds that there are now. It was a focal point, it was a survival point for the people that were here. So it was more than a club then and it's still more than a club now, so it will always be that.

The use of the language of survival is interesting. It highlights the historical significance of the club in providing a safe space within a wider (hostile) environment for the earlier Caribbean migrants, which is then mapped onto the present, showing the continuities of the club and its role in the light of the persistence of racism: 'It was more than a club then and it's still more than a club now, so it will always be that.'

Nicholas, a 17-year-old who played for both the senior and junior sides, referred to the CCC as an important social space for Black people. As he played for another junior cricket team in another part of Yorkshire, he was able to contrast his experiences of playing for White and Black teams. Nicholas had experienced racial abuse from an opposing player while playing junior cricket for his other team, Scholes, which had increased his feelings of isolation at his predominantly White club.

> NICHOLAS: Some teams, if you're batting against them, and you start hitting them all over the place they always have to come out with their racist remarks to try and put you off.... It even happened to me this season when we played a team from Garforth, and I was hitting the opening bowler who has played for Yorkshire [Juniors]. I was hitting him for quite a lot of fours, and then he started to go on and call me names on the pitch ... and then he got me out, and then, he was all 'mouthy mouthy.'
> BC: But how did that make you feel?
> NICHOLAS: Well, it's the first time it's happened, it made me feel kind of funny. I didn't know whether to answer him back or to walk away from him.
> BC: If you were playing for Caribbean do you think he would have said it?
> NICHOLAS: If I were playing for Caribbean he wouldn't have dared say it because if he was saying it to one person he's really saying it to the whole team ... but at Scholes there is only two of us there, and all the rest are White, so it was more easier for him to say it there.

Such incidents compounded his feeling of isolation and otherness in a White setting, and he thus felt more relaxed and secure when at the CCC. It is instructive that Nicholas's (non)response to the racist abuse he received (in this sporting context) almost paralyzes him in his inability to speak or move ('I didn't know whether to answer him back or to walk away'), especially when we consider Fanon's observations on the discursive power of racism: 'overdetermined from without... I am *fixed*' (Fanon, 1986, p. 116). In this sense, the CCC can be seen as providing Nicholas with an environment where his Blackness takes on a lesser significance and offers, in both a symbolic and very real sense, protection from the more overt practices of White racism. [...]

Community, resistance, and cricket

It is important to remember the wider context of the CCC's recent development. Its current ground and clubhouse materialized in the 1980s and can be seen as emerging from a wider Black political struggle that was taking place during this period. Following the violent disturbances of the early 1980s, there was a shift in government spending toward social expenses as a means of trying to placate inner-city tensions. The provision of leisure facilities was a key part of this process, even while government expenditures were generally being squeezed as the welfare state was restructured (Henry, 1993). Although state funding of such leisure provisions has been criticized as a form of 'soft policing' (Hargreaves, 1986) that increased state control of Black and working-class communities and simultaneously diverted attention away from the underlying economic causes of the social deprivation these areas were facing, the outcomes of these policies were more ambiguous. Although it was clear that the primary motive behind such funding was designed to (re)impose social integration, many Black organizations were willing to take the money available and to use it to their own advantage. [. . .]

Ron, who worked for the local council and was instrumental in securing local government funding for the development of the ground and the subsequent building of the clubhouse, was well aware of the underlying political motives of such provision.

> It was after 1981, the uprisings, or the disturbances, whatever you want to call them. The authorities decided that they had to keep the 'natives' happy, and they looked at something that the natives liked, and obviously cricket was what the natives liked.

Ron's deliberately ironic self-description of the 'natives' is instructive. It high-lights how the colonial discourse of British imperialism still resonates as a point of reference within the popular contemporary White imaginary in relation to Black people living in Leeds. Indeed, as late as the 1970s Chapeltown was actually referred to in the local press as 'the colony within' (Farrar, 1996), reinforcing pop-ular local misconceptions of Chapeltown and its residents as alien and potentially violent, a place to be overseen and policed as a colonial settlement.

The 'natives' then, had, after almost 40 years, secured their own ground and pavilion – a physical marker of the club's (and in some ways, Chapeltown's Black communities') presence and progress in the area. However, it is argued here that although the CCC now has a physical presence, that is, a clubhouse and a pitch, the sense in which the club comes to represent the community for some of its members is largely as a symbol, that is to say, it is imagined. [. . .] The language of community, especially for Blacks living in Britain, connotes both political (as a form of resistance) and moral (as a place of transcendence) associations. What we might term 'Black community discourse' (Back, 1996) is used strategically as a way of articulating wider Black struggles within a specific locality by labeling it as a Black area. The Black community discourse can be understood as a narrative that locates a particular area 'as the site of Black struggles and institutions, a place where Black people have fought to make something their own. This construct is also invested with a notion of political agency and locates Black resistance to racism and self-affirmation in this particular area' (Back, 1996, p. 113). Such attempts at estab-lishing (partially) autonomous institutions and spaces, such as the CCC, as part of wider community projects are mechanisms in the development of 'communities of resistance' (Sivanandan, 1990), which are inherently political maneuvers. [. . .]

Thus, given the symbolic significance attached to the club and its central position within the local Black community discourse, the success of the club on the field came to be seen as reflecting on the standing of the Black community of Chapeltown too. For example, during team meetings, management and other senior players would often stress the need for the players to be aware that they were not just playing for themselves, or even the team, but also for the community as a whole: 'for everyone down at Chapeltown' as Ron once put it. Despite the CCC's achievements over the years, the club had not won the Leeds League since its acceptance, after a number of unsuccessful applications, in 1988, and this was a constant source of frustration for many at the club. Both Ron and Earl felt the need for the club to win the league title.

> RON: Because we need to be champions one day.
> EARL: For the community as well as the club.
> RON: And it would lift the community like Earl says.

Errol too acknowledged the importance of the CCC for the Black community of Chapeltown, especially for some of the older members. When asked what importance the club had for the residents of Chapeltown, Errol replied,

> To me it [the CCC] is still important, it's still important, that's my view, I think it's important for the community. Because everybody, especially for the older generation as well, the people who have actually played, it's part of their history, no matter what, you can't take that away from them, because there are times when they go to games and they watch and they say, 'Well, I used to play for these,' so it's important for them.

Another player, Tim, also believed that the club served a wider purpose than merely being a cricket club, in the sense that it could have an important social role and even a moral purpose, especially in relation to offering something positive to Chapeltown's disadvantaged youth. When asked if he felt the CCC was important in any way for Chapeltown, he said,

> TIM: Oh yeah, very important, very important for Chapeltown, very important from a community point of view.
> BC: In what ways?
> TIM: From the club's history, it's nearly 50 years old, I think we should continue. . . . Chapeltown has got this reputation and the Caribbean Cricket Club should be a shining light. We need role models at the club. . . . We should be role models for those kids, we should set examples, we should set standards. I look at Caribbean Cricket Club as a focal point. We've got access to all these kids in the area and we should bring them along and show them what is right.

[. . .]

Cricket and racial contestation

[. . .] Given that the CCC has a predominantly Black membership (and its name, and location, as suggested earlier, signify the club as Black) and given too that it plays its cricket in a league in the heart of Yorkshire (a regional identity historically constructed through a notion of Whiteness), the racial meanings invested in the actual matches are heightened even further. Many of the players felt sure that the opposing teams were well aware of the wider racial significance of the contests and that the cricket matches were more than 'just a game'; the war metaphor was often used to describe the contests.

Overlaid on this of course, as outlined earlier, is the specificity of cricket itself as a cultural practice and its central, almost metaphoric, position as a site of hegemonic struggle between the British and the West Indians. The competition between Black and White men within this context becomes a symbolic and real contestation of masculine and racial pride, and specifically for the Black participants a way of attempting to reassert a unified sense of self, and of rejecting, even if temporarily, the notion that their Black identity is a subordinated, and inferior, identity. [. . .]

These themes emerged constantly during the discussions at the club and the interviews conducted. For instance, referring to opposing White sides, Nigel said, 'I think they see us purely as colour first, end of story, and then the cricket clubs comes [second].' Nigel was therefore dismissive of the notion that the cricket arena was somehow free of racial contestation and significance and that it could bring people together. When I suggested this to him, he replied,

> Oh come on, come on! We are talking about cricket here aren't we Ben? We're talking about the one county that we're based in being the one that always said, [puts on a strong mock Yorkshire accent] 'You can't play for Yorkshire unless you're born in bloody Yorkshire lad!' That's still got to come through and that's been so strong within Yorkshire, the country on its own inside of another country, that's almost how strong they feel, and particularly around cricket.

This passage is important as it pulls together a number of key issues. It shows how a regional identity can become conflated with notions of nation and indeed race. The view that Yorkshire is a 'country on its own inside of another country' is a powerful one that gives the county a particularly strong regional identity. That sport, and in particular cricket, is central to this, and that until recently only those born in Yorkshire could play for Yorkshire, excluding Asian and Black immigrants from being 'true Yorkshiremen' and thus giving the identity a racial connotation, means that the players come to assume representative roles that are charged with social significance; the games themselves become, in effect, Black (West Indian)/White (Yorkshire) contests.

For example, Pete was clear, as he saw it, of the wider significance of the CCC and the matches within a context of a racist society. The relationship of the players to the actual national West Indian Test team went beyond a rhetorical identification and extended to the view that they actually were in some sense part of the

West Indies side:

> PETE: As far as I'm concerned we're just an extension of the West Indies
> national team.
> BC: Is it more than just a cricket game to you?
> PETE: Yes it is. You see I've heard the opposing teams talk you see. I've been
> at a game when we've lost and I've heard the words coming out of the
> dressing room, 'We've beaten the fucking Black bastards dem, again!'
> [thumps steering wheel] So then it takes the game away from being a
> game, it's war then.

Such views were reflected in a number of the interviews undertaken in this study. Errol, who was in his 30s and had played for the club for a number of years and who had also played with a predominantly Asian cricket team, similarly noted the racial, and hence national, significance that was attached to the games: 'They [White teams] don't want a West Indian team to beat them or they don't want an Asian team to beat them. For them it's like, England versus the West Indies, or England versus India.' Errol suggested that White teams would consciously raise their game to ensure they were not beaten by a Black side:

> ERROL: At the end of the day we are living in England. Nobody want us to
> do better. It's like if there were an English [i.e., White] team in the West
> Indies, there's no way that the West Indies players or teams are gonna
> want them to win.
> BC: How do you think other teams see Caribbean?
> ERROL: It's like, to me, they don't want a *Black* team to beat them. We've
> played against teams who never win a game but yet when they're playing
> Caribbeans you'd think that they were unbeatable! ... It's because they
> don't want a Black man to beat them.

We can begin to see here how the wider discourses of the racial signification of sport become constituted in the actual contests themselves. The view that other teams played differently against the CCC because they were seen as a Black club was widely held among the players and supporters. Brett, the first team captain, was again typical when he said,

> If you are wise, it's like any sport, football's the same, if it's a team of Black
> guys playing against a team of White guys they are desperate to beat you. ...
> You get guys, who for the rest of the season they'll never take three wickets
> but against us they've taken five, because they've worked that bit harder, they
> go out there and fight a bit harder, because they're playing Caribbean, it's the
> Black team in the league.

Given the racial signification of the contests, the immense emotional and personal investment made in the games for the Black men was significant. At both a symbolic and very real level, winning became a way of challenging the logic and efficacy of the racism they faced in their day-to-day lives, even if the victories were always, ultimately, transitory. As Bob, an older player in his 40s, acknowledged, racial and masculine pride was at stake in contests between the CCC and other White sides, thus it became paramount for the CCC, and the players themselves, not to lose.

> At the end of the day you don't want to be beaten. You think 'Let's show these lads who's the boss here.' You try your best because you don't want to be beaten because it's like they go away all cocky and that, 'We showed them, they can't play cricket, English game's the best!' all that business. You want to go out there and hopefully shut them up.

Conclusion

Westwood (1990) has argued that as 'a counter to racism black masulinity is called up as part of the cultures of resistance developed by black men in Britain' (p. 61). This article has shown how for a number of Black men, sport, and in particular cricket, can provide a modality through which Black cultural resistance to racism can be achieved. Sports provide an arena whereby Black men can lay claim to a masculine identity as a means of restoring a unified sense of racial identity, freed, if only momentarily, from the emasculating discourses imposed by the ideologies and practices of White racism.

However, we should be cautious not to overstate unproblematically the benefits of such sites of resistance. For one, Black women often occupy marginal positions within sports clubs such as the CCC (especially those that do not have women's teams), which are perhaps more accurately described, as I have tried to make clear throughout, as Black *men's* cricket clubs. Without acknowledging such limitations, the complex positioning of Black women, in particular, within 'white supremacist capitalist patriarchal societies' (hooks, 1994) gets overlooked. Thus, any claims for such cultural practices as being in some way emancipatory must be qualified. Otherwise, as Black feminists have consistently pointed out, the requirements for Black resistance become equated with the need for Black *male* emancipation. The overcoming of the crisis of Black masculinity is frequently misrecognized as the panacea for the Black community as a whole, thereby silencing the voices and needs of Black women; the politics manifest within certain (conservative) Black nationalisms being the most obvious example of this. [. . .]

It is perhaps necessary therefore to understand and explore both the benefits that such forms can have for a number of Black men while simultaneously acknowledging the limitations of sport as a modality of resistance to racism. Only when we have more ethnographically informed analyses in a greater variety of different communities across differing locations will we be able to more fully understand the complexities of Black cultural resistance through sport and its emancipatory possibilities.

Acknowledgement

The author wishes to acknowledge the invaluable assistance, theoretical guidance, and encouragement throughout the research period of Peta Bramham and Sheila Scraton. Special thanks also to Barnor Hesse for constantly pushing me to think at the limits. I would also like to thank Vilna Bashi, Caroline Allen, Max Farrar, and Alan Tomlinson for their insightful comments on a earlier draft of this much revised paper. The usual disclaimers apply.

References

Back, L. (1996). *New ethnicities and urban culture: Racisms and multiculture in young lives*. London: University College London Press.

Birrell, S. (1989). Racial relations theories and sport: Suggestions for a more critical analysis. *Sociology of Sport Journal, 6*, 212–227.

Brah, A. (1996). *Cartographies of diaspora: Contesting identities*. London: Routledge.

Fanon, F. (1986). *Black skin, White masks*. London: Pluto.

Farrar, M. (1981). Riot and revolution: The politics of an inner city. *Revolutionary Socialism, 2*, 6–10.

Farrar, M. (1996). Black communities and processes of exclusion. In G. Haughton & C. Williams (Eds.), *Corporate city? Partnership, participation and partition in urban development in Leeds*. Aldershot, UK: Avebury.

Farrar, M. (1997). Migrant spaces and settler's time: Forming and de-forming an inner city. In S. Westwood & J. Williams (Eds.), *Imaging cities: Scripts, signs, memory*. London: Routledge.

Gilroy, P. (1987). *There ain't no Black in the Union Jack: The cultural politics of race and nation*. London: Hutchinson.

Gilroy, P. (1993). *The Black Atlantic: Modernity and double consciousness*. London: Verso.

Hargreaves, J. (1986). *Sport, power and culture*. Cambridge, UK: Polity.

Henry, I. (1993). *The politics of leisure policy*. London: Macmillan.

Hesse, B. (1997b). White governmentality: Urbanism, nationalism, racism. In S. Westwood & J. Williams (Eds.), *Imaging cities: Scripts, signs, memory*. London: Routledge.

hooks, b. (1992). Representing Whiteness in the Black imagination. In L. Grossberg, C. Nelson, & Treichler, P. (Eds.), *Cultural studies*. London: Routledge.

hooks, b. (1994). *Outlaw culture: Resisting representations*, London: Routledge.

James, C.L.R. (1994). *Beyond a boundary*. London: Serpent's Tail. (Original work published 1963)

Keith, M. (1993). *Race, riots and policing: Lore and disorder in a multi-racist society*. London: University College London Press.

Marqusee, M. (1995) Sport and stereotype: From role model to Muhammad Ali. *Race and Class, 36*, 1–29.

Mercer, K. (1994). *Welcome to the jungle: New positions in Black cultural studies*. London: Routledge.

Messner, M. (1992). *Power at play: Sports and the problem of masculinity*. Boston: Beacon.

Policy Research Institute. (1996). *Community profile of Chapeltown Leeds*. Leeds, UK: Leeds Metropolitan University.

Richards, V. (1991). *Hitting across the line: An autobiography*, London: Headline.

Sivanandan, A. (1982). *A different hunger: Writings on Black resistance*. London: Pluto.

Sivanandan, A. (1990). *Communities of resistance: Writings on Black struggles for socialism.* London: Verso.

Vergès, F. (1996). Chains of madness, chains of colonialism: Fanon and freedom. In A. Read (Ed.), *The fact of Blackness: Frantz Fanon and visual representation.* London: Institute of Contemporary Arts.

Westwood, S. (1990). Racism, Black masculinity and the politics of space. In J. Hearn & D. Morgan (Eds.), *Men, masculinities and social theory.* London: Unwin Hyman.

Wheatley, R. (1992). *100 Years of Leeds League cricket.* Leeds, UK: White Line publishing.

Williams, J. (1994). 'Rangers is a Black club': 'Race,' identity and local football in England. In R. Giulianotti & J. Williams (Eds.), *Game without frontiers: Football, modernity and identity.* Aldershot, UK: Arena.

Zulfiqar, M. (1993). *Land of hope and glory? The presence of African, Asian and Caribbean communities in Leeds,* Leeds, UK: Roots Project.

Seminar questions

Chapter 8

1   Discuss the problematic nature of the following terms: ethnicity, 'race' and black.
2   Describe Maynard's two understandings of difference, one based on experience and the other on postmodernist fragmentation.
3   How can the concept of difference be applied to an understanding of 'race', gender and sport?

Chapter 9

1   Discuss the concept of identity. How did the women in the research identify themselves?
2   What is the relationship between exercise and the construction of gender and ethnic identities and bodies?
3   What key issues need to be addressed by providers of sport and physical activity in minority ethnic communities?

Chapter 10

1   Discuss Carrington's view that black masculinity is a subordinated masculinity.
2   What significance did the players attach to the Caribbean Cricket Club being a black club?
3   Discuss how other sports clubs operate as racialised and gendered spaces.

Part V
Men and masculinities

Introduction

The early feminist critiques of sport concentrated on an understanding of women and sport looking specifically at the inequalities women face in the sporting world. This shifted to a recognition that gender relations were crucial to our understanding of the power relations between women and men and indeed between women and between men. It became clear that if gender inequalities were to be challenged and changed then we needed to have a more comprehensive understanding of where power was held in the relationship. In other words, when considering gender, inequalities and oppression, men and the construction of dominant masculinity must be understood and addressed. Not only is it important for women to know the part played by men and masculinity in the production and reproduction of inequalities, but it is also important for men to take up the challenge and work towards change. To this end there has been a growth in scholarship on men and masculinities which seeks to engage with feminist debates. Within sport sociology, this has involved a critical analysis of male privilege and power in sport. As Messner and Sabo (1990: 13) state:

> A feminist study of men and masculinity, then, aims at developing an analysis of men's problems and limitations compassionately yet within the context of a feminist critique of male privilege.

The chapters in this section problematize the concept of masculinity and explore its social construction in and through sport. Both chapters discuss and critically assess hegemonic masculinity and its hierarchical relationship to different, subordinated masculinities and femininities. The extract from Bob Connell's book provides a concise and accessible introduction to how men and gender have been understood. He analyses the concept of masculinity, showing how masculinities are constructed in relation to one another, through hierarchy and hegemony. Importantly, he notes how collective masculinities are defined in culture and are sustained in institutions. Although not concentrating specifically on sport, his analysis has clear implications for sports cultures and institutions.

Timothy Curry's chapter considers how these theoretical debates are constituted in practice. The empirical data presented shows how hierarchies between men, and between men and women, are played out in men's locker room talk. He argues that sexist locker room talk can reinforce hegemonic masculinity and male privilege. Through participating in sport, young men learn how to adhere to a dominant masculinity that denigrates women and marginalizes men who are perceived as different. Men's talk reveals how masculine identity is affirmed through conversations about women, competition and heterosexuality. The chapter suggests that sport provides an arena for male bonding and the construction of hegemonic masculinity.

After reading these two chapters, students should:

- understand the concept of hegemonic masculinity and its relationship to subordinated masculinities and femininities;
- understand the relationship between dominant forms of masculinity and heterosexuality;
- appreciate the significance of men's social and verbal interaction in sports settings for the reproduction of collective male power.

Reference

Messner, M. and Sabo, D. (1990) *Sport, Men and the Gender Order*, Champaign: Human Kinetics.

Further readings

McKay, J., Messner, M.A. and Sabo, D. (2000) *Masculinities, Gender Relations and Sport: Research on Men and Masculinities*, Thousand Oaks: Sage.

Messner, M. (1997) *The Politics of Masculinities*, London: Sage.

Pronger, B. (1991) *The Arena of Masculinity: Sport, Homosexuality and the Meaning of Sex*, St Martin's Press.

Skelton, A. (1993) 'On being a male PE teacher: the informal culture of students and the construction of hegemonic masculinity', *Gender and Education*, 5(3): 291–303.

11 Debates about men, new research on masculinities*

R. W. Connell

Issues about men and boys

In recent years, questions about men and boys have aroused remarkable media interest, public concern and controversy. [...]

There is no doubt about the historical source of these debates. The new feminism of the 1970s not only gave voice to women's concerns, it challenged all assumptions about the gender system and raised a series of problems about men. Over the decades since, the disturbance in the gender system caused by the women's movement has been felt by very large numbers of men. A growing minority of men has attempted to grapple with these issues in practice or in the realm of ideas.

Concern with questions about boys and men is now world wide. Germany has seen pioneering feminist research on men, programs for male youth, and debates on strategies of change for men. There is an active network of researchers on men and masculinity in Scandinavian countries, where the post of Nordic coordinator for men's studies has recently been created. In 1998 Chile hosted a conference on masculinities in Latin America, which drew researchers and activists from as far apart as Brazil and Nicaragua.

In Japan there have been changes in media images of men, companionate marriages and shared child care, renegotiations of sexuality, and explicit critiques (by men as well as women) of traditional Japanese ideals of masculinity. A new 'men's centre' publishes papers and books exploring new patterns of masculinity and family life. In 1998 the South African feminist journal *Agenda* published an issue on new directions for men in the democratic transition after apartheid. In 1997 UNESCO sponsored a conference in Norway on the implications of male roles and masculinities for the creation of a culture of peace, which drew participants from all over Europe and some other parts of the world.

Concern with issues about masculinity has not only spread to many countries, but also into many fields. Health services are noticing the relevance of men's gender to problems such as road accidents, industrial injury, diet, heart disease and, of course, sexually transmitted diseases. Educators are discussing not just the idea of programs for boys, but also the practical details of how to run them.

* Taken from, The Men and the Boys (2000), Cambridge: Polity Press, pp. 3–5, 10–14 and 29–32.

Criminologists have begun to explore why boys and men dominate the crime statistics, and violence prevention programs are taking increasing notice of gender issues.

Questions about men, boys and gender have thus ceased to be a specialist concern of a small group of intellectuals. They have moved into the public arena, and though media attention will wax and wane, there is no reversing that move.

So the intellectual debate on masculinity now has practical consequences. How we understand men and gender, what we believe about masculinity, what we know (or think we know) about the development of boys, may have large effects – for good or ill – in therapy, education, health services, violence prevention, policing, and social services.

It matters, therefore, to get our understanding of these issues straight. We need to know the facts, connect policy debates with the best available research, and use the most effective theories. [. . .]

Multiple masculinities

It is clear from the new social research as a whole that there is no one pattern of masculinity that is found everywhere. We need to speak of 'masculinities', not masculinity. Different cultures, and different periods of history, construct gender differently.

There is now massive proof of this fact in comparative studies, especially ethnographies (e.g. Cornwall & Lindisfarne 1994). Striking differences exist, for instance, in the relationship of homosexual practice to dominant forms of masculinity. Some societies treat homosexual practices as a regular part of the making of masculinity (Herdt 1984); others regard homosexuality as incompatible with true masculinity.

We might therefore expect that in multicultural societies there will be multiple definitions and dynamics of masculinity. This proves to be true. The importance of ethnicity in the construction of masculinity is emerging strongly in recent work (e.g. Hondagneu-Sotelo & Messner 1994 [USA]; Poynting *et al.* 1998 [Australia]; Tillner 1997 [Austria]).

Diversity is not just a matter of difference between communities. Diversity also exists *within* a given setting. Within the one school, or workplace, or ethnic group, there will be different ways of enacting manhood, different ways of learning to be a man, different conceptions of the self and different ways of using a male body. This is particularly well documented in research on schools (Foley 1990), but can also be observed in workplaces (Messerschmidt 1997) and the military (Barrett 1996).

Hierarchy and hegemony

Different masculinities do not sit side-by-side like dishes on a smorgasbord. There are definite social relations between them. Especially, there are relations of hierarchy, for some masculinities are dominant while others are subordinated or marginalized.

In most of the situations that have been closely studied, there is some hegemonic form of masculinity – the most honoured or desired. For Western popular culture, this is extensively documented in research on media representations of masculinity (McKay & Huber 1992).

The hegemonic form need not be the most common form of masculinity, let alone the most comfortable. Indeed many men live in a state of some tension with, or distance from, the hegemonic masculinity of their culture or community. Other men, such as sporting heroes, are taken as exemplars of hegemonic masculinity and are required to live up to it strenuously – at what may be severe cost, in terms of injury, ill health, and other constraints on life (Messner 1992). The dominance of hegemonic masculinity over other forms may be quiet and implicit, but may also be vehement and violent, as in the case of homophobic violence (Herek & Berrill 1992).

Collective masculinities

The patterns of conduct our society defines as masculine may be seen in the lives of individuals, but they also have an existence beyond the individual. Masculinities are defined collectively in culture, and are sustained in institutions. This fact was visible in Cockburn's (1983) pioneering research on the informal workplace culture of printing workers, and has been confirmed over and over since.

Institutions may construct multiple masculinities and define relationships between them. Barrett's (1996) illuminating study of the 'organizational construction' of hegemonic masculinity in the US Navy shows different forms in the different sub-branches of the one military organization.

This collective process of constructing and enacting masculinities can be traced in an enormous range of settings, from the face-to-face interactions in the classrooms and playgrounds of an elementary school (Thorne 1993) to the august public institutions of imperial Britain at the height of world power (Hearn 1992). In different historical circumstances, of course, different institutions will be more or less prominent in the construction of masculinity. The institutions of competitive sport seem peculiarly important for contemporary western masculinities (Whitson 1990).

Bodies as arenas

Men's bodies do not determine the patterns of masculinity, as biological essentialism and pop psychology would have it. Men's bodies are addressed, defined and disciplined (as in sport: Theberge 1991), and given outlets and pleasures, by the gender order of society.

But men's bodies are not blank slates. The enactment of masculinity reaches certain limits, for instance in the destruction of the industrial worker's body (Donaldson 1991). Masculine conduct combined with a female body is felt to be anomalous or transgressive, like feminine conduct combined with a male body. Research on gender crossing (Bolin 1988) shows that a lot of work must be done to sustain an anomalous gender.

Gender is the way bodies are drawn into history; bodies are arenas for the making of gender patterns. This was a point underplayed by 'male role' discussions, and is underplayed even in some of the more recent research. It is important, then, to register the importance of such processes as violence (Tomsen 1997) and body culture (Klein 1993) in the construction and politics of masculinities.

Active construction

Masculinities are neither programmed in our genes, nor fixed by social structure, prior to social interaction. They come into existence as people act. They are actively produced, using the resources and strategies available in a given social setting.

Thus, the exemplary masculinities of sports professionals are not a product of passive disciplining. As Messner (1992) shows, they result from a sustained, active engagement with the demands of the institutional setting, even to the point of serious bodily damage from 'playing hurt' and accumulated stress. With boys learning masculinities, much of what was previously taken as 'socialization' appears, in detailed studies of schools (Thorne 1993; Walker 1988), as the outcome of intricate and intense manoeuvering in peer groups, classes and adult–child relationships.

Walker (1998a, 1998b), in a study of young working-class men and car culture, gives a striking example of the collective construction of masculinities in adult peer groups. The friendship groups not only draw lines to fend off women's intrusion into masculine social space, but draw in a whole technology as part of the definition of masculinity.

Internal complexity and contradiction

One of the key reasons why masculinities are not fixed is that they are not homogeneous, simple states of being. Close-focus research on masculinities commonly identifies contradictory desires and conduct. A striking example, in Klein's (1993) study of bodybuilders, is the conflict between the heterosexual definition of hegemonic masculinity and the homosexual practice through which some bodybuilders finance the making of an exemplary body. [. . .]

Tomsen (1998) points to another example, the ambivalence in anti-gay violence, which helps to make such violence a systemic feature of contemporary Western life, not just a matter of individual pathology. Poynting et al. (1998) describe, for an ethnic minority, the contradiction between young men's claim to authority and their experience of subordination under the pressure of racism. Masculinities are often in tension, within and without. It seems likely that such tensions are important sources of change.

Dynamics

There is abundant evidence that masculinities do change. Masculinities are created in specific historical circumstances and, as those circumstances change, the gender practices can be contested and reconstructed. [...]

Yet the gender order does not blow away at a breath. Donaldson's (1998) study of ruling-class men shows a major reason why – the persistence of power and wealth, and the active defence of privilege. The eight 'men's movements' which Messner (1997) has traced in the United States have different, and sometimes sharply conflicting, agendas for the remaking of masculinity. The historical process around masculinities is a process of struggle in which, ultimately, large resources are at stake. [...]

Conceptualizing masculinities

Masculinity, understood as a configuration of gender practice in the terms just discussed, is necessarily a social construction. Masculinity *refers* to male bodies (sometimes directly, sometimes symbolically and indirectly), but is not *determined* by male biology. It is, thus, perfectly logical to talk about masculine women or masculinity in women's lives, as well as masculinity in men's lives.

Masculinities are configurations of practice within gender relations, a structure that includes large-scale institutions and economic relations as well as face-to-face relationships and sexuality. Masculinity is institutionalized in this structure, as well as being an aspect of individual character or personality.

Thus we can speak of a specific kind of masculinity being embedded in the gender regime of an institution such as an army, a corporation or a school. A small-scale but closely analyzed example is Walker's (1988) examination of the institutional role of football in maintaining order in an Australian inner-city boys' school. On the larger scale, the state itself institutionalizes particular masculinities and regulates relations between masculinities in the gender order of society.

This activity not only regulates existing gender relations. The state's activity also helps to constitute gender relations and the social categories they define. The best-analyzed example is the role of repressive laws and state-backed medicine in constituting the category of 'the homosexual' in the late nineteenth century (Greenberg 1988). The categories of husband and wife are also partly constituted by state action (e.g. through marriage law). Their meanings and relationships are shaped by a very wide range of state policies – labour market policy, welfare policy, child care and education policy, population policy – as comparative studies of welfare states have shown (O'Connor, Orloff & Shaver 1999).

Further, masculinity exists impersonally in culture as a subject position in the process of representation, in the structures of language and other symbol systems. Individual practice may accept and reproduce this positioning, but may also confront and contest it.

The relationship between personal life and structure constantly emerges as a key issue about masculinity. A striking example is the relationship between boys' engagement in sports and the hierarchical organization of sporting institutions, analyzed in Messner's (1992) research on professional athletes.

I have emphasized earlier the empirical evidence that in any given social setting there is rarely just one masculinity. What used to be called '*the* male role' is best understood as the culturally authoritative or hegemonic pattern of masculinity. But there are generally others. We need ways of understanding the differences, and the relations between different patterns.

Hegemonic masculinity need not be the most common pattern of masculinity. Other masculinities co-exist, or more precisely, are produced at the same time. These include subordinated masculinities, the most important example of which in contemporary European/American culture is gay masculinity. There are also marginalized masculinities, gender forms produced in exploited or oppressed groups such as ethnic minorities, which may share many features with hegemonic masculinity but are socially de-authorized. There are also masculinities which are organized around acceptance of the patriarchal dividend, but are not militant in defence of patriarchy. These might be termed complicit masculinities.

The principal axis around which the varieties of masculinity are organized is the overall social relation between men and women, that is, the structure of gender relations as a whole. A strong cultural opposition between masculine and feminine is characteristic of patriarchal gender orders, commonly expressed in culture as dichotomies and negations. Hegemonic masculinity is thus often defined negatively, as the opposite of femininity. Subordinated masculinities are symbolically assimilated to femininity (e.g. abuse of 'sissies', 'nancy-boys').

Adult masculinities are produced through a complex process of growth and development involving active negotiation in multiple social relationships. Earlier conceptions of 'sex role socialization' oversimplified the social relations and pictured children as much more passive than they are. The process is not so simple. It often involves reversals and dialectics of confrontation and denial, where masculinities are formed in opposition to institutional pressure, as well as through conformity. [. . .]

The result in adulthood is generally a complex personality structure, not a homogeneous one, in which contradictory emotions and commitments co-exist. For instance in adult sexuality, a predatory heterosexuality may co-exist with desire to be nurtured, a pattern that Bishop and Robinson (1998) identify even among the 'clients' of international sex tourism in Thailand. A public heterosexuality may co-exist with a homoerotic desire which is nevertheless feared and denied.

The enactment of masculinity in adult life is partly an outcome of this process of development, which defines a person's capacities for practice, and partly a matter of the social situations in which the person acts. Men whose masculinities are formed around the continuing social subordination of women are likely to act in ways that sustain the patriarchal dividend.

Yet men's interests are divided. This is partly a result of the subordination of some masculinities within the pattern of hegemony, and partly a result of the interplay between gender relations and structures of class, race and nationality. In certain situations men's relationships with particular women or children, or groups including women and children, define interests that are stronger than their shared interest as men. In all these ways men's general interest in patriarchy becomes incoherent or contestable.

Precisely such a contest has been created by the growth of contemporary feminism, presenting a challenge of which virtually all men in Western countries are aware. The result is the growth of new forms of politics addressing masculinity as an object of social action, producing the spectrum of masculinity politics. [. . .]

References

Barrett, F. J. (1996) 'The organizational construction of hegemonic masculinity: the case of the US Navy', *Gender, Work and Organization* 3(3): 129–42.

Bishop, R. and Robinson, L. S. (1998) *Night Market: Sexual Cultures and the Thai Economic Miracle*, New York: Routledge.

Bolin, A. (1988) *In Search of Eve: Transsexual Rites of Passage*, Westport: Bergin and Garvey.

Cockburn, C. (1983) *Brothers: Male Dominance and Technological Change*, London: Pluto.

Cornwall, A. and Lindisfarne, N. (eds) (1994) *Dislocating Masculinity: Comparative Ethnographies*, London: Routledge.

Donaldson, M. (1991) *Time of our Lives: Labour and Love in the Working Class*, Sydney: Allen and Unwin.

Donaldson, M. (1998) 'Growing up very rich: the masculinity of the hegemonic', *Journal of Interdisciplinary Gender Studies* 3(2): 95–112.

Foley, D.E. (1990) *Learning Capitalist Culture: Deep in the Heart of Tejas*, Philadelphia: University of Pennsylvania Press.

Greenberg, D.F. (1988) *The Construction of Homosexuality*, Chicago: University of Chicago Press.

Hearne, J. (1992) *Men in the Public Eye: The Construction and Deconstruction of Public Men and Public Patriarchies*, London: Routledge.

Herdt, G.H. (1984) *Ritualized Homosexuality in Melanesia*, Berkeley: University of California Press.

Herek, G. and Berrill, K. (1992) *Hate Crimes: Confronting Violence Against Lesbians and Gay Men*, Newbury Park: Sage.

Hondagneu-Sotelo, P. and Messner, M. A. (1994) 'Gender displays and men's power: the "new man" and the Mexican immigrant man' in H. Brod and M. Kaufman (eds) *Theorizing Masculinities*, Thousand Oaks: Sage.

Klein, A.M. (1993) *Little Big Men: Bodybuilding Subculture and Gender Construction*, Albany: State University of New York Press.

McKay, J. and Huber, D. (1992) 'Anchoring media images of technology and sport', *Women's Studies International Forum* 15(2): 205–18.

Messershmidt, J.W. (1997) *Crime as Structured Action: Gender, Race, Class and Crime in the Making*, Thousand Oaks: Sage.

Messner, M. (1992) *Power at Play: Sports and the Problem of Masculinity*, Boston: Beacon.

Messner, M. (1997) *The Politics of Masculinities: Men in Movements*, Thousand Oaks: Sage.

O'Connor, J.S., Orloff, A.S. and Shaver, S. (1999) *States, Markets, Families*, Cambridge: Cambridge University Press.

Poynting, S., Noble, G. and Tabar, P. (1998) "If anybody called me a wog they wouldn't be speaking to me alone": Protest Masculinity and Lebanise Youth in Western Sydney', *Journal of Interdisciplinary Gender Studies* 3(2): 76–94.

Theberge, N. (1991) 'Reflections on the body in the sociology of sport', *Quest* 43: 123–34.

Thorne, B. (1993) *Gender Play: Girls and Boys in School*, New Brunswick: Rutgers University Press.

Tillner, G. (1997) 'Masculinity and xenophobia', Paper presented at UNESCO meeting on Male Roles and Masculinities in the Perspective of a Culture of Peace, Oslo.

Tomsen, S. (1997) 'A top night: social protest, masculinity and the culture of drinking violence', *British Journal of Criminology* 37(1): 90–103.

Walker, J.C. (1988) *Louts and Legends: Male Youth Culture in an inner-city school*, Sydney: Allen and Unwin.

Walker, L. (1998a) 'Chivalrous masculinity among juvenile offenders in western Sydney: a new perspective on young working-class men and crime', *Current Issues in Criminal Justice* 9(3): 279–93.

Walker, L. (1998b) 'Under the bonnet: car culture, technological dominance and young men of the working class', *Journal of Interdisciplinary Gender Studies* 3(2): 23–43.

Whitson, D. (1990) 'Sport in the social construction of masculinity', in M.A. Messner and D. F. Sabo (eds) *Sport, Men and the Gender Order: Critical Feminist Perspectives*, Champaign: Human Kinetics Books.

12 Fraternal bonding in the locker room: A profeminist analysis of talk about competition and women*

Timothy Jon Curry

The men's locker room is enshrined in sports mythology as a bastion of privilege and a center of fraternal bonding. The stereotyped view of the locker room is that it is a retreat from the outside world where athletes quietly prepare themselves for competition, noisily celebrate an important victory, or silently suffer a defeat. Given the symbolic importance of this sports shrine, it is surprising that there have been so few actual studies of the dynamics of male bonding in locker rooms. The purpose of this study was to explore a new approach to this aspect of fraternal bonding, by collecting locker room talk fragments and interpreting them from a profeminist perspective. Profeminism in this context meant adapting a feminist perspective to men's experience in sport, giving special attention to sexist and homophobic remarks that reveal important assumptions about masculinity, male dominance, and fraternal bonding.

Although seldom defined explicitly, the fraternal bond is usually considered to be a force, link, or affectionate tie that unites men. It is characterized in the literature by low levels of disclosure and intimacy. Sherrod (1987), for example, suggests that men associate different meanings with friendships than women do, and that men tend to derive friendships from doing things together while women are able to maintain friendships through disclosures. This view implies that men need a reason to become close to one another and are uncomfortable about sharing their feelings.

Some of the activities around which men bond are negative toward women and others who are perceived as outsiders to the fraternal group. For example, Lyman (1987) describes how members of a fraternity bond through sexist joking relationships, and Fine (1987) notes the development of sexist, racist, and homophobic attitudes and jokes even among preadolescent Little Leaguers. Sanday (1990) examines gang rape as a by-product of male bonding in fraternities, and she argues that the homophobic and homosocial environments of such all-male groups make for a conducive environment for aggression toward women.

Sport is an arena well suited for the enactment and perpetuation of the male bond (Messner, 1987). It affords separation and identity building as individual athletes seek status through making the team and winning games (Dunning, 1986), and

* Taken from, *Sociology of Sport Journal* 8(1991): 119–135.

it also provides group activity essential for male bonding (Sherrod, 1987) while not requiring much in the way of intimate disclosures (Sabo & Panepinto, 1990). Feminist scholars have pointed out that the status enhancement available to men through sports is not as available to women, and thus sport serves to legitimate men's domination of women and their control of public life (Bryson, 1987; Farr, 1988). In addition, since most sports are rule bound either by tradition or by explicit formal codes, involvement in sports is part of the typical rights-and-rules orientation of boys' socialization in the United States (Gilligan, 1982).

For young men, sport is also an ideal place to "do gender" – display masculinity in a socially approved fashion (West & Zimmerman, 1987). In fact the male bond is apparently strengthened by an effective display of traditional masculinity and threatened by what is not considered part of standard hegemonic masculinity. For example, as Messner (1989, p. 192) relates, a gay football player who was aggressive and hostile on the field felt "compelled to go along with a lot of locker room garbage because I wanted that image [of attachment to more traditional male traits] – and I know a lot of others who did too ... I know a lot of football players who very quietly and secretly like to paint, or play piano. And they do it quietly, because this to them is threatening if it's known by others." Since men's bonding is based on shared activity rather than on the self-disclosures (Sherrod, 1987), it is unlikely that teammates will probe deeply beneath these surface presentations.

Deconstructing such performances, however, is one way of understanding "the interactional scaffolding of social structure and the social control process that sustains it" in displays of masculinity central to fraternal bonding (West & Zimmerman, 1987, p. 147). Pronger (1990, pp. 192–213) has provided one such deconstruction of doing gender in the locker room from the perspective of a homosexual. He notes the irony involved in maintaining the public façade of heterosexuality while privately experiencing a different reality.

Two other studies of locker rooms emphasized the cohesive side of male bonding through sports, but neither of these studies was concerned specifically with gender displays or with what male athletes say about women (Snyder, 1972; Zurcher, 1982). The recent uproar over the sexual harassment of a woman reporter in the locker room of the NFL's New England Patriots, described by Heymann (1990), suggests that this work is a timely and important undertaking.

Procedures

This study of locker room talk follows Snyder (1972), who collected samples of written messages and slogans affixed to locker room walls. However, since the messages gathered by Snyder were originally selected by coaches and were meant to serve as normative prescriptions that would contribute to winning games, they mostly revealed an idealistic, public side of locker room culture. From reading these slogans one would get the impression that men's sports teams are characterized by harmony, consensus, and "esoteric in-group traditions" (Snyder, 1972, p. 99).

The approach taken here focuses on the spoken aspects of locker room culture – the jokes and put-downs typically involved in fraternal bonding (Fine, 1987; Lyman, 1987). Although this side of locker room culture is ephemeral, situational, and generally not meant for display outside of the all-male peer groups, it is important in understanding how sport contributes to male bonding, status attainment, and hegemonic displays of masculinity.

The talk fragments

The talk fragments were gathered in locker rooms from athletes on two teams participating in contact sports at a large midwestern university with a "big time" sports program. The first team was approached at the beginning of its season for permission to do a field study. Permission was granted and assurances were made that anonymity would be maintained for athletes and coaches. I observed the team as a nonparticipant sport sociologist, both at practices and during competition, for well over a month before the first talk fragments were collected. The talk fragments were gathered over a 2-month period and the locker room was visited frequently to gather field notes. Note gathering in the locker room was terminated upon saturation; however, the team's progress was followed and field observations continued until the end of the season.

Intensive interviews were conducted with some of the athletes and coaches during all 9 months of the research. These interviews concerned not only locker room interaction but also the sport background and life histories of the respondents. Additionally, after the talk fragments were gathered, five of the athletes enrolled in my class on sport sociology and wrote term papers on their experiences in sport. These written documents, along with the interviews and observations made outside the locker room, provided a rich variety of materials for the contextual analysis and interpretation of the conversations held inside the locker room. They also lent insight into how the athletes themselves defined locker room talk.

The talk fragments were collected in plain view of the athletes, who had become accustomed to the presence of a researcher taking notes. Fragments of talk were written down as they occurred and were reconstructed later. Such obvious note taking may have influenced what was said, or more likely what was not said. To minimize the obtrusiveness of the research, eye contact was avoided while taking notes. A comparison between the types of conversations that occurred during note taking versus when note taking was not done yielded few differences. Even so, more talk fragments were gathered from a second locker room as a way of both increasing the validity of the study and protecting the anonymity of the athletes and coaches from the first locker room.

The second locker room

Field notes concerning talk from a second locker room were gathered by a senior who had enjoyed a successful career as a letterman. His presence in the locker room as a participant observer was not obtrusive, and the other student-athletes reacted to him as a peer. He gathered talk fragments over a 3-month period while his team was undergoing conditioning and selection procedures similar in intensity to that of the original team. He met with me every week and described his perceptions of interaction in the locker room. His collection of talk fragments was included as part of a written autobiographical account of his experience in sport while at college. These research procedures were modeled after Zurcher's (1983) study of hashers in a sorority house and Shaw's (1972) autobiographical account of his experience in sport.

One additional point needs to be stressed here: Unlike anecdotal accounts of locker room behavior or studies based on the recollections of former athletes, these conversations were systematically gathered live and in context over a relatively brief period of time. Consequently the stories and jokes may not be as extreme as those remembered by athletes who reflect upon their entire career in sport (e.g., Messner, 1987; Pronger, 1990), or as dramatic as the episode of sexual harassment that took place in the locker room of the New England Patriots (Heymann, 1990).

The strength of this study lies in situating the conversations within the context of the competitive environment of elite collegiate sport rather than capturing the drama of a single moment or the recollections of particularly memorable occasions. In other words, no one study, including this one, can hope to cover the entire gambit of locker room culture and various distinctive idiocultures of different teams (Fine, 1987). A variety of studies that use different methods and incorporate different perspectives are needed for that endeavor.

Profeminist perspective

Messner (1990) has recently argued that a profeminist perspective is needed to overcome male bias in research in the sociology of sport. For decades, Messner claims, male researchers have been prone to writing about sport from a masculine standpoint and have neglected gender issues. He further states that since men have exclusive access to much of the social world of sport, they also have the primary responsibility of providing a more balanced interpretation of that world by paying special attention to gender oppression. He maintains that such balance is best achieved at this point by adopting a value-centered feminist perspective rather than a supposedly value-free but androcentric perspective.

Adopting a feminist standpoint requires assuming that "feminist visions of an egalitarian society are desirable" (Messner, 1990, p. 149). Ultimately, research guided by such an assumption will contribute to a deeper understanding of the costs and the privileges of masculinity and may help build a more just and egalitarian world. Messner does not offer explicit guidelines as to how an andro-centric researcher might begin to undertake such a shift in perspectives, however, although he does refer to a number of exemplary studies.

As a method of consciously adopting a profeminist perspective in this research, a review of feminist literature on sports and socialization was undertaken, feminist colleagues were consulted on early drafts of the manuscript, and a research assistant trained in feminist theory was employed to help with the interpretation of talk fragments. She shared her ideas and observations regarding the talk fragments, written documents, and field notes with me and suggested some additional references and sources that proved useful.

The talk fragments were selected and arranged to provide a sense of the different themes, ideas, and attitudes encountered. In focusing on the talk fragments themselves, two categories emerged (through a grounded theory approach) as especially important for situating and interpreting locker room behavior from a profeminist perspective: (a) the dynamics of competition, status attainment, and bonding among male athletes, and (b) the dynamics of defending one's masculinity through homophobic talk and talk about women as objects. A numbering system for each talk fragment (Athlete 1, 2, Sam, etc.) is used below to keep track of the different speakers. Names have been changed and the numbering system starts over for each talk fragment.

Competition, status attainment and bonding

Locker room talk is mostly about the common interests that derive from the shared identities of male student-athlete. Underlying these interactions is an ever present sense of competition, both for status and position on the team itself and between the team and its opponents. While sport provides an activity to bond around, one's position on the team is never totally secure. An injury or poor performance may raise doubts about one's ability and lead to one's replacement. Such basic insecurities do not promote positive social relationships in the locker room, and they help explain some of the harshness of the talk that the athletes directed toward each other and toward women.

For example, competition can have a subtle influence on the relationships athletes have with others on the team and cause them to be quite tentative, as illustrated by the following statements obtained from two interviews:

> One of the smaller guys on the team was my best friend ... maybe I just like having a little power over [him] ... It doesn't matter if the guy is your best friend, you've got to beat him, or else you are sitting there watching. Nobody wants to watch.

> That's one of my favorite things about the sport, I enjoy the camaraderie. [Who are your friends?] Usually it's just the starters ... you unite behind each other a lot. The other guys don't share the competition with you like the starters do.

The competition can extend beyond sport itself into other domains. It is not unusual for athletes to have as their closest friends men who are not on the team, which helps them maintain some defensive ego boundaries between themselves and the team. It also provides a relief from the constant competition, as one athlete indicates:

> [My] better friends aren't on the team. Probably because we are not always competing. With my [athlete] friends, we are always competing ... like who

gets the best girls, who gets the best grades . . . Seems like [we] are competitive about everything, and it's nice to have some friends that don't care . . . you can just relax.

Competition, emotional control, and bonding

A variety of studies have indicated that male athletes are likely to incorporate competitive motivation as part of their sport identity (e.g., Curry & Weiss, 1989). As competition and status attainment become important for the male athlete in establishing his identity, noninstrumental emotion becomes less useful, perhaps even harmful to his presentation of a conventionally gendered self (Sherrod, 1987). In addition, by defining themselves in terms of what is not feminine, men may come to view emotional displays with disdain or even fear (Herek, 1987). However, control over emotions in sport is made difficult by the passions created by an intense desire to win. One athlete described his feelings of being consumed by competition while in high school and his need to control the emotions:

My junior year, I had become so obsessed with winning the district . . . I was so overcome that I lost control a week before the tournament. I was kicking and screaming and crying on the sofa . . . since then I have never been the same. True, now I work harder than that year but now when I start to get consumed [with something] I get fearful and reevaluate its importance.

As part of learning to control emotions, the athletes have learned to avoid public expressions of emotional caring or concern for one another even as they bond, because such remarks are defined as weak or feminine. For example, the remarks of the following athlete illustrate how this type of socialization can occur through sport. This athlete's father was very determined that his son would do well in sports, so much so that he forced the boy to practice daily and became very angry with the boy's mistakes. To understand his father's behavior, the boy went to his mother:

I would come up from the cellar and be upset with myself, and I would talk to my mother and say, "Why does he yell so much?" and she would say, "He only does it because he loves you."

While the father emphasized adherence to rules and discipline, the boy had to depend on his mother to connect him to his father's love. Distancing from each other emotionally is of course dsyfunctional for the relationships among male athletes and leads to an impoverishment of relationships (Messner, 1987).

Maintaining a "safe" distance from one another also influences what is said and what is not said in front of others about topics of mutual concern, such as grades and women. Failure to address such common problems openly means that they must be dealt with indirectly or by denial. For example, the deriding of academic work by male athletes has been noted by other investigators (Adler & Adler, 1991) and is not typical of female athletes (Meyer, 1990). The reason may be that when athletes make comments that might be construed as asking for help or encouragement, their behavior is considered nonmasculine. They are thus subject to ridicule, as illustrated in the following two talk fragments:

Fragment 1

ATHLETE 1: [Spoken to the athlete who has a locker near him, but loud enough to be heard by others] What did you get on your test?

ATHLETE 2: 13 [pause], that's two D+'s this week. That's a student-athlete for you. [sighs, then laughs quietly]

ATHLETE 1: That's nothing to laugh about.

ATHLETE 2: [contritely] I mean an athlete-student, but things are looking up for me. I'm going to do better this week. How did you do on that test?

ATHLETE 1: Got a 92.

ATHLETE 3: Yeah, who did you cheat off of? [group laughter]

Fragment 2

ATHLETE 1: [To coach, shouted across room] I'm doing real bad in class.

COACH: Congratulations!

ATHLETE 1: [serious tone, but joking] Will you call the professor up and tell him to give me an A?

COACH: [Obviously sarcastically] Sure thing, would tonight at 9 be all right?

Competition and a sense of self

Considering the time-consuming nature of big-time college sports, it is not surprising that they become the central focus of athletes' lives. Approximately 30 hours a week were spent in practice, and often the athletes were too tired after a hard practice to do much else than sleep.

Fragment 3

ATHLETE 1: [collapses on bench] Shit, I'm going to bed right now, and maybe I'll make my 9 o'clock class tomorrow.

ATHLETE 2: 40 minutes straight! I thought he'd never stop the drills.

ATHLETE 1: Left you gasping for air at the end, didn't it?

ATHLETE 2: You mean gasping for energy.

Sports and competition become the greater part of the athlete's world. Through his strivings to excel, to be a part of the team and yet stand out on his own, he develops a conception of who he is. Thus the athlete's sense of self can be seen as being grounded in competition, with few alternative sources of self-gratification (Adler & Adler, 1991). The rewards for such diligence are a heightened sense of self-esteem. When one athlete was asked what he would miss most if he were to leave sports, he declared, "the competition ... the attitude I feel about being [on the team]. It makes me feel special. You're doing something that a lot of people can't do, and wish they could do." In other words, his knowledge of his "self" includes status enhancing presumptions about character building through sport.

This attitude is not atypical. For example, another man claimed, "I can always tell a [refers to athletes in same sport he plays]. They give off cues – good attitude, they are sure of themselves, bold, not insecure." This sense of specialness and status presumption cements the male bond and may temporarily cut across social class and racial differences. Later in life the experiences and good memories associated with fellowship obtained through sport may further sociability and dominance bonding (Farr, 1988). For the elite college athlete, however, this heightened self-esteem is obtained at some costs to other activities. Often academic studies and social or romantic involvements get defined as peripheral to the self and are referred to with contempt in the locker room, as illustrated in the next fragment:

Almost everyone has vacated the locker room for the showers. Sam and a few of his friends are left behind. Sam is red shirting (saving a year's eligibility by not participating on the team except for practices) and will not be traveling with the team. What he is going to do instead is the subject of several jokes once all the coaches have left the locker room:

Fragment 4

ATHLETE 1: What are you going to do, Sam, go to the game?

SAM: I can't, I sold my ticket. [laughs] I'm going to the library so I can study. [cynically] Maybe I'll take my radio so I can listen to the game. [pause] I hate my classes.

ATHLETE 1: Oh, come on, that's not the right attitude.

SAM: And I hope to get laid a few times too.

ATHLETE 1: Hey come on, that's not a nice way to talk.

SAM: How else are you supposed to talk in a locker room?

Sam's comment also leads us directly to the question of peer group influence on presentation of a gendered self. A general rule of male peer groups is that you can say and do some things with your peers that would be inappropriate almost anywhere else. For male athletes this rule translates into an injunction to be insulting and antisocial on occasion (Fine, 1987; Lyman, 1987). You are almost expected to speak sarcastically and offensively in the locker room, as Sam indicates above. Thus, hostile talk about women is blended with jokes and put-downs about classes and each other. In short, while sport leads to self-enhancement, the peer culture of male athletics also fosters antisocial talk, much of which is directed toward the athletes themselves.

Rigidities of the bond

Competition in sports, then, links men together in a status enhancing activity in which aggression is valued (Dunning, 1986). The bond between male athletes is usually felt to be a strong one, yet it is set aside rather easily. The reason for this is that the bond is rigid, with sharply defined boundaries. For example, when speaking about what it is that bonds athletes to their sport and other athletes, a coach remarks,

> They know they are staying in shape, they are part of something. Some of them stay with it because they don't want to be known as quitters. There's no in-between. You're a [team member or not a team member]. The worst guy on the team is still well thought of if he's out there every day going through it. There's no sympathy in that room. No sympathy if you quit. You might die but you're not going to quit.

This rigid definition of who is or is not a team member reflects Gilligan's (1982) concept of a rights/rules moral system for males, which emphasizes individuality, instrumental relations, achievement, and control. In short the male athlete is either on the team or not. There is no grey area: It is clearly a black or white situation. If one follows the "rules," then he has the "right" to participate in bonding. If one does not follow the rules (i.e., quits), he ceases to exist in a bonding capacity. However, as Coakley (1990) has observed, following the rules to their extremes can lead to "positive" deviance, including a refusal to quit in spite of injury. Athlete 1 below endured a number of small and severe injuries, but throughout his ordeal refused to consider leaving the team.

Fragment 5
ATHLETE 1: My shin still hurts, can't get it to stop.
ATHLETE 2: Well, that's it then—time to quit.
ATHLETE 1: Not me, I'm not a quitter.
ATHLETE 2: Oh, come on, I can see through that. You'll quit if you have to.
ATHLETE 1: No way.

Even though injured, an athlete is still a member of the team if he attends practice, even if only to watch the others work out. However, his bond with the others suffers if he cannot participate fully in the sport. Sympathy is felt for such athletes, in that their fate is recognized and understood. As one athlete empathized during an interview, "I feel for the guys who are hurt who are usually starters . . . [They] feel lonely about it, feel like they want to be back out there, feel like they want to prove something."

Perhaps what these athletes need to prove is that they are still a part of the activity around which the bonds are centered. As Sherrod (1987) suggests, the meanings associated with friendship for men are grounded in activities, giving them a reason to bond. Past success or status as a team member is not enough to fully sustain the bond; bonding requires constant maintenance. With boundaries so rigid, the athletes must constantly establish and reestablish their status as members involved in the bond by the only way they know how: through competition.

Rigid definitions of performance requirements in sport combine to form an either/or situation for the athlete and his ability to bond with teammates. If he stays within these boundaries, he is accepted and the bond remains intact. If he fails, he is rejected and the bond is severed. One athlete sums up this position with the following comments: "You lose a lot of respect for guys like that. Seems like anybody who's quit, they just get pushed aside. Like [name deleted], when he used to be [on the team] he hung around with us, and now that he's not, he ain't around anymore." Thus an athlete may find his relations severed with someone he has known for half his life, through participation in sport in junior high and high school, simply because the other person has left the team.

Talk about women

Competitive pressures and insecurities surrounding the male bond influence talk about women. As discussed above, competition provides an activity bond to other men that is rewarding, even though the atmosphere of competition surrounding big-time sports generates anxiety and other strong emotions that the athletes seek to control or channel. Competition for positions or status on the team also curtails or conditions friendships, and peer group culture is compatible with antisocial talk and behavior, some of which is directed at the athletes themselves.

The fraternal bond is threatened by inadequate role performance, quitting the team, or not living up to the demands of masculinity. Consequently, fear of weakening the fraternal bond greatly affects how athletes "do gender" in the locker room and influences the comments they make about women. In this regard, locker room talk may again be characterized both by what is said and what is not said. Conversations that affirm a traditional masculine identity dominate, and these include talk about women as objects, homophobic talk, and talk that is very aggressive and hostile toward women – essentially talk that promotes rape culture.

Woman as person, woman as object

Two additional distinctions now need to be made in categorizing locker room talk about women. One category concerns women as real people, persons with whom the athletes have ongoing social relationships. This category of locker room talk is seldom about sexual acquisition; most often it is about personal concerns athletes might wish to share with their best friend on the team. Because the athletes do not want their comments to be overheard by others who might react with ridicule, this type of talk usually occurs in hushed tones, as described in the following fragment. Talk about women as objects, on the other hand, often refers to sexual conquests. This type of talk is not hushed. Its purpose seems mainly to enhance the athletes' image of themselves to others as practicing heterosexuals.

> *Fragment 6*
> ATHLETE 1 TO 2:   I've got to talk to you about [whispers name]. They go over to an empty corner of the locker room and whisper. They continue to whisper until the coaches arrive. The athletes at the other end of the locker room make comments:

ATHLETE 3: Yeah, tells us what she's got.

ATHLETE 4: Boy, you're in trouble now.

ASSISTANT COACH: You'll have to leave our part of the room. This is where the real men are.

The peer culture of the locker room generally does not support much talk about women as persons. Norms of masculinity discourage talking seriously about social relations, so these types of conversations are infrequent (Fine, 1987; Sabo & Panepinto, 1990). Inevitably, personal revelations will quickly be followed by male athletic posturing, jokes, and put-downs, as in the talk fragment above. While the jokes may be amusing, they do little to enhance personal growth and instead make a real sharing of intimacies quite difficult. The ridicule that follows these interactions also serves to establish the boundaries of gender appropriate behavior. This ridicule tells the athlete that he is getting too close to femaleness, because he is taking relatedness seriously. 'Real men' do not do that. Perhaps just taking the view of women as persons is enough to evoke suspicion in the locker room.

To avoid this suspicion, the athlete may choose to present his attitude toward women in a different way, one that enhances his identity as a "real man." The resulting women-as-objects stories are told with braggadocio or in a teasing manner; they are stage performances usually requiring an audience of more than one, and may be told to no one in particular:

Fragment 7
I was taking a shower with my girlfriend when her parents came home. I never got dressed so fast in my life.

These types of stories elicit knowing smiles or guffaws from the audience, and it is difficult to tell whether or not they are true. In any event the actual truth of such a story is probably less important than the function it serves in buttressing the athlete's claim as a practicing heterosexual.

Fragment 8
ATHLETE 1: How was your Thanksgiving?

ATHLETE 2: Fine, went home.

ATHLETE 1: I bet you spent the time hitting high schools!

ATHLETE 2: Naw, only had to go back to [one place] to find out who was available.

Women's identities as people are of no consequence in these displays. The fact that women are viewed as objects is also evident in the tendency of men to dissect woman's bodies into parts, which are then discussed separately from the whole person. Athlctc 1 in Fragment 9 below is describing a part of a woman's body as if it existed separately from the woman, as if it was in the training room and the woman was not:

> *Fragment 9*
> ATHLETE 1: I just saw the biggest set of Ta-Tas in the training room!
> ATHLETE 2: How big were they?
> ATHLETE 1: Bigger than my mouth.

This perspective toward women highlights the fact that the use of women's bodies is more important than knowing them as people. Perhaps this attitude is also based in the athlete's focus on maintaining control, whether physically through athletic performance or mentally through strict adherence to rules and discipline. Since the male athlete's ideas about control center around physical strength and mental discipline, they stand in sharp contrast to ideas about females, who are generally thought of as physically weak and emotional. Following the implications of these ideas a bit further, women as persons are emotional and cannot be easily controlled; women as objects, however, have no volition and can be more easily controlled.

Doing gender through homophobic talk

From Herek's (1987) notion that through socialization boys learn to be masculine by avoiding that which is feminine or homosexual, it follows that in the locker room an athlete may be singled out if his demeanor is identified as unmasculine in any way. The reasoning may be seen as follows: (a) "real men" are defined by what they are *not* (women and homosexuals); (b) it is useful to maintain a separation from femaleness or gayness so as not to be identified as such; (c) expression of dislike for femaleness or homosexuality demonstrates to oneself and others that one is separate from it and therefore must be masculine. For example, when an athlete's purple designer underwear is discovered, a teammate asks, "and did you get earrings for Christmas?" When he protests, this reply, directed to all of the athletes in the room is offered: "Guess I hit a ... nerve. I won't begin on the footsies today, maybe tomorrow."

This example illustrates that every aspect of the athlete's appearance runs the risk of gender assessment. That which is under suspicion of being at odds with traditional definitions of masculinity threatens the bond and will be questioned. Connell (1990, pp. 88–89) provides further graphic example of gender assessment among athletes. He describes the life of a determinedly heterosexual Australian Iron-Man competitor, whose first coital experience at 17 was both arranged and witnessed by his surf-club friends, and who felt he had to "put on a good show for the boys." Presumably, his performance allowed him and his friends to reaffirm to themselves and others that their sexual preferences remained within the boundaries of the bond.

Not only is being homosexual forbidden, but tolerance of homosexuality is theoretically off limits as well. The sanctions associated with this type of boundary maintenance manifest themselves in jokes and story telling about homosexuals.

Fragment 10

ATHLETE 1: When I was at [high school] we all lined up to watch the other guys come in. Fred pretended to be interested in one of them and said, "I like that one" [he gestures with a limp wrist].... We were all so fucking embarrassed, nobody would give him a ride home. It was the funniest thing!

ATHLETE 2: Yeah, once we all stopped in at [a local bar] and Tom got up to dance with one of the fags, actually took his hand and started to dance! Boy was the fag surprised. [group laughter]

Making fun of homosexuals by mimicking stereotyped gay gender displays brings laughter in the locker room partly because it helps distance the athletes from being categorized as gay themselves. Such hegemonic gender displays also take more aggressive forms. Perhaps male athletes are especially defensive because of the physical closeness and nudity in the locker room and the contact between males in sport itself. This latter idea is evident in the following remarks of a coach:

We do so much touching that some people think we're queer. In 37 years I've never for sure met a queer [athlete]. At [a certain college] we had a [teammate] that some of the fellows thought was queer. I said "pound on him, beat on him, see what happens." He quit after 3 days. He never approached anyone anyway.

Locker room talk promotes rape culture

Maintaining the appearance of a conventional heterosexual male identity, then, is of the utmost importance to the athlete who wants to remain bonded to his teammates. Also, as discussed previously, the perception of women as objects instead of persons encourages expressions of disdain or even hatred toward them on the part of the male athletes. Thus, the striving to do gender appropriately within the constraints of the fraternal bond involves talk that manages to put down women while also ridiculing or teasing each other, as the following fragments indicate:

Fragment 11

ASSISTANT COACH 1: [announcement] Shame to miss the big [football] game, but you have to travel this week to keep you out of trouble. Keep you from getting laid too many times this weekend. Here are the itineraries for the trip. They include a picture of Frank's girlfriend. [Picture is of an obese woman surrounded by children. Frank is one of the best athletes on the team.]

ASSISTANT COACH 2: Yeah, when she sits around the house, she really sits around the house.

ASSISTANT COACH 3: She's so ugly that her mother took her everywhere so she wouldn't have to kiss her good-bye. [group laughter]

Jibes and put-downs about one's girlfriend or lack of sexual success are typified by this exchange. Part of the idealized heterosexual male identity consists of "success" with women, and to challenge that success by poking fun at the athlete's girlfriend is an obvious way to insult him. These jibes were directed at one of the best athletes on the team, whose girlfriend was not in town. It is important to note that these insults were delivered by the assistant coaches, who are making use of their masculine identity as a common bond they share with the student-athletes. By ridiculing one of the better athletes, they are not threatening any of the more vulnerable team members and at the same time they are removing some of the social distance between themselves and the students. After receiving such an insult, the athlete has to think of a comeback to top it or lose this round of insulting. Fine (1987) also noted such escalation of insults in his study of the Little League. This attitude is recognized and understood by other athletes:

Fragment 12
You guys harass around here real good. If you knew my mother's name, you would bring her into it too.

Thus a negative view of women prevails in the locker room and serves to facilitate the bond between athletes and their coaches. At times the competition involved with these exchanges does not involve insults directed at one another. The athletes compete instead to see who can express the most negative attitudes toward women, as illustrated by the final comments from a discussion of different types of women:

Fragment 13
Let me tell you about those [names an ethnic minority] women. They look good until they are 20, then they start pushing out the pups. By the time they're 40, they weigh 400 pounds.

This negative orientation is fed by other related attitudes about women, such as those that concern women's sports, as indicated by the following remarks made by a coach: "[Our sport] has been taking a beating in lots of colleges. It's because of the emphasis on women's sports. Too bad, because [our sport] is cheaper. Could make money ..." (he continues with comments about women's sports not paying their way).

At their extreme, these attitudes promote aggression toward women and create an environment supportive for rape culture (Beneke, 1982; Sanday, 1990). A fairly mild form of this aggression is suggested in the following talk fragment, in which two athletes are talking about Jerry, an athlete who is a frequent butt of their jokes. Jerry has just left the locker room and this conversation occurs when he is out of hearing distance:

Fragment 14
ATHLETE 1: Hey Pete, did you know Jerry is a sexual dynamo?
PETE: Why do you say that?
ATHLETE 1: He said he was with two different girls in the same day and both girls were begging, and I emphasize begging, for him to stop. He said he banged each of them so hard that they begged for him to stop.
PETE: I think he's becoming retarded.
ATHLETE 1: Do you believe he said this to me?
PETE: Well, what did you do?
ATHLETE 1: I laughed in his face.
PETE: What did he do?
ATHLETE 1: Nothing, he just kept telling me about this; it was hilarious.

The preceding fragment can be seen as describing rape in that the women involved with the athlete "begged for him to stop," and in this case the athletes choose to use the story to put down Jerry and thus negate his claim to sexual dynamism. The rape reference is more obvious in the following fragment. To set the scene, the team was visited by high school athletes and their parents; the athletes were being recruited by the coaches. The mother of one recruit drew attention from a group of athletes because she was extremely attractive. This conversation occurs in the locker room just after she left with her son:

Fragment 15
ATHLETE 1: She's too young to be his mother!
ATHLETE 2: Man, I'd hurt her if I got a hold of her.
ATHLETE 3: I'd tear her up.
ATHLETE 4: I'd break her hips. [all laugh]
ATHLETE 3: Yeah, she was hot!

Thus locker room talk about women, though serving a function for the bonding of men, also promotes harmful attitudes and creates an environment supportive of sexual assault and rape. Competition among teammates, the emphasis upon women as objects, sexual conquest as enviable achievement, peer group encouragement of antisocial comments and behavior, and anxiety about proving one's heterosexuality – all of these ideas are combined in the preceding fragment to promote a selfish, hostile, and aggressive approach to sexual encounters with women.

Conclusions

Sex and aggression are familiar themes in men's talk, and it is no surprise to find them of paramount importance in the locker room. Fine's (1987) work with preadolescent Little League baseball players indicated that the conversations of 9 to 12-year-old boys reflected similar concerns. What comes through less clearly in the conversations is the fulfillment that men find in such talk. It is an affirmation of one's masculine identity to be able to hold one's own in conversations about women, to top someone else's joke, or to share a story that one's peers find interesting. In this way the athlete's identity as a man worthy of bonding with is maintained.

College athletes often speak of the rewards of team membership as being an important reason for participating in a sport, and one of the rewards is the give and take of the peer culture in the locker room. The combination of revelation and braggadocio requires a shifting interpretation between fantasy and reality, and the ready willingness to insult means that a false interpretation may subject one to ridicule.

There are no definitive studies that document the effects of participating in locker room culture. On the one hand, behavior in locker rooms is both ephemeral and situational and probably does not reflect the actual values of all the participants. From this perspective, the locker room is just a place to change clothing and to shower, and one should not make too much of what goes on there. In discussing locker room interaction with some of the athletes involved, I found that most distanced themselves from it and denied its importance to them, particularly with respect to devaluing academic work. In some cases locker room talk even served as a negative reference for athletes, who quietly went about their business and avoided involvement. However, it is important to note that no one ever publicly challenged the dominant sexism and homophobia of the locker room. Whatever oppositional thoughts there may have been were muttered quietly or remained private.

On the other hand, there is evidence that years of participating in such a culture desensitizes athletes to women's and gay rights and supports male supremacy rather than egalitarian relationships with women. For instance, Connell's (1990) life history of an Iron-Man indicated that this incredibly fit young man was unable to tolerate a "girl" who stood up for her own interests, and so had a series of girlfriends who were compliant with his needs and schedule. Moreover, Connell observes that this attitude is typical among the other male supremacists who constitute the Australian surfing subculture.

Another illustration is provided by the recent harassment of Lisa Olson in the locker room of the New England Patriots. This episode also supports the idea that locker room talk promotes aggressive antifemale behavior. The details of this case involved grown men parading nude around the seated reporter as she was conducting an interview. Some of the men "modeled themselves" before her, one "adjusted" his genitals and shook his hips in an exaggerated fashion, and one naked player stood arm's length from her and said "Here's what you want. Do you want to take a bite out of this?" – all to the accompaniment of bantering and derisive laughter (Heymann, 1990, p. 9A). No one tried to stop the humiliating activity, nor did management intervene or sincerely apologize until forced to by the NFL Commissioner. In fact, the initial reaction of the team's owner was to support the players. The owner, Victor ("I liked it so much, I bought the company" – Remington) Kiam, was heard to say, "What a classic bitch. No wonder none of the players like her." However, his concern for the sales of his women's shaving products resulted in the following damage control campaign:

> He took out full-page ads in three major U.S. newspapers to protest his inno-cence, offered testimonials from three people who denied he said anything derogatory about Olson, and blamed the Patriots front office personnel for not telling him of the Olson locker room incident sooner.
>
> (Norris, 1991, p. 23)

Finally, Sanday (1990, p. 193) concludes her study of gang rape by fraternity members by indicating that "Sexism is an unavoidable byproduct of a cultural fascination with the virile, sexually powerful hero who dominates everyone, male and female alike." If this is true, then sexism in locker rooms is best understood as part of a larger cultural pattern that supports male supremacy.

It is my view that sexist locker room talk is likely to have a cumulative negative effect on young men because it reinforces the notions of masculine privilege and hegemony, making that world view seem normal and typical. Moreover, it does so in a particularly pernicious fashion. By linking ideas about masculinity with negative attitudes toward women, locker room culture creates a no-win situation for the athlete who wishes to be masculine and who wants to have successful, loving, nurturing relationships with women: "real men" are not nurturant. Similarly, locker room talk provides no encouragement for the "real man" who seeks egalitarian relationships. As Pronger (1990) notes, the myth of masculinity prevalent in the locker room cannot be maintained in the face of equitable relations between men and women or in the acceptance of homosexuality.

Finally, by linking ideas about status attainment with male bonding and mas-culinity, locker room culture makes it more difficult for young men to realize that women also desire success and status attainment through hard work and self-discipline. In other words, through participating in sport young men are taught that discipline and effort are needed for success and that one's acceptance depends on successful performance. But since these lessons are usually learned in all-male groups, they do not generalize easily to women and may create barriers to men's acceptance of women in the workplace.

Acknowledgements

I am grateful to Laurel Richardson, Verta Taylor, Michael Messner, and two anonymous reviewers for the *Sociology of Sport Journal* who provided valuable comments on previous drafts of this manuscript. I also wish to acknowledge the assistance of Kimberly Dill, who served as the research assistant on this project.

References

Adler, P. A., & Adler, P. (1991). *Backboards & blackboards: College athletes and role engulfment.* New York: Columbia University Press.

Beneke, T. (1982). *Men on rape*. New York: St. Martin's Press.

Bryson, L. (1987). Sport and the maintenance of masculine hegemony. *Women's Studies International Forum*, **10**, 349–360.

Coakley, J. J. (1990). *Sport in society: Issues and controversies*. St. Louis: Mosby.

Connell, R. W. (1990). An Iron Man: The body and some contradictions of hegemonic masculinity. In M.A. Messner & D.F. Sabo (Eds.), *Sport, men, and the gender order* (pp. 83–95). Champaign, IL: Human Kinetics.

Curry, T. J., & Weiss, O. (1989). Sport identity and motivation for sport participation: A comparison between American college athletes and Austrian student sport club members. *Sociology of Sport Journal*, **6**, 257–268.

Dunning, E. (1986). Social bonding and violence in sport. In N. Elias & E. Dunning (Eds.), *Quest for excitement: Sport and leisure in the civilizing process* (pp. 224–244). Oxford: Basil Blackwell.

Farr, K. A. (1988). Dominance bonding through the good old boys sociability group. *Sex Roles*, **18**, 259–277.

Fine, G. A. (1987). *With the boys: Little League baseball and preadolescent culture*. Chicago: University of Chicago Press.

Gilligan, C. (1982). *In a different voice: Psychological theory and woman's development*. Cambridge, MA: Harvard University Press.

Herek, G. M. (1987). On heterosexual masculinity: Some psychical consequences of the social construction of gender and sexuality. In M. S. Kimmel (Ed.), *Changing men: New directions in research on men and masculinity* (pp. 68–82). Beverly Hills: Sage.

Heymann, P. B. (1990, Nov. 28). Report describes what happened in locker room. *USA Today*, pp. 9A, 7C.

Lyman, P. (1987). The fraternal bond as a joking relationship: A case study of the role of sexist jokes in male group bonding. In M. S. Kimmel (Ed.), *Changing men: New directions in research on men and masculinity* (pp. 148–163). Beverly Hills: Sage.

Messner, M. A. (1987). The meaning of success: The athletic experience and the development of male identity. In H. Brod (Ed.), *The making of masculinities: The new men's studies* (pp. 193–209). Boston: Allen & Unwin.

Messner, M. A. (1989). Gay athletes and the gay games: An interview with Tom Waddell. In M. S. Kimmel & M. A. Messner (Eds.), *Men's lives* (pp. 190–193). New York: Macmillian.

Messner, M. A. (1990). Men studying masculinity: Some epistemological issues in sport sociology. *Sociology of Sport Journal*, **7**, 136–153.

Meyer, B. B. (1990). From idealism to actualization: The academic performance of female college athletes. *Sociology of Sport Journal*, **7**, 44–57.

Norris, M. (1991, Feb. 2). Mr. nice guy. *T.V. Guide*, pp. 22–29.

Pronger, B. (1990). *The arena of masculinity: Sport, homosexuality, and the meaning of sex*. New York: St. Martin's Press.

Sabo, D. F., & Panepinto, J. (1990). Football ritual and the social reproduction of masculinity. In M.A. Messner & D.F. Sabo (Eds.), *Sport, men, and the gender order* (pp. 115–126). Champaign, IL: Human Kinetics.

Sanday, P. R. (1990). *Fraternity gang rapes: Sex, brotherhood, and privilege on campus*. New York University Press.

Shaw, G. (1972). *Meat on the hoof*. New York: St. Martin's Press.

Sherrod, D. (1987). The bonds of men: Problems and possibilities in close male relationships. In H. Brod (Ed.), *The making of masculinities: The new men's studies* (pp. 213–239). Boston: Allen & Unwin.

Snyder, E. E. (1972). Athletic dressing room slogans as folklore: A means of socialization. *International Review of Sport Sociology*, **7**, 89–100.

West, C., & Zimmerman, D. H. (1987). Doing gender. *Gender & Society*, **1**, 125–149.

Zurcher, L. A. (1983). Dealing with an unacceptable role: Hashers in a sorority house. In L. A. Zurcher (Ed.), *Social roles: Conformity, conflict, and creativity* (pp. 77–89). Beverly Hills: Sage.

Zurcher, L. A. (1982). The staging of emotion: A dramaturgical analysis. *Symbolic Interaction*, **5**, 1–19.

Seminar questions

Chapter 11

1   What is meant by hegemonic masculinity and subordinated masculinities?
2   Why does Connell suggest that institutions of competitive sport are particularly important for contemporary western masculinities?

Chapter 12

1   What examples does Curry use to illustrate men's talk in relation to competition, women and homophobia?
2   What are the potential effects of men's homophobic comments and the objectification of women that Curry's research reveals?

Part VI

Sexualities

Introduction

Sexuality has been central to feminist praxis from second wave radical feminism to more recent engagement with post-structuralism and queer theory. Feminism has demanded women's right to define their own sexuality and has challenged institutional heterosexuality. Work on sexuality and sport applies this understanding through an engagement with issues of lesbianism, homophobia and sexual harassment.

This part explores the manifestation of homophobia in women's sport and physical education. It provides a brief description of the origins of the 'lesbian stereotype', and overviews the changing nature of homophobia in sport. Key concepts of homophobia, heterosexism, and lesbianism are discussed. Both chapters in this section suggest strategies for resisting and challenging homophobia.

Griffin discusses the interconnected nature of homophobia and sexism in women's sport. She looks at how the creation of the 'mannish lesbian' has been used throughout the twentieth century as an effective means to control all women, and maybe particularly, those in sport. She identifies six categories of manifestations of homophobia: silence, denial, apology, promotion of a heterosexy image, attacks on lesbians and preference for male coaches. She examines some of the beliefs that underpin the staying power of the lesbian stigma in sport, and describes strategies for confronting homophobia in women's sports.

The second chapter by Clarke draws on interview data with lesbian physical education teachers about their experiences within a predominantly heterosexist education system and sporting culture. She describes the part that Section 28 of the Local Government Act 1987–88 has played in supporting a homophobic culture in schools, and how lesbian physical education teachers have had to negotiate their professional and personal lives within this climate. She provides details of the strategies which some of the teachers use in order to conceal their lesbian identity. These include strict self-censorship, avoiding personal conversations, distancing themselves from changing rooms and shower facilities and 'playing' the heterosexual.

Both chapters identify the homophobia and heterosexism experienced by lesbian women and the power and stigma of the lesbian label. Yet both chapters also show the strength of resistance in confronting and challenging these power relations.

After reading these chapters, students should:

- understand the historical construction of lesbianism and homophobia;
- recognise the impact of homophobia on women's sporting participation and practice;
- have an awareness of how some teachers experience a lesbian identity in physical education and sport;
- be able to identify strategies for challenging and resisting homophobia.

Further readings

Cahn, S. (1994) *Coming on Strong: Gender and Sexuality in Twentieth Century Women's Sport*, London: Harvard University Press.

Caudwell, J. (1999) 'Women's football in the United Kingdom: theorising gender and unpacking the butch lesbian image', *Journal of Sport and Social Issues* 23(4): 390–402.

Griffin, P. (1998) *Strong Women, Deep Closets: Lesbians and Homophobia in Sport*, Champaign: Human Kinetics.

Lenskyj, H. (1986) *Out of Bounds: Women, Sport and Sexuality*, Toronto: The Women's Press.

Sykes, H. (1996) 'Constr(i)(u)cting lesbian in physical education: feminist and post structural approaches to researching sexuality', *Quest* 48: 459–469.

13 Changing the game: Homophobia, sexism and lesbians in sport*

Pat Griffin

Throughout the history of Western culture, restrictions have been placed on women's sport participation. These restrictions are enforced through sanctions that evolved to match each successive social climate. Women caught merely observing the male athletes competing in the early Greek Olympic Games were put to death. When Baron DeCoubertin revived the Olympic tradition in 1896, women were invited as spectators but barred from participation. Even in the present-day Olympic Games, women may compete in only one third of the events.

Although the death penalty for female spectators was too extreme for the late 19th and early 20th centuries, an increasingly influential medical establishment warned white upper-class women about the debilitating physiological effects of vigorous athleticism, particularly on the reproductive system. Women were cautioned about other 'masculinizing effects' as well, such as deeper voices, facial hair, and overdeveloped arms and legs. The intent of these warnings was to temper and control women's sport participation and to keep women focused on their 'natural' and 'patriotic' roles as wives and mothers (Lenskyj, 1986).

During the 1920s and 1930s, as the predicted dire physical consequences proved untrue, strong social taboos restricting female athleticism evolved. Instead of warnings about facial hair and displaced uteruses, women in sport were intimidated by fears of losing social approval. Close female friendships, accepted and even idealized in the 19th century, became suspect when male sexologists like Freud 'discovered' female sexuality in the early 20th century (Faderman, 1981, 1991; Katz, 1976). In the 1930s, as psychology and psychiatry became respected subfields in medicine, these doctors warned of a new menace. An entire typology was created to diagnose the 'mannish lesbian,' whose depraved sexual appetite and preference for masculine dress and activity were identified as symptoms of psychological disturbance (Newton, 1989). Social commentators in the popular press warned parents about the dangers of allowing impressionable daughters to spend time in all-female environments (Faderman, 1991; Smith-Rosenberg, 1989).

* Taken from, *Quest* 44(2) (1992): 251–265.

As a result, women's colleges and sports teams were assumed to be places where mannish lesbians lurked. Women in sport and physical education especially fit the profile of women to watch out for: they were in groups without men, they were not engaged in activities thought to enhance their abilities to be good wives and mothers, and they were being physically active in sport, a male activity. Because lesbians were assumed to be masculine creatures who rejected their female identity and roles as wives and mothers, athletic women became highly suspect.

The image of the sick, masculine lesbian sexual predator and her association with athleticism persists in the late 20th century. The power of this image to control and intimidate women is as strong today as it was 60 years ago. What accounts for the staying power of a stereotype that is so extreme it should be laughable except that so many people believe it to be accurate? Whose interests are served by stigmatizing lesbians and accusing women in sport of being lesbians? Why does sport participation by women in the late 20th century continue to be so threatening to the social order? How have women in sport responded to associations with lesbians? How effective have these responses been in defusing concern about lesbians in sport?

The purpose of this article is to discuss the issue of lesbians in sport from a feminist perspective that analyzes the function of socially constructed gender roles and sexual identities in maintaining male dominance in North American society. I share the perspective taken by other sport feminists that lesbian and feminist sport participation is a threat to male domination (Bennett, Whitaker, Smith, & Sablove, 1987; Birrell & Richter, 1987; Hall, 1987; Lenskyj, 1986; Messner & Sabo, 1990). In a sexist and heterosexist society (in which heterosexuality is reified as the only normal, natural, and acceptable sexual orientation), women who defy the accepted feminine role or reject a heterosexual identity threaten to upset the imbalance of power enjoyed by white heterosexual men in a patriarchal society (Bryson, 1987). The creation of the mannish lesbian as a pathological condition by early 20th-century male medical doctors provided an effective means to control all women and neutralize challenges to the sexist status quo.

To understand the social stigma associated with lesbian participation in sport, the function of homophobia in maintaining the sexist and heterosexist status quo must be examined (Lenskyj, 1991). Greendorfer (1991) challenged the traditional definition of homophobia as an irrational fear and intolerance of lesbians and gay men. In questioning how irrational homophobia really is, Greendorfer highlighted the systematic and pervasive cultural nature of homophobia. Fear and hatred of lesbians and gay men is more than individual prejudice (Kitzinger, 1987). Homophobia is a powerful political weapon of sexism (Pharr, 1988). The lesbian label is used to define the boundaries of acceptable female behavior in a patriarchal culture: When a woman is called a lesbian, she knows she is out of bounds. Because lesbian identity carries the extreme negative social stigma created by early 20th-century sexologists, most women are loathe to be associated with it. Because women's sport has been labeled a lesbian activity, women in sport are particularly sensitive and vulnerable to the use of the lesbian label to intimidate.

How is homophobia manifested in women's sport?

Manifestations of homophobia in women's sport can be divided into six categories: (a) silence, (b) denial, (c) apology, (d) promotion of a heterosexy image, (e) attacks on lesbians, and (f) preference for male coaches. An exploration of these manifestations illuminates the pervasive nature of prejudice against lesbians in sport and the power of the lesbian stigma to control and marginalize women's sport.

Silence

Silence is the most consistent and enduring manifestation of homophobia in women's sport. From Billie Jean King's revelation of a lesbian relationship in 1981 to the publicity surrounding Penn State women's basketball coach Rene Portland's no-lesbian policy (Lederman, 1991; Longman, 1991), the professional and college sports establishment responds with silence to eruptions of public attention to lesbians in sport. Reporters who attempt to discuss lesbians in sport with sport organizations, athletic directors, coaches, and athletes are typically rebuffed (Lipsyte, 1991), and women in sport wait, hoping the scrutiny will disappear as quickly as possible. Women live in fear that whatever meager gains we have made in sport are always one lesbian scandal away from being wiped out.

Even without the provocation of public scrutiny or threat of scandal, silent avoidance is the strategy of choice. Organizers of coaches' or athletic administrators' conferences rarely schedule programs on homophobia in sport, and when they do, it is always a controversial decision made with fear and concern about the consequences of public dialogue (Krebs, 1984; Lenskyj, 1990). Lesbians in sport are treated like nasty secrets that must be kept locked tightly in the closet. Lesbians, of course, are expected to maintain deep cover at all times. Not surprisingly, most lesbians in sport choose to remain hidden rather than face potential public condemnation. Friends of lesbians protect this secret from outsiders, and the unspoken pact of silence is maintained and passed on to each new generation of women in sport.

Silence has provided some protection. Keeping the closet door locked is an understandable strategy when women in sport are trying to gain social approval in a sexist society and there is no sense that change is possible. Maintaining silence is a survival strategy in a society hostile to women in general and lesbians in particular. How effectively silence enhances sport opportunities for women or defuses homophobia, however, is open to serious question.

Denial

If forced to break silence, many coaches, athletic directors, and athletes resort to denial. High school athletes and their parents often ask college coaches if there are lesbians in their programs. In response, many coaches deny that there are lesbians in sport, at least among athletes or coaches at *their* schools (Fields, 1983). These denials only serve to intensify curiosity and determination to find out who and where these mysterious women are. The closet, it turns out, is made of glass: People know lesbians are in sport despite these denials.

In some cases, parents and athletes who suspect that a respected and loved coach is a lesbian either deny or overlook her sexual identity because they cannot make sense of the apparent contradiction: a lesbian who is competent, loved, and respected. In other instances, a respected lesbian coach is seen as an exception because she does not fit the unflattering lesbian stereotype most people accept as accurate. The end result in any case is to deny the presence of lesbians in sport.

Apology

The third manifestation of homophobia in sport is apology (Felshin, 1974). In an attempt to compensate for an unsavory reputation, women in sport try to promote a feminine image and focus public attention on those who meet white heterosexual standards of beauty. Women in sport have a tradition of assuring ourselves and others that sport participation is consistent with traditional notions of femininity and that women are not masculinized by sport experiences (Gornick, 1971; Hicks, 1979; Locke & Jensen, 1970). To this end, athletes are encouraged, or required in some cases, to engage in the protective camouflage of feminine drag. Professional athletes and college teams are told to wear dresses or attend seminars to learn how to apply makeup, style hair, and select clothes ('Image Lady,' 1987). Athletes are encouraged to be seen with boyfriends and reminded to act like ladies when away from the gym (DePaul University's 1984 women's basketball brochure).

The Women's Sports Foundation (WSF) annual dinner, attended by many well-known professional and amateur female athletes, is preceded by an opportunity for the athletes to get free hairstyling and makeup applications before they sit down to eat with the male corporate sponsors, whose money supports many WSF programs. The men attending the dinner are not offered similar help with their appearance. The message is that female athletes in their natural state are not acceptable or attractive and therefore must be fixed and 'femmed up' to compensate for their athleticism.

Femininity, however, is a code word for heterosexuality. The underlying fear is not that a female athlete or coach will appear too plain or out of style, the real fear is that she will look like a dyke or, even worse, is one. This intense blend of homophobic and sexist standards of feminine attractiveness remind women in sport that to be acceptable, we must monitor our behavior and appearance at all times.

Silence, denial, and apology are defensive reactions that reflect the power of the lesbian label to intimidate women. These responses ensure that women's sport will be held hostage to the *L* word. As long as questions about lesbians in sport are met with silence, denial, and apology, women can be sent scurrying back to our places on the margins of sport, grateful for the modicum of public approval we have achieved and fearful of losing it.

New manifestations of homophobia in women's sport

In the last 10 years, three more responses have developed in reaction to the persistence of the association of sport with lesbians. These manifestations have developed at the same time that women's sport has become more visible, potentially marketable, and increasingly under the control of men and men's sport organizations. Representing an intensified effort to purge the lesbian image, these new strategies reflect a new low in mean-spirited intimidation.

Promotion of a heterosexy image

Where presenting a feminine image previously sufficed, corporate sponsors, professional women's sport organizations, some women's college teams, and individual athletes have moved beyond presenting a feminine image to adopting a more explicit display of heterosex appeal. The Ladies Professional Golf Association's 1989 promotional material featured photographs of its pro golfers posing pin-up style in swimsuits (Diaz, 1989). College sport promotional literature has employed double entendres and sexual innuendo to sell women's teams. The women's basketball promotional brochure from Northwestern State University of Louisiana included a photograph of the women's team dressed in Playboy bunny outfits. The copy crowed 'These girls can play, boy!' and invited basket-ball fans to watch games in the 'Pleasure Palace' (Solomon, 1991). Popular magazines have featured young, professional female athletes, like Monica Seles or Steffi Graf, in cleavage-revealing heterosexual glamour drag (Kiersh, 1990).

In a more muted attempt to project a heterosexual image, stories about married female athletes and coaches routinely include husbands and children in ways rarely seen when male coaches and athletes are profiled. A recent nationally televised basketball game between the women's teams from the University of Texas and the University of Tennessee featured a half-time profile of the coaches as wives and mothers. The popular press also brings us testimonials from female athletes who have had children claiming that their athletic performance has improved since becoming mothers. All of this to reassure the public, and perhaps ourselves as women in sport, that we are normal despite our athletic interests.

Attacks on lesbians in sport

Women in sport endure intense scrutiny of our collective and individual femininity and sexual identities. Innuendo, concern, and prurient curiosity about the sexual identity of female coaches and athletes come from coaches, athletic directors, sports reporters, parents of female athletes, teammates, fans, and the general public (South, Glynn, Rodack, & Capettini, 1990). This manifestation of homophobia is familiar to most people associated with women's sport. Over the last 10 to 12 years, however, concern about lesbians in sport has taken a nasty turn.

Though lesbians in sport have always felt pressure to stay closeted, coaches and athletic directors now openly prohibit lesbian coaches and athletes (Brownworth, 1991; Figel, 1986; Longman, 1991). In a style reminiscent of 1950s McCarthyism, some coaches proclaim their antilesbian policies as an introduction to their programs. Athletes thought to be lesbian are dropped from teams, find themselves benched, or are suddenly ostracized by coaches and teammates (Brownworth, 1991). Coaches impose informal quotas on the number of lesbians, or at least on the number of athletes they think look like lesbians, on their teams (Brownworth, 1991). At some schools, a new coach's heterosexual credentials are scrutinized as carefully as her professional qualifications (Fields, 1983). Coaches thought to be lesbians are fired or intimidated into resigning. These dismissals are not the result of any unethical behavior on the part of the women accused but simply because of assumptions made about their sexual identity.

Collegiate and high school female athletes endure lesbian-baiting (name-calling, taunting, and other forms of harassment) from male athletes, heterosexual teammates, opposing teams, spectators, classmates, and sometimes their own coaches (Brownworth, 1991; Fields, 1983; Spander, 1991; Thomas, 1990). Female coaches thought to be lesbians endure harassing phone calls and antilesbian graffiti slipped under their office doors. During a recent National Collegiate Athletic Association (NCAA) women's basketball championship, it was rumored that a group of male coaches went to the local lesbian bar to spy on lesbian coaches who might be there. Another rumor circulated about a list categorizing Division I women's basketball coaches by their sexual identity so that parents of prospective athletes could use this information to avoid schools where lesbians coach. Whether or not these rumors are true doesn't matter: The rumor itself is intimidating enough to remind women in sport that we are being watched and that if we step out of line, we will be punished.

Negative recruiting is perhaps the most self-serving of all the attacks on lesbians in sport. Negative recruiting occurs when college coaches or athletic department personnel reassure prospective athletes and their parents not only that there are no lesbians in this program but also that there *are* lesbians in a rival school's program (Fields, 1983). By playing on parents' and athletes' fear and ignorance, these coaches imply that young women will be safe in their programs but not at a rival school where bull dykes stalk the locker room in search of fresh young conquests.

Fears about lesbian stereotypes are fueled by a high-profile Christian presence at many national championships and coaches' conferences. The Fellowship of Christian Athletes, which regularly sponsors meal functions for coaches at these events, distributes a free antihomosexual booklet to coaches and athletes. Entitled *Emotional Dependency: A Threat to Close Friendships*, this booklet plays into all of the stereotypes of lesbians (Rentzel, 1987). A drawing of a sad young woman and an older woman on the cover hints at the dangers of close female friendships. Unencumbered by any reasonable factual knowledge about homosexuality, the booklet identifies the symptoms of emotional dependency and how this 'leads' to homosexual relationships. Finally, the path out of this 'counterfeit' intimacy through prayer and discipline is described. The booklet is published by Exodus, a fundamentalist Christian organization devoted to the 'redemption' of homosexuals from their 'disorder.'

By allowing the active participation of antigay organizations in coaches' meetings and championship events, sport governing bodies like the NCAA and the Women's Basketball Coaches' Association are taking an active role in the perpetuation of discrimination against lesbians in sport and the stigmatization of all friendships among women in sport. In this intimidating climate, all women in sport must deal with the double burden of maintaining high-profile heterosexual images and living in terror of being called lesbians.

Preference for male coaches

Many parents, athletes, and athletic administrators prefer that men coach women's teams. This preference reflects a lethal mix of sexism and homophobia. Some people believe, based on gender and lesbian stereotypes, that men are better coaches than women. Although a recent NCAA survey of female athletes (NCAA, 1991) indicated that 61% of the respondents did not have a gender preference for their coaches, respondents were concerned about the images they thought male and female coaches had among their friends and family: 65% believed that female coaches were looked upon favorably by family and friends whereas 84% believed that male coaches were looked on favorably by family and friends.

Recent studies have documented the increase in the number of men coaching women's teams (Acosta & Carpenter, 1988). At least part of this increase can be attributed to homophobia. Thorngren (1991), in a study of female coaches, asked respondents how homophobia affected them. These coaches identified hiring and job retention as problems. They cited examples where men were hired to coach women's teams specifically to change a tarnished or negative (read *lesbian*) team image. Thorngren described this as a 'cloaking' phenomenon, in which a team's lesbian image is hidden or countered by the presence of a male coach. Consistent with this perception, anecdotal reports from other female head coaches reveal that some believe it essential to hire a male assistant coach to lend a heterosexual persona to a women's team. The coaches in Thorngren's study also reported that women (married and single) leave coaching because of the pressure and stress of constantly having to deal with lesbian labels and stereotypes. Looking at the increase in the number of men coaching women's teams over the last 10 years, it is clear how male coaches have benefited from sexism and homophia in women's sport.

Suspicion, collusion, and betrayal among women in sport

The few research studies addressing homophobia or lesbians in sport, as well as informal anecdotal information, have revealed that many women have internalized sexist and homophobic values and beliefs (Blinde, 1990; Griffin, 1987; Guthrie, 1982; Morgan, 1990; Thorngren, 1990, 1991; Woods, 1990). Blinde interviewed women athletes about the pressures and stress they experienced. Many talked about the lesbian image women's sport has and the shame they felt about being female athletes because of that image. Their discomfort with the topic was illustrated by their inability to even say the word *lesbian*. Instead, they made indirect references to *it* as a problem. Athletes talked in ways that clearly indicated they had bought into the negative images of lesbians, even as they denied that there were lesbians on their teams. These athletes also subscribed to the importance of projecting a feminine image and were discomforted by female athletes who didn't look or act feminine.

Quotes selected to accompany the NCAA survey and the Blinde study illustrate the degree to which many female athletes and coaches accept both the negative stigma attached to lesbian identity and the desirability of projecting a traditionally feminine image:

> The negative image of women in intercollegiate sport scares me. I've met too many lesbians in my college career. I don't want to have that image (NCAA)

> Well, if you come and look at our team, I mean, if you saw Jane Doe, she's very pretty. If she walks down the street, everybody screams, you know, screams other things at her. But because she's on the field, it's dykes on spikes. If that isn't a stereotype, then who knows what is (Blinde, p. 12)

> Homosexual females in this profession (coaching) definitely provide models and guidance in its worst for female athletes. I'd rather see a straight male coach females than a gay woman. Homosexual coaches are killing us. (NCAA)

> I don't fit the stereotype. I mean the stereotype based around women that are very masculine and strong and athletic. I wouldn't say I'm pretty in pink, but I am feminine and I appear very feminine and I act that way. (Blinde, p. 12)

These attempts to distance oneself from the lesbian image and to embrace traditional standards of femininity set up a division among women in sport that can devastate friendships among teammates, poison coach–athlete relationships, and taint feelings about one's identity as an athlete and a woman. Some women restrict close friendships with other women to avoid the possibility that someone might think they are lesbians. Other women consciously cultivate high-profile heterosexual images by talking about their relationships with men and being seen with men as often as possible. As long as our energy is devoted to trying to fit into models of athleticism, gender, and sexuality that support a sexist and heterosexist culture, women in sport can be controlled by anyone who chooses to use our fears and insecurities against us.

Underlying beliefs that keep women in sport from challenging homophobia

The ability to understand the staying power of the lesbian stigma in sport is limited by several interconnected beliefs. An examination of these beliefs can reveal how past responses in dealing with lesbians in sport have reinforced the power of the lesbian label to intimidate and control.

A woman's sexual identity is personal

This belief is perhaps the biggest obstacle to understanding women's oppression in a patriarchal culture (Kitzinger, 1987). As long as women's sexual identity is seen as solely a private issue, how the lesbian label is used to intimidate all women and to weaken women's challenges to male-dominated institutions will never be understood. The lesbian label is a political weapon that can be used against any woman who steps out of line. Any woman who defies traditional gender roles is called a lesbian. Any woman who chooses a male-identified career is called a lesbian. Any woman who chooses not to have a sexual relationship with a man is called a lesbian. Any woman who speaks out against sexism is called a lesbian. As long as women are afraid to be called lesbians, this label is an effective tool to control all women and limit women's challenges to sexism. Although lesbians are the targets of attack in women's sport, all women in sport are vicitimized by the use of the lesbian label to intimidate and control.

When a woman's lesbian identity is assumed to be a private matter, homophobia and heterosexism are dismissed. The implication is that these matters are not appropriate topics for professional discussion. As a result, the fear, prejudice, and outright discrimination that thrive in silence are never addressed. A double standard operates, however, for lesbians and heterosexual women in sport. Although open acknowledgment of lesbians in sport is perceived as an inappropriate flaunting of personal life (what you do in the privacy of your home is none of my business), heterosexual women are encouraged to talk about their relationships with men, their children, and their roles as mothers.

Magazine articles about such heterosexual athletes as Chris Evert Mill, Florence Griffiths Joyner, Jackie Joyner Kersey, Joan Benoit, Nancy Lopez, and Mary Decker Slaney have often focused on their weddings, their husbands, or their children. Heterosexual professional athletes are routinely seen celebrating victories by hugging or kissing their husbands, but when Martina Navratilova went into the stands to hug *her* partner after winning the 1990 Wimbledon Championship, she was called a bad role model by former champion Margaret Court. Although heterosexual athletes and coaches are encouraged to display their personal lives to counteract the lesbian image in sport, lesbians are intimidated into invisibility for the same reason.

Claiming to be feminist is tantamount to claiming to be lesbian

Claiming to be feminist is far too political for many women in sport. To successfully address the sexism and heterosexism in sport, however, women must begin to understand the necessity of seeing homophobia as a political issue and claim feminism as the unifying force needed to bring about change in a patriarchal culture. Part of the reluctance to embrace the feminist label is that feminists have been called lesbians in the same way that female athletes have and for the same reason: to intimidate women and prevent them from challenging the sexist status quo. Women in sport are already intimidated by the lesbian label. For many women, living with the athlete, lesbian, and feminist labels is stigma overload.

By accepting the negative stereotypes associated with these labels, women in sport collude in our own oppression. Rather than seeking social approval as a marginal part of sport in a sexist and heterosexist society, we need to be working for social change and control over our sport destinies. The image of an unrepentant lesbian feminist athlete is a patriarchal nightmare. She is a woman who has discovered her physical and political strength and who refuses to be intimidated by labels. Unfortunately, this image scares women in sport as much as it does those who benefit from the maintenance of the sexist and heterosexist status quo.

The problem is lesbians in sport who call attention to themselves

People who believe this assume that as long as lesbians are invisible, our presence will be tolerated and women's sport will progress. The issue for these people is not that there are lesbians in sport but how visible we are. Buying into silence this way has never worked. Other than Martina Navratilova, lesbians in sport are already deeply closeted (Bull, 1991; Muscatine, 1991). This careful camouflage of lesbians has not made women's sport less suspect or less vulnerable to intimidation. Despite efforts to keep the focus on the pretty ones or the ones with husbands and children, women in sport still carry the lesbian stigma into every gym and onto every playing field.

Women in sport must begin to understand that it wouldn't matter if there were no lesbians in sport. The lesbian label would still be used to intimidate and control women's athletics. The energy expended in making lesbians invisible and projecting a happy heterosexual image keeps women in sport fighting among ourselves rather than confronting the heterosexism and sexism that our responses unintentionally serve.

Lesbians are bad role models and sexual predators

This belief buys into all the unsavory lesbian stereotypes left over from the late 19th-century medical doctors who made homosexuality pathological and the early 20th-century sexologists who made female friendships morbid. In reality, there are already numerous closeted lesbians in sport who are highly admired role models. It is the perversity of prejudice that merely knowing about the sexual identity of these admired women instantly turns them into unfit role models.

The sexual-predator stereotype is a particularly pernicious slander on lesbians in sport (South et al., 1990). There is no evidence that lesbians are sexual predators. In fact, statistics on sexual harassment, rape, sexual abuse, and other forms of violence and intimidation show that these offenses are overwhelmingly heterosexual male assaults against women and girls. If we need to be concerned about sexual offenses among coaches or athletes, a better case could be made that it is heterosexual men who should be watched carefully. Blinde (1989) reported that many female athletes, like their male counterparts, are subjected to academic, physical, social, and emotional exploitation by their coaches. When men coach women in a heterosexist and sexist culture, there is the additional potential for sexual and gender-based exploitation when the unequal gender dynamics in the larger society are played out in the coach–athlete relationship.

It is difficult to imagine anyone in women's sport, regardless of sexual identity, condoning coercive sexual relationships of any kind. Even consensual sexual relationships between coaches and athletes involve inherent power differences that make such relationships questionable and can have a negative impact on the athlete as well as on the rest of the team. This kind of behavior should be addressed regardless of the gender or sexual identity of the coaches and athletes involved instead of assuming that lesbian athletes or coaches present a greater problem than others.

Being called lesbian or being associated with lesbians is the worst thing that can happen in women's sport

As long as women in sport buy into the power of the lesbian lable to intimidate us, we will never control our sport experience. Blaming lesbians for women's sports' bad image and failure to gain more popularity divides women and keeps us fighting among ourselves. In this way, we collude in maintaining our marginal status by keeping alive the power of the lesbian label to intimidate women into silence, betrayal, and denial. This keeps our energies directed inward rather than outward at the sexism that homophobia serves. Blaming lesbians keeps all women in their place, scurrying to present an image that is acceptable in a sexist and heterosexist society. This keeps our attention diverted from asking other questions: Why are strong female athletes and coaches so threatening to a patriarchal society? Whose interests are served by trivializing and stigmatizing women in sport?

Women in sport need to redefine the problem. Instead of naming and blaming lesbians in sport as the problem, we need to focus our attention on sexism, heterosexism, and homophobia. As part of this renaming process, we need to take the sting out of the lesbian label. Women in sport must stop jumping to the back of the closet and slamming the door every time someone calls us dykes. We need to challenge the use of the lesbian label to intimidate all women in sport.

Women's sport can progress without dealing with homophobia

If progress is measured by the extent to which we, as women in sport, control our sporting destinies, take pride in our athletic identities, and tolerate diversity among ourselves, then we are no better off now than we ever have been. We have responded to questions about lesbians in sport with silence, denial, and apology. When these responses fail to divert attention away from the lesbian issue, we have promoted a heterosexy image, attacked lesbians, and hired male coaches. All of these responses call on women to accommodate, assimilate, and collude with the values of a sexist and heterosexist society. All require compromise and deception. The bargain struck is that in return for our silence and our complicity, we are allowed a small piece of the action in a sports world that has been defined by men to serve male-identified values.

We have never considered any alternatives to this cycle of silence, denial, and apology to the outside world while policing the ranks inside. We have never looked inside ourselves to understand our fear and confront it. We have never tried to analyze the political meaning of our fear. We have never stood up to the accusations and threats that keep us in our place.

What do we have to pass on to the next generation of young girls who love to run and throw and catch? What is the value of nicer uniforms, a few extra tournaments, and occasional pictures in the back of the sports section if we can't pass on a sport experience with less silence and fear?

Strategies for confronting homophobia in women's sport

What, then, are the alternatives to silence, apology, denial, promoting a heterosexy image, attacking lesbians, and hiring male coaches? How can women in sport begin confronting homophobia rather than perpetuating it? If our goal is to defuse the lesbian label and to strip it of its power to intimidate women in sport, then we must break the silence, not to condemn lesbians but to condemn those who use the lesbian label to intimidate. Our failure to speak out against homophobia signals our consent to the fear, ignorance, and discrimination that flourishes in that silence. If our goal is to create a vision of sport in which all women have an opportunity to proudly claim their athletic identity and control their athletic experience, then we must begin to build that future now.

Institutional policy

Sport governing organizations and school athletic departments need to enact explicit nondiscrimination and antiharassment policies that include sexual orientation as a protected category. This is a first step in establishing an organizational climate in which discrimination against lesbians (or gay men) is not tolerated. Most sport governing organizations have not instituted such policies and, when asked by reporters if they are planning to, avoid taking a stand (Brownworth, 1991; Longman, 1991). In addition to nondiscrimination policies, professional standards of conduct for coaches must be developed that outline behavioral expectations regardless of gender or sexual orientation. Sexual harassment policies and the procedures for filing such complaints must be made clear to coaches, athletes, and administrators. As with standards of professional conduct, these policies should apply to everyone.

Education

Everyone associated with physical education and athletics must learn more about homophobia, sexism, and heterosexism. Conferences for coaches, teachers, and administrators should include educational programs focused on understanding homophobia and developing strategies for addressing homophobia in sport.

Athletic departments must sponsor educational programs for athletes that focus not only on homophobia but on other issues of social diversity as well. Because prejudice and fear affect the quality of athletes' sport experience and their relationships with teammates and coaches, educational programs focused on these issues are appropriate for athletic department sponsorship and should be an integral part of the college athletic experience.

Visibility

One of the most effective tools in counteracting homophobia is increased lesbian and gay visibility. Stereotypes and the fear and hatred they perpetuate will lose their power as more lesbian and gay people in sport disclose their identities. Although some people will never accept diversity of sexual identity in sport or in the general population, research indicates that, for most people, contact with 'out' lesbian and gay people who embrace their sexual identities reduces prejudice (Herek, 1985).

The athletic world desperately needs more lesbian and gay coaches and athletes to step out of the closet. So far only a handful of athletes or coaches, most notably Martina Navratilova, have had the courage to publicly affirm their lesbian or gay identity (Brown, 1991; Brownworth, 1991; Bull, 1991; Burke, 1991; Muscatine, 1991). The generally accepting, if not warm, reaction of tennis fans to Martina's courage and honesty should be encouraging to the many closeted lesbian and gay people in sport. Unfortunately, the fear that keeps most lesbian and gay sportspeople in the closet is not ungrounded: Coming out as a lesbian or gay athlete or coach is a risk in a heterosexist and sexist society (Brown 1991; Brownworth 1991; Burton-Nelson, 1991; Hicks, 1979; Muscatine, 1991). The paradox is that more lesbian and gay people need to risk coming out if homosexuality is to be demystified in North American society.

Another aspect of visibility is the willingness of heterosexual athletes and coaches, as allies of lesbian and gay people, to speak out against homophobia and heterosexism. In the same way that it is important for white people to speak out against racism and for men to speak out against sexism, it is important for heterosexual people to object to antigay harassment, discrimination, and prejudice. It isn't enough to provide silent, private support for lesbian friends. To remain silent signals consent. Speaking out against homophobia is a challenge for heterosexual women in sport that requires them to understand how homophobia is used against them as well as against lesbians. Speaking out against homophobia also requires that heterosexual women confront their own discomfort with being associated with lesbians or being called lesbian because that is what will happen when they speak out: The lesbian label will be used to try and intimidate them back into silence.

Solidarity

Heterosexual and lesbian women must understand that the only way to overcome homophobia, heterosexism, and sexism in sport is to work in coalition with each other. As long as fear and blame prevent women in sport from finding common ground, we will always be controlled by people whose interests are served by our division. Our energy will be focused on social approval rather than on social change, and on keeping what little we have rather than on getting what we deserve.

Pressure tactics

Unfortunately, meaningful social change never happens without tension and resistance. Every civil and human rights struggle in the United States has required the mobilization of political pressure exerted on people with power to force them to confront injustice. Addressing sexism, heterosexism, and homophobia in women's sport will be no different. Taking a stand will mean being prepared to use the media, collect petitions, lobby officials, picket, write letters, file official complaints, and take advantage of other pressure tactics.

Conclusion

Eliminating the insidious trio of sexism, heterosexism, and homophobia in women's sport will take a sustained commitment to social justice that will challenge much of what has been accepted as natural about gender and sexuality. Addressing sexism, heterosexism, and homophobia in women's sport requires that past conceptions of gender and sexuality be recognized as social constructions that confer privilege and normalcy on particular social groups: men and heterosexuals. Other social groups (women, lesbians, and gay men) are defined as inferior or deviant and are denied access to the social resources and status conferred on heterosexual men.

Sport in the late 20th century is, perhaps, the last arena in which men can hope to differentiate themselves from women. In sport, men learn to value a traditional heterosexual masculinity that embraces male domination and denigrates women's values (Messner & Sabo, 1990). If sport is to maintain its meaning as a masculine ritual in a patriarchal society, women must be made to feel like trespassers Women's sport participation must be trivialized and controlled (Bennett *et al.*, 1987). The lesbian label, with its unsavory stigma, is an effective tool to achieve these goals.

If women in sport in the 21st century are to have a sport experience free of intimidation, fear, shame, and betrayal; then, as citizens of the 20th century, we must begin to reevaluate our beliefs, prejudices, and practices. We must begin to challenge the sexist, heterosexist, and homophobic status quo as it lives in our heads, on our teams, and in our schools. A generation of young girls; our daughters, nieces, younger sisters, and students; is depending on us.

References

Acosta, V., & Carpenter, L. (1988). Status of women in athletics: Causes and changes. *Journal of Health, Physical Education, Recreation & Dance*, **56**(6), 35–37.

Bennett, R., Whitaker, G., Smith, N., & Sablove, A. (1987). Changing the rules of the game: Reflections toward a feminist analysis of sport. *Women's Studies International Forum*, **10**(4), 369–380.

Birrell, S., & Richter, D. (1987). Is a diamond forever? Feminist transformations of sport. *Women's Studies International Forum*, **10**(4), 395–410.

Blinde, E. (1989). Unequal exchange and exploitation in college sport: The case of the female athlete. *Arena Review*, **13**(2), 110–123.

Blinde, E. (1990, March). *Pressure and stress in women's college sports: Views from Athletes.* Paper presented at the annual convention of the American Alliance for Health, Physical Education, Recreation and Dance, New Orelans.

Brown, K. (1991). Homophobia in women's sports. *Deneuve*, **1**(2), 4–6, 29.

Brownworth, V. (1991, June 4). Bigotry on the home team: Lesbians face harsh penalities in the sports world. *The Advocate: The National Gay and Lesbian Newsmagazine*, pp. 34–39.

Bryson, L. (1987). Sport and the maintenance of male hegemony. *Women's Studies International Forum*, **10**(4), 349–360.

Bull, C. (1991, December 31). The magic of Martina. *The Advocate: The National Gay and Lesbian Newsmagazine*, pp. 38–40.

Burke, G. (1991, September 18). Dodgers wanted me to get married. *USA Today*, p. 10C.

Burton-Nelson, M. (1991). *Are we winning yet?* New York: Random House.

Diaz, J. (1989, February 13). Find the golf here? *Sports Illustrated*, pp. 58–64.

Faderman, L. (1981). *Surpassing the love of men: Romantic friendship and love between women from the Renaissance to the present.* New York: Morrow.

Faderman, L. (1991). *Odd girls and twilight lovers: A history of lesbian life in twentieth-century America.* New York: Columbia University Press.

Felshin, J. (1974). The triple option . . . for women in sport. *Quest*, **21**, 36–40.

Fields, C. (1983, October 26). Allegations of lesbianism being used to intimidate, female academics say. *Chronicle of Higher Education*, pp. 1, 18–19.

Figel, B. (1986, June 16). Lesbians in the world of athletics. *Chicago Sun-Times*, p. 119.

Gornick, V. (1971, May 18). Ladies of the links. *Look*, pp. 69–76.

Greendorfer, S. (1991, April). *Analyzing homophobia: Its weapons and impacts.* Paper presented at the annual convention of the American Alliance for Health, Physical Education, Recreation and Dance, San Francisco.

Griffin, P. (1987, August). *Lesbians, homophobia, and women's sport: An exploratory analysis.* Paper presented at the annual meeting of the American Psychological Association, New York.

Guthrie, S. (1982). *Homophobia: Its impact on women in sport and physical education.* Unpublished master's thesis, California State University, Long Beach.

Hall, A. (Ed.) (1987). The gendering of sport, leisure, and physical education [Special issue]. *Women's Studies International Forum*, **10**(4).

Herek, G. (1985). Beyond 'homophobia': A social psychological perspective on attitudes toward lesbians and gay men. In J. DeCecco (Ed.), *Bashers, baiters, and bigots: Homophobia in American society* (pp. 1–22). New York: Harrington Park Press.

Hicks, B. (1979, October/November). Lesbian athletes. *Christopher Street*, pp. 42–50.

Image lady. (1987, July). *Golf Illustrated*, p. 9.

Katz, J. (1976). *Gay American History*, New York: Avon.

Kiersh, E. (1990, April). Graf's dash. *Vogue*, pp. 348–353, 420.

Kitzinger, C. (1987). *The social construction of lesbianism.* Newbury Park, CA: Sage.

Krebs, P. (1984). At the starting blocks: Women athletes' new agenda. *Off our backs*, **14**(1), 1–3.

Lederman, D. (1991, June 5). Penn State's coach's comments about lesbian athletes may be used to test university's new policy on bias. *Chronicle of Higher Education*, pp. A27–28.

Lenskyj, H. (1986). *Out of bounds: Women, sport, and sexuality.* Toronto: Women's Press.

Lenskyj, H. (1990). Combatting homophobia in sports. *Off our backs,* **20**(6), 2–3.

Lenskyj, H. (1991). Combatting homophobia in sport and physical education. *Sociology of Sport Journal,* **8**(1), 61–69.

Lipsyte, R. (1991, May 24). Gay bias moves off the sidelines. *New York Times,* p. B1.

Locke, L., & Jensen, M. (1970, Fall). Heterosexuality of women in physical education. *The Foil,* pp. 30–34.

Longman, J. (1991, March 10). Lions women's basketball coach is used to fighting and winning. *Philadelphia Inquirer,* pp. 1G, 6G.

Messner, M., & Sabo, D. (Eds.) (1990). *Sport, men, and the gender order: Critical feminist perspectives.* Champaign, IL: Human Kinetics.

Morgan, E. (1990). *Lesbianism and feminism in women's athletics: Intersection, bridge, or gap?* Unpublished manuscript, Brown University, Providence.

Muscatine, A. (1991, November/December). To tell the truth, Navratilova takes consequences. *Women's SportsPages,* pp. 8–9. (Available from Women's SportsPages, P.O. Box 151534, Chevy Chase, MD 20825)

National Collegiate Athletic Association, (1991). *NCAA study on women's intercollegiate athletics: Perceived barriers of women in intercollegiate athletic careers.* Overland Park, KS: Author.

Newton, E. (1989). The mannish lesbian: Radclyffe Hall and the new woman. In M. Duberman, M. Vicinus, & G. Chauncey (Eds.), *Hidden form history: Reclaiming the gay and lesbian past* (pp. 281–293), New York: New American Library.

Pharr, S. (1988). *Homophobia: A weapon of sexism.* Inverness, CA: Chardon Press.

Rentzel, L. (1987). *Emotional dependency: A threat to close friendships.* San Rafael, CA: Exodus International.

Smith-Rosenberg, C. (1989). Discourses of sexuality and subjectivity: The new woman, 1870–1936. In M. Duberman, M. Vicinus, & G. Chauncey (Eds.). *Hidden from history: Reclaiming the gay and lesbian past* (pp. 261–280). New York: New American Library.

Solomon, A. (1991, March 20). Passing game. *Village Voice,* p. 92.

South, J., Glynn, M., Rodack, J., & Capettini, R. (1990, July 31). Explosive gay scandal rocks women's tennis. *National Enquirer,* pp. 20–21.

Spander, D. (1991, September 1). It's a question of acceptability. *Sacramento Bee,* pp. D1, D14–15.

Thomas, R. (1990, December 12). Two women at Brooklyn College file rights complaint. *New York Times,* p. 22.

Thorngren, C. (1990, April). *Pressure and stress in women's college sport: Views from coaches.* Paper presented at the annual convention of the American Alliance for Health, Physical Education, Recreation and Dance, New Orleans.

Thorngren, C. (1991, April). *Homophobia and women coaches: Controls and constraints.* Paper presented at the annual convention of the American Alliance for Health, Physical Education, Recreation and Dance, San Francisco.

Woods, S. (1990). The contextual realities of being a lesbian physical education teacher: Living in two worlds (Doctoral dissertation, University of Massachusetts, Amherst, 1989). *Dissertation Abstracts International,* **51**(3), 788.

14 Outlaws in sport and education? Exploring the sporting and education experiences of lesbian Physical Education teachers*

Gill Clarke

> Another brick to add to the wall – the longer I live, the more people I get
> involved with, the more complicated and painful it gets. I hate lying, deceiving,
> misleading, but I'm so damn good at it, I do it to myself all the time.
>
> (Harriet, 28 February, 1995)

Introduction

Living a lesbian existence in a heterosexist and homophobic world as Harriet
reveals can be both complicated and painful. This paper illustrates the complexities of the teaching and sporting lives of lesbian physical education teachers in
secondary schools in England. In so doing, it reveals how they manage their lesbian identity in order to appear to comply with dominant discourses of hegemonic
heterosexuality and femininity.

The social and political context

Before illustrating some of these identity management strategies, it is necessary to
locate these women's lives within their social, cultural and political context since
this impacts on the way that they live their lives and how they should be understood.
The current political climate for lesbians continues to be a chilly one, although on
the surface there may appear to have been some advances for homosexuals, for
example: the lowering of the age of consent for gay men from 21 to 18 – as opposed
to a heterosexual age of consent of 16; lesbian heroines in soaps, Dyke TV and so
on. I would argue that these are but superficial changes which, in many ways, mask
the rise and power of the New Right and the pursuit of traditional family values
and the desire to return to some mythical golden age of the family. Anne Marie
Smith (1995) makes a powerful case for a recognition of the Right's evisceration of
liberal democracy. She traces the emergence of a new type of homophobia which
masquerades as a type of liberal democratic "tolerance"; this pseudo-tolerance she
argues is reserved for the "good homosexual", not the dangerous queer. This is

---

* Taken from, S. Parker (eds) (1995) *Leisure, Sport and Education*, Eastbourne: LSA Publications.

the homosexual that knows their place, that can assimilate (cf. to the discourses of racism) and return to the closet. Section 28 of the Local Government Act 1987–8 has done much to keep teachers in the "good homosexual's" closet. This legislation – passed in the Thatcher years when there was an attempt to gain political mileage by linking the left wing of the Labour party with pro-gay policies (see Miller, 1995: p. 503) – stated that:

> A local authority shall not – (a) intentionally promote homosexuality or publish material with the intention of promoting homosexuality; (b) promote the teaching in any maintained school of the acceptability of homosexuality as a pretended family relationship.
>
> (Smith, 1994: p. 183)

It is clear how this repressive legislation portrays lesbians and gays in a negative light and serves to legitimate hegemonic discourses of heterosexuality and to fuel prejudice and hatred.

Though it has been argued that Section 28 is vaguely worded and "Imprecisely drafted and dangerously open to misinterpretation, its implications are far-reaching. Already operating to encourage damaging self censorship, Section 28 strikes at the civil liberties of us all" (Colvin with Hawksley, 1989, Back cover). The impact of this legislation has been to make many teachers afraid of disclosing their (homo)sexuality for fear of reprisal and job loss – hence, as is later illustrated, the compulsion many feel to employ heterosexual passing strategies so as to conceal their real identity. Despite the fact that Section 28 may be only of symbolic power as "The scope of . . . (its) provision has yet to be interpreted by the courts . . ." (OutRage and Stonewall, 1994: p. 33), it continues to impact negatively on the identities of lesbians and gay men.

Nevertheless, in the conservative and politically sensitive world of education it should be noted that these fears appear to have some grounding. Take for instance the case of Hackney headteacher Jane Brown who turned down the offer of subsidised tickets to her school to see Romeo and Juliet at the Royal Opera House for a number of reasons, including her much-quoted reason that the ballet was "entirely about heterosexual love". Despite the fact that there were other very good educational and economic reasons put forward for not taking up the offer, the press got hold of the story. When they:

> . . . discovered where – and with whom – Jane Brown lived. Her defence was detonated. The woman was dyke. That explained everything!
>
> (Campbell, 1995: p. 18)

The *Sun* referred to her as a "hatchet faced dyke" and announced the story on their front page with the heading "ROMEO, ROMEO, where art thou homo?". Such was the witch hunt of the tabloid press that Jane Brown was forced to leave her home and go into hiding in order to escape – not only this media persecution, but also from the death threats that she had received. After nearly eighteen months the investigation was concluded, and Jane Brown was exonerated. It is perhaps no wonder that many lesbian and gay teachers feel threatened by what happened to Jane Brown. This then is the backdrop against which these lesbian lives must be interpreted: this is their lived reality.

Lesbian teachers

The stories and scenarios that are portrayed in this paper emanate from research into the lives and lifestyles of lesbian physical education teachers. The vignettes are derived from questionnaires and in-depth interviews/conversations with 14 white able bodied women. The questionnaire was distributed in the summer of 1995 and focused on their sporting pastimes, and the interviews were conducted between 1993 and 1995, focusing on: lesbian identity, activities of teaching, interaction with pupils and relationships with colleagues. These areas for discussion grew out of my experiences as a "good" lesbian teacher [that is, I think I passed fairly convincingly as (pseudo) heterosexual] and out of my reading of Pat Griffin's (1992) and Madiha Didi Khayatt's (1992) research into the lives of lesbian teachers in North America. The women in this research are aged between 23 and 47 and their teaching experience varies from just over one year to over 25 years. At the time of the interviews they taught in a variety of schools from: mixed Comprehensives, Roman Catholic, Church of England to Independent schools. In order to preserve their anonymity, all the women were from the outset given a pseudonym; they were also informed in writing of the procedures that would be adopted to maintain this confidentiality and how the information was to be subsequently used. This was essential as none of the teachers were totally out about their sexuality in school. I make no claim here that these women are necessarily representative, indeed I believe there is no generic lesbian women, nor am I arguing for any false universalism of their experiences.

Covering our tracks: strategies for concealing a lesbian identity

The following section illustrates some of the strategies employed by these teachers to conceal their identities from both colleagues and pupils. None of the teachers were totally open about their sexuality at school; for most, their lesbianism was carefully concealed from all but a very small number of "trusted" colleagues. Indeed for some of the teachers, their true identity was known to no-one within the school. All the teachers feared that should their lesbianism be revealed then they would be likely to be viewed differently and in a non-positive light by both colleagues and pupils, and that ultimately they would lose their job. To avoid this, they constructed sometimes quite complex boundaries around themselves in order to deflect any suspicion about their sexuality. This meant that they had to be constantly vigilant about the public persona they presented: hence they felt the need to "live two lives" and to endure the stress and strain that this entailed. These two lives were the school life and the home life – the former required that a pseudo-heterosexual lifestyle was portrayed, and the latter for some of the women also required at times the adoption of similar strategies. Fay, for instance, commented on the need to "cover her tracks" and the resultant stress that this created. She described how:

> When you go into school you know it is different... I find it very difficult to cope with because you know my sexuality to me is a very important part of me and then all of a sudden you are faced with here we go, back again to the conservatism of it all and we are covering our tracks by not saying who we live with, who we go out with, what we do at weekends. You are only choosing to tell the bits that aren't going to tell a story.

We can see from this statement how "covering our tracks" involves a number of different ploys, including strict self censorship. This self censorship necessitates a monitoring of what is said about the self and others and a holding back of significant parts of the self. Thus certain situations within school become the possible sites for exposure and unwelcome attention. Hence these social situations might be avoided for fear of revealing too much about the self – thus for example conversations in staffrooms were often consciously avoided when heterosexual staff were talking about their families, children and so on. Gabby described how she distanced herself:

> ... by not talking about my personal life (and by) ... not getting involved in anything socially at school where staff would be taking their partners. .... So in that kind of way I look after myself.

"Looking after myself" also involved the ability to deflect questions about boyfriends from both colleagues and pupils. This heterosexual presumption was dealt with in a variety of ways; for example, Harriet revealed how she would sometimes lie, even though she didn't like to do so because in a way she felt that this was a "putting down" of herself. She also described how she was asked directly by some of the lower school pupils if she had a boyfriend and how she felt so much on the spot that she told them that she did have a boyfriend. Another strategy that she sometimes felt compelled to employ in order to deflect suspicion was to "be overtly flirtatious with young male staff". Others also described how their "street cred" was improved if they were seen by staff or pupils in the company of men. For some, the invention of mythical men did much to preserve their pseudo straight identity. It is clear from these brief scenarios how compulsory heterosexuality remains the order of the day in the public world of the school, and how not only must tracks be covered but in some instances false trails laid.

The staffroom, as previously mentioned, provided another site for possible exposure when conversation on occasions turned to issues to do with homosexuality. Many of the women believed that if they were to join in such conversations then their identity was further at risk due to attention being directed at them. Thus not only did such conversations have to be side-stepped but also homophobic jokes had to be endured and openly tolerated, for few felt able to challenge such abuse.

One of the women, Ivy, felt safer to do so because she was the Equal Opportunities officer for the school so this enabled her to challenge under the "Equal Opps. umbrella". For most, this keeping silent was both frustrating and upsetting. Harriet commented on how she had an argument with somebody at work who knew about her sexuality:

> ... it does get me down when they start sort of gay bashing in the staffroom or in the pub and she says, "well why don't you say something?" – but I can't, you know, you've got a family, you've got a husband and two boys to hide behind almost but I haven't so I can't. I really feel that I can't.

For two of the teachers who had been married it was possible to hide behind their married title. Maud admitted that she had kept the title "Mrs", albeit probably subconsciously, to hide behind, though most of her colleagues knew that she was divorced. Ivy felt that the "Mrs" title was a buffer for women, and as a lesbian it was an even greater buffer. It was a title that she said she wouldn't lose at all, although she conceded that on her own private letters to businesses she always referred to herself as Ms. She posited the view that:

> If you are a Miss there are certain connotations drawn, either spinster or the lesbian/feminist type, but if you are a Mrs you have conformed to the rules of society, and if you haven't got a husband then it doesn't really matter. You actually have been at one point ... you are accepted.

Caroline, although single, also commented on how she too thought that the title "Mrs" provided a cover from the gaining of a lesbian reputation that she felt "Miss" in physical education often suffer from.

Teachers at risk?

The very physicality of the subject and the centrality of the body to physical education pose particular threats to lesbian teachers. In a homophobic and heterosexist world where New Right discourses about the family hold hegemonic power over other lifestyles, to be a lesbian teacher working with children is to be seen by some as Lucy remarked as "a paedophile or pervert". All the teachers feared such accusations and went to great lengths to avoid getting "too close" to pupils. Fay remarked that:

> ... it is different for PE teachers because you are involved with the physical side of things. It has got to be worse, it's not like you teach English or you teach Humanities or whatever, you teach PE. There has got to be a different stigma attached to it and everything else that goes with it, and I think this is what people are afraid of. ... I think it frightens a lot of people that if that was found out, they would think you were molesting or you were some kind of

pervert. You know the only reason you are teaching PE is because you can see all the kids undress.

All the teachers who had to supervise pupils changing and showering after lessons were extremely anxious about how their presence in these situations would be perceived. Thus they sought to distance themselves from these locations and in particular the showering ritual by remaining in their offices or in the background. For one of the teachers – Gabby – These fears became a nightmare when she was called into the Headmaster's office after a pupil had complained:

> ...that I watched her in the showers ...I'd always thought that when I was in that situation, which was my worst nightmare, that I would go bright red because I am rubbish at lying, and I didn't. I just felt the colour drain from my face and I looked absolutely shell-shocked ...and the Head said "we're only asking about this because we want to disprove it". They (the parents) complained to the Local Authority, ...I was absolutely gobsmacked and they (the Head and Deputy) said they were meeting with the parents in a weeks time about it and there were other things they were meeting about as well, and the parents didn't bring it up. The Head wrote a letter to the Authority saying that as far as he was concerned any claim made about me was completely unsubstantiated and the school was prepared to support me to the last ...but that was a very nervous moment.

Other "nervous moments" were sometimes caused when the teachers had to support female pupils, Ethel described how she felt vulnerable when she had to support pupils in gymnastics or help pupils to hold a racket or a piece of athletics equipment correctly, generally any situation where she came into physical contact with a pupil caused her anxiety.

As regards the vulnerability of heterosexual teachers in these situations, it was acknowledged that they too could be at risk, but it was generally felt that it was not to the same extent as lesbian teachers. Kay remarked "no teacher likes to be faced by this situation – but the problem is very sensitive and a threatening one to a lesbian teacher". For as Annie commented:

> [It's] Not to the same degree because any false allegation would be less believed if the governors found they had a lovely boyfriend but if the governors found you had a lovely girlfriend I'm sure it would open some homophobic doors.

The homophobia and heterosexism that these teachers experience in their daily lives was – as we shall see for some of them – not dissimilar to that found on the sports field. Ivy observed, "Why should sport be any different to anything else?!"

Sporting a difference

Most of the women were involved in some form of sport outside of their working lives; they participated in a wide variety of activities, some played just for fun, whilst others competed at various levels from club to international. Their motivations for involvement varied slightly, but almost all said that they participated because they enjoyed being active and the social contacts that they made whilst engaged in sport or physical activity.

Some of the women were out about their sexuality to some extent in their chosen activities, (only two were totally out) and in these cases it was only to a small group of people. Kay, for instance, revealed that her sexuality was not admitted to all, but that she had disclosed it to a small few. Those who were not out gave a variety of reasons including:

> My sexuality has never been something that I wished to discuss with my team mates.
>
> (Ethel)

> I would find it job threatening to be out to anyone on an ad hoc basis. My status as a PE teacher would soon come out. I fear for my job if it got back to school.
>
> (Ivy)

Within the activity or the club that they were involved with most believed or knew that there were other lesbians also involved. For the vast majority of the women this had not been a factor when they were choosing their activity. Kay commented: "I became involved in this sport long before I knew the meaning of sex!!"; and Ethel said: "I play my sport for the sake of the sport, not because it will introduce me to other lesbians. Hockey was important in my life *before* I became aware of my sexuality".

Like their lives in school, compulsory heterosexuality also impacted upon their sporting experiences in that most of the women still feel the need to conceal their lesbianism, through conforming with dominant discourses of hegemonic heterosexuality and femininity.

Harassment and anti-lesbian comments

This research has provided considerable evidence of anti-lesbianism within sporting activities; many of the women had had direct experience of verbal abuse. For example, Barbara recalled how a supporter had shouted "lezz" when she'd scored a goal, Caroline described how other netballers had mocked the county coach who was a closet lesbian. Deb remembered how she had umpired a mixed tournament and drunken men had made anti-lesbian comments along the side line. Ethel recounted how on several occasions when training or preparing for a game when people had walked past the pitch they had made comments such as: "look at the lezzies, there must be a few lesbians out there". However, she also said that she had never experienced anti-lesbian comments on the pitch. Harriet revealed that the captain of the men's hockey 1st. XI said that the majority of the men's teams didn't attend social functions because of the high proportion of lesbians in the women's teams who attend the social functions and are not discrete in displaying their sexual preferences. Lucy recollected that homophobic comments had been made when she was younger, but nothing had been directed at her personally, but she remembered being made aware that lesbian activity was not approved of by her peers at that time. Naomi had also heard homophobic comments, though again they had not been directed at her personally; at social events she had been aware of negative comments and jokes being made about lesbians.

What do these scenarios tell us about lesbian women in sport? I would contend that although these are the experiences of only a small group of lesbian women, they are not necessarily atypical. The sporting arena has historically been the prerogative of men and the training ground for the development of hegemonic masculinity, it was an arena women entered at their peril. For the Victorians, a woman was a frail character, whose femininity and reproductive role was to be protected; sport was seen as potentially deleterious to her health and child bearing functions. This legacy has been a long time passing – as the history, for instance, of the Modern Olympics bears witness: women continue to compete in lesser numbers and in fewer events than men. For those women who dared to enter this male domain, their performances were subject to the scrutiny of the male gaze, which in many cases trivialised their performances and also suggested that where they performed well then they must be some sort of freak of nature, indeed possibly a man! What I am trying to do in this historical snapshot is to illustrate that women in sport have not had an easy time, and this has been particularly so in those sports that have traditionally not been seen as stereotypically feminine. Thus whilst it may be socially acceptable for a woman to be a successful gymnast/ice skater, it may be less acceptable for her to be a successful rugby/football player. The former carry an acceptable (heterosexual) feminine image whereas the latter do not: that is, the image is not feminine, therefore it must be masculine, and hence women engaged in such sport must be masculine and therefore lesbian. As Messner and Sabo (1994, p: 110) comment:

> Lesbianism is thus recast by heterosexist culture as an emulation of masculinity. In contrast male homosexuality is considered a negation of masculinity.

It is perhaps no wonder that many women would feel uncomfortable playing in sports in an environment where their sexuality is likely to be questioned. Therefore, it is not surprising that many women within sport seek to distance themselves from any possible suggestion of or association with lesbianism through the making and confirming of their femininity and their (hetero)sexuality overtly visible. Thus we often see evidence of what has been described as hyperfemininity (see Felshin, 1974 and Lenskyj, 1994) – that is, the wearing of make-up, jewellery and other adornments to proclaim a so called "normal sexuality". This is not confined to the way that the athlete presents herself; it is also replicated by the way that the media portray women in sport; very often it is not their performance that is commented on but the fact that they are a mother, wife and so on. Reference is also frequently made to what they are wearing and to their appearance. As sport is now big global business, the media moguls and sponsors are increasingly all powerful in determining what constitutes an acceptable, marketable image and product. It is clear from the female sporting superstars who have made it that heterosexuality and hyper-femininity are the order of the day. When Martina Navratilova came out as a lesbian she lost millions of dollars in sponsorship and endorsements. By this stage of her career arguably she could afford to, but how many others could? Most then choose to keep their lesbianism carefully hidden for fear of their careers being destroyed.

The world of sport as has been illustrated in this paper is not a welcoming one for lesbian participants. What is also disturbing is that within this sporting world we have largely failed to discuss and address the difficulties that lesbian women face within this arena. There have been some notable exceptions to this claim (see for example the work of Griffin and Lenskyj). But whilst we remain silent, I would argue that we continue to perpetuate and reinforce myths, stereotypes and fears about lesbian women in sport. Through these practices we deny them the right to participate openly and fully in sport. This right to participate should be a basic human right and not something reserved for the heterosexual majority.

It is apparent that at all levels of sporting participation, lesbian women feel the need to remain invisible if they are to survive. This has also meant that when they were aware of homophobia or anti-lesbianism they did not always feel able to challenge it. Harriet indicated how she was:

> ... resigned to being put down, and am not always surprised or deeply hurt by it when I hear it now – if you hear it often enough you begin to believe it and accept it.

It's OK as long as we don't draw attention to ourselves

This final section seeks to analyse the lesbian sporting experience. What is evident from the vignettes portrayed here is that sport for these lesbian women seems in general to be another arena where they still cannot be themselves. Or perhaps they can be, but at a price – so as long as they don't draw attention to themselves, and know how to be a "good" lesbian in sport they are "tolerated". But as we saw previously, the moment they reveal their sexual preferences they are not welcome. Harriet described how "a member of our women's first eleven wished to transfer to the other major club in [the town] but they have discussed her transfer and have denied it, on the grounds of her sexuality". Clearly, this woman would seem not to be a "good" lesbian. Others too have found their sporting progress curtailed when they failed to display heterosexual credentials. As Lenskyj (1992, p: 28) states:

> ... there is ample evidence that the women in sport and physical education who are lesbian have to survive in a most inhospitable climate because of the

pervasiveness of homophobia, which often takes the form of discriminatory hiring and firing practices.

Indeed, Gert Hekma's (1994) research into the discrimination that Dutch lesbian women and gay men experience in organized sports in Holland was pointedly titled: "*Als ze maar niet provoceren*" ('If they don't provoke'), a comment that was made by two sports clubs who said that they had no problems with gays and lesbians as long as they did not provoke. This would appear to mean that it's OK to be a lesbian or gay man in sport, but don't make it obvious, don't do anything that will give your (homo) sexuality away. It is clear from this small scale research that these women make every attempt not to make their sexuality obvious; for instance, only two of the 14 women interviewed were totally out in their sports; the remainder were either out to only a small group of friends or to none of their team mates. For those who were out to a certain extent, this was not necessarily a positive experience. Harriet revealed that her team mates at hockey found out more by mistake than design and that she wished they didn't know. She made it clear that she has no intention of telling those with whom she plays other sports. Further to this, she commented:

> When some of my married, heterosexual friends at hockey found out about me, they quickly changed their way of relating to me and talking to me. I felt let down obviously and, but I also felt "dirty", like I really was doing something wrong.

This feeling "dirty" reveals still further the power of the lesbian label to intimidate women regardless of their sexuality. However, it should not be thought from these examples that lesbian women are powerless – rather, by virtue of living a lesbian existence they are challenging compulsory heterosexuality. And for some women, the lesbian label is a powerful source of unity and pride. Lenskyj (1994, p: 365) reveals how:

> Lesbian sporting leagues organized on feminist principles provide one example of the potential for sport to be reclaimed . . . (and) to include the celebration of female physicality and sexuality.

Though Lenskyj is referring to sporting leagues in North America, it should be noted that there are a number of lesbian sporting teams, for example: "Dynamo dykes" (volleyball), "South London Studs" (football), 'The London Amazons" (softball) and "London Hiking Dykes" (a lesbian walking group). What is indicated, though, by Harriet is that lesbianism is something to be feared and avoided in case of contamination. Again in the light of such views, it is no wonder that many women may fear even entry to the sports field. I find these fears and phobias in some ways paradoxical, and in many ways confusing. If LeVay's (see Vines, 1992: p. 2) claims are accepted – that homosexuals are *born*, not *made*, since sexual orientation is established in the womb as a result of the action of hormones on the brain of the developing foetus – how then can anybody become "contaminated"? They've either already "got" it (that is lesbianism), or they haven't! What I also find interesting, yet troubling, is the scrutiny with which we interrogate lesbianism, yet in the main heterosexuality has largely escaped this. (A notable exception is the work by Sue Wilkinson and Celia Kitzinger.) In reflecting on Harriet's words, what is perhaps most disturbing is how she is led to feel, that it is something wrong and dirty that she is engaged in. In the light of her feelings and the actions of homophobic heterosexuals it is no wonder that the suicide rate for young lesbians and gays is higher than for other groups. Are lesbian women really so dangerous? Certainly there seems to be a belief that we are, that we threaten the cultural norms of heterosexuality and patriarchal power, and that other women need to be protected from us. Where, might we ask, is the evidence that supports these views?

The impact of the events described above is abundantly clear; to be out is a personal risk, the costs of which many understandably are not prepared to face. These concerns, I would argue, serve to keep most sporting lesbians invisible and silent and preserves the privileging of the hegemonic heterosexual order.

It should be noted, though, that this is not the case for all lesbian women: some have found the space within sport to occupy the ground that they wish – as Yvonne Zipter (1988) clearly describes in "Diamonds are a dyke's best friend". And more latterly this is illustrated by Susan Fox Rogers (1994) in "Sportsdykes: stories from on and off the field". Both books celebrate and explore the lesbian sports experience. Zipter writes about dykes in softball, ". . . assessing its [softball] place and function in our community nation-wide, why most of us love it (but some of us don't), its origins, foibles, and pitfalls" (Zipter, 1988: p. 14). Rogers, on the other hand, has edited a rather eclectic collection of articles which range "From serious investigative journalism to works of lyrical fiction, the life of the 'girl jock' is vividly revealed . . ." (Rogers, 1994: Front book jacket).

Before closing, I want to return to some of the findings of Hekma's (1994) research since they are relevant to my own findings. Perhaps most telling was his conclusion that discrimination against lesbians and gay men occurs regularly in organized sport. Though the women interviewed for this research had not all been subject to homophobic comments and so on, the majority thought that it was common in sport. Hekma found that the most common form of abuse took that of verbal comments. This too was evidenced by the women in this study, and took the form of remarks made by spectators or passers by. Some of the women were also subjected to anti-lesbian comments from their team-mates rather than the opposition. By way of contrast, some of the women had had no experience of homophobia – but I would suggest that this may be associated with the fact that they are so deeply hidden in the closet, that nobody knows they are there.

In conclusion, it can be seen how – for this group of women – a lesbian existence is perceived as somewhat perilous. The conservative world of education and in particular physical education makes for a precarious existence for lesbian teachers. To survive requires that these teachers are able to at least "pass" as heterosexual and to cover their lesbian tracks. The sporting world for these women is not so dissimilar to that of education. The homophobia and heterosexism faced by these women has led them in the main to continue to conceal their lesbian identity. What is manifest from both these worlds is the power of the lesbian label to force women into narrowly prescribed gender roles; it is a power that few feel able to confront and challenge. Until we remove the power and stigma of the lesbian label, little is likely to change.

References

Clarke, G. (1994) "The research that dare not speak its name: doing controversial research in physical education", Conference Proceedings of the 10th Commonwealth & Scientific Congress University of Victoria, Canada.

Cahn, S. K. (1994) *Coming on strong: Gender and sexuality in twentieth-century women's sport*. New York: The Free Press.

Campbell, B. (1995) "Hard lessons", *Diva* (Aug/Sept): pp. 18–21.

Colvin, M. with Hawksley, J. (1989) *Section 28: A practical guide to the law and its implications*. London: National Council for Civil Liberties.

Dewar, A. (1993) "Would all the generic women in sport please stand up? Challenges facing feminist sport sociology", *Quest*, Vol. 45, No. 2: pp. 211–229.

Epstein, D. (ed) (1994) *Challenging lesbian and gay inequalities in education*. Buckingham: Open University Press.

Felshin, J. (1974) "The dialectic of woman and sport", in E. W. Gerber, J. Felshin, P. Berlin and W. Wyrick (eds) *The American woman in sport*. USA: Addison-Wesley Publishing Company, pp. 179–279.

Gerber, E. W., Felshin, J., Berlin, P. and Wyrick, W. (1974) *The American woman in sport*. USA: Addison-Wesley Publishing Company.

Griffin, P. (1991) "Identity management strategies among lesbian and gay educators", *Qualitative Studies in Education*, Vol. 4, No. 3: pp. 189–202.

Griffin, P. (1992) "From hiding out to coming out: Empowering lesbian and gay educators", in K. M. Harbeck (ed) *Coming out of the classroom closet: gay and lesbian students, teachers, and curricula*. New York: Harrington Park Press.

Hargreaves, J. (1994) *Sporting females: Critical issues in the history and sociology of women's sports*. London: Routledge.

Hekma, G. (1994) *Als ze maar niet provoceren. Discriminatie van homoseksuele mannen en lesbische vrouwen in de georganiseerde sport*. Amsterdam: Het Spinhuis.

Khayatt, M. D. (1992) *Lesbian teachers: An invisible presence*. USA: State University of New York Press.

Kitzinger, C. (1987) *The social construction of lesbianism*. London: Sage Publications.

Kolnes, L. (1995) "Heterosexuality as an organizing principle in women's sport" *International Review for Sociology of Sport*, Vol. 30, No. 1: pp. 61–77.

Lather, P. (1986) "Issues of validity in openly ideological research: between a rock and a hard place", *Interchange*, Vol. 17, No. 4, Winter: pp. 63–84.

Lenskyj, H. (1990) "Combating homophobia in sports", *Off Our Backs*, Vol. 20, No. 6: pp. 2–3.

Lenskyj, H. (1992) "Unsafe at home base: Women's experiences of sexual harassment in university sport and physical education", *Women in Sport and Physical Activity Journal*, Vol. 1, No. 1, Spring: pp. 19–33.

Lenskyj, H. (1994) "Sexuality and femininity in sport contexts: Issues and alternatives", *Journal of Sport and Social Issues*, November, Vol. 18, No. 4: pp. 357–376.

Messner, M. and Sabo, D. (1994) *Sex, violence and power in sports: rethinking masculinity.* USA: The Crossing Press.

Miller, N. (1995) *Out of the past: Gay and lesbian history from 1869 to the present.* UK: Vintage.

Moses, A. E. (1978) *Identity management in lesbian women.* USA: Praeger Publishers.

Pharr, S. (1988) *Homophobia: A weapon of sexism.* USA: Chardon Press.

Rich, A. (1980) "Compulsory heterosexuality and lesbian existence", *Signs: Journal of Women in Culture and Society*, Vol. 5, No. 4: pp. 631–660.

Rogers, S. F. (ed) (1994) *Sportsdykes: Stories from on and off the field.* New York: St Martin's Press.

Sears, J. T. (1992) "Researching the other/searching for self: Qualitative research on (homo)sexuality in education", *Theory into Practice*, Vol. XXX1, No. 2, Spring: pp. 147–156.

Smith, A. M. (1994) *New Right discourse on race and sexuality: Britain, 1968–1990.* Great Britain: Cambridge University Press.

Smith, A. M. (1995) "Resisting the 'New Homophobia' and the Right's evisceration of liberal democracy", paper presented at the New Sexual Agendas Conference, Middlesex University, 14–15 July.

Smith, D. E. (1987) *The everyday world as problematic: A feminist sociology.* Milton Keynes: Open University Press.

Sparkes, A. C. (ed) (1992) *Research in physical education and sport: Exploring alternative visions.* London: Falmer Press.

Sparkes, A. C. (1994) "Self, silence and invisibility as a beginning teacher: A life history of lesbian experience", *British Journal of Sociology of Education*, Vol. 15, No. 1: pp. 93–118.

Squirrell, G. (1989a) "In passing...teachers and sexual orientation", in S. Acker (ed) *Teachers, gender and careers.* London: Falmer Press.

Squirrell, G. (1989b) "Teachers and issues of sexual orientation", *Gender and Education*, Vol. 1, No. 1: pp. 17–34.

Troiden, R. R. (1988) *Gay and lesbian identity: A sociological analysis.* New York: General Hall, Inc.

Vallee, M., Redwood, H. and Evenden, M. (1992) *Out, proud and militant: The fight for lesbian and gay rights and the fight for socialism.* London: Militant.

Vines, G. (1992) "Obscure origins of desire", *New Scientist*, 28 November, No. 3: pp. 2–8.

Wilkinson, S. and Kitzinger, C. (eds) (1993) *Heterosexuality: A feminism and psychology reader.* London: Sage Publications Ltd.

Woods, S. (1992) "Describing the experience of lesbian physical educators: A phenomenological study", in A. Sparkes (ed) *Research in physical education and sport: Exploring alternative visions.* London: Falmer Press.

Zipter, Y. (1988) *Diamonds are a dyke's best friend.* USA: Firebrand Books.

Seminar questions

Chapter 13

1 How is homophobia manifested in women's sport? How applicable are Griffin's categories for understanding homophobia in men's sports?
2 What are the underlying beliefs that Griffin argues keep women in sport from challenging homophobia? To what extent are these beliefs still evident in today's sport and are there others that you can identify?

Chapter 14

1 How do physical education teachers experience a lesbian identity in school and sport?
2 To what extent do the resistances of lesbian teachers evident in Clark's research challenge homophobia?

Part VII
Bodies, physicality and power

Introduction

Although the body is central to sport and physical education, it has received little critical analysis within the sociology of sport. An emphasis on the body has tended to be the prerogative of the scientific disciplines such as biomechanics, physiology and so on. As Ann Hall (1996: 50) argues:

> Female bodies have always been central to feminism, but sporting bodies have not . . . feminists have rarely paid attention to female *sporting* bodies, nor have they always seen the relevance of physicality, or empowerment through physical activity, to feminist politics.

The chapters in this part provide examples of recent engagement with these debates by sports scholars. Each of the chapter focuses in some way on the body, physicality and power, although each takes quite a different approach. The first two chapters, one by David Whitson and the other by Camilla Obel, consider the complexities of gendered physicalities and empowerment but do so from different theoretical positions. The final chapter by Celia Brackenridge deals with a very sensitive and under researched area – gender relations, violence and abuse in sport. This is also centrally about power, but again, she approaches this from a different position to the first two authors concentrating specifically on the abuse of power.

David Whitson discusses the relationship between physical and social power and how gendered subjectivities are embodied in individuals. Sport is seen to have been important, both historically and in contemporary practice, in naturalizing gendered bodily practices. Males and females have learnt to live their bodies in active and passive ways. Whitson explores the potential of 'new' sports to offer empowering experiences to both women and men. He also discusses the potential of these 'new' sports to 'do' femininity and masculinity in a variety of different ways. In these circumstances power can be embodied in ways not necessarily tied to domination or gender.

Camilla Obel concentrates on bodybuilding for women which is seen by many as rejecting the traditional categories of gender. She discusses conceptualizations of gender, sexuality and the body, arguing for the collapse of gender as an unambiguous principle. She suggests that there are different readings of the identity work involved in the sport of bodybuilding. One reading suggests that female bodybuilders present a challenge to a traditional understanding of gender. However, this is critiqued through an alternative reading drawing on ethnographic empirical research with bodybuilders. This work suggests that there are far more contradictions and ambiguities experienced by women in the sport. There is the potential for women bodybuilders to both collude with and resist dominant notions of gender. Indeed, Obel argues that it is men's bodybuilding that has the greater potential to challenge traditional understandings of gender. This paper draws on post-structural analysis and Foucault's work on power and resistance and provides an interesting contrast to Whitson's analysis of power and empowerment.

In the final chapter, Celia Brackenridge explores the definition of violence, arguing for one that includes the violence done to women in and out of sport. She highlights the fact that often violence in sport is defined as violence 'on the field' primarily between athletes. She presents evidence to suggest that violence to women in sport is far more prevalent than has been currently thought. She links the rise in violence against women to their challenge to men's dominance both in and out of sport. In doing this she argues that men's violence needs to be seen not solely as an individual issue but as systemic to the institution of sport. The chapter provides important definitional and theoretical discussion and also provides some strategies for challenging violence against women in sport.

After reading these three chapters, students should:

- be able to assess the role of sport in the embodiment of gender and power relations;
- understand the relationship between physicality, empowerment and sport;
- appreciate the relationship between gender, violence and abuse in sport.

Reference

Hall, M. A. (1996) *Feminism and Sporting Bodies*, Champaign: Human Kinetics.

Further readings

Brackenridge, C. (2001) *Spoilsports: Understanding and Preventing Sexual Exploitation in Sport*, London: Routledge.
Gilroy, S. (1989) 'The embody-ment of power: gender and physical activity', *Leisure Studies* 8(2): 163–72.
McDermott, L. (1996) 'Towards a feminist understanding of physicality within the context of women's physically active and sporting lives', *Sociology of Sport Journal* 13: 12–30.
Messner, M. (1988) 'Sport and male domination: the female athlete as contested ideological terrain', *Sociology of Sport Journal* 5(3): 197–211.
Wright, J. and Dewar, A. (1997) 'On pleasure and pain: women speak out about physical activity', in G. Clarke and B. Humberstone (eds) *Researching Women and Sport*, London: Macmillan.

15 The embodiment of gender: Discipline, domination, and empowerment*

David Whitson

> I watch my daughter. From morning to night her body is her home. She lives in it and with it. When she runs around the kitchen she uses all of her self. She feels pleasure and expresses it without hesitation . . . I sometimes feel she is more a model for me than I am for her.
>
> (A mother, quoted in Boston Women's Health Book Collective, 1976, p. 40)

> When we were kids there was release in playing, the sweetness of being able to move and control your body. . . . I felt released because I could move around anybody. I was free.
>
> (Hockey player Eric Nesterenko, quoted in Terkel, 1974, p. 383)

These reflections remind us of the virtual identity of body and self that we mostly take for granted in childhood. We ran, climbed, skipped, and threw, and in these activities of early childhood we discovered things about ourselves and what we could do in the world. We took an innocent pleasure in learning to move and control our bodies and experienced a growing sense of self that was intimately connected with our experience of our bodies, both what we could do and what we looked like. Yet the two recollections, one by a woman and the other by a man, serve not only to remind us how most of us become alienated from our bodies in adult life: they also point out how differently the childhoods of girls and boys come to be structured: by discourses of femininity and masculinity and by gendered practices of play that teach us to inhabit and experience our bodies in profoundly different ways.

In the first section of this chapter, I briefly review these practices and the ideologies that have justified and, for many, naturalized such differences. The encouragement and the institutional support that boys generally enjoy in any efforts they make to develop physical strength and sports skills are contrasted with the historical construction of femininity as prettiness and vulnerability and the ambiguous messages that are encountered even today by strong, active females. In the second section, I examine the challenges associated with the broadening of opportunities

* Taken and abridged from, S. Birrell and C. Cole (eds) (1994) *Women, Sport and Culture*, Champaign: Human Kinetics.

for physical empowerment and ask what "the embodiment of power" (Gilroy, 1989) means – for women and for men. Feminist and masculinist discourses of sport pose the question of how and indeed whether empowerment, the confident sense of self that comes from being skilled in the use of one's body, can be detached from an emphasis on force and domination, which are integral to the body contact sports that comprise the "major games" of male popular culture. Finally, I examine the current popularity of newer sports and other forms of noncombative physical practice, activities ranging from dance and yoga to aerobics and various forms of exercise in natural environments (Bloch, 1987). For although critics are correct to point out the commodification, the sexual imagery, and the individualism that are all present in the marketing of fitness (and the social marketing of wellness), it is still important to distinguish between marketing discourse and the expanded experiences of their bodies and themselves that many women and men – of different ages, body types, and social locations – enjoy and explore in these new activities.

Embody-ing power: masculinizing and feminizing practices

> Through football I learned . . . how my body could be used as a force, how my shoulders, back, hips and legs, driven in a straight line against a ball carrier's thighs, could topple him easily. As early as nine years old, I began to know my own body in ways that only an athlete or a dancer know[s] it.
>
> (Oriard, 1982, pp. 18–19)

This recollection by Michael Oriard, a former Kansas City Chief-turned-English professor, illustrates what Bob Connell's essay "Men's Bodies" (1983) has articulated in a more general way, namely how childhood sports teach boys to use their bodies in skilled, forceful ways while providing them a detailed and accurate knowledge of their physical capacities and limits. Boys learn how to develop force (through leverage, coordination, and follow-through) and to transmit this power through their limbs or through extensions, like ball bats and golf clubs. In contrast, Iris Young (1980) has suggested that the movement patterns of most girls are characterized by their partiality, by their failure to take the sort of advantage described by Oriard of the torque that is generated when the entire body is mobilized into a throw, a swing, or a tackle:

> Not only is there a typical style of throwing like a girl, but there is a more or less typical style of running like a girl, climbing like a girl, swinging like a girl, hitting like a girl. They have in common, first, that the whole body is not put into fluid and directed motion, but rather, in swinging and hitting, for example, the motion is concentrated in one body part; and second, that the woman's motion tends not to reach, extend, lean, stretch, and follow through in the direction of her intention. (p. 143)

What is meant by the phrase "throwing like a girl," Young suggests, is precisely the tendency of many girls not to put their whole bodies into the motion, unlike most boys. Likewise, she suggests that when women who are not used to physical work are faced with physical tasks, they frequently fail to use the strength they do have to the fullest. She argues, drawing on de Beauvoir and Merleau-Ponty, that these partial and half-hearted movement patterns derive ultimately from discourses and practices that have encouraged the woman to experience her body as an object-for-others, whereas men have learned to experience themselves in the active, forceful ways depicted so clearly by Oriard: to act, instead of being looked at and acted upon. She begins from Merleau-Ponty's proposition that human subjectivity, one's fundamental experience of one's self in the world and one's basic orientation to the external world (to other people as well as the object world) is rooted in the lived body and in how one learns to live one's body. For Merleau-Ponty (1962; also see Young, 1980, pp. 140–142, 146–148), *I*, *I can*, and *I cannot* are all embodied experiences, and one's sense of oneself as an active person is developed precisely through experiences of mastering one's body and realizing one's intentions in physical movements in and through space.

Young proceeds to argue, following de Beauvoir (1974), that women historically have been taught to embody what she calls "inhibited intentionality," in which feminine body comportment, feminine movement patterns, and tentative uses of space all say *I cannot* in the very act of trying. In such movement habits, says de Beauvoir, women embody the contradictory nature of their experience in patriarchal societies, a contradiction between their phenomenal experience of themselves as active subjects and their social construction as objects for others. "Femininity" here is not an essence that all women have naturally or even that some have more than others. It is, rather, a product of discourses, practices, and social relations that construct the situation of women in patriarchal societies in ways that typically disable women in relation to men. [...]

The "typical" effect of the feminizing practices that construct the female body as object is to inhibit women, at the same time that many kinds of masculinizing practice teach boys to live their bodies and to experience themselves in active and powerful ways. Sport is only one of these masculinizing practices; but Connell (1983) underlines how important sport is in the formative experience of boys, and histories of "athleticism" in the English boys' schools remind us that organized sports has always been about teaching boys to be power-full people, through experiences of physical discipline and accomplishment. In contrast, Sheila Fletcher (1984) has described how, while the private schools of the Victorian period were using sport to teach "manliness" to upper-class boys, upper-class girls were learning to be "ladies." [...]

Here it may be worth referring to what developmental psychologist John Shotter (1984) has called a "political economy of developmental opportunities" in which some people, because of their social location, have access to more and different kinds of developmental opportunities than others. Despite the economic language, moreover, Shotter is clear that it is not simply a matter of class or financial resources. The development of "personal powers" and the sense of self that results involves other people (initially parents, and subsequently "society") recognizing what is skilled and valuable in what a child does spontaneously, and holding it up for the child's own recognition and pleasure. Out of the latter, Shotter suggests, comes a boy's or girl's desire to develop natural capacities into personal skills; but within the prevailing discourses and engendering practices outlined above, boys and girls are typically (though not always) offered very different kinds of developmental opportunities, and often with the "best" of intentions.

Indeed, even when parental support is strong and training and competitive opportunities are available, Young (1979) suggests that as the girl athlete enters adolescence, "she increasingly experiences the sexually objectifying gaze of men" (p. 47). She cannot help becoming aware that many people, women as well as men, are assessing her more in terms of her looks than her accomplishments, and that according to the standards that are applied to her and to other women, "femininity" and power are incompatible. Blye Frank's work (1991) reminds us that adolescent males are also very much concerned with their looks and with projecting a masculine body image; but the important difference is that "masculinity" equates precisely with appearing physically powerful and strong (see Connell, 1983). This is why teenaged boys often spend much time in body-building and martial arts. However for girls, it becomes difficult not to want to develop "habits of feminine body comportment – walking like a girl, standing and sitting like a girl, gesturing like a girl, and so on" (Young, 1980, p. 153), habits in which women learn to embody male expectations of weakness and incompetence. There are differences, of course, in the extent to which individual women want to, or indeed can, conform their body comportment to these male-defined images of femininity. However, the discourse of masculine strength and feminine weakness continues to constitute both expectations and self-expectations, and Young's point is that to whatever extent a female is induced into pursuing a feminine persona, the more likely it is that she will feel ambivalent about her own strength and will actually *become* more inhibited and tentative in her movement patterns. "To the degree that we choose ourselves as body-objects, we find it difficult to become enthusiastic body subjects and frequently do not desire to challenge our bodies in sport" (1979: 48). [. . .]

Discourses of masculine strength and feminine weakness and the ways of being that they help to normalize have also been addressed by Catherine MacKinnon (1987), who suggests (like Young) that male ideas and images of femininity have been all too commonly embodied in women who become weak and vulnerable. In her view, it is not only that many women choose to live their bodies as vulnerable and in doing so actually render themselves more vulnerable, although this is clearly important. It is also that received ideas that say women cannot do certain physical things or push themselves in certain kinds of physical training without harm (e.g., in weight training or distance running) become self-fulfilling prophecies. "The notion that women cannot do certain things, cannot break certain records, cannot engage in certain physical pursuits has been part of preventing women from doing these things" (p. 119). This is one way of understanding the power of ideology. Today, of course, women have dramatically surpassed what were once thought their limits both in strength and aerobic events; and the women who have done so have created new kinds of role models, new images of possibility that open the imagination to still greater levels of accomplishment. MacKinnon goes on to suggest, though, that the women who have embodied these accomplishments have done more than challenge received notions about women in sport. In living their bodies as skilled and forceful subjects rather than as objects of the male gaze, and especially in embodying power themselves, they challenge one of the fundamental sources of male power, the ideological equation of physical power itself with masculinity.

Empowerment: domination and pleasure

MacKinnon goes on to propose, however, that the meanings and practices that have been naturalized in much of men's sport may not be what women want and that a closer analysis of just what is empowering and pleasurable in physical activity is called for. [. . .]

A useful starting point is MacKinnon's observation that from a feminist's perspective, sport for men looks like a form of combat. Even in sports that don't involve direct personal confrontation, many men are intensely competitive; and in those that do involve body contact, sport is a narrative of pitting oneself against an individual on the other side and prevailing in the contest, dominating and subduing one's opponent. MacKinnon's comments here articulate directly with the observations of Bob Connell and his colleagues on why football (and other body contact sports) remain important masculinizing practices in Western societies. [. . .]

What we are talking about here is a traditionally masculine way of embodying power, where this means the capacity to achieve one's ends, by force if necessary, even in the face of opposition. At its best, this model of masculinity defines the "real" man as a person of few words, but with a powerful sense of his own abilities and the toughness and physical competence to handle any difficulties or challenges. Male sports heroes were long presented as embodiments of this kind of masculinity, as indeed movies and television have often presented an older kind of Western hero or police detective.[1] [. . .]

Here we can begin to see why combative sports and aggressive players have been celebrated among many men. The devaluation of physical work and the ascendancy of intellectual and interpersonal skills in a service and information society, the entry of women into many workplaces and the increasing economic independence of women, and the gradual willingness of the law to intervene in domestic violence: All of these contribute to the erosion of a world in which a powerful male body could translate into social power. Body contact sports are now one of the few areas of public life in which force and intimidation are still allowed to triumph, where men who love to hit can still enjoy doing so, and others will celebrate their toughness and their willingness to pay the price. [. . .]

However, MacKinnon proposes, and of course she is not alone, that there is more to sport than combat and more to empowerment through physical activity than learning to hit effectively. If the constitutive structure and the basic story line of our major team games involve the domination of opponents and the control of territory through force. MacKinnon suggests that this vision of sport leaves out "some rather major elements" of the sporting experience. These include the pleasures that can be taken in smooth, powerful motion (e.g., in running or swimming), in coordination and fine motor skills, in self-awareness and self-possession, in partnership and shared fun (see Nelson, 1991). These are experiences that both men and women can and do enjoy, MacKinnon suggests, *but they are seldom allowed to be the central purpose of male sport* (1987, p. 121).

Empowerment, in this alternative discourse, means learning how to move in coordinated and increasingly skillful ways and often how to coordinate your own movements with those of others. It may mean learning how to use equipment, like sticks, racquets, or skis, as extensions of your limbs, for example, in the well-struck golf or tennis shot or in the grace and skill or different skiing disciplines. It may even mean learning how to generate force and power and to take advantage of these in competitive games. But the pleasure and the sense of accomplishment are in the skills and a competent, confident sense of self, rather than in the domination of others. It may even be that for many women today, a confident, less vulnerable sense of self will require knowledge of how to mobilize force in self-defense. However, even this typically involves learning how to use one's body skillfully, just as it has for generations of smaller men. This is consistent with Young's discussion, and it is not inconsistent with a definition of "personal power" as self-discovery: that is, experimenting with, then developing through skilled practice, and finally enjoying what we can do with our bodies. This is what developmental psychologists describe as mastery play, or the development of natural talents into skills that we can draw on, when necessary, and can enjoy the feel of, whenever we care to use them (see Shotter, 1973, 1974).

Certainly there are numerous accounts in which men describe enjoying particular moments of embodied skill in this way. Eric Nesterenko, in the comments quoted at the beginning of this chapter, goes on to talk about the pleasure he still took in skating, in leaning into turns, defying the forces of gravity with his sense of balance and his "feel" for just what his body would allow him to do (Terkel, 1974). Some of my favorite accounts, because they recall experiences I can recognize, are by runners who describe the pleasures of fast runs and the pleasures of partnership with other runners, who are part of these experiences and help to make them happen.[2] However, accounts of "flow" and the enjoyment of skill and of moments of embodied self-awareness are familiar in the literature of skiing, tennis, surfing, swimming, and, doubtless, of other sports as well. Even in games like football and hockey, former athletes Oriard and Nesterenko convey clearly the pleasures they took in the skills of these games. However, their overall experiences amply confirm MacKinnon's point that this kind of enjoyment was seldom allowed to be their central purpose. Normally, it was subordinated to the quest for victory, a quest that demanded an emphasis on force – and a capacity to absorb force and play through pain – in pursuit of domination. Both the personal and academic literatures underline that this becomes the norm in organized male sport at an early age.

There are also many accounts in which women talk of the pleasures they have found in skilled physical performance and of the sense of empowerment they have experienced when doing so. [. . .] Just as is true for men, there is a range of activities in which women speak of enjoying the feelings that come with skill, of taking pleasure in movement and in partnership, and of discovering new aspects of themselves in the process. Indeed, it may be worth remarking that for some women, martial arts have provided a context in which they have learned to express force and to overcome the sort of partial, tentative movement habits described by Young (1980). At the other end of a kind of continuum, dance and yoga have also become popular disciplines through which women (and increasing numbers of men) have learned to know their bodies and to live them as subjects. Here, the emphasis is very much on skill and on body awareness, on the integration of mind and body as self. Charlotte Bloch (1987) suggests that over the last 10 to 15 years, some remarkable shifts have occurred in what she calls the dominant body culture, not the least of which has been the emergence of new sports and the popularity of modes of exercise (some old and some new) that are alternatives to sport's traditional emphasis on competition and combat. Included here might be yoga and other body-consciousness movements (e.g., t'ai chi, Feldenkrais), aerobics and other dance-based activities, bodybuilding, skateboarding and rollerskating, jogging and cycling, as well as a variety of wilderness and outdoor activities. None of these are combative activities, and those that do lend themselves to competitions can also be enjoyed either as modes of wilderness travel or simply as pastimes in which to enjoy the athleticism of one's body, of playing with one's own skills. All of these activities are enjoyed by women and men, both separately and together. [. . .]

However, Birrell and Richter's discussion (1987) of feminist transformations of baseball – not a body contact sport but in other ways very representative of the culture of male team sports – can make some points about competition and skill, and about their place in the pleasures of sport and physical activity. First, Birrell and Richter show that a competitive game can be played without the single-minded quest for victory that has spoiled many women's experiences of the "male model" of sport. They do not devalue competition; indeed, several women speak of enjoying the challenge of a good game, adding that the experience is less satisfying when players fool around or do not try. Still, they argue that the emphasis on winning that informs the standard discourse of male sport produces a variety of practices that override any sense of good opponents as partners, who bring out the best in us, and that often blot out the pleasure that might be felt when using physical skills. Here, their analysis recalls MacKinnon's point that the quest for domination produces a structure of meanings and practices (Birrell and Richter call it "a rationalistic structure") in which partnership and having fun together, and pleasure in skill and self-exploration, are not allowed to be the primary purposes of sporting participation (see Nelson, 1991).

Secondly, there is the issue of skill. Feminist baseball teams as a matter of principle do not wish to reproduce the hierarchies based on skill that characterize the social relations of so many teams. They want to actively support less skilled and less experienced players, that is, to provide a supportive atmosphere in which less confident women can make mistakes while learning to feel more at home with their bodies and with the game. Nonetheless, few would go so far as to agree with the antiskill slogan worn by one team: "Every error helps another woman." Women who are skilled (or who want to develop skills) are bothered by this objection to skill. They have been empowered themselves precisely through learning *how* to do confidently and well things that they were once very tentative and apprehensive about, and their skills are an important source of the pleasures they derive from the game. Yet we need to recognize that the hegemony of the rational, instrumental approach to skill development has often meant authoritarian regimens of practice in which "no pain, no gain" has been the guiding principle. These take the fun, and the sense of playing with out bodies, out of sport. In reaction against this, it is not surprising that the notion that "anything worth doing is worth doing badly" (George Bernard Shaw) has some appeal. Yet on balance, the observations of Birrell and Richter (1987) as well as those of other women who have written about empowerment through physical activity (Gilroy, 1989; Theberge, 1987), suggest that the development of some level of skill and fitness are necessary foundations of any enjoyment of physical practices. [. . .]

Finally, there is the issue of physical domination. The experiences of self-discipline and strength and endurance celebrated by Lenskyj and Granskog, and likewise the pride in skill and in competitive achievement described by Birrell and Richter, do not necessarily (and typically do not) involve the physical domination of another person. Neither does the language of empowerment they use have much in common with that often used by football or hockey people when talking about the demands of their sports and what power means in the context of a body contact sport.[3] This raises the issue of the relative place of experiences of skill and strength (both physical and mental, and the integration of the two), as opposed to the physical domination of other people, in experiences of personal power or empowerment, as well as the further issue of how and why the capacity to dominate has been ideologically constructed as a cornerstone of masculine identities. Beyond this, we must reflect on the relative balance of force and skill in the constitutive structure of sports and physical activities, especially those that are widely followed in our popular culture. We must ask ourselves about the cultural meanings of these textual activities and their effect on discourses of masculinity and femininity and on the gender order. Adapting Connell's observation (1983) that the demands of every sport involve a particular balance between force and skill, it can be suggested that the more it is force that is decisive, the more a physically dominating, hegemonic masculinity can be publicly celebrated and the more likely that the culture of sport will be part of the defense of the existing gender order.

These are not new issues, of course, but they remain important ones, if only because changes in sport and body culture are uneven and difficult to read with confidence. One of the points made both by Birrell and Richter and by MacKinnon is that for feminist reconstructions of sporting and physical practices to have a broader effect (among women and men alike), popular understandings of empowerment and the powerful body must move away from the traditional masculine preoccupation with force and domination toward a new emphasis on personal experiences of skill and of pleasure in motion, and on sharing these experiences with others. On the surface, the burgeoning interest in noncontact sports and other modes of competitive exercise suggest that this is actually happening. Women are much better represented in all of these activities than they are in the traditional team games (in some, of course, they are the major participants); and if Young (1979) is correct, the physical empowerment of more women and the entry into sport of greater numbers of women will steadily contribute toward breaking down the masculinist connotations of sport itself. Yet there remains the distinct possibility that the traditional male games will retain their privileged place in popular culture, and some critics have raised important questions about aspects of the growth of aerobics and other "participation sports."

New activities, old problems?

To bring the questions into focus, consider the running and jogging boom that has swept the western world over the last quarter century. It may be hard to realize today that it all began in the 1960s in the desire of disparate and anonymous individuals to enjoy a simple form of exercise without the disciplines and expectations of organized tract and field. People honked and pointed at runners on the streets; there were a few "fun runs"; *Runners World* was a mimeographed cult sheet in California. But in less than 10 years, the running industry boomed, replete with fashions, mass marathons, and its own "promotional culture"[4] proliferation of multinational sport shoe companies now bring out more "new and improved" models each year than does the automotive industry, as well as accessories that were undreamt of 10 years ago. Individuals market themselves as experts in everything from the psychology of running to race organization services. *Runners World* is now only one of several glossy vehicles for the promotion of all these wares, as well as the personalities and training programs of a new elite. It's important to recognize that running has been reconstructed so that it attracts many participants who were and are excluded from high-performance tract athletics, especially men and women who are past their physical prime. Yet as Mike Featherstone (1982) has noted, the growth of running cannot be disconnected from the growth of a promotional discourse in which a series of themes – progress, mobility, self-realization, and self-control – were articulated with running in ways that spoke to the circumstances and aspirations of many young adults formed in the affluent postwar years.

Not dissimilar phenomena can be observed in the growth of activities like mountain biking, triathlon, and cross-country skiing. In teams of skill and endurance, all of these "lifestyle sports" offer pleasure in physicality. They typically also offer real pleasure in their environment and often in companionship and in subcultural solidarity. They offer these pleasures to women and men alike, and importantly to older women and men who can pursue "personal bests" at their own pace, with the personal meanings and the sense of empowerment depicted in Granskog's (1991) discussion of the Ironman Triathlon:

> The Ironman represents for many the opportunity to express the reality that ordinary people from all walks of life can indeed achieve extraordinary athletic accomplishments. In many ways one might argue that the entire process is a ... quest to test one's limits and beyond. (p. 13)

At the same time, all of these sports have also become quickly commodified, both fashion conscious and fashion-able; the equipment and the typical venues themselves often require considerable disposable income. Jeremy Howell (1991) echoes Featherstone, suggesting that the promotional discourse that has associated lifestyle sports with upwardly mobile, self-actualizing individuals has helped to insert the fit body into our images of "success" in ways that are not unproblematic. Robert Crawford (1985) has suggested that this equation of fitness and health with success and conspicuous consumption does indeed create self-expectations and obsessions – "healthism" – that become the source of health problems such as eating disorders and injuries, which in the former case affect women in particular.

Arguably of greatest significance, though, is the growth of aerobics. This is because, even more so that running and cross-country skiing, this activity has been part of the legitimation of physical activity for women. Indeed, in its constitutive links with dance and music, its potential of popularizing a radical break with the hegemony of competitive physical activities is perhaps unique. Yet although it has been the context for much that is positive – new opportunities for adult women to experience physical empowerment, as well as opportunities for support and friendship like those that have always been available to men – aerobics, too, has proved easy to incorporate, to commodify, and in some distinctive ways. There has been the familiar commercialization of the activity, particularly the fashionable clothing and the fitness club itself. Beyond this, the marketing of fitness as an aid to sex appeal articulates easily with the objectification of the female body. Marg MacNeill's (1988) discussion of the sexual imagery and the commodification of the fit female body underlines this all too clearly.

However, focusing entirely on the incorporative capacities of the system down-plays the extent to which there have been real gains associated with these changes in the dominant body culture. If anything of what Young (1979, 1980) and MacKinnon (1987) have said is correct (about the empowering potential of women learning to use their bodies actively), surely it is important that millions of women who, in the sporting culture of earlier periods, would not have taken part in vigorous and challenging physical activities, now want to do so. It also seems an advance that they can choose from a much broader range of activities and social environments – from baseball to yoga – to find a way of being physical that is enjoyable and wholly their own. It further seems important that the increasing range of wilderness and aerobic activities, and their increasing legitimacy of dance and yoga for men, has opened up many spaces in which men, too, can experience different kinds of physicality and ways of being strong other than through use of force. The cumulative effect of these changes can only contribute to reinforcing the legitimacy of other ways of being male, despite predictable innuendo and resistance from males who would defend hegemonic masculinity. Moreover, the new availability of noncombative forms of exercise has also clearly spoken to the needs of millions of middle-aged men, for whom the body used to be little more than a briefcase for other, more serious kinds of ambitions, something we attended to only if it broke down before the book got written or the deal closed.

With regard to aerobics, although the critiques of the commodification and sexualization of these activities are important, it is also important to note the very real pleasure that so many women clearly find in these kinds of classes, and not only in the commercial ones, but in the thousands of much less visible classes in schools and community centers, where the atmosphere is usually quite different from that of "20-Minute Workout." Bruce and Markula (1989) suggest that women's pleasure in these classes is both real and widespread, and they reiterate both the empowerment issue and the sense of partnership in doing physical things with other women, which was cited by Birrell and Richter. Both of these issues are reinforced in Susan Willis's discussion of "working out" (1990); and though she revisits the critical question raised by MacNeill and Featherstone, she considers that the remarkable success of *Our Bodies, Ourselves* highlights just how important the body and physicality are to women today. The new availability of appropriate and enjoyable forms of exercise has been especially important, she suggests, to middle-aged and older women, who were completely neglected in the exercise discourses and practices of earlier periods. [. . .]

Concluding remarks

In this chapter I have sought to explicate how gendered identities are both social and historical constructs and how gendered subjectivities are embodied by individuals as they grow from childhood into adult sexual identities. Masculinity and femininity become personally embodied in the ways described previously; yet this always occurs in specific social contexts that historically have privileged masculinity over femininity and particular ways of being male or female over other ways. Sports and other texts of physical competence have been important in this, insofar as they have naturalized norms of male strength and female weakness and have actively reproduced these through developmental practices that have taught males and females to live in their bodies in active or passive ways. Body contact games, in particular, have historically naturalized an aggressive way of "doing masculinity" (Frank, 1991) in which physical domination is legitimated; over time, these confrontative sports have become important masculinizing practices that initiate young males into a hierarchy of gendered identities in which the capacity to dominate is honored and physical power confers social power.

I have tried to make a case for the importance of a variety of other physical practices, some new (or at least newly popular, e.g., some of the aerobic and wilderness sports) and others of a longer history (e.g., dance and other non-competitive movement forms, aerobics, and other exercise practices). In all of these activities, the challenges and the pleasures are in skill and self-possession rather than confrontation and offer empowering experiences to women and men alike. They have also constituted cultural texts in which different ways of being female and male, different ways of "doing" femininity and masculinity, are modelled and legitimized, and texts in which the embodiment of strength, skill, and discipline and the subjective empowerment described by Granskog and others are equated neither with gender nor with the domination of others.

We must acknowledge that, in commercial culture, many of these activities have been promoted in part by articulating them with other, less progressive themes (with fashion, individuation, consumption), and that in this process, the experience of personal transformation is typically detached from the socially transformative dimension of modernism suggested by Gruneau. However, I want to close by recalling that Stuart Hall (1984) suggests that it has been an all too common mistake on the left to see the commodification of leisure (I would add "fitness") as entirely manipulative, as if the consumers of leisure goods and experiences were passive dupes. In Hall's view, this position, like that of earlier critics of mass culture, overlooks the extent to which new forms of leisure consumption have opened up for many people – and especially women and young people – opportunities and lives that are somewhat less limited and constrained than were those of their counterparts only a few generations ago. Hall considers that the left cannot simply decry the commercialism that surrounds leisure products and experiences that people patently want, even though market segmentation now means that alternative and subcultural practices and styles are quickly articulated with other, more ambiguous social identities. Indeed, Mariana Valverde (1991), following Hall, has proposed that subjectivity "ought not to be seen either as constructed by ideology or as flowing from some inner source of coherent meaning" (p. 182). Subject positions, she suggests, are multidimensional, and they are constructed out of our responses to a number of distinct and often competing cultural discourses (e.g., feminism and traditional texts of feminine sexuality; Julia Roberts vs *Thelma and Louise*) that converge upon us with greater or lesser effectiveness. Thus, the degrees of enthusiasm with which the texts of identity made available through the marketplace (e.g., the slim and fit woman, the mountain biker, the skateboarder or surfer) are taken up by individuals will depend on the other subject positions that are already part of our identities and the variety of alternative subject positions available to us in our particular time and social location. This underlines the importance of those sports and other physical practices that encourage femininity and masculinity to be embodied in a variety of shapes and ways and that allow power to be embodied in ways not tied to domination or gender. In any event, the texts and images of physical being that succeed in making an effective place for themselves in popular culture – and today, this means commercial culture – are likely to be more important than ever in the formulation of gendered identities.

Notes

1 I am indebted to Rick Gruneau for this idea.
2 See Joe Henderson's *Thoughts on the Run* (1972) and Ian Jackson's *Yoga and the Athlete* (1975), both published by Runner's World Publications, Mountain View, CA. See also Mike Spino's classic "Running: A Spiritual Experience" in J. Scott (Ed.), *The athletic revolution*, New York: Free Press, 1972, pp. 222–225.
3 Oriard offers a self-critical reflection on the physical combat of line play in football, but there are numerous football accounts that reflect straightforward pride in the capacity to dominate. For hockey, see Robert Faulkner's "Making violence by doing work: Selves,

situations, and the world of professional hockey" in D. Landers (Ed.), *Social problems in athletics*, Champaign, IL: University of Illinois Press, 1976, pp. 93–112.
4 The term comes from Andy Wernick (1991), though he does not discuss this particular example.

References

Birrell, S., & Richter, D. (1987). Is a diamond forever? Feminist transformations of sport. *Women's Studies International Forum*, **10**(4), 395–409.

Bloch, C. (1987). Everyday life, sensuality, and body culture. *Women's Studies International Forum*, **10**(4), 433–442.

Boston Women's Health Book Collective. (1976). *Our Bodies, Ourselves*. New York: Simon & Schuster.

Bruce, T., & Markula, P. (1989, November). Female pleasure: The enjoyment of aerobics. Paper presented at North American Society for the Sociology of Sport, Washington, DC.

Connell, R.W. (1983). Men's bodies. In R.W. Connell, *Which way is up?* (pp. 17–32). Sydney: Allen & Unwin.

Connell, R.W., Ashenden, D.J., Kessler, S., & Dowsett, G.W. (1982). *Making the difference*. Sydney: Allen & Unwin.

Crawford, R. (1985). A cultural account of "health": Control, release, and the social body. In P. McKinlay (Ed.) *Issues in the political economy of health care* (pp. 60–103). New York: Tavistock.

de Beauvoir, S. (1974). *The second sex*. New York: Vintage Books.

Featherstone, M. (1982). The body in consumer culture. *Theory, Culture & Society*, **1**(2), 18–33.

Fletcher, S. (1984). *Women first: The female tradition in English physical education*. London: Athlone.

Frank, B. (1991, November). Sports, looks, and a woman: What every guy needs to be masculine. Paper presented at North American Society for the Sociology of Sport, Milwaukee, WI.

Gilroy, S. (1989). The embody-ment of power. Gender and physical activity *Leisure Studies*, **8**(2), 163–172.

Granskog, J. (1991, November). In search of the ultimate: Ritual aspects of the Hawaiian Ironman Triathlon. Paper presented at North American Society for the Sociology of Sport, Milwaukee, WI.

Gruneau, R. (1993). The critique of sport in modernity: Theorizing power, culture, and the politics of the body. In E. Dunning & J. Maguire (Eds.), *The sports process* (pp. 85–109). Champaign, IL: Human Kinetics.

Hall, S. (1984, January). The culture gap. *Marxism Today*, pp. 18–22.

Howell, J. (1991). "A Revolution in Motion": Advertising and the politics of nostalgia. *Sociology of Sport Journal*, **8**(3), 258–271.

MacNeill, M. (1988). Active women, media representations, and ideology. In J. Harvey & H. Cantelon (Eds.), *Not just a game* (pp. 195–211). Ottawa: University of Ottawa Press.

MacKinnon, C. (1987). Women, self-possession, and sport. In *Feminism unmodified: Discourses on life and law* (pp. 117–124). Cambridge, MA: Harvard University Press.

Merleau-Ponty, M. (1962). *Phenomenology of perception*. New York: Humanities Press.

Nelson, M.B. (1991), *Are we winning yet?* New York: Random House.

Orates, J.C. (1987). *On boxing*. Garden City, NJ: Doubleday.

Oriard, M. (1982). *The end of autumn*. Garden City. NJ: Doubleday.

Shotter, J. (1973). Prolegomena to an understanding of play *Journal for Theory of Social Behaviour*, **3**(1), 47–89.

Shotter, J. (1974). The development of personal powers. In M. Richards (Ed.), *The integration of a child into a social world* (p. 215–244). Cambridge: Cambridge University Press.

Shotter, J. (1984). *Social accountability and selfhood*. London: Blackwell.

Theberge, N. (1987). Sport and women's empowerment. *Women's Studies International Forum*, **10**(4), 387–393.

Terkel, S. (1974). *Working*. New York: Avon Books.

Valverde, M. (1991). As if subjects existed: Analyzing social discourses. *Canadian Review of Sociology and Anthropology*, **28**(2), 173–187.

Willis, S. (1990). Work(ing) out. *Cultural Studies*, **4**(1), 1–18.

Young, I. (1979). The exclusion of women from sport: Conceptual and existential dimensions. *Philosophy in Context*, **9**, 44–53.

Young, I. (1980). Throwing like a girl: A phenomenology of feminine body comportment, motility, and spatiality. *Human Studies*, **3**, 137–156.

16 Collapsing gender in competitive bodybuilding: Researching contradictions and ambiguity in sport*

Camilla Obel

Research into the sport of bodybuilding provides information about the construction – "sculpturing" – of bodies through sport practices. I will argue in this chapter
that it can also challenge conceptions of "natural" bodies as well as theoretical
arguments about gendered and disciplined bodies. Attention given to the development of the body's muscularity by male and female bodybuilders produces images
of bodies which potentially cross boundaries between the received understandings
of the "masculine" and the "feminine" and in doing so question the "naturalness"
of bodies. The ambiguity as to what the bodies of bodybuilders represent with
respect to expressions of gender, and the apparent explosion of the physical limits
of the body, points towards the need for analyses which aim to depict this ambiguity rather than favouring certain readings of body images over others. As such,
bodybuilding is a challenge to categorical ways of thinking about masculinity,
femininity and the body. In this chapter I will explore the gendered discourses
which bodybuilders utilize. My attention is directed at their use of "masculinity"
and "femininity" to explain the appearances of the body.

Studies of sport have emphasized the idea that dominant representations of
bodies of sports persons provide important sources of differentiated gender identification and identity work (see for example Heaven and Rowe 1990). In this
chapter I suggest that readings of body images as either feminine or masculine,
images which either reaffirm or contradict the sexuality of the sports performer,
are problematic. Firstly, readings of gender by a researcher, might emphasize
a particular reading of the bodies under investigation. However, these might, in
turn, actually contradict the meanings favoured by the individual performers themselves. Secondly, the notion of gender itself is problematic. For example, readings
of gender representations in bodybuilding have uncritically suggested that at any
one time it is possible to identify a dominant understanding of masculinity and
femininity which the bodies of bodybuilders can be measured against in order to
present bodybuilding as either contradicting or reaffirming this prevailing exegesis
of gender (see for example Guthrie and Castelnuovo 1992). While the constitution
of masculinity and femininity is often critiqued in sports studies (see for example

* Taken and abridged from, *International Review for the Sociology of Sport*, 31(2) (1996): 185–203.

Jennifer Hargreaves 1986), and research has suggested that dominant understandings of gender has been challenged by new cultural representations like those of bodybuilding (see for example John Hargreaves 1987, p. 155), such challenges might never in fact challenge the theoretical position that gender is primarily produced and encouraged in order to control bodies and populations. This can be seen in analyses of sports which incorporate a reading of Michel Foucault's work that emphasises the control and domination of bodies in modern societies identified in the desires and pleasures produced through self-discipline and self-surveillance by sports practitioners (Hargreaves 1987; Miller 1990).

I will argue that research into bodybuilding suggests that gender is ambiguous and shifting depending on the institutional context in which it is produced (Wuthnow 1989). The focus in the paper is on gender as collectively produced in action as opposed to individually managed more or less successfully. An argument is also made for a study of bodybuilding that is grounded in ethnographies (see the work on men's bodybuilding by Klein, and the work on women's bodybuilding by Bolin) which are sensitive to ambiguity and contradiction (see Cole 1991), and is interested in aspects of resistance rather than control (Foucault 1980a), and open to a multiplicity of readings of gender representations (see Schulze 1990). The aim of this paper is to show how a study of bodybuilding can provide accounts of gender as utilised and produced in order to credit the sport with identity and "respectability". It is in the pursuit of respectability that notions of gender become ambiguous. I also suggest that in the pursuit of bodybuilding identities, understandings of gender and body practices may be challenged, shifted or supported.

Muscular femininity and the sport of bodybuilding

The research into the sport of bodybuilding which I conducted over the period 1991–1992 was initially inspired by debates surrounding female bodybuilders. Images of Ms Olympias and other images of female athletes with muscular physiques inspired a small, concerned debate in the New Zealand media which mirrored similar debates in other countries about "excessively" muscular women (Huggett 1991; Lucas 1991). The debates expressed a general disbelief concerning the intentions of such women and a concern with the physical and psychological well-being of these women. In 1991 a New Zealand magazine quoted a psychologist saying that the obsession with body image he had found some bodybuilders expressing could be compared with obsessions voiced by anorexia sufferers:

> Some psychologists say that the "anorexia to starve yourself" is de-feminising: you lose all your feminine bulges. And some bodybuilding women seem to be de-feminising, not by seeking to be the pre-adolescent figure, but rather by masculinising themselves; if you don't want to be a woman there are two ways to go about it. You starve yourself so you look like a child or you go bodybuilding to look like a man. It's the same disturbed body image.
>
> (Huggett 1991, p. 20)

The same article quoted an American study which found that of all sports examined, bodybuilding had the highest incidence of people with a distorted body image. Likewise, in a New Zealand fashion magazine a sports doctor voiced concern regarding the health status of female bodybuilders.

> Body-builders have often attracted criticism about the lengths to which they'll go to achieve sporting success. American studies have shown female competitors to suffer from eating problems such as anorexia and bulimia (uncontrollable self-starvation and vomiting, respectively), dehydration, amenorrhoea (loss of periods), infertility, and premature osteoporosis (brittle bones), as well as other wide-ranging problems related to anabolic-steroid use.
>
> (Lucas 1991, p. 62)

Medical discourses in general view the image of female bodybuilders as "unnatural" and "unhealthy" and bodybuilding practices as potentially dangerous. There appears to be a "danger" point at which a female bodybuilder ceases to be female and becomes associated too closely with the image of the male. This situation brings the gender of male bodybuilders into question as differences in body image between men and women appear to be minimized in bodybuilding. As a result, identification and articulation of sexual identity appear disrupted and confused as specific body images incorporate a view of bodies as literally "worked" as opposed to "natural". Bodybuilding suggests, then, that a gender dichotomy cannot be articulated on to a base line of natural, biological bodies.

Readings of the image of the muscular female bodybuilder suggest that binary oppositions between the masculine and the feminine and between nature and culture are disrupted. An example of such a reading is presented by Annette Kuhn (1988, p. 17) who states that muscles have been "re-invented" in bodybuilding with the effect that female bodybuilders can be seen to transgress the boundaries of sexual difference:

> ... when women enter the arena of bodybuilding, a twofold challenge to the natural order is posed. Not only is the naturalness of the body called into question: but when women have muscles, the natural order of gender is under threat as well. Muscles are rather like drag, for female bodybuilders especially: while muscles can be assumed, like clothing, women's assumption of muscles implies a transgression of the proper boundaries of sexual difference.

Kuhn suggests that images of female bodybuilders disrupt the opposition between the masculine and the feminine. I want to suggest, however, that how gender is realised is extremely complex. That rather than a threatening femininity being openly produced, women bodybuilders actually resist being interpreted as threatening. Or put in another way, the sport of bodybuilding is normalized by women taking it up, rather than by men.

Readings of bodybuilding which suggest confusion and a threat to a gender order do not take into account the experiences of bodybuilders nor the language and practices of competitive bodybuilding which have attempted to resolve such ambiguity. The readings are those of authors and not the bodybuilders. However, if one shifts the focus to the bodybuilders then it can be seen that their discourse constitutes masculinity and femininity in opposition. Gender differences have to be worked at and articulated in performance. Since organised, competitive bodybuilding differs from locality to locality, from country to country and from one competitive organization to another, these differences make it difficult to generalise about the pursuit as one sport. However, rules distinguishing between men and women competitors do not vary significantly between contests. The most dramatic distinction between competitive men's and women's bodybuilding is the compulsory pose event which comprises one of the two to four main events in all bodybuilding contests. Men perform seven compulsory poses while women perform only five of these seven poses. The front and back lat spread poses were early in the history of women's competitive bodybuilding identified as "unfeminine" and abandoned in contests. [...]

Providing clearly identifiable gendered bodybuilding images has been a concern from the commencement of women's competitive bodybuilding. Women's competitive bodybuilding, which began in the late 1970s to early 1980s, incorporated the gender-differentiated rules but these were not enough to combat concerns expressed about "masculine-like" females. Contest rules were altered to include a notion of "femininity" to ensure that women competitors would display clearly identifiable feminine characteristics when performing. [...]

Interpreting women's bodybuilding: the case of Bev Francis

Several commentaries on the contradiction of femininity and muscularity in bodybuilding have been made (Bolin 1992a, 1992b, 1992c: Guthrie and Castelnuovo 1992; Holmlund 1989; Klein 1985b; Kuhn 1988; Mansfield and McGinn 1993; Miller and Penz 1991; Nelson 1991; Pally 1985; Schulze 1990). Some of these accounts trace Bev Francis' bodybuilding career from the beginning in 1983 when she first appeared in a Miss Olympia contest. Mansfield and McGinn (1993) argue that Bev Francis changed her body image in order to fulfil the twin constraints of "aesthetics and safe femininity". Dobbins writing in Muscle and Fitness gave this description of the controversy that has characterized Bev Francis' bodybuilding career:

> Bev showed up at Caesar's Palace for the filming of Pumping Iron II [in 1983] with a blocky, muscular body developed by years of powerlifting but which she had shrunk and depleted by several months of incredible overtraining and starvation. For some time afterwards Bev became the new "horrible example" in women's bodybuilding, but she came back to silence her critics. After taking time to win more powerlifting titles. Bev returned to bodybuilding, followed a real program of competition training, shaped her body, improved her symmetry and brought her proportions into line to the point where she

was able to win the IFBB World Women's Professional Bodybuilding Championship; defeating none other than the superaesthetic Anja Langer. (1990, p. 191)

While Dobbins seems critical of the femininity requirement included in contest rules, his account of Francis' career suggests that it was the powerlifting practices which prevented her from winning contests. In other words, Dobbins suggests that had Francis followed bodybuilding practices, there would not have been ambiguity with respect to that which the image of her body represents. Although new definitions of contest rules may no longer emphasise femininity as a requirement, women competitors must still pay tribute to an aesthetic body image which, according to Mansfield and McGinn, "does not exclude a feminine aesthetic but rather includes it together with an emphasis on aesthetic muscularity". [. . .]

In an interview with the most successful New Zealand bodybuilder, Siobahn O'Neill, the issue of changing judging criteria in women's bodybuilding was also raised.

> There is no doubt that the changing direction of women's bodybuilding will work to O'Neill's advantage as she strives to establish a professional career. She will benefit from moves towards accentuating the female form, and away from excessive bulk. . . . "I was told [by officials at the 1991 world amateur championships, where O'Neill placed seventh] I already had enough size. I just had to get more refined. I had been really tempted to use steroids before the worlds because I didn't know if I was big enough," she admits. "It was a huge relief to know I didn't need to get freaky big."
>
> (Umbers 1992, p. 38)

[. . .] While Bev Francis did not compete in the 1992 Ms Olympia (she came second in 1991), her view on the ideal female bodybuilding physique in the following quote, could be interpreted to support the suggestion made by the ESPN commentator, namely that Francis did not fulfil the requirements for an ideal female bodybuilding physique. In Nelson's (1991 p. 107) chapter on women's bodybuilding "You Can't Just Be Muscular" Bev Francis was quoted as having said: "My idea of the perfect female bodybuilder is [one with] a body that is muscularly as close to the male's as possible, but with the expression and the personality of a female coming out."

I want to argue that writers have stressed the idea that Francis represents a threat to women's bodybuilding. This emphasis effectively ignores that Francis, like Weider, has attempted to reassure that women's bodybuilding is compatible with an attractive and acceptable femininity. In her bodybuilding manual Bev Francis' Power Bodybuilding (1989) Francis did not comment on the way she changed her looks; however she did mention femininity once in relation to what appears to be an artistic perspective to "onstage personal appearance" as well as an issue of avoiding "gender confusion". [. . .]

Mansfield and McGinn (1993, p. 63) provide this reading of the changes Bev Francis made to her appearances over the period from the filming of the Pumping

Iron II film in 1983 to the late 1980s and early 1990s when she gained sporting success:

> Over the years her waist and hips have become more slender, and the proportions of her body have changed to become more symmetrical, the development of her leg muscles has toned down, she has brought out the "detail" of her musculature rather than concentrating on pure size and mass, she uses make-up and nail polish, and has grown, lightened and curled her hair.

While Bev Francis did not comment directly on the femininity requirements which she, according to Mansfield and McGinn attempted to fulfil, she did emphasise in her manual that bodybuilders should not show off their muscles everywhere as that may present an undesirable image of the sport.

> I believe there are two places where you have a right to show off your hard-earned muscles – at the beach and at bodybuilding competitions. In all other situations, I personally dress conservatively – often in loose clothing and long-sleeved tops, which reveal very little of my muscular development. One thing that immediately turns off someone outside of the sport is to see a puffed-up bodybuilder in a tank top and shorts, lats spread to the hilt, every muscle tensed, strutting along the streets. You'll do a lot more for the sport if you present yourself as a relaxed, intelligent person. No one has to be a muscle-head, unless she wants to. Spend some time developing aspects of your personality that have nothing to do with the sport, and try to come across as a well-adjusted, pleasant person. You'll speak well for the sport of bodybuilding if you do so.
>
> (Francis 1989, p. 134)

The point that I want to make regarding Francis' career, which has been interpreted by writers as epitomizing concern with gender in bodybuilding, is that rather than focusing on how Francis appeared "threatening" and resisting of a traditional femininity, Francis herself emphasises that "passing" as a woman elsewhere is important. Apart from working hard towards aligning her training methods and body image to that of an ideal female bodybuilding physique, she emphasises the need to defuse the tension between muscularity and safe femininity. It is this emphasis on femininity specific work which effectively normalises women's bodybuilding as well as the sport of bodybuilding in general.

Mansfield and McGinn (1993) argue that the constraints placed on competitive female bodybuilders appear to create a situation whereby "the proclamation of gender must be made very loudly indeed" in order to counter-balance their musculature. The point which needs to be emphasised, however, is that while bodybuilding competitors must conform to rules and regulations constituted upon sexual differences, the notion of gender is also produced and embraced by female bodybuilders to make their bodies and thus identities accepted. This use of gender to affirm an acceptable femininity is revealed by a female bodybuilder. [. . .]

There are two kinds of woman – your Marylin Monroe type and your ancient Greek, Michelangelo type, the sculptured women. We can be just as feminine if not more so than the other type. Most bodybuilding women are very feminine. We make a point of it – we're not butch. The female bodybuilder is into being a woman – she's sculpturing her body to look like a woman's body. Men turn around and look. When you are healthy, fit and shaped up you've got this sparkle. It turns everybody on, male and female alike.

(Huggett 1991, p. 16)

Women's bodybuilding provides a source of pleasure to those involved as well as to spectators and has been celebrated as well as criticised by feminists for being respectively radical or colluding (Guthrie and Castelnuovo 1992; Kuhn 1988; Miller and Penz 1991; Schulze 1990). The point that I want to make is that women's bodybuilding provides an example of how the politics of gender are constituted within particular contexts through the negotiation and articulation by the practitioners. The analysis of gender in women's bodybuilding presented in this paper, with the career of Bev Francis as a case in point, has highlighted that female competitors negotiate their "nature" and thus the idea of "gender". If dominant discourses of sport and gender articulate that women and sport in general, and women and muscles in particular, present a contradiction, the ambiguity which surrounds the female bodybuilder cannot but constitute her as "unnatural" and threatening. The resolution to this within the competitive bodybuilding community involves encouraging women to accentuate an aesthetic ("feminine") appearance. Thus, while women's bodybuilding can be presented as contradicting a dominant notion of femininity and questioning taken-for-granted assumptions about sexual identity, through studying how female bodybuilders compete as well as what they say about their bodies, identities and sport, it can also be presented as reinforcing a more "conservative" or traditional notion of femininity. The complexity of these interlocked readings suggests that women's bodybuilding can highlight the complex construction of bodies, gender and sexual identity. While gender traditionally has been applied in analyses of sports pursued by women in order to highlight how relations of gender prevent women from participating in sports on the same basis as men, this analysis argues that gender should be considered a cultural product constituted in action by individuals, groups and institutions in order to present specific social practices and identities as meaningful. [...]

Masculinity and feminising practices in men's bodybuilding

Research on men's bodybuilding is extensive. For example, Aycock (1992), Bednarek (1985), Dutton and Laura (1989), Fussell (1993), Gillett and White (1992), Goldberg (1992), Klein (1981, 1985a, 1986, 1987, 1989, 1992, 1993), Lingis (1988) as well as Gaines and Butler's "insider" account of bodybuilding (1974). While the scope of research into such issues as the construction of bodies and the politics of gender and sexuality raised by women's bodybuilding has been recognised recently, studies of men's bodybuilding has tended to focus on such issues as deviance, narcissism, fascism, homophobia (Klein 1987, 1989, 1993). Apart from the ambiguity of pursuing feminising practices in men's competitive bodybuilding which this part of the paper identifies, at least two other issues have been identified as potentially threatening to a "wholesome" image of the sport. Accounts of steroid abuse and links to the homosexual community in men's bodybuilding (Klein 1986, 1989) for example, have prompted the Weider corporation to proclaim health and heterosexuality as cognate to the sport. [. . .]

Apart from appealing to other practices than those identified as specific to sport and thus creating concern with cultural respectability within the bodybuilding community, this paper suggests that few analyses have actually linked the practices and experiences of men's competitive bodybuilding with issues of gender ambiguity. In contrast to accounts of female bodybuilding which often incorporate male bodybuilding in analyses, few accounts of men's bodybuilding attempt to analyse male bodybuilding in relation to female bodybuilding. Such an analysis can highlight how the sexual identity of male bodybuilders can be viewed as ambiguous not only as a consequence of women taking up the sport but also through the competitive bodybuilding practices pursued by male bodybuilders themselves.

In one reading situating women and men bodybuilders side by side produces a dichotomy which effectively "normalises" men's bodybuilding. In this reading concerns about the image of women bodybuilders sustain an account in which men's bodybuilding is viewed as the "norm" in the sport and women bodybuilders are viewed as "freaks". This account provides for readings of the female as "other" to the "given" male. While this paper has suggested that such a reading does not take into account that practices and experiences of women's competitive bodybuilding need to be identified as non-threatening and thus "normalising" to the sport, neither does the reading take into account the practices and experiences of male bodybuilders. Thus, upon researching practices performed by competitive male bodybuilders a different picture emerges which highlights how practices of appearance enhancement, an essential prerequisite in competitive bodybuilding, include practices which can be identified as "feminine" or femininity work. This situation produces ambiguity with respect to the sexual identity of male bodybuilders.

The body of the male bodybuilder, like the body of female bodybuilders, disrupts the dichotomy of nature/culture in bodybuilding discourses and practices while retaining a position of superiority in relation to female bodybuilders. The bodybuilding community, like most co-sexed sports, is characterised by relations of gender which place women in an inferior position (Klein 1985b). Women are not excluded from the sport; however the inclusion of women in the sport, marked by the establishment of the Miss Olympia contests in 1980 (which later changed to the less sexualized title of Ms Olympia) was characterised by gender-differentiated contest rules. Apart from the current situation where men perform "all" the seven mandatory poses in contests and women only five, competitive bodybuilding rules allow female competitors to have breast implants while all other implants as well as performance enhancing drugs are considered illegal.

While breasts are constructed as essentially a natural feminine characteristic in bodybuilding discourses, they can be cultivated by female bodybuilders who might not find themselves "feminine enough" or unable to live up to the "aesthetic" standards required in contests rules. Carla Dunlap (winner of the Miss Olympia contest in 1983) made this comment about the necessity for women to have breasts:

> I found that in bodybuilding, because you were sending so many mixed signals, if [people] looked at you and did not see a face they immediately recognized as female, the next place they looked was at your chest, and if you didn't have recognizable breasts, then you had to in some way communicate your femininity.'
>
> (Nelson 1991, pp. 105–106)

The breast implant "allowance" made for women bodybuilders again sustains a situation where the male body is constructed as the norm and "naturally" suited for the sport.

It should be noted however, that competitive body physiques and performance by male contestants are not considered exclusively "natural" male attributes. Achieving a competitive appearance is hard work. Such an ideal competitive body image for male bodybuilders is described by Joe Weider (1984, p. 63) in one of his bodybuilding manuals:

> While many champs don't possess the classically handsome facial features of a Tom Selleck, they all invariably make the most of their natural attributes by appearing well-groomed onstage at every competition. This clean-cut appearance used to be called "the Mr. America look," and it's definitely a quality that you should work hard to achieve.

Ways of achieving a well-groomed and clean-cut appearance include the "feminine" practices of dieting (see Bolin (1992c) for an extensive discussion of dieting by both female and male bodybuilders); shaving off all body hair; applying tanning lotions or sun bathing; carefully selecting posing costume to accentuate strong body features and to hide weak points; rehearsing posing routines in front of mirrors; taking dance/ballet classes to improve posing performance as well as getting advice from professional choreographers on posing routines. [. . .]

Arnold Schwarzenegger, who is known for taking ballet classes to improve on his posing routine (the introduction to the film Pumping Iron shows Schwarzenegger and Ed Corney practicing their posing with a female ballet dancer). [. . .]

All of these techniques which can improve the performance of bodybuilders are knowledges and experiences characteristically held by women. The appearance-enhancing practices that competitive male bodybuilders perform can thus be characterised as a feminising process.

The analysis of the body politics of men's bodybuilding presented in this paper suggests that, while the image of the male bodybuilder can be interpreted as "normal" in relation to the female bodybuilder and the male body "naturally" suited for the sport, both male and female bodybuilders must re-work their bodies in order to compete for titles of best bodybuilding body and performance. For the male bodybuilder this work involves developing skills which can be identified as feminine, and thus the masculinity of male bodybuilders is called into question. Bodybuilding discourses emphasise the need to develop such "feminine" skills by characterising them as necessary in order to achieve a *handsome, clean-cut* and *well groomed* appearance. Thus, in a bodybuilding discourse terms like these attempt to resolve the tension between feminine skills and men's bodybuilding through aligning the products of such skills with masculine attributes.

Researching contradictions and ambiguity in sport

This chapter has suggested that the confrontation of nature and culture, which bodybuilding brings to the surface, can challenge and potentially bring about changes in perceptions of the "nature" of bodies, masculinity and femininity, thus facilitating new readings of how subjectivities can be negotiated through body work. In constructing a specific femininity, the female bodybuilder's muscularity "mocks" traditional notions of masculinity through "emulating" an "excessive" muscularity, and thus resists a traditional notion of femininity. At the same time bodybuilding's gender segregated contest rules reinforce a traditional notion of femininity, and female bodybuilders emphasise that bodybuilding enables them to be attractive and feminine. While the body of the male bodybuilder can be read as a "text" on "hyper-masculinity", this paper suggests that in processes of objectification to increase his competitive chances, the competitive male body-builder "mimics" traditional femininity work and contradicts traditional notions of masculinity.

Through this analysis of competitive bodybuilding, the flexibility and shifting nature of the language and practices of bodybuilders as well as readings of gender representations have been highlighted. The discussions of women's and men's bodybuilding in this paper support the suggestion made in writings of Michel Foucault on resistance. Although Foucault's work did not include research into sport, the analyses he made of disciplinary practices of large institutions can be of use in studies of sport in general (Miller 1990, Jennifer Hargreaves 1986), and bodybuilding in particular (Aycock 1992; Bolin 1992c: Gillett and White 1992; Guthrie and Castelnuovo 1992; Kuhn 1988; Mansfield and McGinn 1993; Miller and Penz 1991). The theoretical argument that can be presented on the basis of the discussions presented in this paper suggests that the social practices of body discipline performed by bodybuilders enable the articulation of specific gendered body images produced in particular social contexts.

The focus on resistance, cultural development and change goes beyond textual analyses which tend to produce readings of representations which emphasise con-trol. With this focus in mind the effectiveness of power relations in bodybuilding or the appeal of the sport should not be considered fundamentally as the ability to dominate and create "docile bodies", as, for example, Fussell (1993: 595) suggests:

> Buy the Bodybuilding Lifestyles or Shape, become a walking, talking – actually, lip-synching – cliché. Become a replicant. Add to the three D's of gymspeak ('Discipline, Dedication, Determination') a fourth: Decapitation.

As opposed to this reading. Foucault (1980a, p. 95) argued that ". . . where there is power there is resistance, or rather consequently, this resistance is never in a position of exteriority to power." Foucault (1980b, p. 56) specified this statement in this discussion of the relationship between power and resistance in relation to body work, and the potential for new cultural developments:

> Mastery and awareness of one's body can be acquired only through the effect of an investment of power in the body: gymnastics, exercise, muscle building, nudism, glorification of the body beautiful. All of this belongs to the pathway leading to the desire of one's body, by way of the insistent, meticulous work of power on the bodies of children or soldiers, the healthy bodies. But once power produces this effect, there inevitably emerges the responding claims and affirmations, those of one's own body against power, of health against the economic system, of pleasure against the moral norms of sexuality, marriage, decency. Suddenly, what had made power strong becomes used to attack it. Power, after investing itself in the body, finds itself exposed to a counterattack in that same body.

The theoretical position discussed above supports the analysis presented in this paper that bodybuilders acquire desired body skills through daily subjecting their bodies to strenuous disciplinary practices, and in doing so challenge notions of gendered body images and practices. Furthermore, the discussions of bodybuilding presented here also indicate that the pleasures derived through defying traditional body images and adopting "cross-gendered" body practices can be underscored by different readings of bodybuilding. Readings of women's bodybuilding have emphasised both resisting and colluding aspects of women's bodybuilding. Some writers have argued that women's competitive bodybuilding is dominated by a traditional "gender order" which Bev Francis has resisted while a more careful reading of Francis' and other female bodybuilders' accounts of women's body-building – as non-threatening – has not been explored adequately. I have also argued that issues of gender in men's competitive bodybuilding have not been researched extensively. The readings I have presented in this paper suggest that the acquisition of "feminine" skills in men's bodybuilding makes men's bodybuilding, rather than women's bodybuilding, a threat to a traditional understanding of gender.

The focus of this chapter has been to collapse gender as an unambiguous prin-ciple and to discuss "new" or more appropriate ways of conducting studies of gender representations in sport. I have argued above that analyses of sport can benefit from Foucault's work on resistance because his conceptualisation of how power works goes beyond a focus on control. Power relations in Foucault's work are characterised as complex sets of processes which constantly encounter resistances. A study of gender relations in bodybuilding can highlight such complex processes. In this chapter I have argued that contradictions and ambiguity surrounding body practices and gender representations should be viewed as possibilities for studies which seek to explore how particular body practices engage with a variety of read-ings in order to create and hold semiotic and social territory (Schulze 1990, p. 78).

The theoretical conclusion of this chapter is thus that contrasting discourses which bring to the surface confrontations of nature/culture only suggest opportunities for complex cultural developments. Local studies into social practices sensitive to ambiguity, contradiction and disruptions may bring forward knowledges of complex cultural developments like those identified in bodybuilding. Cole (1991: 46) also notes this in her discussion of sports studies in general:

> Rather than obscuring contradictions, inconsistencies, and disruptions contradictions or unexpected practices are considered and reported because they are seen as opportunities for, but not guarantees of, conceptual developments: consequently, total commitment to theory is at least temporarily suspended – challenging theoretical authority.

Through gaining respectability as a sport, bodybuilding may encounter more resistances "from within" as standards and rules regarding the sport may become more formalised. It is not a coincidence that at the "top" of the sport the Weider brothers work towards gaining Olympic status for the sport while many bodybuilders might argue that this will ruin the appeal of the sport.

> The bodybuilding sport that my brother Ben and I helped to create is basically a dignified, conservative and very artistic sport. Through my publications contest promotion and other means, I have spent millions portraying the human body in all its majesty, strength and elegance. By developing the sport along these lines, we have made it acceptable both here and abroad. As a sport, it is getting the kind of recognition we hope will soon gain it acceptance by the International Olympic Committee.
>
> (Weider 1991, p. 7)

I have suggested that this recognition has been accompanied by new problems of gender ambivalence.

Notes

1 This chapter is based on a thesis entitled "Negotiating nature: Bodybuilding and the Art of Being Some Body" by Camilla Obel, presented for the degree of M.A. in Sociology. Canterbury University, New Zealand, 1993. I am grateful for the constructive criticism by Dr. Jan Cameron and Dr. Terry Austrin on earlier drafts of this chapter.

2 Benarek (1985, pp. 239–240) states that studies of personality profiles of bodybuilders, which date back to the 1940s and revealed male bodybuilders indicating feelings of inferiority, lack of masculinity, narcissistic and homosexual tendencies, have been debunked in later studies from the 1970–80s. However, the focus on socio-psychological insecurity among male bodybuilders has re-surfaced again in research by Klein in particular (1987; 1989; 1993).

References

Aycock, Alan, 1992: "The Confession of the Flesh: Disciplinary Gaze in Casual Bodybuilding". In: *Play & Culture*. Vol. 5:338–357.

Bednarek, Joachim, 1985: "Pumping Iron or Pulling Strings: Different Ways of Working Out and Getting Involved in Body-Building". In: *International Review for the Sociology of Sport*. Vol. 20(4):239–259.

Bolin, Anne, 1992a: "Vandalized Vanity: Feminine Physiques Betrayed and Portrayed". In: F. Mascia-Lees (ed.): *Tatoo, torture, adornment and disfigurement: The denaturalization of the body in culture and text*. Albany. NY; SUNY Press.

Bolin, Anne, 1992b: "Beauty or beast: The subversive soma". In: C. Ballerino Cohen (ed.): *Body Contours: Deciphering scripts of gender and power*. New Brunswick. NJ; Rutgers University Press.

Bolin, Anne, 1992c: "Flex Appeal, Food and Fat: Competitive Bodybuilding, Gender and Diet". In: *Play & Culture*, Vol. 5:378–400.

Cole, Cheryl L., 1991: "The Politics of Cultural Reproduction: Visions of Fields/Fields of Visions". In: *International Review for the Sociology of Sport*. Vol. 26(1):37–50.

Dobbins, Bill, 1990: "Ms Olympia: Alive & Well". In: *Muscle & Fitness*, Vol. 51(1).

Dutton, K. R. and Laura. R. S., 1989: "Towards a History of Bodybuilding". In: *Sporting Traditions* Vol. 6(1):25–41.

Foucault, Michel, 1980a: *The History of Sexuality*. Vol. 1. New York: Pantheon.

Foucault, Michel, 1980b: *Power/Knowledge: Selected Interviews and Other Writings 1972–77* (ed.) Colin Gordon, Brighton: Harvester Press.

Francis, Bev, 1989: *Bev Francis's Power Bodybuilding*, New York: Sterling Publ.

Fussell, Sam, 1993: "Body Builder Americanus". In: Laurence Goldstein (ed.): *The Male Body* (Part One). Michigan Quarterly Review. Vol. 32(4) (Special Issue).

Gaines. Charles and Butler, George, 1974: *Pumping Iron. The Art and sport of Bodybuilding*. New York: Simon and Schuster.

Goldberg, Jonathan, 1992: "Recalling Totalities: The Mirrored Stages of Arnold Schwarzenegger". In: *difference: A Journal of Feminist Cultural Studies*. Vol. 4(1):172–204.

Guthrie, Sharon R. and Castelnuovo, Shirley, 1992: "Elite Women Bodybuilders: Models of Resistance or Compliance?". In: *Play & Culture*. Vol. 5:401–408.

Hargreaves, Jennifer, 1986: "Where's the virtue? Where's the Grace? A discussion of the Social Production of Gender Relations in and through Sport". In: *Theory, Culture & Society*, 3(1):109–121.

Hargreaves, John, 1987: "The body, sport and power relations". In: John Horne, David Jary and Alan Tomlinson (eds.): *Sport, Leisure and Social Relations, Sociological Review Monograph 33*, London: Routledge & Kegan Paul, pp. 139–159.

Heaven, Patrick and Rowe, David, 1990: "Gender, Sport and Body Image". In: David Rowe and Geoff Lawrence (eds.): *Sport and Leisure Trends in Australian Popular Culture*, Sydney: HBJ Publishers. pp. 59–73.

Holmlund, Christine Anne, 1989: "Visible Difference and Flex Appeal: The Body, Sex, Sexuality and Race in the Pumping Iron Films". In: *Cinema Journal* Vol. 28(4):38–51.

Huggett, Paul, 1991: "The Body Perfect". In: *The New Zealand Listener, TV and Radio Times*, September 16–22, pp. 14–20.

Klein, Alan M., 1981: "The Master Blaster: Empire Building & Body Building". In: *Arena Review*, Vol. 5(3):29–32.

Klein, Alan M., 1985a: "Muscle Manor: The Use of Sport Metaphor and History in Sport Sociology". In: *Journal of Sport and Social Issues*, Vol. 9:4–17.

Klein, Alan, M., 1985b: "Pumping Iron". In: *Society*, Vol. 22(4):68–75.

Klein, Alan M., 1986: "Pumping Irony: Crisis and Contradiction in Bodybuilding". In: *Sociology of Sports Journal*. Vol. 3:112–133.

Klein, Alan M., 1987: "Fear and Self-Loathing in Southern California: Narcissism and Fascism in Bodybuilding Subculture". In: *Journal of Psychoanalytical Anthropology*, Vol. 10(2):117–137.

Klein, Alan M., 1989: "Managing Deviance: Hustling, Homophobia, and the Bodybuilding Subculture". In: *Deviant Behavior*, Vol. 10:11–27.

Klein, Alan M., 1992: "Man Makes Himself: Alienation and Self-Objectification in Bodybuilding". In: *Play & Culture*, Vol. 5:326–337.

Klein, Alan M., 1993: *Little Big Men: Bodybuilding Subculture and Gender Construction*, Albany; State University of New York Press.

Kuhn, Annette, 1988: "The Body and Cinema: Some Problems for Feminism". In: Susan Sheridan (ed.): *Grafts: Essays in Feminist Cultural theory*. London; Verso. pp. 11–23.

Lingis, A., 1988: "Orchids and Muscles". In: William J. Morgan and Klaus V. Meier (eds.): *Philosophical Inquiry in Sport*. Champaign, Illinois; Human Kinetics Publ., pp. 125–136.

Lucas, Janet, 1991: "Living Sculptures". In: *More*, Oct., pp. 60–64.

Mansfield, Alan and McGinn, Barbara, 1993: "Pumping Irony: The Muscular and the Feminine". In: Sue Scott and David Morgan (eds.): *Body Matters: Essays on the Sociology of the Body*. London: The Falmer Press. pp. 49–68.

Miller, Toby, 1990: "Sport, Media and Masculinity". In: David Rowe and Geoff Lawrence (eds.): *Sport and Leisure – Trends in Australian Popular Culture*. Sydney; HBJ Publishers, pp. 96–108.

Miller, Leslie and Penz, Otto, 1991: "Talking Bodies: Female Bodybuilders Colonize a Male Preserve". In: *Quest*, 43:148–163.

Nelson, Maria Burton, 1991: "You Can't Just Be Muscular". In: *Are We Winning Yet? How Women are Changing Sports are Changing Women*. New York: Random House, pp. 97–116.

Obel, Camilla, 1992: *Negotiating Nature: Bodybuilding and the Art of Being Some Body*, unpublished M.A. Thesis. Sociology Department, Canterbury University, Christchurch, New Zealand.

Pally, Marcia, 1985: "Women of Iron". In: *Film Comment*, Vol. 21 (July–Aug.): 60–64.

Schulze, Laurie, 1990: "On the Muscle". In: Jane Gaines and Charlotte Herzog (eds): *Fabrications, Costume and the Female Body*, New York; Routledge, Chap. 4, pp. 59–78.

Schwarzenegger, Arnold, 1984: *Arnold's Bodybuilding for Men*. New York: Simon and Schuster.

Umbers, Lee, 1992: "O'Neil shapes up to THE PROFESSIONALS: In *NZ Sports Monthly*, May, pp. 38–39.

Weider, Joe. 1984: *Competitive Bodybuilding*, Chicago: Contemporary Books.

Weider, Joe. 1985: *Pumping Up. Supershaping The Female Physique*. New York: Sterling Publ.

Weider, Joe, 1991: "Preserving Body Elegance". In: *Muscle & Fitness*, Editorial (Month unknown):7

Wuthnow, R., 1988: *Communities of Discourse: Ideology and Social Structure in the Reformation, the Enlightenment and European Socialism*. Harvard University Press.

17 Men loving men hating women: The crisis of masculinity and violence to women in sport*

Celia Brackenridge

Introduction

> ... violence against women is not an inevitable outgrowth of male biology, male sexuality, or male hormones. It is 'male conditioning' not the 'condition of being male', that appears to be the problem ... it is partly men's insecurity about their masculinity that promotes abusive behaviour towards women.
>
> (Heise in Lancaster and di Leonardo 1997: 424–5)

In this chapter I shall argue that we are hampered in our understanding of violence in sport by narrow definitions of fair play, especially in the literature on children's sports. Casting fair play as 'fairness between players' leaves us in difficulties when things go wrong on the field of play since we tend then to look for the causes and solutions of these problems amongst the players themselves. In other words, we use micro-social, often pathological, tools to try to understand the problems of cheating, aggression and violence when macro-social analyses are also needed. I am arguing, therefore, that social psychology and the psychology of the individual too often dominate our thinking on these issues yet offer impoverished accounts of violence *unless* social and cultural perspectives are also considered.

Sexual violence is one of the many expressions of unfairness in sport but one which, until very recently, has been absent from both the research and policy agendas in sport. Violence, I suggest, is *also* narrowly defined in ways that draw our attention to public examples of aggressive outbursts by men but which render invisible sexual violations privately perpetrated by them on women and children. This approach to violence applies both inside and outside sport. It is the reason that there is far greater investment in social policy initiatives to deal with 'the problem of male violence' and far less to deal with the private suffering of women and children (see Figure 17.1). In short, then, naughty boys draw political interest and large sums of research and policy money whereas suffering women and girls do not.

---

* This chapter is drawn and abridged from Spoilsports: Understanding and Preventing Sexual Exploitation in Sport (2001) Taylor & Francis and from a paper in the proceedings of the 2000 European Fair Play Congress in Israel.

OUTSIDE SPORT		INSIDE SPORT	
Public spaces **'street'**	**Private spaces** **'home'**	**Public spaces** **'arena'**	**Private spaces** **'locker room'**
Violence between young men	Domestic violence to women and children	Violence between players on the field	Bullying, harassment and sexual exploitation between peers and by authority figures

Figure 17.1 Public and private sexual exploitation and violence inside and outside sport.

Sport is a sex segregated social institution. The separation of sports into male and female on biological grounds is reinforced by powerful ideological and political mechanisms. Woven into these sex and gender divisions is the heterosexual imperative that privileges particular expressions of masculinity above others and above all types of femininity. Social domination through violence is, of course, not exclusively based on gender and sexuality, although these are the focus of this paper: race, class and disability issues are also associated with violence, although their association with sexual violence in sport is under-researched.

Sexual violence in and around sport is closely linked to two projects of recent times, one theoretical and one socio-political. The first is the body project, which has come to dominate theoretical accounts of the structure-agency interface (Theberge 1991; Shilling 1993; Hall 1993). The second is the project – some might say rearguard action – of developing and maintaining the privileges of heterosexual masculinity. Individual and collective violent responses can ensue whenever this latter project is threatened, whether by the incursion of women into sport, the exposure of homosexuality in sport, or by individual men's own failure to live up to the heterosexual masculine standard. My purpose here is to consider why this situation has arisen and what might be done to alleviate it. I will suggest that both institutional and personal violence to women *in* sport are examples of violence *through* sport that are consequences of the crisis of masculinity that has been brought about by late modernity.

Definitions

Sex discrimination, sexual harassment and sexual abuse in sport emerged as social problems in the 1970s, 1980s and 1990s respectively: they are presented here as a continuum of sexual violence, each conceptualized discretely but linked functionally (see Figure 17.2). Each stems from an abuse of power, whether personal, institutional or both. One of the most important aspects of power is the power

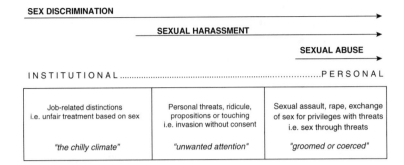

Figure 17.2 The sexual violence continuum.

to name or to resist definitions made by those in power. With reference to sexual exploitation, both within and beyond sport, the power of men to define what counts as violence and what does not, leaves us with narrow definitions that invariably benefit men. For example, defining sexual violence only as more extreme, injury-provoking outbursts excludes the wide range of everyday invasions by men, made without consent, into women's life spaces. It ignores institutional violence of discrimination in pay, resources, career provision and safety and the emotional and psychological abuses of neglect, deprivation, insensitivity and oppression that many women suffer day by day, week by week, year by year from their male partners and colleagues. My definition of violence (following Hearn 1996; 1998; Kelly 1988) as 'that which violates' is then a controversial one but one which allows us to address violence in sport as a systemic issue rather than merely an interpersonal one.

I shall focus on sexual violence to women and girls by men in sport but want to stress at the outset that boys are also sexually exploited in sport settings. Certainly, most of the research data on sexual exploitation in sport concerns its effects on girls and young women. This is not because boys and young men escape such problems, as official statistics demonstrate (Ferguson and Mullen 1999).

I shall not address sexual exploitation by women authority figures in sport since so few women are in positions of power and since we have almost no research evidence on this theme to draw from at this point.

Evidence of sexual violence to women in sport

What is the evidence for violence to women and girls in sport? Recent empirical studies in Canada, The Netherlands, Denmark, Holland and Britain indicate that the gains in gender equity of the past thirty years are probably illusory. Rather than being strangers, the perpetrators of serious sexual exploitation are usually known to their victims, and studies outside sport confirm the pattern that rapists are more likely to be known than unknown to the victim (Watson 1996). Women in sport, especially those at the elite level, face sexual harassment and abuse from their athlete peers, their non-athlete peers and from their coaches.

Very few sport-specific data on the incidence and prevalence of sexual exploitation are available. Under-reporting is a common problem in research studies of rape, for obvious reasons of confidentiality and post-disclosure victimization. According to Donnelly (1999) there are several strong indicators that the incidence of sexual harassment in sport is under-reported, which he suggests is related to sport culture. Lenskyj (1992: 21) adds:

> Like women working in other traditionally male-dominated fields, many female athletes appear to grow resigned to the frequent acts of verbal and physical harassment in the sport context.

The figures available suggest that large numbers of young people enter sport clubs and programmes having already experienced the stresses and trauma of sexual exploitation within their own. Since it is known that sex offenders target the vulnerable, these individuals, especially if intensely committed to sporting goals, are likely to be especially susceptible to sexual approaches either by unscrupulous authority figures or by bullying peers (Brackenridge and Kirby 1997).

The first national level survey of sexual harassment in sport, amongst 1,200 Canadian Olympians (Kirby and Greaves 1996), showed that sexual harassment and abuse by authority figures were widespread practices. Twenty-nine per cent of all respondents ($n = 266$) complained of having experienced upsetting sexual comments or advances. Twenty-two per cent replied that they had had sexual intercourse with persons in positions of authority in sport. Nine per cent reported they had experienced *forced* sexual intercourse, or rape, with such persons. Twenty-three of them were under 16 years of age at the time of the sexual assault, in other words they had experienced *child* sexual assault (defined as rape in some countries). Sexually exploitative behaviours were differentially experienced by gender in this study. Females demonstrated: a higher degree of vulnerability; higher awareness of the issues; more instances of abuse and harassment; and wider variation of abuses than did their male athlete peers. Fifty-five per cent of the female athletes reported experiencing upsetting putdowns (humiliation) in sport.

Reviewing several studies in sport, MacGregor (1998) suggested that between 40 and 50 per cent of sport participants, experience a negative and uncomfortable environment in their encounters with other people in these settings, caused by everything from mild harassment to sexual abuse. A Danish study across twelve different sports (Toftegaard 1998), of 275 coaches and 250 sports students' attitudes towards harassment and abuse, found that 25 per cent of athletes either knew about, or had themselves experienced when under 18 years old, sexual harassment or abuse by a coach. The coaches were clear what was right and wrong but their behaviour did not always match their expressed attitudes. Nearly 6 per cent were in doubt about whether having a relationship with an athlete under eighteen was 'completely unacceptable' even though it is illegal in Denmark and carries a four year jail sentence. Twenty per cent had had a sexual relationship with one of their athletes above eighteen years of age and 66 per cent thought that this was acceptable: six coaches (2.6 per cent) said they had actually had such a relationship with an athlete under 18. It was the youngest coaches who were least aware of how, and under which circumstances, such problems could occur. In Australia, from a screening questionnaire given to 1,100 elite athletes, Leahy (1999) reported that 2 per cent of men and 27 per cent women had experienced sexual *harassment* in sport and 3 per cent of men and 12 per cent of women reported *abuse* experiences.

Mindful of the limitations of surveys for studying this very sensitive topic, Fasting, Brackenridge and Sundgot Borgen (2000) carried out a study of sexual harassment patterns amongst 660 elite females in 58 sport disciplines in Norway and compared the results with those from an age-matched control sample of non-elite athletes[2], with follow-up qualitative interviews. In the survey, the athletes were asked about their experiences of sexual harassment outside, as well as inside, sport. The athletes actually experienced less sexual harassment overall from inside (28 per cent) than from outside sport (39 per cent). Overall, 51 per cent of respondents reported that they experienced sexual harassment, from both within and outside sport, mainly from men. 'Ridicule' was the most common form of harassment from other athletes and 'unwanted touching' from authority figures.

The fact that ridicule was experienced by so many female athletes in this study, both by peers in sport and people outside sport, is of great concern. Holman (1994; 1995) also found evidence of more harassment from peer athletes than from coaches in her Canadian study and Crosset *et al.* (1995) found that male American student-athletes were over-represented in sexual assaults on campus in comparison with their non-athletic peers. Robinson's account of abuses in Canadian ice hockey also illustrate vividly that there is a high tolerance for sexual bullying in sport by peer athletes (Robinson 1998). According to the Norwegian results, males were over-represented in all categories of sexual harasser (authority figures in sport, peers in sport and others from outside sport). It seems that, in spite of the many positive strides towards gender equity in recent years, both in sport and in society at large, female elite athletes still may not be totally accepted by society or even by their male athlete peers.

Among the oldest participants in the Norwegian study (over 23 years), the control group had experienced more sexual harassment than the athletes. One possible explanation for this finding may be that, as they grow older, elite athletes become more adept at protecting themselves and are thereby able to avoid potential harassment situations. Conversely, it may be that the athletes become more habituated to sexual harassment in their sports and thus *less* likely to name or report it. In these circumstances, sexual harassment becomes the price for reaching elite athlete status.

Striking, yet counter-intuitive findings from the Norwegian data, were that athletes who participated in 'masculine' sports had more often experienced sexual harassment (59 per cent) than participants in 'feminine' (50 per cent) or 'gender-neutral' (46 per cent) sports, and that female athletes in sports with the most clothing cover experienced the most ridicule. Clearly, a great deal more work needs to be done on this issue before any confidence can be based in claims about 'risky sports' but these data point towards some explanations of sexual exploitation. One is that such sports are also associated with the masculine heritage and male dominance in sport: women playing previously male-only or overtly masculine sports represent a threat to that dominant status and also provoke homophobic prejudice. Sadly, despite the advances made in women's sport over the past two decades, the notion of 'gender appropriateness' (Metheny 1963; Lenskyj 1986) appears to be alive and well in sport. Perhaps the most worrying finding from the Norwegian study was that significantly more of the female athletes had experienced sexual harassment from an authority figure in sport (15 per cent), such as coaches, instructors, managers and so on, than the controls had done from supervisors or teachers in the workplace (9 per cent). This indicates that authority figures in sport may exhibit behaviour towards athletes that is not tolerated or accepted in workplaces or educational institutions. It is no surprise that those countries most associated with liberal social policy, fair play and gender equity have done the most research into this subject. Given the findings from Norway, one of the leading nations in working for gender equity, the situation in other countries is likely to give much greater cause for concern.

This, then, is the picture of sexual violence to women in sport as far as we know it on the basis of current research. Of course we cannot say for certain whether the situation has become better or worse over time since no previous, baselines studies of sexual harassment and abuse in sport have been conducted.

The conditions and consequences of late modernity

> ... it is partly men's insecurity about their masculinity that promotes abusive behaviour toward women.
>
> (Heise in Lancaster and di Leonardo (1997: 425))

As constructions of sexuality in late modernity fragment along with other former certainties, men's sport is faced with a particular challenge. It is founded on the modern ideologies of social structures rooted in fixed (male) authority. If not completely irrelevant, we are certainly struggling to find relevance for these ideologies today. According to Messner and Sabo (1990: 9)

> Sport ... is an institution created by and for men ... it has served to bolster a sagging ideology of male superiority and has thus helped to reconstitute masculine hegemony in the 19th and 20th centuries.

Unlike many other major cultural forms, such as music, theatre or literature, in sport heterosexuality is an 'organizing principle' (Kolnes 1995). Sex segregation is embedded in the constitutive systems of sport and in the ideological and cultural domination enjoyed by heterosexual men. Adherence to the process of man-making through sport is still one of the most pervasive features of contemporary western culture. Messner and others have noted that sexuality and gender have been differently constructed for women and for men, with sports for men being consonant with masculinity and heterosexuality but sports for women being dissonant with both femininity and heterosexuality. This has been extensively reported as the 'apologetic' (Felshin 1974), whereby females have to 'justify' the threat to their (hetero)sexual identity posed by their participation in sport. They do this by adopting overtly feminine clothing, jewellery or other trappings of traditional heterosexuality. In other words, stereotypical notions of masculine and feminine are also expected to align along the gender divide. More recently, queer theorists have examined the false binaries that characterize sport ideology, the male-female, gay-straight, win-loss relations of sporting practice.

In sport, traditional heterosexual masculinity is made and re-made through the convergence of the physical and the cultural. But in order to preserve its ideological and political dominance heterosexual men's sport has gone to enormous lengths to exclude women (and gay men), to vilify them and to undermine their own sporting aspirations. Control of women's public sexuality extends to definitions of acceptable dress, hairstyles, make up and type of sport. In private, women's sexual development is controlled through use of the contraceptive pill, restrictive diets and sanctioned social lives. Personal ridicule experienced by female athletes is reinforced by powerful cultural messages and structural exclusions of women from the bases of power in sport. This does not happen to *all* female athletes or in *all* sport organizations, of course, but the overall effect impinges on the experiences of all female athletes.

As in other all-male institutions, in the homosocial world of men's sport there is lack of empathy with women, lack of concern for intimacy with women and lack of respect for women (Curry 1991, 1998). There is often also conflicted sexuality, whereby men used their masculinity as a commodity in exchange relations with other men. One explanation for this behaviour is that it ensures the male (sport) group will look after the man who is insecure about his sexuality. Such individuals, however, have to 'pass' as straight at all costs to ensure their continued acceptance into the hyper masculine sub-world of their sport.

In his research into amateur bodybuilders, Alan Klein (1990) found that many were male prostitutes who identified themselves as straight but did not have straight sex for years. Klein describes male athletes as the 'gatekeepers of masculinity' (1990: 132). He quotes one American Football star who came out as gay and said

> . . . how could any man come through [the NFL] as purely heterosexual after spending so much time idealizing and worshipping the male body, while denigrating and ridiculing the female.
>
> (Kopay and Young 1997, cited in Klein 1990: 132)

. . . and Robinson quotes Malszecki (1998: 89) who said: 'The role of women is to nourish the man emotionally so he can withstand the dysfunctional relationship he has with men.'

The ability to inflict and to tolerate pain is another mechanism of male sport that renders inferior/feminine anyone unable or unwilling to comply with these norms. This establishes yet further social distance between heterosexual males in sport and 'others'. This hyper masculine, heterosexual culture of sport, with its sexually intense initiation rituals, excessive use of alcohol and demeaning attitudes towards women, can remove inhibitions for sexual abuse and assault, both by males to females (singly or in groups) and by males to other males (Benedict 1997; Robinson 1998).

Peer support for sexual assault and rape is an important influence on actual behaviour, especially in social settings described above, where alcohol is freely consumed, and where males attempt to overcome their fears about expressing intimacy. In many sports, the associated 'social life' is a major attraction to participants and a central part of the overall sporting experience.

Robinson (1998) described numerous cases of sexual degradation, assault and rape in social settings by Canadian male ice hockey players.

> In the rape culture of the [ice] hockey locker room, . . . females are referred to as 'groupies', 'puck bunnies', 'pucks' and 'dirties' among the players . . .
>
> (Robinson 1998: 5)

The theory of masculine crisis

Mariah Burton Nelson's book *The Stronger Women Get, The More Men Love Football* (1994) depicts vividly the retreat into hyper masculine sport that has been provoked by women's incursion into sport and other areas of public life. Football, in all its formulations but archetypally in the American code, combines being male with sanctioned violence (Benedict 1997). Together, these ingredients develop cultural domination by males and cultural inferiority in females.

The greater the crisis for traditional heterosexual masculinity, then, the greater the violent response to women in sport. Thus, violence by men to women in sport is, simultaneously, a method by which to maintain power and a celebration of the making and re-making of threatened masculinity. One female survivor of sexual abuse in sport said:

> . . . the men in power know very well that this is going on, often they've done it themselves . . . They are sitting there married to women who they had coached themselves . . . they're collaborating in the whole process rather than stopping it . . . even the most ethical men often vicariously enjoy the sexual dalliances of other men . . . there's something about knowing that this is going on that they get off on it, they appreciate, so they will deliberately look the other way.

That sport is a prime site for the (re)production of heterosexual masculinity has been persuasively argued by many eminent feminists and pro-feminists in recent years (Lenskyj 1992; Hall 1996; Messner 1992, 1996; Messner and Sabo 1994). These arguments are used to examine how men legitimize sexually exploitative practices in sport as part of the heterosexual masculine identity (re)formation process.

Liz Kelly (1988) has argued that the purpose of sexual violence to women is control, not sex, and that institutionalized surveillance of women's sexuality is legitimized in western patriarchy. The heterosexual imperative ensures that, even in the absence of men, women in sport are under constant surveillance so that their conformity to social expectations may be monitored. Dress, language, gestures and interpersonal behaviour are all, therefore, subordinated and socially controlled unless women choose to resist actively. Since men control the financial and political infrastructure of sport, however, the price of overt or sustained resistance by women may be loss of access to competitive opportunities, funds or facilities. One parent reported her daughter's experience of sexual harassment by a coach to me as follows:

> ... [she] decided that she would never be left alone with him again ... she attended one more [practice] and was dropped ...The [governing body] closed ranks to support him ... They said they'd investigated and there was no case to answer. He carried on coaching with a female chaperone.

As if to underline their alliance with dominant heterosexual masculine culture, some sport sub-worlds foster exaggerated sexualization through, for example, allowing violent or degrading 'hazing' (initiation) rituals (Robinson 1998) and illegal drinking in a sexist and/or homophobic atmosphere (Curry 1998). In these conditions, young athletes are likely to be most at risk of abuse by their athlete peers and leaders (Crosset *et al.* 1995). The excesses of male locker room culture have been well documented (Messner and Sabo 1990; Curry 1991; Messner 1992), underpinned by Hearn's pioneering analysis of organization sexuality (Hearn *et al.* 1989). In such a climate, interpersonal boundaries are all-too-easily eroded and personal and sexual liberties taken by sexual aggressors.

The motivation for such sexual abuses is not sexual gratification but the achievement of power through the humiliation of others. Humiliation plays an important part in obedience training and may be manifested through physical, sexual or psychological denigration. Such controlling behaviour is frequently legitimated within sport where the superior knowledge of the coach is deemed to give him licence to require complete obedience from the athlete, whether male or female.

Whereas sport sociology has paid close attention to men's violences to men in respect of on-field brutality, injury, 'deviance', off-field brawling and spectator/fan 'hooliganism' (Young 1991; Dunning 1999) it has paid relatively little attention to men's violences towards women. Use of language to demean and control men, for example the naming of male athletes as female ('pussy', 'wimp', 'big girl's blouse', 'limp-wristed', 'sisters') affirms the importance of heterosexual masculinity and its opposition to femininity (Curry 1991; 1998). It also confirms male athletes' lack of respect for women, which is a precursor to sexual exploitation.

The family-like social system of the sports club is often mentioned by athlete survivors of sexual harassment and abuse as nurturing yet also controlling. Unless challenged, the sports club can become a dysfunctional, surrogate family system in which the hetero-patriarchal authority of the coach is used to render all others (women, children, gay men) powerless. Faced with a sexually exploitative authority figure the athlete has an impossible choice. If she speaks out her integrity remains in tact but her survival in elite competitive sport is hazarded. If she allows the abuse to continue without reporting it, her personal and sexual integrity is violated but her performance in sport might be salvaged. Where she is emotionally attached to the authority figure, then, she may rationalize sexual contact as a reciprocal sign of affection.

Just as competitive fitness in sport must be constantly maintained, the borders between female (and gay male) resistance and heterosexual male control are constantly in flux, being negotiated and re-negotiated through advance and retreat. Pressure for women to have equal membership rights in sports clubs, the abolition of the so-called gender verification test (supposed to identify males masquerading as females), and quotas for women's representation in major sporting organizations, are all examples of threats to traditional male supremacy in sport. Sex discrimination and sexual harassment in sport are expressions of men's concerns about loss of power; sexual abuses are their most extreme attempts to (re)gain that power.

> Lots of coaches who are now very successful started with the women's team ... [the women] had potentially good coaches, who were successful, but [the coaches] had a very poor opinion of [them] ... it's just [that] a coach has much more respect when he's dealing with a men's team.
>
> (Female survivor of sexual harassment in sport)

As women press their claims for sexual equality in the workplace and gain increasing prominence in public life, so they are either 'rendered invisible' or more publicly sexualized and eroticized, for example through pornography (Burton Nelson 1994). Catherine McKinnon calls this the 'eroticization of dominance' (cited in Hearn 1998: 7) that links sexuality to violence: it underpins both *sexual abuses that appear not to be violent and physical abuses that appear not to be sexual.*

Sexual violence in sport arises from a combination of both personal and cultural factors. It is allowed to blight sport because of a general systems failure in which 'collective blindness' (Smith 1995) to the issue is compounded by lack of knowledge and lack of political will for change. Since sport reflects its wider social context, however, these conditions are culturally endemic in Western capitalist societies and not special to the institution of sport.

Human rights, human wrongs ... transforming violent gender relations in sport

In order to eradicate all forms of gendered violence in sport, sport organizations need to move beyond liberal gender equity policies and to embed practical anti-harassment and ethics principles in their work. This requires complete constitutional overhaul and cultural change in the major sport organizations if women and gay men are ever to assume their human rights. Educational programmes that address coaching styles, personal relationships, language and behaviour in sport are important (and cost effective) mechanisms for change but, on their own, they will not bring about sustainable improvements in the organizational culture of sport. Systemic problems require systemic solutions. So, in addition to the work on personal attitudes and interpersonal behaviour, we need to look at macro-level initiatives, both structural and cultural.

Structural initiatives include constitutional change to give wider representation to women at all levels and in all roles in sport, especially in visible leadership positions within sport organizations. By this I do not mean token numbers, like those currently identified in the IOC's targets for women, but the critical mass of 40 per cent minimum that is required by, for example, the Swedish public committee system. Policies and procedures in sport organizations also need to be brought into line with international and national statutes for equal rights and human rights, such that women, sexual minorities and children are also fully represented. Monitoring and evaluation of policies for improved human rights is essential.

Structural levers are available to the governing bodies of world sport, such as the giving or withholding of grants, the awarding or not of competition venues, and the banning of non-compliant states or organizations. Cultural initiatives include active resistance to pornographic and infantilising imagery of females in sport, so commonly seen in the media. There also needs to be open discussion about sexual issues, including sexual exploitation of women, gay men and children in sport. Athlete empowerment is also needed, extending beyond simply having a voice in selection or a right to resist sexual coercion, to a full opportunity to influence decision-making throughout every sport. Whether there is the political will to implement such initiatives is debatable, since most of the major sport organizations are run by self-selecting (male) oligarchies who are reluctant to give up their power.

Conclusions

Sexual access to women and girls comprises many processes through which males define females as sexually available. In sport, which arguably suffers from a cultural time lag in comparison with other social institutions, this access is still legitimized through the dominant ideology of heterosexuality as 'normal' (sexual practice) and male sexuality as 'natural' (biologically driven). The hierarchical gender-power relations which characterize the social institution of sport, and by which women's sport, historically, has been systematically belittled, excluded, undermined or ignored, are now under severe threat from the disrupting forces of late modernity. As traditional social categories fracture and diversify, so the certainties of sport as a site of heterosexual masculine identity formation are challenged. This has led to a gender backlash within sport as men struggle to come to terms with women's emerging power in the executive suite, the gym and the stadium.

Notes

1 All quotations from personal interviews are anonymized.
2 The project was part of a much larger study of the medical issues of the 'female athlete triad' (eating disorders, menstrual irregularity and osteoporosis), carried out for the Norwegian Olympic Committee.

Acknowledgement

Thanks to Kari Fasting for her research collaboration.

References

Benedict, J. (1997) *Public Heroes, Private Felons. Athletes and Crimes Against Women*, Boston: Northwestern University Press.

Brackenridge, C. H. (1997) '"He owned me basically": Women's experience of sexual abuse in sport', *International Review for the Sociology of Sport* 32(2): 115–30.

Brackenridge, C. H. and Kirby, S. (1997) 'Playing safe? Assessing the risk of sexual abuse to young elite athletes', *International Review for the Sociology of Sport* 32(4): 407–18.

Burton Nelson, M. (1994) *The Stronger Women Get, the More Men Love Football: Sexism and the American Culture of Sports*, New York: Harcourt Brace.

Christopherson, J., Furniss, T., O'Mahoney, B., Peake, A., Armstrong, H. and Hollows, A. (1989) *Working with Sexually Abused Boys: An Introduction for Practitioners*, London: National Children's Bureau.

Crosset, T., Benedict, J. R. and McDonald, M. A. (1995) 'Male student-athletes reported for sexual assault: a survey of campus police departments and judicial affairs offices', *Journal of Sport and Social Issues* 19(2): 126–40.

Curry, T. (1991) 'Fraternal bonding in the locker room: a profeminist analysis of talk about competition and women', *Sociology of Sport Journal* 8(2): 119–35.

Curry, T. (1998) 'Beyond the locker room: campus bars and college athletes', *Sociology of Sport Journal* 15(3): 205–15.

Donnelly, P. (1999) 'Who's fair game?: Sport, sexual harassment and abuse', in P. White and K. Young (eds) *Sport and Gender in Canada*, Toronto: Oxford University Press.

Dunning, E. (1999) *Sport Matters: Sociological Studies of Sport, Violence and Civilisation*, London: Routledge.

Fasting. K., Brackenridge, C. H. and Sundgot Borgen, J. (2000) *Sexual Harassment In and Outside Sport*, Oslo: Norwegian Olympic Committee.

Felshin, J. (1974) 'The dialectic of woman and sport' in E. Gerber, J. Felshin, P. Berlin and W. Wyrick (eds) *The American Women in Sport*, London: Addison-Wesley.

Fergusson, D. M. and Mullen, P. E. (1999) 'Childhood sexual abuse: an evidence based perspective', Vol. 40, *Developmental Clinical Psychology and Psychiatry*, London: Sage.

Hall, M. A. (1993) 'Feminism, theory and the body: A response to Cole', *Journal of Sport and Social Issues* 17(2): 98–105.

Hall, M. A. (1996) *Feminism and Sporting Bodies: Essays on Theory and Practice*, Champaign, IL: Human Kinetics.

Hearn, J. (1996) 'Men's violence to known women: men's accounts and men's policy developments' in B. Fawcett, B. Featherstone, J. Hearn, and C. Toft (eds) (1996) *Violence and Gender Relations: Theories and Interventions*, London: Sage.

Hearn, J. (1998) *The Violences of Men*, London: Sage.

Hearn, J., Sheppard, D., Tancred-Sheriff, P. and Burrell, G. (eds) (1989) *The Sexuality of Organisation*, London: Sage.

Heise, L. L. (1997) 'Violence, sexuality and women's lives', in R. Lancaster and M. di Leonardo (eds) *The Gender and Sexuality Reader: Culture, History, Political Economy*, London: Routledge.

Holman, M. (1994) 'Sexual harassment in athletics: listening to the athletes for solutions', unpublished paper presented to the annual conference of North American Society for the Sociology of Sport Conference.

Holman, M. (1995) 'Female and male athletes' accounts and meanings of sexual harassment in Canadian interuniversity athletics', unpublished PhD thesis, University of Windsor, Ontario, Canada.

Kelly, L. (1988) *Surviving Sexual Violence*, Cambridge: Polity Press.

Kirby, S. and Greaves, L. (1996) 'Foul play: Sexual abuse and harassment in sport, paper presented to the pre-olympic scientific congress, Dallas, USA July 11–14.

Klein, A. M. (1990) 'Little big man: hustling, gender narcissism, and bodybuilding subculture', in M. A. Messner and D. F. Sabo (eds) *Sport, Men and the Gender Order* Champaign, IL: Human Kinetics.

Kolnes, L. (1995) 'Heterosexuality as an organising principle in women's sports', *International Review for the Sociology of Sport* 30: 61–80.

Leahy, T. (1999) Personal communication, E.mail, November 28th.

Lenskyj, H. J. (1986) *Out of Bounds: Women, Sport and Sexuality*, Toronto: The Women's Press.

Lenskyj, H. J. (1992) 'Unsafe at home base: women's experiences of sexual harassment in university sport and physical education', *Women in Sport and Physical Activity Journal* 1(1): 19–34.

MacGregor, M. (1998) 'Harassment and abuse in sport and recreation', *CAHPERD Journal de L'Acsepld*, Summer, 64(2): 4–13.

Messner, M. (1992) *Power at Play: Sports and the Problem of Masculinity*, Boston: Beacon Press.

Messner, M. (1996) 'Studying up on sex', *Sociology of Sport Journal* 13: 221–37.

Messner, M. and Sabo, D. (eds) (1990) *Sport, Men and the Gender Order*, Champaign, IL: Human Kinetics.

Messner, M. and Sabo, D. (1994) *Sex, Violence and Power in Sports: Rethinking Masculinity*, Freedom, California: Crossing Press.

Metheny, E. (1963) *Connotations of Movement in Sport and Dance*, Dubuque, Iowa: Brown.

Robinson, L. (1998) *Crossing the Line: Sexual Harassment and Abuse in Canada's National Sport*, Toronto: McClelland and Stewart Inc.

Sexual Exploitation: Rape, Child Sexual Abuse, and Workplace Harassment, London: Sage Library of Social Research, Vol. 155.

Shilling, C. (1993) *The Body and Social Theory*, London: Sage.

Smith, G. (1995) 'Child abuse: a feeling of failure', *The Guardian* 'Society', August 9th, pp. 6–7.

Theberge, N. (1991) 'Reflections on the body in the sociology of sport', *Quest* 43: 123–34.

Toftegaard, J. (1998) 'Den forbudte zone' ('The Forbidden Zone'), unpublished M.A. thesis, Institut for Idraet, Copenhagen, Denmark.

Watson, L. (1996) *Victims of Violent Crime Recorded by the Police, England and Wales 1990–94*, Home Office Statistical Findings Issue 1/96, London: Home Office Research and Statistics Directorate.

Young, K. (1991) 'Sport and collective violence', *Exercise and Sport Sciences Reviews* 19: 539–87.

Seminar questions

Chapter 15

1 What is the relationship between sport and physicality for both men and women?
2 How can different sports contribute to the physical and social empowerment of women?

Chapter 16

1 How does Obel use the story of Bev Francis' career in bodybuilding to highlight gender contradictions and ambiguities?
2 What are the feminising practices in men's bodybuilding?
3 Why does Obel argue that men's bodybuilding, rather than women's bodybuilding, is more of a threat to a traditional understanding of gender?

Chapter 17

1 How has our understanding of violence in sport been hampered by narrow definitions? How useful is Brackenridge's sexual violence continuum in moving the debate forward?
2 What is the relationship between hegemonic heterosexual masculinity and sexual violence towards women in sport?
3 How convincing are Brackenridge's arguments that sexual violence towards women in sport is related to a crisis in hegemonic masculinity?

Part VIII

Policy and politics

Introduction

A central feature to feminism has been the notion of *praxis* that is the interconnectedness of theory and action or practice. In relation to gender and sport, feminist praxis has been crucial to the struggles and gains women have made in the sporting world. The majority of the policy developments and practical initiatives have been liberal in philosophy and strategy, that is, concentrating on equal access and opportunity issues. The changes that have taken place have been at both a macro institutional level and at the more micro level of individuals. The final part of the book begins with a copy of the Windhoek 1998 Call for Action that developed from the 1994 Brighton Declaration on Women and Sport (United Kingdom Sports Council 1998). This statement resulted from the second World conference on women and sport and called for action throughout the world to further the development of equal opportunities for girls and women to participate fully in sport in its broadest sense. This is an example of action being taken at an international level by key academics and practitioners involved at a policy level. In contrast there have been many struggles and initiatives by individuals and by groups of women at a local level. These tend to be more grassroots in their orientation but are just as important having the potential to create real change for the specific women involved.

The two chapters we have chosen for the *Reader* reflect some of the debates raised by both macro policy decisions and processes and those initiated by sports women struggling to achieve gender equity. The first chapter by Margaret Talbot provides a useful critique of different approaches to gender and sport policy and goes on to provide examples of patriarchal bureaucratic processes in action in international sports organizations. She draws on research undertaken at the 1994 Commonwealth Games and also her own reflective experiences with the European Sports Conference and the International Working Groups on Women and Sport. These latter experiences were with the working parties that produced the Brighton Declaration on Women and Sport and the Windhoek Agreement. The chapter provides a fascinating insight into policy processes and their implementation and the implications these have for gender equity and sport.

In contrast, the chapter by Nancy Theberge focuses specifically on one sport, ice hockey, and women's struggles for legitimacy in a sport historically defined and dominated by men. She traces the development of women's ice hockey to its inclusion for the first time in the Olympic games in 1998. This inclusion is seen to increase the ideological struggle over the gendering of sport with the women involved under pressure to be tough in the game and feminine off the ice. She argues that both the Olympic stage and commercial pressures highlight the distinctions between the women's and the men's games and heighten the debate about women's engagement in certain sports and the gendering of hockey players. Whilst these debates are being played out in a sport known to symbolize masculinity (described by Theberge as 'cold, rugged, hard'), they would appear to be very pertinent to other sports in which women are making inroads onto the national and international scene (soccer, American football, baseball, rugby etc.).

After reading these two chapters, students should:

- be aware of gender stratification and power in sports organizations;
- understand the development and impact of gender equity policies in sport;
- recognize patriarchal processes and their effects on sportswomen's opportunities;
- be able to discuss the ideological struggle over the gendering of women's ice hockey;
- be able to apply the debates within women's ice hockey to other sporting contexts.

Further readings

Birrell, S. and Ritcher, D. M. (1987) 'Is a diamond forever? Feminist transformations in sport, *Women Studies International Forum* 10(4): 395–409.

Hall, M. A. (1995) 'Feminist activism in sport: a comparative study of women's sport' in A. Tomlinson (ed) *Gender, Sport and Leisure: Continuities and Challenges*, Brighton: Chelsea School Research Centre, University of Brighton.

United Kingdom Sports Council (1998) *Women and Sport from Brighton to Windhoek: Facing the Challenge*, London: United Kingdom Sports Council.

Women's Sports Foundation (1999) *National Action Plan: Women's and Girls' Sport and Physical Activity*, London: Women's Sports Foundation/Sport England.

WWW sources

Women's Sport Foundation: *http://www.wsf.org.uk*

Canadian Association for the Advancement of Women and Sport and Physical Activity (CAAWS): *http://caaws.ca/main.htp*

Women Sport International: *http://www.de.psu.ed/wsi/index.htm*

Women's Sports Foundation (United States): *www.lifetimetv.com/wosport.index.html*

The Windhoek call for action

The 400 delegates from 74 countries present at the 2nd World Conference on Women and Sport held in Windhoek, Namibia, May 19–22, 1998 called for action throughout the world to further the development of equal opportunities for girls and women to participate fully in sport in its broadest sense. This call reflected an overwhelming desire on the part of all delegates to seek greater co-operation and co-ordination between the many agencies and organizations responsible for women's issues, and recognized and stressed the importance that sport can and should play in the advancement of girls and women.

The Conference recognized the need for linkages into existing international instruments, in particular the Beijing platform for Action and the UN convention on the elimination of all forms of discrimination against women, that impact directly and indirectly on advancement of girls and women.

The Conference celebrated the successes achieved by and for girls and women since the endorsement of the Brighton Declaration in 1994. These success stories demonstrate clearly the potential of sport to impact positively on the lives of girls and women.

This Call for Action is addressed to all men and women in those national and international sport organizations, governments, public authorities, development agencies, schools, businesses, educational and research institutions, and women's organizations, who are responsible for, or who directly influence the conduct, development or promotion of sport, or who are in any way involved in the employment, education, management, training, development or care of girls and women in sport.

In addition to re-affirming the principles of the Brighton Declaration, the Conference delegates called for action in the following areas:

1 Develop action plans with objectives and targets to implement the principles of the Brighton Declaration, and monitor and report upon their implementation.
2 Reach out beyond the current boundaries of the sport sector to the global women's equality movement and develop closer partnerships between sport and women's organizations on the one side, and representatives from sectors such as education, youth, health, human rights and employment on the other.

Develop strategies that help other sectors obtain their objectives through the medium of sport and at the same time further sport objectives.

3   Promote and share information about the positive contribution that girls' and women's involvement in sport makes, *inter alia*, to social, health and economic issues.

4   Build the capacity of women as leaders and decision makers and ensure that women play meaningful and visible roles in sport at all levels. Create mechanisms that ensure that young women have a voice in the development of policies and programmes that affect them.

5   Avert the "world crisis in physical education" by establishing and strengthening quality physical education programmes as a key means for positive introduction to young girls of the skills and other benefits they can acquire through sport. Further, create policies and mechanisms that ensure progression from school to community-based activity.

6   Encourage the media to portray positively and significantly cover the breadth, depth, quality and benefits of girls' and women's involvement in sport.

7   Ensure a safe and supportive environment for girls and women participating in sport at all levels by taking steps to eliminate all forms of harassment and abuse, violence and exploitation, and gender testing.

8   Ensure that policies and programmes provide opportunities for all girls and women in full recognition of the differences and diversity among them – including such factors as race, ability, age, religion, sexual orientation, ethnicity, language, culture or their status as an indigenous person.

9   Recognize the importance of governments to sport development and urge them to develop appropriate legislation, public policy and funding monitored through gender impact analysis to ensure gender equality in all aspects of sport.

10   Ensure that Official Development Assistance programmes provide equal opportunities for girls' and women's development and recognize the potential of sport to achieve development objectives.

11   Encourage more women to become researchers in sport, and more research to be undertaken on critical issues relating to women in sport.

Windhoek, Namibia
May 22, 1998

18 Playing with patriarchy: The gendered dynamics of sports organizations*

Margaret Talbot

Gender and sport policy

There have been many gender analyses of the distribution of power in sports organizations, and discussions of how the gender hegemonies of these sports organizations affect women's opportunities to play and work in sport (Hall 1996; Hargreaves 1994; Talbot 1990*a*). However, sports policies are constructed often without awareness of structural gender inequalities, and in policy formation, the tendency has been to adopt a 'women and sport' approach (see Figure 18.1).

In 'women and sport' approaches, it is assumed that if women can learn new behaviours (i.e., to be more assertive, to learn sports skills while they are children, to be more confident, competitive etc.), then access to sport, whether as participant or as worker, will be unproblematic. Gender inequities in sports organizations are 'explained', if they are recognized at all, by the **social** barriers which women face, such as family responsibilities and pressure on time. The way sport itself is constituted or managed is not often seen to provide barriers. If barriers are recognized, they are frequently defended by the argument that they are so fundamental to the identity of the sport or the sports organization, that they must not be changed (Abrams and Talbot 1995; Talbot 1988; 1990*a*; 1990*b*; 1994). These institutionalized

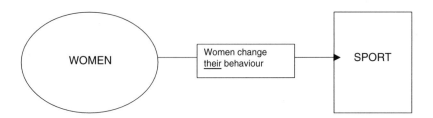

Figure 18.1 'Women and sport' approach.

* An earlier version of this chapter was presented as a keynote chapter at the European Women and Sport 2000 Conference: *Women, Sport and Culture – how to change the sports culture*? Helsinki 8 June 2000.

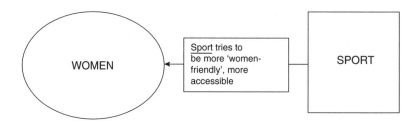

Figure 18.2 'Women-friendly' sport.

barriers prevent effective development and action, and serve to exclude large numbers of people, including many women. Sports organizations which claim to embrace the values of equity and inclusiveness cannot afford, if their policies are to be effective, to ignore structural inequalities, or refuse to recognize their own part in perpetuating them (Figure 18.2).

Where sports organizations are prepared to analyse critically the ways they operate, the ways they make policy, and the ways in which national and international policy processes influence or are influenced by these sites of power (Hall 1996; Hargreaves 1994; Talbot 1991), action can be taken to make sport more accessible to women. Leaders of sport organizations may not have considered, for example, the exclusionary effects of holding meetings in locations which are difficult to reach by public transport; or of holding meetings in early weekday evenings – the very time when women with family responsibilities are most in demand and on call.

However, in some cases, organizational practices appear to be designed to maintain the (male) status quo. Some women, who have been elected as members of committees or boards of sport organizations, have faced continued resistance to their inclusion and their contributions. Written evidence of their experiences remain scarce, because in most cases they withdraw from the system altogether. But it is likely that, as in corporate senior management (Marshall 1995), organizational cultures which are based on the locker room and replicated in the board room, do in fact marginalize women's experience, career prospects and contributions. Evidence needs to be collected of women's experiences in such situations, and used creatively with those who control sport, to show that sport is failing to utilize women's experiences and contributions effectively.

Women (and any other group new to involvement in sport at senior level) face new and changing challenges. Even if they are able to use the nominations, elections and appointment systems which continue to be dominated in sports organizations by men (Fasting 1993; Talbot 1990*a*; 1997; 2001), increasingly they need to negotiate new pressures for specialist knowledge and experience. Since the 1970s, many government agencies have attempted to influence sports organizations at national level, by implementing **rational planning (strategic) approaches**.

Such approaches were adopted, partly to compete with the successes of the state-controlled national sports organizations of the Eastern and Communist countries; and partly to secure some accountability from voluntary national organizations, for the government funding used to develop sport at national level. As the demands of performance in international sport became greater, with implications for hugely increased budgets, governments saw the opportunity and need to use the funding to force, coerce or negotiate organizational change in national sports organizations (Abrams *et al.* 1996; Macintosh and Whitson 1990). The risks and perceived waste of resources observed in community development approaches (Averley 1995) have led to preoccupation with the quantitative measures and performance indicators of rational planning. In the UK, this is represented in national sports policy as 'more people, more places, more medals' (English Sports Council 1997).

The two contrasting models in Figure 18.3 of managing projects and programmes can leave many people stranded, unable to understand why their efforts are misunderstood and unappreciated. This may be particularly true of those working in education and development, whose ideologies reflect the aim of empowerment and capacity-building: more women work in these areas of sport provision than in other areas of sport like facility management, local government senior management, senior levels of national sports organizations. There is a need for more knowledge about the dynamics of people's responses to finding themselves in alien management contexts in sport. It would be particularly interesting to know whether senior managers even acknowledge the desirability of community development approaches, and how people working in the field learn to play the strategic development game to their own advantage.

Rational planning, which centralizes the importance of strategic planning, now dominates national approaches to sport. (Rational planning stems from the idea of a rational society in, e.g., the work of Habermas 1972; Giddens 1979; 1987). At first sight, rationality should **increase** the awareness that a sport cannot afford to ignore either the talents or the demands of more than half of the population. But the processes of organizational change, where existing stakeholders do their best to protect, secure or defend positions of power, and where gatekeeping practices can resist change, mean that leaders of organizations effectively marginalize

STRATEGIC PLANNING	COMMUNITY DEVELOPMENT
Characterized by:	**Characterized by:**
• top-down	• bottom-up
• rationality and tidiness	• coping with diversity, irrationality, passion
• agenda-setting by major stake holders	• capacity-building – structures, leaders, participants
• prescription/direction	
• outcomes must justify investment	• non-directive – empowerment – resources
	• trust and acknowledgement of risk

Figure 18.3 Contrasting models.

considerations of gender equity (Abrams and Talbot 1995; Macintosh and Whitson 1990; Talbot 2001). Macintosh and Whitson (1990) provide examples of the gender dynamics of sports organizations, and warn that rational planning approaches tend to render invisible, commitment to sports equity. Moving away from 'gentlemen's clubs' and 'kitchen table organizations' (Slack and Hinings 1987), towards rationally planned organizations, can further restrict women's opportunities and reduce awareness of gender equity requirements.

Ironically, it could be argued that women have a special role to play, in using their superior capacity for consensus styles of management (Marshall 1995), in balancing the tensions between strategic management and community development. This tension-management includes appreciating and helping colleagues to understand both strategic and local objectives; providing focus, including imperatives, priorities and urgencies; ensuring adequate support structures, towards stability and effective use of staff time; empowerment and contracting of specific tasks; and leadership and advocacy. The development of these skills could place women in very good positions as organizations begin to realize the needs to manage these tensions.

Patriarchal bureaucratic processes in international sports organizations

This chapter provides examples of patriarchal bureaucratic processes in action in international sports organizations. Just as researchers in gender and management (Franks 1999; Maddock 1999; Marshall 1995) have begun to change management practice by recording and analysing women's experiences in relation to men's ('development through a gender lens'), those in sport need also to record the gendered processes of management in sport. Since problems within malestream culture are commonly experienced by women alone, these problems are difficult to address. However, this kind of research can support reflective practice, and thus provide support and affirmation to those people trying to change organizations, both from within and from outside.

The examples in this chapter are taken largely from research undertaken around the 1994 Commonwealth Games, and my own reflective experiences with the European Sports Conference and International Working Groups on Women and Sport. The research project, 'Commonwealth Women and Sport' (Talbot 1997) was commissioned by the Commonwealth Secretariat in mid-1994, shortly after the Brighton Conference. Its purposes were to provide a basis for informing Commonwealth policy and strategy related to development aid through sport, and it was to serve as an extension of the Secretariat policy priority of development aid for women in the Commonwealth. The Commonwealth Secretariat's view of sport is clear:

> Sport imparts values and principles which help form a foundation for broader Commonwealth understanding – principles such as: the equality and dignity

of the individual; non-discrimination on the basis of race, sex, colour, creed, economic status or political belief; fair play.

Commonwealth Secretariat 1991: 2

In recognition of the central place of the Commonwealth Games in the identity and public perceptions of the Commonwealth (McMurtry 1990), the research project was to forge closer links between the Secretariat and the Commonwealth Games Federation, and between international and Commonwealth women's sports networks and the Secretariat's Non-Governmental Organizations (NGO) Desk Officer. The Commonwealth Games research, because of the strong but informal influence of the Commonwealth Secretariat on the Commonwealth Games Federation, has enabled research which has focused directly on policy processes, rather than policy outcomes or products. At the 1994 Games, we collected data in several ways, to explore the opportunities and barriers to women offered by Commonwealth sport:

- documentary analysis,
- questionnaires to all women competitors, national general team managers and national delegates to the Commonwealth Games Federation (CGF) General Assembly,
- interviews with 6 of the 7 women general team managers at the Games,
- conversations with women athletes and officials,
- observation of the CGF General Assembly, the Games events (both competitive and ritual) and the meetings of the Commonwealth Heads of Government Meeting (CHOGM) Committee of Development Through Sport.

The other area of experience was provided by my active involvement at a European level. During the 1990s, women in Europe utilized the opportunities offered by the increasing unification of European interests across East and West. The 1989 Council of Europe Seminar on women and sport in the UK (Sports Council 1989) led to the establishment of a Working Group on Women and Sport by the European Sports Conference (ESC). The Working Group mapped the position of women in European sport and established overall aims and strategic goals towards gender equity in European sport, which were unanimously adopted at the European Sports Conference in Oslo in 1991 (ESC 1991). The data (Fasting 1991; 1993) showed clearly that there were very few women in powerful or decision-making positions in either the national or pan-European structures of sport, and that there was still much to be done to ensure that women could enjoy the levels of opportunity which the European Sports Charter (ESC 1993) represented. This example illustrates the way in which clear evidence of inequity can be used to secure support for intervention to be made.

In 1993, the European Women and Sport Group (EWS) secured a place on the Executive Board of the ESC. In May 1994, 200 delegates from more than 80 countries – many of them Ministers or directors of national sports agencies – gathered in Brighton for a conference 'Women, Sport and the Challenge of Change'. The

Brighton Conference turned out to be a watershed in international policy for women and sport. The organizing group had intended that the Conference should leave a lasting legacy, as well as provide much needed support for, and establish networks between, the women and men working towards gender equity in sport across the world. The result was the Brighton Declaration on Women and Sport (1994). The Brighton Declaration, since its adoption by the Conference, has been formally endorsed or adopted by dozens of international sports organizations, including the Commonwealth Games Federation, and many national sports agencies, including those of Commonwealth countries.

However, sports organizations commonly fail to own the issue of under-representation of women (Abrams and Talbot 1995; Hall *et al.* 1989; McKay 1992; 1998; Talbot 2001). The conventional wisdom is that, if there were sufficient women of the right calibre, and if women were willing to come forward into positions in organizations, then they would be better represented in sports institutions and federations. But leaders of these organizations commonly fail to recognize or acknowledge that their own long established procedures and practices, created in the main by all-male groups for all-male sport, actually prevent women from making the contribution which their sports participation warrants.

This tendency is characteristic of international and national sports organizations, whose structures, procedures and constitutions seem designed to prevent change or response to changing contexts. Inclusion of 'new blood' is effectively resisted, and constitutions are frequently used as barriers behind which existing officers or boards take refuge, rather than as aids to effective or business-like management of an organization's affairs.

International sports organizations are dependant on national sport organizations for nominations for positions, and often for financial contributions. This reinforces the difficulties faced by women in securing positions of influence or being elected into executive positions. (The same is true for other groups whose participation is seen as marginal or recent.) Positions are frequently subject to long established and jealously guarded systems of largely male patronage. 'Reward' for years of voluntary work is commonly the basis for election.

The most intractable problem is the unwillingness of most sports organizations to accept that gender inequity is their concern (see also McKay 1998; Salman 1997; Talbot 2001). The tendency of conservative organizations is to reproduce in their own image ('masculinity-as-culture'), which results in entrenched resistance to change. 'National Sports Organizations see any necessary changes as coming from the women themselves' (Whitson and Macintosh 1989: 41). Despite positive guidelines which have been produced to facilitate gender equity work with national sports organizations (Abrams *et al.* 1996; Canadian Association for the Advancement of Women in Sport (CAAWS) 1995), there remains much to be done before all those in positions of power accept responsibility for ensuring that women enjoy as many and as rich opportunities as men in sport. Nevertheless, some actions and interventions have been shown to be effective in improving women's opportunities, as participants, and as members of sports-related professions and occupations (CAAWS 1994; Fasting 1993).

The potential for change?

What is clear for all countries and all international organizations, is that both political will and effective leverage are required if sports organizations and institutions are to change the practices of (predominantly male) generations. Examples of good practice then can be used as appropriate in different contexts. However, it should be recognized that an intervention that has been effective in one society or structure, may be ineffective – or even counterproductive – in another.

For example, the Nordic countries are often seen as examples of good practice in terms of legislation, policies and practices which encourage gender equity; but the adoption of female officer quotas, which have been so successful in Nordic sports federations, frequently produce very hostile reactions in other countries, with frequent denials of the logical arguments for equity which previously may have been accepted. In Sweden, there is powerful legislation on gender equity and a long tradition of women playing a major role in public life, yet

> ... the ambition for an advance towards equality has not been received only in a positive spirit in sport ... it has produced reactions that show representatives with a very conservative view of women are to be found in the sports movement ...
>
> Swedish Sports Confederation 1990

The relationships between sports policy and legislation, both national and international, which aim to prevent gender discrimination are clearly very important, but have been little explored. It is interesting that in Britain, European Union law has often been more effective, and certainly more radical, than national legislation. Progress towards gender equity is at different stages and phases in different countries, and strategies for change have brought about different degrees of success. One universal constant is that sport lags behind all other areas of social or cultural life (even the Church!), in awareness of, commitment to and effective implementation towards gender equity. Sports organizations remain 'highly patriarchal, nationalistic, and confirming of existing hierarchies and inequalities' (Kidd 1987: 6). Jennifer Hargreaves (1994) maintains that 'it is a *system* of power based on gender' (p. 222), and that sport's history and the ways that it was developed, continue to disadvantage women:

> Women experience similar problems in struggling for recognition in all sports and events from which they have traditionally been excluded. In the early stages there is no history to draw upon; no role models or networking arrangements exist for interested participants; there are no female organizations of coaches; there is always resistance and a certain amount of ridicule; and it is impossible to secure financial backing. The longer men practically and ideologically appropriate an activity, the more difficult it is for women to take part.
>
> Hargreaves 1994: p. 279

The data collected at the 1994 Commonwealth Games (Talbot 1997) illustrate many aspects of organizational resistance to measures to promote gender equity. The inherently conservative structures and procedures of organizations are exploited by gatekeepers, who formally and informally protect these Commonwealth sports organizations as white, male, middle class, and largely English-speaking. This is reflected in the people who are elected or appointed to positions, and by the staff employed by Commonwealth and national organizations. The gendered ideologies of both sport and women were powerful in Games events and staffing. Women volunteer officials wore short white pleated skirts, which many resented ('they treat us like Barbie dolls'), and wore colour-coded blazers reflecting different tasks and different levels of seniority. By contrast, male volunteers, whichever level of seniority they occupied, all wore white trousers and the teal-blue blazers which corresponded with the women's highest 'rank'.

Gendered hierarchies and definitions of sports performance were also apparent, both in decision-making, and in the perceptions of the women competitors at the Games, as recorded in their responses to the questionnaires. As an English badminton player said: 'Nearly all the administrators, managers and coaches are men and deep down they resent the successful women athletes, and they, therefore, make their lives in sport very difficult.' This was echoed by a Jamaican track and field athlete: 'The country doesn't really want to support female athletes in any form of sports'.

Observation of events leading up to and during the Games provided further evidence of this gendered hierarchy of the values of 'performance'. The CGF General Assembly debated what new events should be included in the 1998 Commonwealth Games. It had been agreed at the previous Assembly that netball should be added, as a means of redressing the gender inequity caused by so many events in wrestling and boxing, at that time, both male-only sports in the Commonwealth Games. This led to the host country, Malaysia, proposing several other team sports for the 1998 Games – men's and women's hockey, and rugby sevens and cricket – both for men only. When questioned about why these sports were to be men only, the idea of women's rugby was given very short shrift. Cricket was considered in a slightly more focused way, but still illustrated these gendered hierarchies of performance. The Games representative replied, judiciously, that events in the Games must be at world class level; that he did not think many 'ladies' played cricket in the world (the Women's World Cup had recently taken place); and that of course 'we do not want ladies just frolicking about'! It was not surprising that a Brunei woman badminton competitor had internalized these hegemonic relationships, in recording in her questionnaire response, her feeling that such treatment was unfair: 'Respect women's sport as much as men's. Women should get the same attention and direction as men. We might not fully achieve the same standard as men but we all deserve to expose our ability'.

There were other challenges to stereotypes from the women competitors, one of which directly contradicts a commonly held assumption about gender and religion, at least among these elite athletes. Given some of the myths about religion, women and sport, the women competitors showed strikingly limited influence from religion. Less than 2 percent of the competitors (none from Asia) saw this as a barrier. It should be borne in mind that women who achieve sports success at international level have declared their position regarding public performance and religious observances which would prevent women taking part in certain events or wearing certain types of dress. It should be acknowledged, however, that a more accurate picture of the influence of religion would be gathered from study of the perceptions of women who are not competing at international level, or who do not play sport at all (see, e.g., Ikulayo 1991; Salman 1997).

The Commonwealth Games are somewhat more acceptable to some religious leaders than other world events. This is partly because there are single-sex competitions in sports where dress code is not an issue (e.g., shooting and lawn bowls), and possibly also because it is thought that it is easier to ensure women's safety and honour within the 'friendly Games'. This distinctive provision for women, however, seems not to be fully appreciated by the senior officials of the CGF, or by its national members.

The dynamics of exclusion of women from sport were frequently expressed in their questionnaire responses by the women competitors, despite their own achievements within the system:

Tennis is for rich men's daughters

Sierra Leone athlete, 22

Little support is given to women in my country. Why? Because our families believe women are meant to stay home and make good mothers and house-wifes.

Nigerian athlete, 26

Some sports (i.e., athletics) provide very equal opportunities, whereas others are still very male dominated. It is appalling that 3 Commonwealth Games sports are for men only (weightlifting, boxing, wrestling).

Australian athlete, 36

The 1994 women competitors' responses demonstrated clear recognition of social and structural inequalities, and of the failure of their national sports organizations to cater for them effectively or equitably. Their responses provide a clear pattern of the distribution of the resources of sport – time, spaces, coaching, sports science, financial support, even basic nutrition in some countries – being markedly worse for women than men competitors at the same levels of achievement (Talbot 1997).

The data provides useful means of questioning the effectiveness of many national and international sports policies and structures. The following aspects of sports provision were cited by the women competitors as 'poor' or as 'not existing' in their countries:

Primary Physical Education	24%
Secondary Physical Education	18%
Junior Sport	25%
Adult recreational sport	17%
Coaching and training	21%
Sports science support	40%
Facilities	24%
Sports scholarships	59%

All these were cited as barriers to women's sports participation, and in almost all cases, the provision was seen as poorer for women. These are structural barriers within sports structures and therefore, are capable of being changed by intervention strategies or new provision. There are indeed social and cultural barriers, but the elite sports women saw these as less of a problem than they would be for those women who did not or could not play sport.

The women who were General Team Managers (GTMs) for their countries at the 1994 Games were interviewed in the research. For smaller countries with small teams, the task of GTM involves direct control of and care for athletes, officials and coaches; for the larger teams, this is a complex, demanding and highly responsible role, including management of sport-specific team managers and large numbers of athletes. Our purpose was to explore women GTMs' perceptions, as achieving women in sport, of the opportunities and barriers for women in sport, and their views on why there were so few women at that level in national and international sports organizations. They were asked, not only about their own backgrounds and experience in sport, but also their interpretations of the reasons for their appointments as GTMs. Their views on national sports and gender equity policy, and its effects on sports opportunities for women, and the effectiveness of sport itself to recognize and deal with some of the issues they raised, were all addressed.

The list of seven countries (of 64 competing countries) whose teams were headed by women GTMs at the 1994 Commonwealth Games was interesting, since it included the 'big three' – the Commonwealth countries with the largest teams (both men and women). These were Canada, the host country; Australia, which also turned out to be the most successful team in terms of number of medals; and England. Together, these three women had overall responsibility for 794 athletes, almost 33 percent of the total competitors at the Commonwealth Games in 1994. The other four national teams headed by a female GTM were Brunei, Falkland Islands, Norfolk Islands and Swaziland – all countries with relatively small teams, and, in fact, relatively small populations. However, these seven women GTMs were responsible for a total of 845 competitors – almost 35 percent of all those at the Games.

Both the national GTMs and Delegates to the CGF General Assembly cited perceptions of provision and barriers to women's sports achievement which were similar to those expressed by the women competitors. Generally speaking, the opinions and perceptions of women competitors and GTMs were closer to each other than were the opinions of National Delegates, to either women competitors or GTMs. This illustrates one of the criticisms commonly made of administrators, that they are out of touch with their athletes. The women GTMs' views showed clearly that they had reflected critically on the traditionally male forms of leadership in sport, and had adopted alternatives:

> I think probably women make better team managers than men, because I think there really is, because of the crisis situation, a real need to have a calmness, to almost have a nurturing to really understand the kind of pressure and stress that people are under, so that's one area I really think is critical. I think another area, is we really need a shared philosophy that everybody understands with some real common vision, common values because if you don't have this, with a thousand decisions every day, they can't be running to the Chef every time and saying what about this, and what about that, there needs to be an understanding and a philosophy and therefore almost empowering to allow others to make the decisions, and I think that again in the hierarchical, patriarchal stuff that does not usually happen.
>
> It is important that the athletes are treated as people holistically and so if they need counselling, or entertainment or whatever. We have for years just treated them as a piece of meat, get out there and perform, that's all they are is a machine so now we are really much broader than that.

The GTMs were very conscious of how few women had been appointed at senior levels in national and international structures, and were well aware of the very real barriers, both structural and informal, which faced women within Commonwealth Games organizations. They were also willing to articulate their impatience and dissatisfaction with organizations which they felt were years behind others:

> Women are just not coming up through the ranks, really; well, certainly in England the way we are stuck unless the governing body put the representative on our Council it is very difficult to come up through the ranks. For some of the others, it's being a Secretary General, a natural progression, but how many get there in the first place?

The long-standing barrier to women being appointed in international sports organizations, posed by the systems of nominations from largely male-dominated national organizations, had been also a long-standing irritant to these women. They perceived an unwritten requirement for decades of male patronage before any appointments were likely:

> Age can make a big difference – this organization is so traditional that you have to be at least over 85, at least over 60 to have earned the respect that you feel is due to you, male or female if you are newcomers.

The people who sit on the committees have been there so long that they are clubs more than associations. I don't think it is to keep anybody out but it is just the fact that they have been there so long they are there to stay. In our country there is a huge amount of ability and even though they need people to do a good job, if you do a good job they will give you a good position, but then they'll do their best to get you out. Don't expect any reward or recognition. It's a strange system.

This is a slow process. When I went to the CGF meeting in Barcelona, I was the only woman delegate there from a country and I bet half of them, at least half of the men delegates could not even look at me, they looked through me, or looked at me as 'well who is this?'.

This feeling of being invisible (or inaudible) had irritated another of the women GTMs:

A woman is still regarded as a low class citizen and even though they are turning to women more and more to run sports affairs, yet we have still the unspoken low social status. We have a lot of women helpers but they are never really recognized and the ones who do the work are not recognized as the ones who sit on the Association.

I think almost everywhere in the world is dominated by men. There are only certain areas in sport where women are more prominent, but mostly a lot of them are men. I think it is especially good for us because we come from a very strong Muslim country where Islam is the official religion so it says a lot for the stereotyped image of Islamic countries that women play a role – still they allow a woman to be a team manager. Most of the others are western countries, except for Swaziland and Brunei. Western countries of course you have to understand that the role of women is much stronger here.

As well as the difficulties experienced because of the structural barriers in Commonwealth Games associations and societies, national governing bodies of sport, and the CGF itself, these women GTMs saw the dominant culture of the CGF ('a very traditional British white male organization') as problematic particularly for women:

Most of them say 'Gentlemen we will adjourn now' and it drives me crazy.

Another woman GTM pointed out the cultural barriers that remain to prevent women, especially those with children and unsupportive husbands, from staying involved in sports administration, let alone progressing through the various levels to be representatives of any kind. For women who are financially and legally dependent on men, the capacity to devote time to sport in either voluntary or paid positions, is therefore very limited.

The GTM from Brunei pointed out that the way international sport itself is organized and administered can, albeit inadvertently, present barriers to some women's participation and involvement. In spite of her own Islamic country providing good employment opportunities for competent women in sports administration, there were constraints for their active participation in international sport because of the particular activities which were selected, and the dress codes which were tolerated or even required by international federations. Another GTM had reflected on the dangers of international sports organizations continuing to operate as they always have done:

> In order to be sustainable, we can no longer have the hierarchical, patriarchal decision making structures. Just to bring the CGA together to have an AGM costs $50,000 just in air fares. We need to change the way we manage sport, use the technology better, like teleconferencing.

Conclusion

The focus of this chapter has been on policy processes and implementation (Hogwood and Gunn 1984; Talbot 2001). It is possible here, only to provide examples of patriarchal processes and their effects on women athletes and sports workers' opportunities in European and Commonwealth sport. It is important to recognize that rational planning and more informal patriarchal interpretations of it, are enacted through decisions about structures, personnel and resources, as well as through policies and procedures. In turn, these are mediated and shaped by ideologies of culture, race and gender. The hegemonies of gender, race/culture; state and NGO relations; formal and informal uses of power; and the ideologies of nationhood, sports performance and masculinity, femininity and motherhood – all have powerful effects on the bureaucratic processes and dynamics of sports organizations and their officers' actions and decisions. The effects of decisions about women and their involvement in sport, are immense. It is our task to change perceptions of what is 'allowable, possible and/or pleasurable' (Hargreaves 1990), so that women can make their distinctive and valuable contributions to the development of sport. One woman GTM interviewed at the 1994 Commonwealth Games, illuminates the way forward:

> But some of the changes are in terms of women's leadership style. You don't have to sit on the Board with your suits, and move and second, and follow rules of order. You can talk about consensus, and in fact the outcome of how you manage the organization is more important than the profit and the structures – I think we have to do this regardless of gender, but when it does the women will emerge as the leaders, because we are much more capable of that style. I mean there are fewer egos involved and the need to be President and to be seen and glorified as the President. **I think it is the dawning of our era**. (my emphasis)

References

Abrams, J., Long, J., Talbot, M. and Welch, M. (1996) *Organisational Change in National Governing Bodies of Sport*, Leading the Way Series, Leeds Metropolitan University.

Abrams, J. and Talbot, M. (1995) *Organizational Change and Sports Governing Bodies: a Review of the Literature*, Leading the Way Series, Leeds Metropolitan University.

Averley, H. (1995) 'Community development in sport', chapter presented at *First National Conference on Sports Development*, Newcastle, Northern Ireland: Northern Ireland Sports Council.

Brighton Declaration on Women and Sport (1994) London: Sports Council.

Canadian Association for the Advancement of Women in Sport (1994) *Women in Sport*, Gloucester, Ontario: CAAWS.

Canadian Association for the Advancement of Women in Sport (1995) *Guidelines for National Sports Organizations*, Ottawa: CAAWS.

Commonwealth Secretariat (1991) *Working Party on Strengthening Commonwealth Sport: Final Report*, London: Commonwealth Secretariat.

English Sports Council (1997) *Strategy for Sport*, London.

European Sports Conference (1993) *European Sports Charter*.

European Sports Conference (1991) *The New Europe and Future Sports Co-operation*, Report of the X ESC, Oslo.

Fasting, K. (1993) *Women and Sport. Monitoring Progress Towards Equality: a European Survey*, Oslo: Norwegian Confederation of Sport, Women's Commission.

Fasting, K. (1991) Setting the Scene, in European Sports Conference (op. cit.), pp. 135–144.

Franks, S. (1999) *Having None of It: Women, Men and the Future of Work*, London: Granta Publications.

Giddens, A. (1979) *Critical Problems in Social Theory*, London: Macmillan.

Giddens, A. (1987) *The Nation State and Violence*, Berkley, California: University of California Press.

Habermas, J. (1972) *Knowledge and Human Interest*, London: Heinemann.

Hall, M. A. (1996) *Feminism and Sporting Bodies*, Leeds, Human Kinetics.

Hall, M. A., Cullen, D. and Slack, T. (1989) 'Organizational elites recreating themselves: the gender structure of national sports organizations', *Quest* 41(1): 28–45.

Hargreaves, J. (1990) 'Gender on the Sport Agenda', *International Review of Sociology of Sport* 25(2): 287–308.

Hargreaves, J. (1994) *Sporting Females: Critical Issues in the History and Sociology of Women's Sports*, London: Routledge.

Hogwood, B. and Gunn, L. (1984) *Policy Analysis for the Real World*, Oxford University Press.

Ikulayo, P. (1991) 'Women and Sport in Nigeria', *Sport in Africa*, 1: 21–24.

Kidd, B. (1987) 'The Olympic Movement and the sports-media complex', in R. Jackson and T. McPhail (eds) *The Olympic Movement and the Mass Media: Past, Present and Future Issues*, Conference Proceedings, University of Calgary, pp. 13–20.

Macintosh, D. and Whitson, D. (1990) *The Game Planners: Transforming Canada's Sport System*, Montreal/Kingston: McGill/Queen's University Press.

Maddock, S. (1999) *Challenging Women: Gender, Culture and Organizations*, London: Sage.

McKay, J. (1998) *Managing Gender: Affirmative Action and Organizational Power in Australian, Canadian and New Zealand Sport*, New York: State University of New York Press.

McKay, J. (1992) *Why So Few? Women Executives in Australian Sport*, Department of Anthropology and Sociology, University of Queensland.

McMurtry, R. (1990) cited in *Commonwealth Heads of Government Committee for Co-operation in Sport Report*, London: Commonwealth Secretariat.

Marshal, J. (1995) 'Gender and management: a critical view of research', *British Journal of Management* 6: 53–66.

Salman, W. (1997) *Woman and Sport in Malaysia*, Masters by Research thesis, Leeds: Faculty of Cultural & Educational Studies, Leeds Metropolitan University.

Slack, T. and Hinings, B. (1987) *The Organization and Administration of Sport*, London: Sports Dynamics.

Sports Council (1989) *Taking the Lead*, Proceedings of Council of Europe Conference, London: Sports Council.

Swedish Sports Confederation (1990) *A Plan for Equality Between Men and Women in Sport in the 1990s*, Stockholm.

Talbot, M. (2001) 'Femocrats, technocrats and bureaucrats: women's contested place in the Olympic movement', in M.Talbot (ed.), *Gender, Power and Culture: A Centenary Celebration of Women in the Olympics*, Meyer & Meyer Sport, Cologne.

Talbot, M. (1997) *Commonwealth Women and Sport: Opportunities and Barriers*, London: Commonwealth Secretariat.

Talbot, M. (1994) Managing the Process: the work of the European Sports Conference Group on Women and Sport, in Sports Council (ed.) *Women, Sport and the Challenge of Change*, International Conference Report, London: Sports Council

Talbot, M. (1991) 'Intervention in debate on women and sport', European Sports Conference.

Talbot, M. (1990*a*) 'Women and sports administration: Plus ca change . . .?', Chapter presented at General Assembly of International Sports Federations conference, Monaco.

Talbot, M. (1990*b*) 'Women, sport and power', Keynote Chapter presented at 'First World Summit on Women and the Many Faces of Power' conference, Montreal.

Talbot, M. (1988) 'Their own worst enemy? Women and leisure provision,' in Erica Wimbush and Margaret Talbot (eds), *Relative Freedoms*, Milton Keynes: Open University Press.

19 Challenging the gendered space of sport: Women's ice hockey and the struggle for legitimacy

Nancy Theberge

One of the main sites for the contemporary challenge to the gendered landscape of sport is ice hockey. Ice hockey is often celebrated as an aspect of popular culture that unites Canadians in a particularly powerful way. Well known literary references describe the sport as 'the Canadian specific', 'our common passion', 'the language that pervades Canada', and 'the game of our lives' (Gruneau and Whitson 1993: 3).

These constructions of hockey as a pan-Canadian practice mask the deeply gendered character of the sport. From its origins in the late nineteenth century, hockey quickly emerged as one of the key signifiers of masculinity in Canadian life (Gruneau and Whitson 1993). The sport embodies a particular version of masculinity – cold, rugged and hard – and has been dominated by men.

Historical accounts locate the first women's hockey game in 1891, or shortly after the formal beginnings of the men's game (McFarlane 1994). In the early twentieth century, women's hockey prospered in some areas of the country, only to fall victim to the retrenchment in women's sport that took place in the 1940s when, as one observer has put it, 'a long time out began' in women's hockey (McFarlane 1994: 103). A revival began in the 1960s, which accelerated in subsequent decades. In Canada, a key event was the inauguration of the women's national championships in 1982. This was followed by major developments in international competition, including the first World Championships in 1990 (with subsequent World Championships in 1992, 1994, and annually since 1997, with the exception of during Olympic years) and inclusion on the Olympic programme in 1998.

The effort by women to claim a place in hockey has been marked by struggle. A symbol, and site, of the struggle over access is the ice rink. Although the mythology of hockey in Canada celebrates legions of rosy cheeked children – almost always boys – playing hockey on frozen backyards and ponds, the reality is that the sport is now largely practised in indoor arenas. These arenas serve as 'men's cultural centres' (Kidd 1990), in that they offer a setting that celebrates masculinity and where the roles girls and women play are usually supportive: they watch their brothers', sons' and husbands' games, staff the concession stands and take tickets.

In their examination of the culture and organization of Canadian hockey, Etue and Williams (1966) discuss the ongoing struggle to gain access to ice arenas, most of which are community owned. Many rinks allocate ice time on the basis of previous year's use, ensuring a continuation of the practice of favouring long established male hockey programmes. In one account of the operation of this policy, advocates for women's hockey were told by managers of a community rink that allocating ice time to groups who used it the previous year 'worked for them, so they saw no reason to change' (Etue and Williams 1996: 166).

Another commonly employed policy that continues male privilege involves residency requirements. Many communities require teams using public facilities to include a minimum percentage of residents from the community. While the policy ostensibly is intended to ensure that access is provided to local ratepayers, it reflects conditions in men's hockey, where the large number of participants ensures that teams have no problem filling rosters with local residents (and even with this, residency requirements are often ignored.) In women's hockey, still struggling to become established and with teams needing to recruit from a broader geographical area than in men's hockey, residency requirements can function as a means of exclusion. Nonetheless, women's hockey programmes continue to encounter problems in securing ice time because of residency rules (Etue and Williams 1996: 166–7).

Difficulties in gaining access to ice time are both a material barrier and a metaphor for the broader struggle by women to disrupt the gendered space of sport. For many supporters, a major step forward in this effort was the inclusion of women's hockey in the Olympics in 1998. Olympic status has conferred upon hockey a measure of credibility and sense of having 'arrived.' At the same time, however, appearance on the most celebrated stage of international sport and developments associated with this appearance have raised the stakes in the struggle by women to claim a place in the masculine preserve of sport. This chapter examines some key aspects of this struggle. Before proceeding to this discussion, some background information is provided on the development of women's hockey and issues in the construction of the sport.

The development of women's hockey

While women's hockey has seen impressive development in recent decades, this progress is uneven. Internationally, the leaders are Canada, which has won all the World Championships through to the year 2000, and the US, which finished second at all the World Championships. These two countries switched places at the Olympics, with the US winning gold and Canada silver. At all the World Championships and at the Olympics, Finland won bronze. Other countries which competed at the Olympics, based on standings at the 1997 World Championships, were China and Sweden. Japan competed as host country.

Progress in women's hockey has barely dented the advantage enjoyed by the men's game. In their 1996 book, *On the Edge: Women Making Hockey History*, Etue and Williams review the state of development in several North American, European and Asian countries. In all the countries they discuss, support for women's involvement lags well behind that accorded to men, judged by a variety of measures, including dollars expended by the national federation, number of participants and number of programs (Etue and Williams 1996: 274–300).

Since the publication of Etue and Williams' account, there has been important progress. In North America recent years have seen the expansion of university hockey programs and the inauguration of national university women's hockey championships in both Canada and the United States. Another important development was the establishment of the National Women's Hockey League, comprised of the best club teams from Ontario and Quebec.[1] This league, while not professional in the sense of providing salaries to players, nonetheless is a major step forward in the organization of elite level women's hockey. The calibre of competition is extremely high and teams receive varying amounts of corporate sponsorship and growing, if still limited, media coverage.

Issues in the construction of hockey

One of the key issues in the cultural struggle around the gendering of hockey involves the practice of the sport. The rules of play in men's and women's hockey are essentially the same, with one major difference. The rules of women's hockey prohibit intentional body checking, that is, intentional efforts to hit or 'take out' an opponent. There is nonetheless considerable body contact in women's hockey, both intentional and unintentional (or as it is termed in the sport, 'incidental'), as players try to outmanoeuvre and out muscle one another. At the same time, women's games are noticeably different from the full contact games played at the elite levels of men's hockey in that without body checking, the forceful collisions that are a defining feature of men's hockey are largely absent.

It is generally agreed that the prohibition of body checking results in a game in which speed, strategy and playing skills are featured more prominently than in a full contact game, which emphasizes power and force. On other counts, however, the prohibition of body contact is the subject of debate. Underlying much of the debate is disagreement about the relation between women's and men's hockey. Some see body checking as just one aspect of the aggressive physicality that characterizes the men's game, including the fighting that frequently occurs in North American professional hockey. Critics fear that the inclusion of body checking in the women's game would inevitably lead to an increase in other forms of unacceptable aggression.

Others argue that there is no inevitable relationship between body checking and violence and that the model of men's hockey need not extend to the women's game. In support of this they point to the fact that women's hockey already has severe penalties – usually multiple game suspensions – that effectively eliminate fighting and other forms of aggressive physicality. So long as these sanctions are in place, it is argued, introducing body checking will not lead to an increased incidence of other, undesirable features of men's hockey.[2]

Admission to the Olympics: raising the stakes in the battle for legitimacy

The admission of women's hockey to the Olympics was the culmination of a period of rapid ascension within the international sporting arena. The first international women's hockey tournament was held in 1987, outside Toronto. This event was organized by the Ontario Women's Hockey Association, which has been a leader in the organization of hockey in Canada. It is notable that the tournament had no formal sponsorship or sanctioning from the national governing body, the Canadian Amateur Hockey Association (now the Canadian Hockey Association) or the International Ice Hockey Federation (IIHF). The IIHF did, however, send observers to the tournament and the success of the event, along with continued pressure from supporters, led the IIHF to sanction the first official World Championships, in Canada in 1990 (Etue and Williams 1996: 240–1).

Following the inauguration of World Championships, supporters turned their attention to the Olympics. Aided by pressure to redress the gender imbalance in the Olympics, which included no women's team sports in the Winter Games, in 1992 the International Olympic Committee voted to include women's hockey on the Olympic programme. While this decision was made too late for the 1994 Games in Lillehamer, women's hockey was included in the programme for the 1998 Games in Nagano.

The impact of Olympic status on women's hockey has been profound. In the fall of 1992, I began a research project that involved field work with a team playing at the elite levels of the sport and interviews with players and coaches from this team and elsewhere in women's hockey (Theberge 2000). This work continued for nearly two years, through the summer of 1994 and thus it coincided with the beginning of the 'Olympic era' in women's hockey. In interviews and in informal discussions conducted as part of my research, players and coaches frequently remarked on the legitimacy that Olympic status conferred on their sport and on them as participants. Many players, from teenagers to veterans in their late twenties and thirties, identified competing in the Olympics as their ultimate goal in hockey.

Olympic status has also intensified the instrumentalism which has increasingly come to characterize the sport. For most of the past century, women played hockey for the fun and satisfaction it provided. With the development of international play culminating in entry into the Olympics, the conditions of involvement have changed dramatically. Etue and Williams (1996) identify the 1990 World Championships as a key turning point. In a profile of members of the Canadian team that won this event, they describe the contrasts among players:

> Women in the past had played for the sheer love of the game and the fun and sense of community that came from belonging to a team. The newer players, however, were less drawn by the social aspects of team play and more by the athletic heights it allowed them to reach. This distinction would emerge fully with future world championships and, eventually, the long dreamed of Olympics.
>
> (Etue and Williams 1996: 20)

While the impact of the Olympics was evident within the sport for several years prior to 1998, it was not until the pre-Olympic year of 1997 that public interest and most crucially media attention began to intensify. The pre-Olympic buildup began with the 1997 World Championships, held in April in Kitchener, Ontario. With support from different levels of government, the event was well promoted and generated considerable following. Two of the games were nationally broadcast in Canada, including the dramatic gold medal game between Canada and the US that went into overtime. The interest generated by the World Championships picked up again some months later. In the fall of 1997 and early 1998, as part of their pre-Olympic preparations, the Canadian and American teams played each other 13 times, in exhibitions and tournaments held in the two countries. Each of these games was an occasion to promote the sport in communities across North America. One of the games was played in January, 1998 before an audience of more than 15,000 as part of the National Hockey League's All Star weekend festivities.

The buildup culminated with the Olympic Games in February. For those within the sport who had worked over the last decade to see women's hockey featured on the world stage, the realization of this dream began with the opening ceremony. Live television broadcast of this spectacle featured interviews with Canadian women hockey players and a dramatic moment when one of the veteran players on the team bared her hips on national television to show a tattoo of the Olympic rings.

The publicity of the Olympics also brought unprecedented scrutiny. The uneven development of the sport internationally, evident in earlier World Championships, was now on display on the very public stage of the Olympics. Three games played on the first day of competition ended in a combined score of 24–0; the second day saw combined scores of 20–2. This inevitably brought criticism, including a column in a major Canadian newspaper headlined 'Women's Hockey is Not Ready for the World.' Toronto *Globe and Mail* writer Allan Maki argued that 'They shouldn't be playing women's hockey at the Nagano Olympics. The games have been awful, as one sided as a firing squad.' He continued:

> The truth is women's hockey was fast-tracked into the Games to draw more female viewers and sponsors. It simply isn't ready. There aren't enough quality players competing on a world-wide basis . . . . There is marginal excitement. The competition has been two parts predictable, one part embarrassing. The Japanese were happy to lose to Canada by 13 goals because the last time the two countries played the score was 18–0. This is progress, said the Japanese. It's not. Women's hockey should not have been put on the Olympic schedule this quickly. Given a little more time, the women's game could have stolen the show and taken itself to a higher level.
>
> (Maki 1998: O8)

Other commentary described early round competition as a 'travesty' (Mayoh 1998: 14). In drawing attention to the disparity in international play, these remarks were a public statement of conditions that had long been recognized in the women's hockey community. At the 1997 World Championships, one of the most respected coaches in Canadian women's hockey told me that three of the teams in the premiere Canadian league would be competitive at this tournament; that is, three Canadian club teams could play with the world leaders. This view is shared by others familiar with elite level women's hockey. Within the Canadian women's hockey community, acknowledgement of uneven competition at the world level is generally seen not as the basis of criticism but as an indication of the lack of support the sport receives and the need to improve conditions.

Criticism of the uneven early round play was countered by references to similar conditions in men's hockey during the early years of Olympic competition. In 1924 in Chamonix, France, the Canadian men won games by scores of 33–0, 30–0, 22–0 and 19–2. Some took the occasion of the first Olympic women's hockey tournament to call for greater support from the hockey establishment. A Canadian member of the women's committee of the IIHF noted:

> I wish the IIHF would take more of a leadership role. If they put a little effort into developing women's hockey in the heartland of Europe, it wouldn't be long before you'd have six or seven legitimate contenders there.
>
> (quoted in Mayoh 1998: 14)

Criticism gave way to praise as the Olympic tournament reached the much anticipated gold medal game between Canada and the US, won by the Americans, 3–1. This game, which capped a long standing rivalry between the teams, showcased the sport at its best – play was skilled, physical and intense. And the Olympic stage ensured media attention. The gold medal game was televised in Canada live at 4 a.m. and again on tape delay the following afternoon. In the US, where tape delayed broadcast has become the norm for Olympic telecasts, the game was broadcast several days later in its entirety.

The gold medal game also received extensive print media attention, including coverage in two US newspapers with national circulation, *USA Today* and the *New York Times*. The *Times* featured a cover photo of the victorious US team on the day following the gold medal game. In addition, a long and thoughtful piece by veteran sportswriter Robert Lipsyte explored the significance of the game for the gendered landscape of hockey and by extension, sport. The article trumpeted the gold medal game as 'the final public knell of the artificial construction of what is masculine and feminine in sports'. Lipsyte described the American players as 'warriors, hard-charging competitors who came to win, not just play.' Moreover, he suggested:

> Something about their sport – cold, difficult, brutal, artistic – made their gold medal win more symbolic than the ones won (by American women) in soccer, softball and basketball. Ice hockey, after all, would seem to be the stereotypical male sport
>
> (Lipsyte 1998: S1)

The 1998 Olympic women's hockey tournament highlighted key aspects of the struggle facing women who wish to challenge the gendered space of sport. For most of this century, women played ice hockey in obscurity. With Olympic entry and surrounding developments, the conditions of participation have changed dramatically. Having made it to the 'show', women athletes are now subjected to increased scrutiny, leading to both praise for outstanding performances and criticism for allegedly failing to make the grade.[3] This scrutiny is an instance of what Michael Messner (1988: 206) has described as a revised strategy by oppositional groups in which the attitude toward women in sport seems to be 'They want to be treated equally with men? Well, let's see what they can do.'

Continued struggles over the gendering of sport[4]

Another aspect of the heightened scrutiny now applied to women's hockey involves the long standing struggle over the gendering of sport and athletes. In the months leading up to the Olympics, this concern took on a new life as women's hockey, and a few individual players, received unprecedented attention from media and corporate interests (though this attention was still minimal in comparison to that accorded men's sport and men's hockey in particular).[5] This interest has dramatized the ideological struggle over gender and sport in two ways. First, corporate interest in the marketability of women's hockey has heightened concern about the gendered construction of players. As one observer of women's hockey in the new era of corporate interest put it, in order to be marketable, players must be 'tough on the ice but pretty and feminine off it.'[6]

The most striking evidence of the emphasis on appearance in promoting women's hockey was the prominence of one member of the Canadian Olympic team, Cassie Campbell, who was featured in several contexts, including Canadian Hockey Association promotional campaigns and commercial endorsements. In addition, she appeared on the covers of two national magazines in conjunction with stories that were not about her specifically but the Olympic team and women's hockey generally.[7] Campbell, who is generally thought to be particularly attractive, was by far the most prominently featured member of the Canadian Women's Olympic Hockey team. For this, she has been dubbed by her teammates and others as the 'poster girl' for women's hockey. In a television news magazine piece on women's hockey broadcast shortly before the Olympics, Campbell was asked about her prominence and its basis in her appearance. She responded that she wouldn't be a poster girl if she weren't also a good hockey player.[8] In this she is almost certainly correct and bears testimony to the emergence of a revised apologetic, in which women athletes are now free to celebrate their athleticism, so long as they remain 'feminine' off the ice, fields and courts (Festle 1996: 285).

The heightened interest in women's hockey led to renewed debate about the construction of the game. This is the second way in which ideological struggle has been intensified. This discussion has (perhaps inevitably) involved comparisons between the men's and women's games. Observers remain divided on the attraction of the version of hockey played by women. Representative commentary was provided in two television pieces that aired on Canadian television in the weeks before the Olympics. 'She Shoots, She Scores', a news magazine piece, indicated that the Canadian Hockey Association favours the ban on intentional body checking because it has made the game more acceptable to players and their parents. The same point was made in 'The Game of Her Life', a documentary on the Canadian Women's Olympic Hockey team produced by the National Film Board of Canada in association with the Canadian Broadcasting Corporation. Shannon Miller, the coach of the Olympic team, discussed the attraction of the full contact game and said that as a player she enjoyed playing full contact.[9] Nonetheless, Miller argued, the exclusion of body checking has been a 'tremendous move' for the development of women's hockey.[10]

Additional commentary came from Ken Dryden, a former National Hockey League star and current President of the Toronto Maple Leafs of the NHL, who has written widely on hockey and is a vocal critic of fighting in the men's game. Dryden spoke of the 'delicate dilemma' posed by girls wanting to play a sport that looks and feels like hockey. He argued that the current game, which has incidental body contact but no intentional body checking, meets this description.[11]

Others question this view and 'She Shoots, She Scores' noted that social pressure for a 'safe, clean women's game' is countered by 'market potential for something else.' Unidentified fans interviewed in the program describe the attraction of the 'rough and tumble game' that features fighting and the desirability of seeing women players 'drop the gloves' – the hallmark of a fight in the NHL. Additional commentary suggesting confusion about the gendering of sport came from the editor of the recently established *Sports Illustrated: Women/Sport*, Sandra Bailey. Bailey indicated that while women's muscle definition has now become desirable, this is so only within limits and 'we still want women to be much more in the role they grew up with.' At the same time, she argued, public acceptance of alternative versions of sport is limited and hockey played by rules different from the men's game will be a hard sell.[12]

Discussions of the construction of hockey are often hampered by an uncritical association of body checking with other forms of gratuitous violence. This was evident in my own research. On several occasions in informal conversations and interviews, when I asked individuals about body checking, they responded by talking about fighting. This association came most frequently from younger players who have no experience or even knowledge of women's hockey with intentional body checking.[13] A similar tendency was evident in 'She Shoots, She Scores', the documentary referred to above. In the examination of physicality in women's hockey, Ken Dryden, a knowledgeable observer and thoughtful critic, distinguished between contact and gratuitous violence. But the framing of the discussion and commentary through much of the segment failed to distinguish between the two.

As indicated previously, there is debate about the relationship between the inclusion of body checking and fighting and other undesirable practices. But the dominance of the National Hockey League model of hockey provides the standard against which other versions of the sport are inevitably compared, leading to a too frequent association of intensely physical play and fighting (Theberge 1997; 2000). As efforts are made to promote women's hockey to a wider audience which is less familiar with the women's game, by advertising and other corporate executives whose expertise lies in marketing rather than hockey, failure to appreciate the distinction between intense physical play and fighting and other forms of gratuitous violence is likely to be more pronounced. This will only exacerbate the ideological struggle – and confusion – surrounding the association of gender, sport and physicality.

Conclusion

The prominence of ice hockey in Canadian cultural life and its symbolism as a 'flag carrier of masculinity' (Bryson 1990: 174) have made the contemporary struggle by women to claim a space particularly meaningful. For many supporters, the appearance of women's hockey in the 1998 Olympics was the culmination of a dream that marked arrival among the elite of sport. This appearance, however, has also provided the context for renewed questioning of the legitimacy of women's presence in the masculine preserve of sport. When interest in women's ice hockey was confined to a few players and supporters, the quality of play was of little concern beyond this circle. Placed on the international stage of the Olympics, lopsided scores – the outcome of uneven development – became a focus of attention and the basis of criticism.

Inclusion in the Olympics has also raised the stakes in the ideological struggle over the gendering of sport. The Olympic stage is the centrepiece of international corporate sport. Appearance on this stage inevitably brings pressure to secure media interest and commercial sponsorship. Again in contrast to when women's hockey was a well kept secret, promoters now concern themselves with 'marketability' and key to this concern is the issue of gender. Poster girls may be tough on the ice but there is intense pressure to be feminine off it.

In ice hockey, the conception of toughness is contested in a particularly meaningful way in the rules around body contact. Perhaps the ultimate ideological battlefield in hockey lies in the distinctions between the practice of the men's and women's games. The Olympic stage and commercial pressures have highlighted these distinctions and coming years will likely witness heightened debate about the practice of hockey and gendering of hockey players.

Notes

1 In the 2000–2001 season a team from Vancouver played an exhibition schedule in the NWHL, with plans to join the League on a regular basis in 2001–2002.
2 For an extended discussion of this issue, see Theberge (2000).
3 Another example of a sport that came under criticism for lack of competitive depth in its inaugural Olympic appearance is weightlifting. Like women's ice hockey, weightlifting has long been colonized as a masculine preserve and has particular cultural importance as a signifier of masculinity. At the 2000 Olympic Games in Sydney, there was a significant gap (66 pounds) between the performances of the gold and bronze medal

winners. An article in the American magazine *Sports Illustrated* quoted a 'male insider who did not want to be identified' who criticized the lack of depth in the competition as 'ridiculous.' With considerably more perspective on this issue, the article went on to comment 'Well, duh. It's a new sport, so there will be more depth by the Athens games in 2004 and more still by 2008' (McCallum, 2000).

4 The discussion in this section is adapted from Theberge, 2000. See Chapter 9, 'Female Gladiators and the Road Ahead.'

5 The 1998 Olympic men's hockey tournament was the first in which National Hockey League players participated. With the inclusion of Canadian NHL players, the men's tournament thus finally included the best Canadians. In Canada publicity around the men's team was extensive and by some accounts excessive. For example, selections to the men's team were announced in an elaborately staged nationally televised ceremony before an NHL game in Ottawa some months before the Olympics. As this event took place during the NHL season, the Olympic team members were scattered across North America competing with their professional teams. The ceremony consisted of a parade of children, selected to stand in for the players, who skated to centre ice under the glare of a spotlight, each representing an NHL player who at that moment was plying his trade somewhere else.

6 Quoted in 'She Shoots, She Scores', broadcast on the magazine segment of the CBC National News on January 16, 1998.

7 The cover photos were in conjunction with Gwen Smith, 'She Shoots, She Scores', *Elm Street*, November/December, 1997, pp. 32–44; and Peter Kuitenbrower, 'Gold & Girls', *Chatelaine*, February, 1998, pp. 36–43.

8 Cassie Campbell, interviewed in 'She Shoots, She Scores.'

9 Until the late 1980s, the rules regarding body checking in hockey varied across Canada. In Ontario, senior women's hockey was played with body checking until 1989. In international hockey, body checking was prohibited in 1992.

10 Shannon Miller, interviewed in 'The Game of Her Life.'

11 Ken Dryden interviewed in 'She Shoots, She Scores.'

12 Sandra Bailey interviewed in 'She Shoots, She Scores.'

13 As indicated in note 8, until the late 1980s, senior women's hockey was played with body checking. Many veteran players have played full contact hockey, including body checking. Among younger players, only a small minority who have played at the elite levels of boys hockey have experience playing the full contact game with body checking.

References

Bryson, L. (1990) 'Challenges to male hegemony in sport', in M. Messner and D. Sabo (eds) *Sport, Men and the Gender Order*, Champaign Il: Human Kinetics.

Etue, E. and Williams, M. (1996). *On the Edge: Women Making Hockey History*, Toronto: Second Story.

Festle, J. (1996) *Playing Nice: Politics and Apologies in Women's Sports*, New York: Columbia.

Gruneau, R. and Whitson, D. (1993) *Hockey Night in Canada: Sport, Identities and Cultural Politics*, Toronto: Garamond.

Kidd, B. (1990). 'The men's cultural centre: sport and the dynamic of women's oppression/men's repression', in M. Messner and D. Sabo (eds) *Sport, Men, and the Gender Order*, Champaign Il: Human Kinetics.

Lipsyte, R. (1998) 'Nagano's legacy: female gladiators', *New York Times*, February 22: p. S1, 13.

Maki, A. (1998) 'Women's hockey is not ready for the world,' *Toronto Globe and Mail*, February 10, 1998: p. O8.

Mayoh, (1998) 'Women's hockey deserved promotion to Olympics', *Hipcheck* 1(2): 14, March/April.

McCallum, J. (2000). 'American beauties', *Sports Illustrated*, October 2, 2000.

McFarlane, J. (1994) *Proud Past, Bright Future: One Hundred Years of Canadian Women's Hockey*, Toronto: Stoddart.

Messner, M. (1988) 'Sports and male domination: the female athlete as contested ideological terrain', *Sociology of Sport Journal* 5(3): 197–211.

Theberge, N. (1997) 'It's part of the game: physicality and the production of gender in women's ice hockey', *Gender & Society* 11(1): 69–87.

Theberge, N. (2000) *Higher Goals: Women's Ice Hockey and the Politics of Gender*, Albany: State University of New York Press.

Seminar questions

Chapter 18

1   Critically assess the different approaches to gender and sport policy.
2   What were the main examples of organisational resistance to measures to promote gender equity?
3   How can gender equity be achieved in sport? What examples are there of successful struggles and resistances that have produced change?

Chapter 19

1   What have been the key areas of contestation and struggle faced by women as they moved into the game of ice hockey?
2   To what extent does the development of women's ice hockey challenge the prevailing gender order in sport?
3   Have women entering other 'men's' sports faced similar struggles to those experienced by the women ice hockey players?

Index